MW00582194

MPLS and VPN Architectures, Volume II

Jim Guichard, CCIE No. 2069
Ivan Pepelnjak, CCIE No. 1354
Jeff Apcar

Cisco Press
201 West 103rd Street
Indianapolis, IN 46290 USA

MPLS and VPN Architectures, Volume II

Jim Guichard, CCIE No. 2069

Ivan Pepelnjak, CCIE No. 1354

Jeff Apcar

Copyright© 2003 Cisco Systems, Inc.

Cisco Press logo is a trademark of Cisco Systems, Inc.

Published by:
Cisco Press
201 West 103rd Street
Indianapolis, IN 46290 USA

All rights reserved. No part of this book may be reproduced or transmitted in any form or by any means, electronic or mechanical, including photocopying, recording, or by any information storage and retrieval system, without written permission from the publisher, except for the inclusion of brief quotations in a review.

Printed in the United States of America 1 2 3 4 5 6 7 8 9 0

Library of Congress Cataloging-in-Publication Number: 619472051122

ISBN: 1-58705-112-5

Warning and Disclaimer

This book is designed to provide information about MPLS and VPN architectures. Every effort has been made to make this book as complete and as accurate as possible, but no warranty or fitness is implied.

The information is provided on an "as is" basis. The authors, Cisco Press, and Cisco Systems, Inc. shall have neither liability nor responsibility to any person or entity with respect to any loss or damages arising from the information contained in this book or from the use of the discs or programs that may accompany it.

The opinions expressed in this book belong to the authors and are not necessarily those of Cisco Systems, Inc.

Trademark Acknowledgments

All terms mentioned in this book that are known to be trademarks or service marks have been appropriately capitalized. Cisco Press or Cisco Systems, Inc. cannot attest to the accuracy of this information. Use of a term in this book should not be regarded as affecting the validity of any trademark or service mark.

Feedback Information

At Cisco Press, our goal is to create in-depth technical books of the highest quality and value. Each book is crafted with care and precision, undergoing rigorous development that involves the unique expertise of members from the professional technical community.

Readers' feedback is a natural continuation of this process. If you have any comments regarding how we could improve the quality of this book, or otherwise alter it to better suit your needs, you can contact us through e-mail at feedback@ciscopress.com. Please make sure to include the book title and ISBN in your message.

We greatly appreciate your assistance.

Publisher	John Wait
Editor-In-Chief	John Kane
Cisco Representative	Anthony Wolfenden
Cisco Press Program Manager	Sonia Torres Chavez
Manager, Marketing Communications, Cisco Systems	Scott Miller
Cisco Marketing Program Manager	Edie Quiroz
Acquisitions Editor	Amy Moss
Production Manager	Patrick Kanouse
Development Editor	Grant Munroe
Project Editor	Lori Lyons
Copy Editor	Karen A. Gill
Technical Editors	Matt Birkner, Dan Tappan
Content Editor	Monique Morrow
Team Coordinator	Tammi Ross
Book Designer	Gina Rexrode
Cover Designer	Louisa Adair
Production Team	Mark Shirar
Indexer	Tim Wright

Corporate Headquarters
Cisco Systems, Inc.
170 West Tasman Drive
San Jose, CA 95134-1706
USA
www.cisco.com
Tel: 408 526-4000
    800 553-NETS (6387)
Fax: 408 526-4100

European Headquarters
Cisco Systems International BV
Haarlerbergpark
Haarlerbergweg 13-19
1101 CH Amsterdam
The Netherlands
www-europe.cisco.com
Tel: 31 0 20 357 1000
Fax: 31 0 20 357 1100

Americas Headquarters
Cisco Systems, Inc.
170 West Tasman Drive
San Jose, CA 95134-1706
USA
www.cisco.com
Tel: 408 526-7660
Fax: 408 527-0883

Asia Pacific Headquarters
Cisco Systems, Inc.
Capital Tower
168 Robinson Road
#22-01 to #29-01
Singapore 068912
www.cisco.com
Tel: +65 6317 7777
Fax: +65 6317 7799

Cisco Systems has more than 200 offices in the following countries and regions. Addresses, phone numbers, and fax numbers are listed on the
Cisco.com Web site at www.cisco.com/go/offices.

Argentina • Australia • Austria • Belgium • Brazil • Bulgaria • Canada • Chile • China PRC • Colombia • Costa Rica • Croatia • Czech Republic
Denmark • Dubai, UAE • Finland • France • Germany • Greece • Hong Kong SAR • Hungary • India • Indonesia • Ireland • Israel • Italy
Japan • Korea • Luxembourg • Malaysia • Mexico • The Netherlands • New Zealand • Norway • Peru • Philippines • Poland • Portugal
Puerto Rico • Romania • Russia • Saudi Arabia • Scotland • Singapore • Slovakia • Slovenia • South Africa • Spain • Sweden
Switzerland • Taiwan • Thailand • Turkey • Ukraine • United Kingdom • United States • Venezuela • Vietnam • Zimbabwe

Copyright © 2003 Cisco Systems, Inc. All rights reserved. CCIP, CCSP, the Cisco Arrow logo, the Cisco *Powered* Network mark, the Cisco Systems Verified logo, Cisco Unity, Follow Me Browsing, FormShare, iQ Net Readiness Scorecard, Networking Academy, and ScriptShare are trademarks of Cisco Systems, Inc.; Changing the Way We Work, Live, Play, and Learn, The Fastest Way to Increase Your Internet Quotient, and iQuick Study are service marks of Cisco Systems, Inc.; and Aironet, ASIST, BPX, Catalyst, CCDA, CCDP, CCIE, CCNA, CCNP, Cisco, the Cisco Certified Internetwork Expert logo, Cisco IOS, the Cisco IOS logo, Cisco Press, Cisco Systems, Cisco Systems Capital, the Cisco Systems logo, Empowering the Internet Generation, Enterprise/Solver, EtherChannel, EtherSwitch, Fast Step, GigaStack, Internet Quotient, IOS, IP/TV, iQ Expertise, the iQ logo, LightStream, MGX, MICA, the Networkers logo, Network Registrar, *Packet*, PIX, Post-Routing, Pre-Routing, RateMUX, Registrar, SlideCast, SMARTnet, StrataView Plus, Stratm, SwitchProbe, TeleRouter, TransPath, and VCO are registered trademarks of Cisco Systems, Inc. and/or its affiliates in the U.S. and certain other countries.

All other trademarks mentioned in this document or Web site are the property of their respective owners. The use of the word partner does not imply a partnership relationship between Cisco and any other company. (0303R)

Printed in the USA

About the Authors

Jim Guichard, CCIE No. 2069, is a Technical Leader II within the Internet Technologies Division (ITD) at Cisco Systems. During the past six years at Cisco and previously at IBM, Jim has been involved in the design, implementation, and planning of many large-scale WAN and LAN networks. His breadth of industry knowledge, hands-on experience, and understanding of complex internetworking architectures have enabled him to provide valued assistance to many of Cisco's larger service provider customers. His previous publications include *MPLS and VPN Architectures* , by Cisco Press.

Ivan Pepelnjak, CCIE No. 1354, is the Chief Technology Advisor and member of the board with NIL Data Communications (www.NIL.si), a high-tech data communications company that focuses on providing high-value services in new-world service provider technologies.

Ivan has more than 10 years of experience in designing, installing, troubleshooting, and operating large corporate and service provider WAN and LAN networks, several of them already deploying MPLS-based virtual private networks (VPNs). He is the author or lead developer of a number of highly successful advanced IP courses covering MPLS/VPN, BGP, OSPF, and IP QoS, and he is the architect of NIL's remote lab solution. Ivan's previous publications include *MPLS and VPN Architectures* and *EIGRP Network Design Solutions* , by Cisco Press.

Jeff Apcar is a Senior Design Consulting Engineer in the Asia Pacific Advanced Services group at Cisco Systems. He is one of the Cisco lead consultants on MPLS in the region and has designed MPLS networks for many service providers in AsiaPac using packet-based and cell-based MPLS. Jeff has also designed and maintained large IP router networks (500+ nodes) and has a broad and deep range of skills covering many facets of networking communications.

Jeff has more than 24 years of experience in data communications and holds Dip. Tech (Information Processing) and B.App.Sc (Computing Science) (Hons) from the University of Technology, Sydney, Australia.

About the Technical Reviewers

Matthew H. Birkner, CCIE No. 3719, is a Technical Leader at Cisco Systems, specializing in IP and MPLS network design. He has influenced multiple large carrier and enterprise designs worldwide. Matt has spoken at Cisco Networkers on MPLS VPN technologies in both the U.S. and EMEA over the past few years. A "double CCIE", he has published the Cisco Press book, Cisco Internetwork Design. Matt holds a BSEE from Tufts University, where he majored in electrical engineering.

Dan Tappan is a distinguished engineer at Cisco Systems. He has 20 years of experience with internetworking, having worked on the ARPANET transition from NCP to TCP at Bolt, Beranek, and Newman. For the past several years, Dan has been the technical lead for Cisco's implementation of MPLS (tag switching) and MPLS/VPNs.

About the Content Reviewer

Monique Morrow is currently CTO Consulting Engineer at Cisco Systems, Inc. She has 20 years of experience in IP internetworking that includes design, implementation of complex customer projects, and service development for service providers. Monique has been involved in developing managed network services such as remote access and LAN switching in a service provider environment. She has worked for both enterprise and service provider companies in the United States and in Europe. She led the Engineering Project team for one of the first European MPLS-VPN deployments in 1999 for a European service provider.

Dedications

To my wife Sadie, for putting up with me writing another book and the long lonely nights associated with such an undertaking. To my children Aimee and Thomas, who always help to keep me smiling.—Jim

To my wife Karmen, who was always there when I needed encouragement or support. To my children Maja and Monika, who waited patiently for my attention on too many occasions.—Ivan

To my wife Anne, who is an exceptional person in every way. To my children Caitlin, Conor, and especially Ronan: Despite his constant efforts to reboot my PC, I managed to lose a draft only once.—Jeff

Acknowledgments

Every major project is a result of teamwork, and this book is no exception. We'd like to thank everyone who helped us in the long writing process: our development editor, Grant Munroe, who helped us with the intricacies of writing a book; the rest of the editorial team from Cisco Press; and especially our reviewers, Dan Tappan, Matt Birkner, and Monique Morrow. They not only corrected our errors and omissions, but they also included several useful suggestions to improve the quality of this publication.

Jeff would like to thank his management team Tony Simonsen, Michael Lim, and Steve Smith, for providing the time and encouragement to do the book. Also special thanks to the guys in the AsiaPac Lab Group, Nick Stathakis, Ron Masson, and George Lerantges, who let him hog lots of gear. Last, Jeff would like to thank Jim and Ivan for inviting him to collaborate with them.

Finally, this book would never have been written without the continuous support and patience of our families, especially our wives, Sadie, Karmen, and Anne.

Contents at a Glance

Table of Contents

Introduction

Since our first MPLS book (*MPLS and VPN Architectures*) was published by Cisco Press a few years ago, MPLS has matured from a hot leading-edge technology—supporting Internet services and leased-line–based VPN solution—to a set of solutions that are successfully deployed in large-scale service provider networks worldwide. A number of additional solutions had to be developed to support the needs of these networks, and many additional IOS services were made VPN-aware to enable the service providers to deploy the services they were already offering within the new architectural framework. Therefore, it was a natural step to continue on the path we charted with the first book and describe the enhancements made to MPLS architecture or its implementation in Cisco IOS in *MPLS and VPN Architectures: Volume II*.

Who Should Read This Book?

This book is not designed to be an introduction to Multiprotocol Label Switching (MPLS) or virtual private networks (VPNs); Volume I (*MPLS and VPN Architectures*) provides you with that knowledge. This book is intended to tremendously increase your knowledge of advanced MPLS VPN deployment scenarios and enable you to deploy MPLS and MPLS VPN solutions in a variety of complex designs. Anyone who is involved in design, deployment, or troubleshooting of advanced or large-scale MPLS or MPLS VPN networks should read it.

How This Book Is Organized

Although this book could be read cover-to-cover, it is designed to be flexible and allow you to easily move between chapters and sections of chapters to cover just the material that you need more information on. If you do intend to read them all, the order in the book is an excellent sequence to use.

Part I: Introduction

Chapter 1, "MPLS VPN Architecture Overview," serves as a refresher to the information contained within MPLS and VPN Architectures. It does not describe the MPLS or MPLS VPN technology in detail; if you need baseline MPLS or MPLS VPN knowledge, read *MPLS and VPN Architectures*: Volume I first.

Part II: Advanced PE-CE Connectivity

Chapter 2, "Remote Access to an MPLS VPN," discusses integration of access technologies such as dial, DSL, and cable into an MPLS VPN backbone. This chapter shows how you can integrate various access technologies into the backbone, thereby providing VPN service to many types of customers.

Chapter 3, "PE-CE Routing Protocol Enhancements and Advanced Features," builds on Volume 1 of the *MPLS and VPN Architectures* book and introduces more advanced options/features for OSPF connectivity as well as support for IS-IS and EIGRP routing protocols.

Chapter 4, "Virtual Router Connectivity," discusses the use of the VRF constructs to build virtual router type connectivity, extending the VRF concept to the CE router. This chapter also discusses new VRF-related features, including VRF-lite and PE-based network address translation (PE-NAT).

Part III: Advanced Deployment Scenarios

Chapter 5, "Protecting the MPLS-VPN Backbone," looks at various security issues within the backbone and describes the necessary steps that a service provider must take to protect the backbone and any attached VPN sites.

Chapter 6, "Large-Scale Routing and Multiple Service Provider Connectivity," describes the advanced features, designs, and topologies that were made possible with the enhancements to Cisco IOS since the first MPLS and VPN Architectures book was written.

Chapter 7, "Multicast VPN," discusses the deployment of IP multicast between VPN client sites.

Chapter 8, "IP Version 6 Across an MPLS Backbone," discusses a model (6PE) that gives the service providers an option to provide IPv6 connectivity across an MPLS-enabled IPv4 backbone.

Part IV: Troubleshooting

Chapter 9, "Troubleshooting of MPLS-Based Solutions," provides a streamlined methodology for identifying faults in MPLS solutions and troubleshooting an MPLS VPN backbone.

Icons Used in This Book

Throughout this book, you will see the following icons used for networking devices:

The following icons are used for peripherals and other devices:

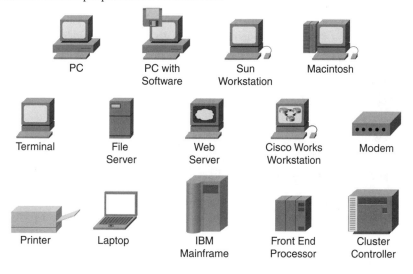

The following icons are used for networks and network connections:

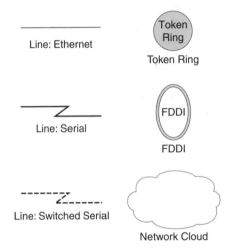

Line: Ethernet

Token Ring

Line: Serial

FDDI

Line: Switched Serial

Network Cloud

Command Syntax Conventions

The conventions used to present command syntax in this book are the same conventions used in the IOS Command Reference. The Command Reference describes these conventions as follows:

- Vertical bars (|) separate alternative, mutually exclusive elements.

- Square brackets [ ] indicate optional elements.

- Braces { } indicate a required choice.

- Braces within brackets [{ }] indicate a required choice within an optional element.

- Boldface indicates commands and keywords that are entered literally as shown. In actual configuration examples and output (not general command syntax), boldface indicates commands that are manually input by the user (such as a show command).

Italics indicate arguments for which you supply actual values.

CHAPTER 1

MPLS VPN Architecture Overview

Virtual private networks (VPNs) have recently received a lot of attention from equipment manufacturers, consultants, network designers, service providers, large enterprises, and end users due to their cost advantages over traditional enterprise networks. As with most technologies, the foundation for today's VPN networks and underlying technologies was created more than 20 years ago. During its development, end users discovered that it made financial sense to replace links between sites in their own private network with virtual connections across a shared infrastructure. The assumption for doing this was that a shared environment (or VPN) is equivalent in terms of security and privacy to the network (links) it was replacing.

This chapter reviews the basic Multiprotocol Label Switching (MPLS) and MPLS-based VPN concepts and terminologies to ensure an understanding of the terms used in this book. It also covers the latest developments in the MPLS VPN arena and how they enable the service provider to offer new MPLS-based services, such as remote access into an MPLS-based VPN or Internet Protocol (IP) multicast within a VPN. These developments are also described in depth in later chapters.

NOTE   You can find more in-depth descriptions of these concepts and additional MPLS or VPN background information in Ivan Pepelnjak and Jim Guichard's *MPLS and VPN Architectures* (Volume I), published by Cisco Press, which is a prerequisite to understanding this book.

MPLS VPN Terminology

Since the early days of X.25 and Frame Relay (the two technologies initially used to deploy VPN services), many different technologies have been proposed as the basis to enable a VPN infrastructure. These ranged from Layer 2 technologies (X.25, Frame Relay, and Asynchronous Transfer Mode [ATM]) to Layer 3 technologies (primarily IP) or even Layer 7 technologies. IBM once had a product that transported IP datagrams over Systems Network Architecture (SNA) application sessions, and TGV (a company later acquired by Cisco Systems) had implemented IP transport over DECnet sessions. Not surprisingly, with such a variety of implementation proposals, the overall terminology in the field has changed dramatically. This book uses the terminology introduced with the MPLS-based VPN.

MPLS VPN-based terminology is based on a clear distinction between the service provider network (P-network) and the customer network (C-network), as shown in Figure 1-1.

Figure 1-1   *MPLS VPN-Based Terminology*

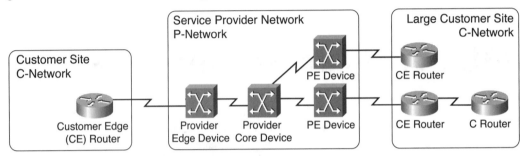

The P-network is always topologically contiguous, whereas the C-network is usually clearly delineated into a number of *sites* (contiguous parts of the customer network that are connected in some way other than through the VPN service). Note that a site does not need to be geographically contained; if the customer is using a VPN service for its international connectivity only, a site could span a whole country.

The devices that link the customer sites to the P-network are called *customer edge* (CE) *devices*, whereas the service provider devices to which the CE routers connect are called *provider edge* (PE) *devices*. In most cases, the P-network is made up of more than just the PE routers. These other devices are called P devices (or, if the P-network is implemented with Layer 3 technology, P routers). Similarly, the additional Layer 3 devices in the customer sites that have no direct connectivity to the P-network are called C routers.

VPN technologies have evolved into two major approaches toward implementing VPN services:

- **Connection-oriented VPN**—The PE devices provide virtual leased lines between the CE devices. These virtual leased lines are called *virtual circuits* (VCs). The VCs can be permanent, established out-of-band by the service provider network management team (called *permanent virtual circuits,* or *PVCs*). They can also be temporary, established on demand by the CE devices through a signaling protocol that the PE devices understand. (These VCs are called *switched virtual circuits,* or *SVCs*).

- **Connectionless VPN**—The PE devices participate in the connectionless data transport between CE devices. It is unnecessary for the service provider or the customer to establish VCs in these VPNs, except perhaps between the PE and CE routers if the service provider uses switched WAN as its access network technology.

Connection-Oriented VPNs

Connection-oriented VPNs were the first ones to be introduced. They offer a number of clear advantages, including the following:

- The service provider does not need to understand the customer's network; the service provider just provides virtual circuits between the customer sites.

- The service provider is not involved in the customer's routing (as shown in Figures 1-2 and 1-3), and it doesn't need to know which Layer 3 protocols the customer is deploying. Consider, for example, the network shown in Figure 1-2. The VPN network is implemented with Frame Relay VCs; therefore, the service provider is unaware of the routing protocols that the customer is using. From the customer's routing perspective, the customer routers are directly adjacent (linked with virtual point-to-point links), as shown in Figure 1-3.

Figure 1-2   *Connection-Oriented VPN: Physical Topology*

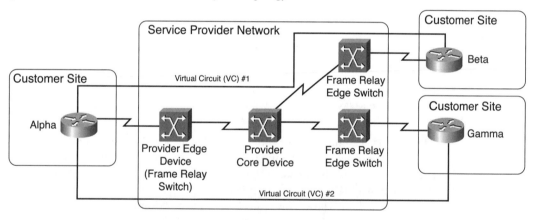

Figure 1-3   *Connection-Oriented VPN: Customer Routing Perspective*

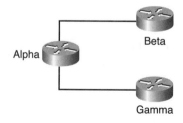

Connection-oriented VPNs also have several obvious disadvantages:

- All VCs between the customer sites have to be provisioned, either manually by the service provider network management team or by the CE devices. Even if the VCs are established automatically by the CE devices, these devices need to be configured with enough information to establish the links through the signaling protocol of choice.

- The CE routers must exchange the routing information with other CE routers, resulting in more router adjacencies, slower convergence, and generally more complex routing setups.

NOTE   If you are interested in more of the advantages and disadvantages of connection-oriented or connectionless VPNs, you can find them in Chapter 8, "Virtual Private Network (VPN) Implementation Options," of Jim Guichard and Ivan Pepelnjak's *MPLS and VPN Architectures* (Volume I), published by Cisco Press, 2002.

Modern connection-oriented VPNs are implemented with a variety of different technologies, including the following:

- They can be implemented with traditional connection-oriented Layer 2 technologies (X.25, Frame Relay, or ATM) or with connectionless Layer 2 technologies, such as virtual LANs (VLANs).

- They can also be implemented with *tunnels* that are established over public Layer 3 infrastructure (usually over public IP infrastructure—most commonly the Internet). These VPNs can use Layer 3 over Layer 3 tunnels, such as generic routing encapsulation (GRE), which is described in RFC 2784, or tunnels based on IP security (IPSec) technology. These VPNs can also use Layer 2 over Layer 3 tunnels, which are most commonly found in dial-up access networks to implement virtual private dialup networks (VPDNs).

Connectionless VPNs

Contrary to connection-oriented VPNs, connectionless VPNs propagate individual datagrams that the CE devices send across the P-network. This approach, although highly scalable as proven by today's Internet, does impose a number of limitations on the customers:

- The customers can use only the Layer 3 protocol that the service provider supports. This was a serious drawback a few years ago, but it is quickly becoming a moot issue because most networking devices now support IPv4.

- The customers must use addresses coordinated with the service provider. In a connectionless network, every P device must be able to forward every individual datagram to its final destination; therefore, each datagram must have a unique destination address, known to every P device, as shown in Figure 1-4.

Figure 1-4   *Packet Propagation on Connectionless VPNs*

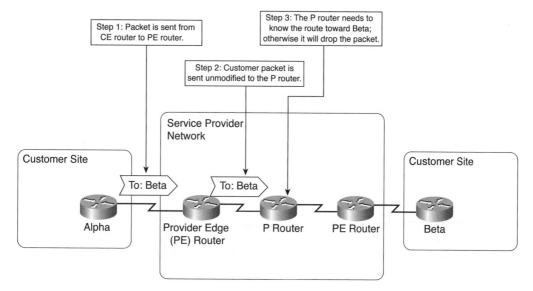

The simplicity of CE router configuration in a connectionless VPN world, as well as the capability to support IP-based VPN services together with public IP services on the common infrastructure, prompted many service providers to consider the rollout of connectionless VPN services. However, the acceptance of these services was initially quite low because the customers were unwilling to renumber their existing network infrastructure to comply with the service provider's addressing requirement. Clearly, a different VPN technology was needed that would combine the benefits of a connectionless VPN (simple CE router configuration and lack of explicit provisioning of the virtual circuits) with the benefits of a connection-oriented VPN (such as the support of overlapping address spaces and the simplicity of data forwarding in the P devices).

MPLS-Based VPNs

MPLS-based VPN technology uses a combination of connection-oriented and connectionless VPN technologies, including the following features:

- The interface between the CE routers and the PE routers is connectionless. No additional configuration is needed on the CE devices.

- The PE routers use a modified IP forwarding paradigm; a distinct IP routing and forwarding table (called *virtual routing and forwarding* table, or *VRF*) is created for each customer.

- The customer's addresses are extended with 64-bit *route distinguishers* to make nonunique 32-bit IP addresses globally unique within the service providers' backbone. The resulting 96-bit addresses are called *VPNv4* addresses.

- A single routing protocol is run between the PE routers for all VPN customers. Modified *Border Gateway Protocol* (BGP) with multiprotocol extensions is used in this function.

- The PE routers use MPLS-based VCs (called *label-switched paths,* or *LSPs*) to transport the customer's datagrams between PE routers. Additional MPLS labels are inserted in front of the customer's IP datagrams to ensure their proper forwarding from ingress PE routers toward the destination CE router.

- The LSPs between all PE routers are established automatically based on the IP topology of the P-network. It is unnecessary to configure or manually establish these paths.

- The mapping between the customer's destination addresses and LSPs leading toward the egress PE routers is performed automatically based on the BGP next-hops.

The following sections will briefly refresh your MPLS and MPLS VPN knowledge. For more in-depth discussion of the MPLS and MPLS VPN technology, please refer to Cisco Press's *MPLS and VPN Architectures* (Volume I). For more details on ATM-based MPLS implementations, refer to *Advanced MPLS Design and Implementation*, published by Cisco Press.

The MPLS Technology

In essence, the MPLS technology combines the richness of IP routing and the simplicity of hop-by-hop label switching of Frame Relay or ATM to provide the seamless integration of the connection-oriented forwarding with the IP world. Due to their dual nature (they operate on both the IP layer as well as the label-switching layer), the MPLS devices are called *label switch routers* (LSRs). This section describes the typical operation of MPLS devices, focusing on the simplest MPLS application: forwarding of IP datagrams across an MPLS network.

All devices in an MPLS network run IP routing protocols on their *control plane* to build IP routing tables. In MPLS devices that support IP forwarding, the IP routing tables are used to build IP forwarding tables, also called *forwarding information base* (FIB). In MPLS devices that support only label forwarding (such as the ATM switches with MPLS functionality), the IP routing FIB does not exist. The IP routing operation of the MPLS control plane is shown in Figure 1-5.

Figure 1-5   *LSRs Build the IP Routing Table*

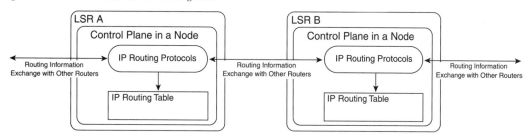

After the IP routing tables have been built, MPLS labels are assigned to individual entries in the IP routing table (individual IP prefixes) and propagated to adjacent MPLS devices through a *Label Distribution Protocol* (LDP).

NOTE   In usual MPLS operation, labels are not assigned to BGP destinations because the router always reaches BGP destinations through recursive lookup on BGP next-hop. Therefore, BGP destinations can be reached through the label that is associated with the BGP next-hop for those destinations.

Each MPLS device uses its own local label space; globally unique labels or centralized label assignment is unnecessary, making MPLS extremely robust and scalable. Every label assigned by an MPLS device is entered as an input label in its *label forwarding information base* (LFIB), which is the forwarding table used for label switching. The label assignment and distribution of an MPLS device are illustrated in Figure 1-6.

Figure 1-6 *Control Plane Operations in an LSR*

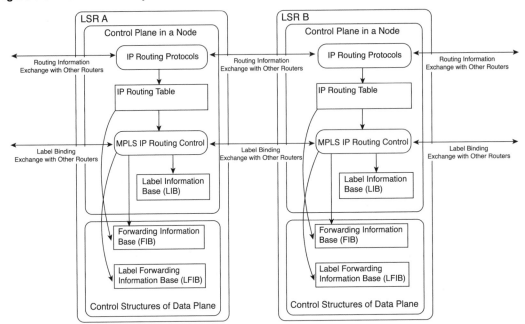

Most label assignments, both local as well as those made by adjacent devices, are entered into a table called the *label information base* (LIB). The label that the IP next-hop assigns for a particular IP prefix is entered as an output label in the local LFIB to enable pure label forwarding. In devices that support IP forwarding, such a label is also entered into the FIB to support IP-to-label forwarding.

After the IP routing tables, IP forwarding tables, and label forwarding tables have been built, the MPLS devices can start to forward IP traffic. All MPLS devices must support label forwarding; whenever they receive a labeled packet, they perform a label lookup in the LFIB, replace the input label with the output label, and forward the labeled packet to the next-hop LSR. Some MPLS devices (ingress LSRs) can receive IP datagrams, perform a lookup in the FIB, insert an MPLS label stack in front of the IP datagram based on information stored in the FIB, and forward the labeled packet to the next-hop LSR. The PE router within the MPLS VPN architecture is an example of such a device.

Other MPLS devices (egress LSR) can receive labeled packets, perform an LFIB lookup, and (based on the absence of an output label in the LFIB) remove the label from the ingress labeled datagram and forward the IP datagram to the next-hop IP router. In most cases, all LSRs in an MPLS network can act as both ingress and egress LSRs, the notable exception being ATM switches acting as LSRs. The various paths that an IP datagram or a labeled datagram can take through an LSR are displayed in Figure 1-7.

Figure 1-7   *Packet Forwarding in an LSR*

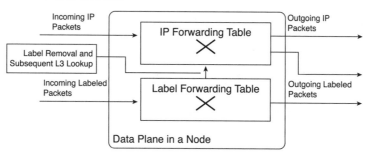

The basic principle of MPLS has been extended to a variety of other applications, including these:

- **MPLS traffic engineering (TE)**—The modified link-state routing protocols (OSPF and ISIS) are used to discover free resources in the network, labels are assigned through the *Resource Reservation Protocol* (RSVP), and the global FIB is modified based on MPLS TE labels.

- **MPLS VPNs**—Many FIBs are created (one or more per VPN customer), and Multiprotocol BGP is used to distribute the customer routing information and MPLS labels across the network.

- **MPLS quality of service (QoS) in ATM environments**—The standard LDP is modified to assign up to four labels for each IP prefix, with each label serving a different QoS class.

New MPLS applications are constantly emerging. For example, one of the new MPLS applications (also covered in this book) enables IPv6 transport across an MPLS network; IPv6 routing protocols are used to build IPv6 routing tables, which are then used as the basis for label assignment and distribution.

The large variety of different MPLS applications still adhere to the common framework. Each application might have its own "routing protocol," its own LDP, and its own forwarding database. However, the MPLS applications all share a common LFIB, enabling the LSRs to transparently integrate new MPLS applications without affecting the existing services, as shown in Figure 1-8.

Figure 1-8 *Multiple MPLS Applications in a Single LSR*

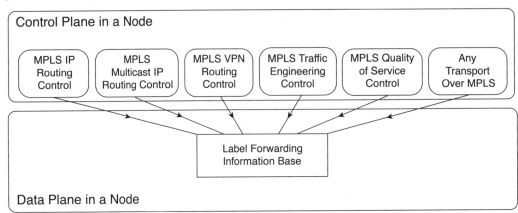

The MPLS VPN Technology

As discussed previously, MPLS-based VPNs use a combination of connectionless VPNs between the customers and service providers (thus minimizing the provisioning complexity and cost) with connection-oriented VPNs in the network core (reducing the overhead on the P devices). Furthermore, several additional mechanisms have been implemented to allow the customers to use overlapping address spaces.

In a typical MPLS-VPN network, the CE routers and PE routers exchange the customer routes using any suitable IP routing protocol. These routes are inserted into VRFs on the PE routers, which guarantees the perfect isolation between customers. This process is illustrated in Figure 1-9, which details the internal structure of a PE router (San Jose) to which two VPN customers are connected (FastFood and EuroBank) and which also connects to a P router (Washington).

When customer routes are placed into VRFs, the PE routers allocate a separate MPLS label that will be needed for VPN data forwarding to each customer route. The customer routes and associated MPLS labels are transported across the P-network using multiprotocol BGP. The customer IP addresses are augmented with a 64-bit route distinguisher before being inserted into the provider's BGP to ensure global uniqueness of potentially nonunique customer addresses. Additional BGP attributes (extended BGP communities) are used to control the exchange of routes between VRFs to allow the service providers to build VPN topologies that are almost impossible to build with any other VPN technology.

NOTE

You can find detailed descriptions of these topologies and implementation guidelines in the *MPLS and VPN Architectures* (Volume I) book.

Figure 1-9   *Virtual Routing Tables in a PE Router*

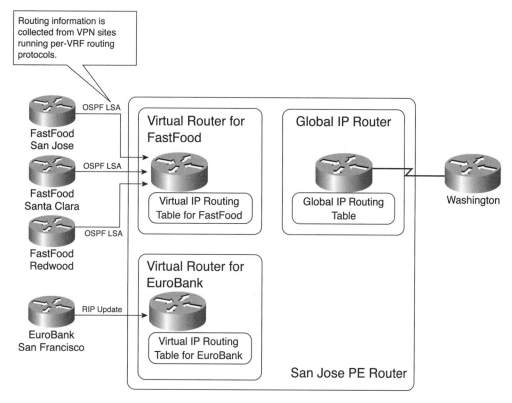

The extended BGP communities are also used to implement additional MPLS VPN features, including *automatic route filtering* with the site-of-origin (SOO) community or automatic propagation of Open Shortest Path First (OSPF) route attributes across the BGP backbone. (OSPF support is described in more detail in Chapter 3, "PE-CE Routing Protocol Enhancements and Advanced Features.")

VPN packet forwarding across the MPLS VPN backbone is implemented with MPLS forwarding using an MPLS label stack imposed in the IP datagram by the ingress PE router. The first label in the stack is the label assigned to the IP address of the egress PE router (BGP next-hop) in the service provider core. The second label is the label assigned to the customer route by the egress PE router. The first label is usually removed one hop before the egress PE router through a process called *penultimate hop popping*. The egress PE router then performs label lookup on the VPN label, removes the VPN label, and forwards the packet to the CE router. The whole process is illustrated in Figure 1-10.

Figure 1-10 *VPN Packet Propagation in an MPLS VPN Network*

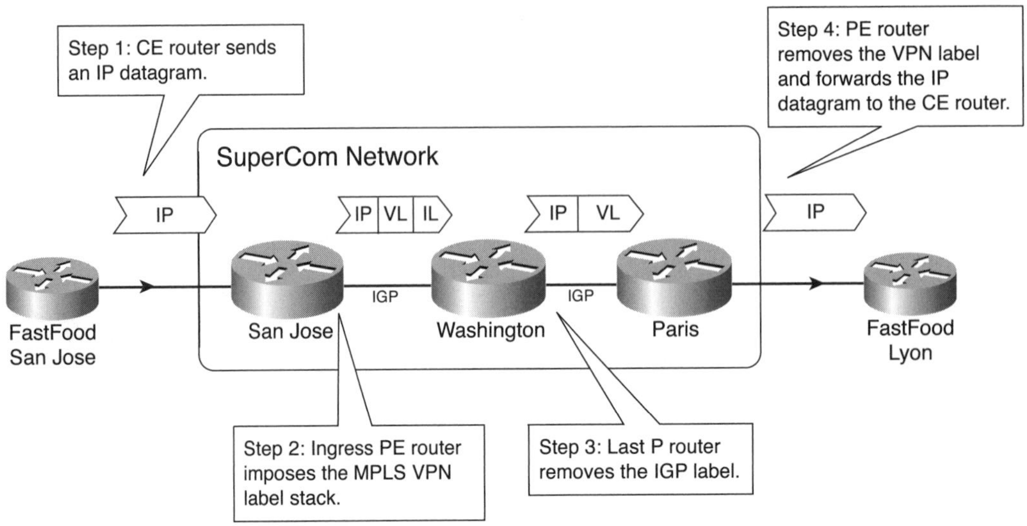

An IP datagram, sent from San Jose to Lyon, is forwarded across the service provider backbone in a number of steps:

1 An IP datagram is sent from the CE router to the PE router.

2 The PE router performs an IP lookup and prepends an MPLS header consisting of two labels: a label assigned via LDP (also known as IGP label, or IL), identifying the path toward the egress PE router (Paris); and a VPN label (VL) assigned by the Paris PE router.

3 The penultimate router in the service provider network removes the IGP label, leaving only the VPN label in the MPLS header.

4 The egress PE router performs label lookup on the VPN label, removes the MPLS header, and forwards the IP datagram to the Lyon CE router.

New MPLS VPN Developments

Many service providers worldwide have enthusiastically embraced the MPLS and MPLS VPN technologies as they enable the service providers to deploy the two most common applications—Internet access and VPN services—on a common network infrastructure. The diversity of their infrastructures, access layer technologies, and IP routing setups, as well as the new services these service providers would like to deploy, have triggered the development of several new MPLS-related features, including these:

• Tight integration of access technologies such as dial-up, digital subscriber line (DSL), and cable with MPLS VPN

- New routing protocol options and support for additional VPN routing protocols
- Transport of additional Layer 3 protocols over MPLS

Each of these is discussed in the following sections.

Access Technology Integration with MPLS VPN

The initial implementation of MPLS VPN technology supported customer sites that were connected primarily to the service provider backbone through a permanent connection. These connections were implemented with Layer 2 technology, which was well established in the IOS code base. Although you could, with skill, support other access technologies (most notably, dial-up users), a number of supporting technologies were not MPLS VPN-enabled, forcing the service providers to accept compromises they would rather avoid.

Tighter integration of MPLS VPN with access technologies was implemented by making several additional Cisco IOS services VPN-aware:

- Virtual-Profile Cisco Express Forwarding (CEF)
- Overlapping address pools
- On-demand address pools (ODAP)
- Framed Route VRF Aware
- Per VRF authentication, authorization, and accounting (AAA)
- VRF-aware large-scale dial out (LSDO)
- VPN-ID
- DHCP relay—MPLS VPN support

All these features and the access technology integration with MPLS VPN is described in detail Chapter 2, "Remote Access to an MPLS VPN."

New Routing Protocol Options

New Cisco IOS releases extend the range of IP routing protocols that are supported between the PE routers and the CE routers. Enhanced IGRP (EIGRP) and Integrated Intermediate System-to-Intermediate System (Integrated IS-IS) are supported, as well as additional OSPF connectivity options, including virtual OSPF links between PE routers (*sham links*). Furthermore, Cisco IOS supports IP Multicast inside the MPLS VPN and per-VRF network address translation (NAT) on the PE router. These new features are described in Chapters 3, "PE-CE Routing Protocol Enhancements and Advanced Features," 4, "Virtual Router Connectivity," and 7, "Multicast VPN."

New Layer-3 Protocols Transported Over MPLS

IP version 6 (IPv6), also known as IP: The Next Generation (IPng), has joined IPv4 as another Layer 3 protocol that can be transported across an MPLS backbone. MPLS support for globally routed IPv6 is described in Chapter 8, "IPv6 Across an MPLS Backbone."

Summary

Many service providers that wanted to minimize their costs of provisioning and operations by offering all their services (VPN and public Internet) over a common infrastructure have enthusiastically embraced MPLS-based VPN networks. Furthermore, these service providers have achieved significant cost savings due to the provisioning simplicity offered by MPLS VPN's integration with the benefits of both connectionless and connection-oriented VPN approaches.

An end-to-end MPLS VPN solution is, like any other VPN solution, divided into the central P-network to which a large number of customer sites (sites in the C-network) are attached. The customer sites are attached to the PE devices (PE routers) through CE devices (CE routers). Each PE router contains several virtual routing and forwarding tables (VRFs)—at least one per VPN customer. These tables are used together with Multiprotocol BGP run between the PE routers to exchange customer routes and to propagate customer datagrams across the MPLS VPN network. The PE routers perform the label imposition (ingress PE router) and removal (egress PE router). The central devices in the MPLS VPN network (P routers) perform simple label switching.

MPLS-based VPNs have been significantly enhanced since their initial rollout. The new MPLS VPN features allow better integration of access technologies, support of additional PE-CE routing protocols, as well as support of new transport options across MPLS backbones (transport of IPv6 and legacy Layer 2 technologies).

CHAPTER 2

Remote Access to an MPLS VPN

The initial service offerings for Multiprotocol Label Switching (MPLS) virtual private networks (VPNs) were provided to customers through fixed connections to the provider edge (PE) router by using technologies such as leased line, Frame Relay, Asynchronous Transfer Mode (ATM) permanent virtual circuits (PVCs), or last mile Ethernet. The provision of remote or off-net access to the MPLS VPN was incumbent upon the customer having the appropriate access infrastructure in place to cater to his mobile or remote workforce. Therefore, the ability for an MPLS VPN service provider to supply MPLS VPN value-added services (which, in turn, generates more revenue) to remote users was completely dependent on the customer's remote access network and the geographic coverage that the network provided. This is illustrated in Figure 2-1.

Figure 2-1 *Remote Access Provided by Customer*

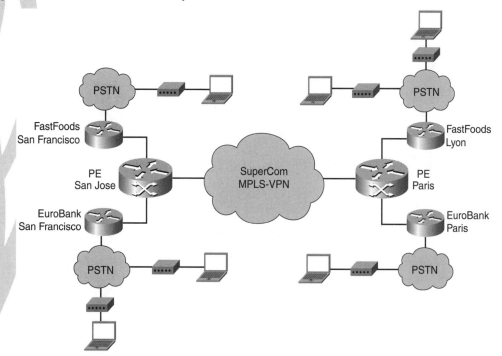

In this scenario, the SuperCom network provides only fixed-line access to the EuroBank and FastFoods customer edge (CE) routers. Remote access is provided by using EuroBank and FastFoods hardware at their remote locations.

To provide a scalable and complete end-to-end VPN service, the service provider must have a network infrastructure that is capable of integrating remote access directly into an MPLS VPN network. Such an infrastructure can enable remote users to seamlessly access their corporate VPNs through a service provider point of presence (POP), not a customer POP. The advantage of this is that a service provider can offer a value-add service by leasing wholesale dial access to many VPN customers. The VPN customers can be ISPs or large enterprises that want to provide access to remote users but avoid the need for maintaining their own separate and expensive access network. The same service provider remote access network can be sold as a unique service to many VPN customers (build once, sell many), which decreases the customer's operating costs and increases the revenue of the service provider. This is illustrated in Figure 2-2.

Figure 2-2   *Remote Access Provided by a Service Provider*

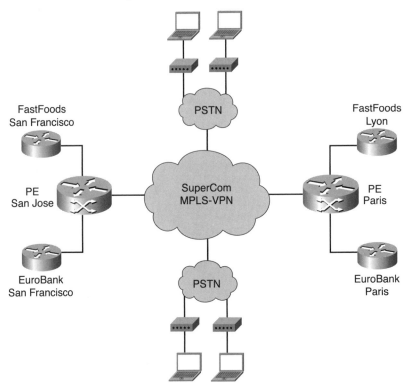

In this scenario, SuperCom provides remote access services terminating into the MPLS VPN network. This remote access network allows any EuroBank or FastFoods remote user direct access to his VPNs, which alleviates the need for EuroBank and FastFoods to provide a separate remote access infrastructure.

Service providers will invariably use one or more of the following access technologies to provide remote access to an MPLS VPN:

- Public Switched Telephone Network (PSTN)
- Integrated Services Digital Network (ISDN)
- Asymmetric digital subscriber line (ADSL)
- Data-over Cable Service Interface Specifications (DOCSIS), or simply called cable

These access technologies are used in conjunction with various protocols and procedures to provide the remote access service. The protocols and procedures include the following:

- Point-to-Point Protocol (PPP)
- Layer 2 Tunneling Protocol (L2TP)
- Virtual private dialup network (VPDN)
- Remote Authentication Dial-In User Service (RADIUS)
- Dynamic Host Configuration Protocol (DHCP)

The first part of this chapter provides an overview of each of these protocols and procedures to provide you with a foundation for understanding how remote access is provided to an MPLS VPN. The second part of this chapter covers the following remote access scenarios and features:

- Dial-in access to an MPLS VPN via VPDN (L2TP) or direct ISDN
- Large-scale dial-out access from an MPLS VPN via L2TP or direct ISDN
- Dial backup to an MPLS VPN
- Digital subscriber line (DSL) access to an MPLS VPN by using various encapsulation methods
- Cable access to an MPLS VPN
- Advanced features, such as on-demand address pools, per-VRF AAA, and VRF-aware DHCP relay

Feature Enhancements for MPLS VPN Remote Access

Several new features and enhancements were made to Cisco IOS so that MPLS VPN services could be provisioned over various remote access technologies. Most of these features are incorporated into the detailed examples provided throughout this chapter or are addressed in the later section, "Advanced Features for MPLS VPN Remote Access." The features can be summarized as follows:

- **Virtual-profile Cisco Express Forwarding (CEF)**—PPP sessions that terminate on a Cisco router through an L2TP tunnel or direct ISDN interface do so via a virtual-access interface. The virtual-access interface is an instance of a virtual-profile or a virtual-template. Each system has a maximum of 25 virtual-templates; virtual-profiles do not have this limitation; therefore, they are preferred because they are more scalable and flexible. The virtual-profile CEF feature allows these interfaces to be CEF switched, which is a prerequisite for MPLS.

- **Overlapping address pools**—Previously, per-router local address pools could only be specified in the global IP routing instance. This meant that all VRFs as well as all global interfaces shared a single local pool to provide interface addresses for PPP sessions. The overlapping pool feature allows the same IP address range to be used concurrently in different VRFs, thereby providing better utilization of the IP address space.

- **On-demand address pools (ODAP)**—Instead of configuring pool address ranges locally, the ODAP feature allows a central RADIUS server to provide VRF-aware pool addresses as required. In this way, the local pool can expand and contract based on usage, and the RADIUS server can provide better address management by allocating subnets where they are needed.

- **Framed Route VRF aware**—When a remote CE router dials into a PE router via a PPP session, there must be a mechanism to allow the remote subnet to be injected into the VRF for the duration of the call. This is done through the Framed-Route RADIUS attribute or the corresponding cisco-avpair "ip:route" attribute. This attribute usually applies to the global routing table; however, enhancements have been made so that Cisco IOS can determine whether it should be applied to a VRF.

- **Per VRF authentication, authorization, and accounting (AAA)**—This feature allows RADIUS information to be sent directly to a customer RADIUS server that is located within the VRF. Previously, the only way to get to a customer RADIUS server was to use a proxy via the service provider RADIUS server reachable in the global routing table.

- **VRF-aware large-scale dial out (LSDO)**—This feature allows the LSDO solution to operate within the context of a VRF. VRF-aware LSDO allows multiple VRFs to use the same dialer interface on a router with individual profiles downloaded from an AAA server.

- **VPN-ID**—This feature allows remote access applications such as a RADIUS or DHCP server to identify the VPN that originates a RADIUS or DHCP request. The VPN-ID feature is based on RFC 2685.

- **DHCP Relay—MPLS VPN Support**—This feature allows a single DHCP server to identify and service many VRFs by supplying addresses from distinct IP address pools. Creating different namespaces within the server separates address pools. Either the VRF name or the VPN ID identifies these namespaces. The DHCP server can reside in the global routing table or in any customer or shared services VRF.

Overview of Access Protocols and Procedures

This section briefly describes the typical protocols that are used in remote access technologies. It serves as a refresher or an introduction to those of you who are not intimately familiar with these protocols. For a more in-depth description of remote access protocols and Cisco IOS configuration guidelines, please refer to Cisco Connect Online (www.cisco.com) under the Technologies section.

PPP

PPP is fundamental to the deployment of nearly all the remote access scenarios discussed in this chapter. PPP provides a link layer service (Layer 2 of the OSI model) between two devices (in this case, the customer device and the PE router), and it can operate over a variety of physical media such as ISDN, ADSL, leased line, and virtual circuits such as ATM PVCs and L2TP tunnels. PPP provides a datagram service only; reliable transport is the responsibility of the higher layers in the protocol stack. The connection that PPP operates over can be either fixed or switched (dial-up) and running in asynchronous or synchronous bit serial mode. The only requirement for PPP is that the circuit provided be full duplex. An advantage of PPP is that it can support many different network protocols (Layer 3 of the OSI hierarchy), such as IP, DECnet, AppleTalk, and OSI simultaneously over the same link.

PPP is a layered protocol that has three components:

- An encapsulation component that is used to transmit datagrams over the specified physical layer.

- A Link Control Protocol (LCP) to establish, configure, and test the link as well as negotiate capabilities.

- One or more NCPs used to negotiate optional configuration parameters and facilities for the network layer. There is one Network Control Protocol (NCP) for each protocol supported by PPP.

NOTE   The device that terminates PPP sessions in a service provider network is called a *network access server (NAS)*. A NAS is capable of terminating many connections over a variety of physical media. Among other examples, a NAS could be a Cisco Systems 7200 acting as a PE router with switched ISDN connections or a Cisco Systems AS5300 universal access concentrator terminating dial-in ISDN or analog modem calls.

To establish a link for point-to-point communication, each endpoint uses LCP to open the connection, negotiate capabilities, and configure the link appropriately. Examples of capabilities that can be negotiated are the maximum receive unit (MRU), compression of certain PPP fields, and Password Authentication Protocol (PAP) or Challenge Handshake Authentication Protocol (CHAP).

Optionally, you can assess the link quality to determine whether the network protocols can be activated. If the link quality is not of acceptable quality, then LCP can hold off passing to the NCP phase. When the LCP phase is completed, the relevant NCP for that protocol must separately negotiate each network layer protocol. For example, the NCP for IP called Internet Protocol Control Protocol (IPCP) can negotiate options such as IP addresses to be used at each end of the link, DNS server addresses, and the compression protocol. LCP and NCP are both extensible protocols; therefore, new features and options can be easily added when required. Figure 2-3 shows where LCP and NCP fit in the PPP model.

Figure 2-3   *PPP Model*

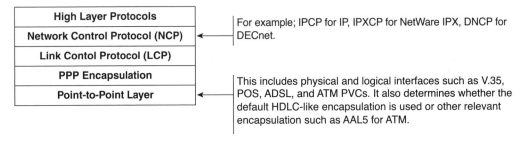

The LCP layer also provides the optional authentication function, which is a fundamental requirement when providing remote access services. Authentication takes place after the link has been established and prior to the NCP negotiation phase.

As previously mentioned, LCP has two authentication protocols available: PAP and CHAP. PAP is a simple two-way handshake protocol. The username/password is repeatedly sent across the link from the originating end until an acknowledgement is received. PAP sends passwords in clear text; there is no protection from playback or trial and error attacks (such as trying to guess passwords from the outside).

CHAP is a more robust authentication protocol that uses a three-way handshake to verify the identity of the remote end. The authentication is done initially when the link is established and might be periodically repeated. CHAP is the preferred authentication method and will be used in examples throughout this chapter. The three-way handshake operates as follows:

- The local peer sends a challenge message to the remote peer
- The remote peer combines the challenge with a shared secret key and responds with a value calculated by using a one-way hash function (such as a message-digest algorithm MD5).
- The local peer then compares the returned hash value with what it expected to receive. (It calculates its own value by using the hash function.)
- If the hash values match, the authentication is acknowledged; otherwise, the connection is terminated.

NOTE   The password, or "secret key" as it is referred to, is never sent across the link. Only the hashed response of the secret is transmitted. Because CHAP can be used to authenticate many different remote systems, the challenge/response packet can also contain a name (usually the hostname) that will be used to index a list of secret keys or passwords.

Figure 2-4 illustrates CHAP in operation. A remote FastFoods user has dialed into the San Jose NAS. SanJose_NAS will send a challenge message to the FastFoods_Mobile1 PC asking for its secret. FastFoods_Mobile1 will use information in the challenge message as well as the secret that is locally stored to send a response back. The response message will contain the name of the FastFoods remote user (FastFoods_Mobile1) as well as the encrypted secret (*whatsthebuzz*). The SanJose_NAS will then compare the response received from FastFoods_Mobile1 with the name/secret pair stored either locally on the NAS server or on a RADIUS/AAA server. If the encrypted versions of the secrets match, then an accept message is sent back and the NCP layer can proceed. This handshake can be periodically repeated during the call.

Figure 2-4   *CHAP Three-Way Handshake*

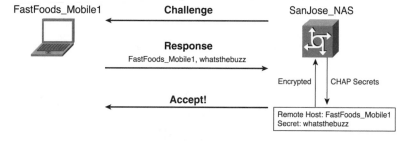

L2TP

In a typical PPP connection, the Layer 2 termination point and the PPP session endpoint reside on the same physical device. For example, a user could obtain a connection to the NAS by way of an analog dial-up or ISDN connection and then run PPP over that connection. In this case, the Layer 2 and PPP session would terminate on the NAS as shown in Figure 2-5.

Figure 2-5   *PPP Endpoints*

L2TP allows the PPP session endpoint to be divorced from the Layer 2 termination point. This means that a PPP session can be extended across the Internet or an ISP network. While traversing an IP backbone, the PPP session is carried inside an L2TP tunnel. The PPP session can pass through many intermediate nodes before terminating on the target remote access server. L2TP allows the remote client to communicate with the remote server by using PPP as if the two were directly connected. The network infrastructure is transparent to either end of the PPP session. The device that terminates the Layer 2 connection and originates the L2TP tunnel is called the *L2TP Access Concentrator (LAC)*. The device that terminates the L2TP tunnel and the original PPP session from the remote client is called the *L2TP Network Server (LNS)*. The LAC passes packets between the remote client and the LNS.

NOTE   L2TP allows the creation of a virtual private dialup network (VPDN) to connect a remote client to its corporate network by using a shared infrastructure, which could be the Internet or a service provider's network. VPDNs are described in the following section.

Figure 2-6 illustrates the basic concept of an L2TP tunnel.

Figure 2-6   *PPP Session Through an L2TP Connection*

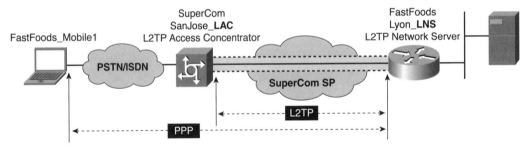

In this scenario, FastFoods has a remote client called FastFoods_Mobile1 that needs to communicate directly with a server that is located at the FastFoods Lyon site. The nearest dial-in POP to the FastFoods mobile user is provided by SuperCom in San Jose. The Lyon server is reachable through a FastFoods router that is directly connected to the SuperCom network in Paris. Therefore, when FastFoods_Mobile1 calls into the SuperCom LAC in San Jose, the San Jose LAC will exchange PPP messages with FastFoods_Mobile1 and communicate by way of L2TP requests and responses with FastFood's Lyon_LNS to set up an L2TP tunnel. The PPP session will be established between FastFoods_Mobile1 and the Lyon_LNS.

PPP frames from FastFoods_Mobile1 will be accepted by the SanJose_LAC, stripped of any linked framing or transparency bytes, encapsulated in L2TP, and forwarded over the appropriate tunnel toward Lyon_LNS. The LNS will accept these L2TP frames, strip the L2TP encapsulation, and process the incoming PPP frames.

VPDN

A *VPDN* is a network that connects a remote access client to a private network by using a shared or public IP infrastructure. A VPDN uses a tunnel protocol, such as L2TP, Point-to-Point Tunneling Protocol (PPTP), or Layer 2 Forwarding (L2F) to extend the Layer 2 and higher parts of the network connection from a remote user across an ISP network to a private network. VPDNs allow a service provider to share its common remote access infrastructure among many remote clients. Each client can dial in to a service provider NAS/LAC and be connected to the private corporate network based on the logon domain name or the number that was dialed (by using the dialed number identification service, or DNIS).

Figure 2-7 describes the VPDN process. It is essentially the same scenario as described in Figure 2-6, except that the protocol exchanges are fully detailed. It uses a combination of PPP, L2TP, and RADIUS to provide the virtual private dial-in service.

Figure 2-7   *VPDN Process*

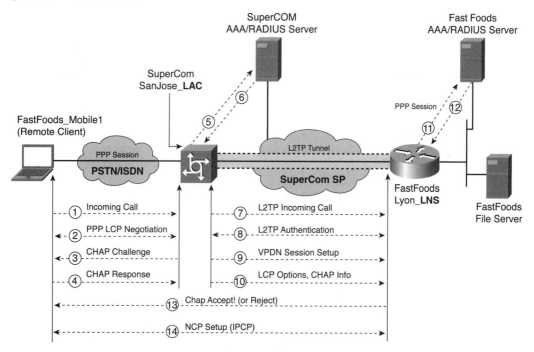

The following steps outline what happens during the VPDN process:

Step 1   The FastFoods remote client initiates a PPP call to the SuperCom San Jose LAC via PSTN or ISDN.

Step 2   The remote client and the LAC begin to negotiate PPP options by using LCP. This covers elements such as the authentication method (CHAP or PAP), compression, and the PPP multilink.

Step 3   Assuming that CHAP was selected, the LAC sends a challenge message.

Step 4   The FastFoods remote client responds with its username (assume it is mobile1@fastfoods.com) and password. The LAC partially authenticates the user by using the information it has received in the CHAP response.

Step 5   The LAC checks whether the FastFoods remote client is a VPDN user. It determines this by examining the username (mobile1), domain name (fastfoods.com), or called number (DNIS). This information can either be stored locally (configured statically) on the LAC or it can be retrieved from the SuperCom RADIUS server. In our example, the information is forwarded via a RADIUS request to the SuperCom RADIUS server.

Step 6   The RADIUS server has an entry for the domain name of the FastFoods remote client; therefore, the client is a VPDN user. The RADIUS server replies to the LAC with a message containing the IP address of the FastFoods LNS and other information to allow the LAC to create an L2TP tunnel to the specific LNS.

NOTE   If the remote client were determined not to be a VPDN client, then authentication would continue on the LAC. In this case, it would be likely that this customer would be subscribing to Internet access or some other SuperCom common service and would be connected directly to the global routing space of SuperCom.

Step 7   If the L2TP tunnel does not already exist, the SanJose_LAC builds a tunnel to the FastFoods Lyon_LNS by using L2TP control messages. Only one tunnel is built for each domain. For example, all fastfoods.com that subsequently dial in use the same tunnel.

Step 8   L2TP provides an optional CHAP-like authentication mechanism during tunnel establishment. The LNS can check to see if the LAC can open a tunnel (via local configuration) to it and both the LAC and LNS can authenticate each other using a shared secret configured locally or on a RADIUS server. Alternatively, the LNS can accept the tunnel without any authentication.

Step 9   After the tunnel is created, a VPDN session is created over the L2TP tunnel for the FastFoods remote client. Each remote client is associated with a unique VPDN session on an L2TP tunnel.

NOTE An L2TP tunnel can support many VPDN sessions for the same domain. Therefore, any further FastFoods remote clients that called into the San Jose LAC would be forwarded through the same L2TP tunnel to the Lyon LNS.

Step 10 The San Jose LAC then forwards the partially authenticated CHAP response from the FastFoods client. This includes the username/ password information (mobile1@fastfoods.com) and the LCP-negotiated parameters.

Step 11 The LNS creates a virtual-access interface based on a virtual-template for the VPDN session. The remote user information is authenticated by the FastFoods Radius server (or username/password information configured statically on the LNS can be used).

Step 12 The FastFoods RADIUS server returns the appropriate response/ authorization and any other relevant information.

Step 13 The FastFoods Lyon LNS then sends a CHAP response back to the FastFoods remote client through the L2TP tunnel.

Step 14 After the CHAP response is successful, the NCP phase, in this case using IPCP, is performed. When the PPP sessions are functioning, the LAC acts as a go-between for the FastFoods remote client and the LNS.

The combination of PPP, L2TP, and VPDN are the basic building blocks for enabling remote access to MPLS VPNs. Some modifications and feature enhancements are required to support L2TP directly into VRFs, and these will be discussed in detail in the remote access to MPLS VPN examples later in this chapter.

RADIUS

RADIUS provides a distributed client/server system that prevents unauthorized access to facilities, such as dial-in services or individual hosts. RADIUS is a protocol that provides AAA services to a network. User permissions and configuration information are stored on a centralized RADIUS/AAA server.

NOTE   In this chapter, a *RADIUS server* refers to an AAA server that uses the RADIUS protocol.

A NAS operates as a RADIUS client. The client is responsible for passing user information to designated RADIUS servers and then acting on the response that is returned. RADIUS servers are responsible for receiving user connection requests, authenticating the user, and returning all configuration information that is necessary for the client to deliver service to the remote access user. The RADIUS server can also provide accounting services to measure the amount of resources that each remote access user consumes. Figure 2-8 shows the types of RADIUS messages.

Figure 2-8 *RADIUS Messages*

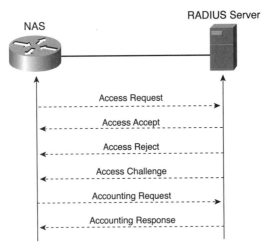

The RADIUS message types are described as follows:

- **Access Request**—These packets are sent to a RADIUS server. They convey information that is used to determine whether a user is allowed access to a specific NAS (such as the username) and any special services requested for that user.

- **Access Accept**—These packets are sent by the RADIUS server. They provide specific configuration information in a series of attributes that are necessary to begin delivery of service to the user.

- **Access Reject**—These packets are sent by the RADIUS server to reject the access-request due to invalid information in the request. For example, a nonexistent username or a bad password would be rejected.

- **Access Challenge**—These packets allow the RADIUS server to send the user a challenge requiring a response.

- **Accounting Request**—These packets are sent from a client (typically a NAS or its proxy) to a RADIUS accounting server. They convey information that provides accounting for a user service.

- **Accounting Response**—These packets are sent from the RADIUS accounting server to the client to acknowledge that the Accounting Request has been received and recorded successfully.

The RADIUS standard and its extensions specify a large number of attributes that can be exchanged between a RADIUS client and a RADIUS server (where they are usually stored in the server database). These attributes are referred to as *attribute value* (AV) pairs. A RADIUS request from the NAS and the corresponding reply from the server carry a series of attributes. Within a RADIUS packet, these attributes are encoded using the type-length-value (TLV) format, as shown in Figure 2-9.

Figure 2-9   *RADIUS Attribute Format*

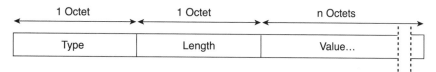

Examples of RADIUS attributes are:

- username (type = 1; value is a string)
- user-password (type = 2; value is a string)
- frame-protocol (type = 7; value can be 1 for PPP, 2 for SLIP, and so on)

For a comprehensive list of attributes, please refer to the RADIUS specification detailed in RFC 2138. To provide specific support for proprietary vendor information, the RADIUS standard defines a vendor-specific attribute with a type value of 26. *Vendor-specific attributes* (VSAs) allow vendors to support their own extended attributes that are unsuitable for general use. The standard states that the information within this attribute should be encoded as a sequence of vendor TLVs. Cisco Systems Inc. complies with the suggested format, and the Cisco VSA is shown in Figure 2-10.

Figure 2-10   *Cisco VSA*

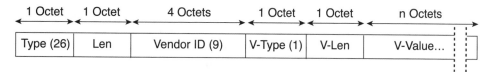

The Vendor ID takes its value from the SMI Network Management Private Enterprise Code definition. The Vendor ID for Cisco Systems Inc., has a value of 9. The Vendor Type (v-type) field has a value of 1, which defines this Cisco VSA as the "cisco-avpair." The Vendor Value (v-value) is a string that consists of the following format:

protocol : attribute sep value

where

> **Protocol** is a value of the Cisco protocol attribute for a particular type of authorization.
>
> **Attribute** and **value** are an appropriate attribute-value (AV) pair.
>
> **sep** is = for mandatory attributes and * for optional attributes.

The cisco-avpairs are used extensively when providing remote access to MPLS VPNs. Table 2-1 shows some examples of cisco-avpairs.

Table 2-1 *Examples of Cisco avpairs*

Attribute	Value
cisco-avpair	ip: addr-pool=main_pool
cisco-avpair	vpdn: ip-addresses=10.1.1.1
cisco-avpair	lcp: interface-config=ip vrf forwarding <vrfname>\n ip unnumbered Loopback

The first example causes the IP address pool, preconfigured as main_pool on the NAS, to be used during IP authorization (the IPCP phase). The next example defines an endpoint of a tunnel (that is, the LNS, 10.1.1.1) to be used. The last example allows any valid interface command to be configured dynamically on the router. This example defines a VRF and uses the IP address defined on the loopback0 interface (this must exist on the LNS).

DHCP

DHCP allows a device such as a PC to be dynamically configured with network information such as an IP address, DNS, and WINS server addresses from a central location. DHCP removes the burden of managing and coordinating IP addressing, which can be a time-consuming task for large networks. In addition, DHCP allows PC users to move between different IP subnets (such as different offices) and still receive the correct network information each time they connect to the IP network.

DHCP is a client/server protocol that uses Bootstrap Protocol (BOOTP) messages for its requests. DHCP messages from client to server are carried in BOOTP requests, whereas server to client messages are carried in BOOTP replies. The DHCP message consists of a series of options such as gateway address, allocated address, subnet mask, DNS server address, domain name, and so on. Figure 2-11 shows the basic steps for DHCP operation between a PC client and a DHCP server on the same LAN.

NOTE   BOOTP is an older protocol that provided functionality similar to DHCP, although in a severely limited fashion. DHCP is, in fact, an extension of BOOTP, mostly specifying new attributes that can be exchanged between the clients and the servers and new message types needed to support the more robust IP address allocation offered by DHCP.

The following steps illustrate the DHCP operation:

Step 1   The PC client broadcasts a DHCP DISCOVER message requesting an address allocation. The message will be received by all DHCP servers connected to the LAN (although we have shown only one).

Figure 2-11   *DHCP Operation*

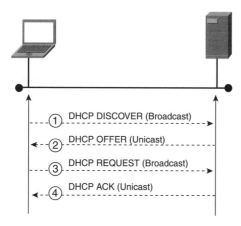

Step 2   The DHCP server issues a DHCP OFFER message containing the IP address, domain name, DNS, lease time, and so on in a unicast message back to the PC. Note that several DHCP Offer messages might be dependant on the number of DHCP servers connected to the LAN.

Step 3   The PC selects a received offer (usually the first or only one). At this point, the offer has not been formally accepted, but the DHCP server usually reserves the address (for a short period) until it receives a formal request from the PC. The PC formally requests the address offered by broadcasting a DHCP REQUEST. A broadcast is used so that the message serves as a reject to any other DHCP servers that made offers.

Step 4   The DHCP server confirms that the IP address has been allocated by responding with a DHCP ACK message that also includes other network configuration parameters.

The following are other messages that can be sent:

- **DHCP DECLINE**—Client to server, indicating that the network address is already in use or there is another issue.

- **DHCP RELEASE**—Client to server, indicating that the network address is to be relinquished and the remaining lease cancelled.

- **DHCP NAK**—Server to client, indicating that the client's notion of network address is incorrect (for example, the client has moved to a new subnet) or the client's lease has expired.

- **DHCP INFORM**—Client to server, asking only for local configuration parameters; the client already has an externally configured network address.

DHCP Relay Agents

The previous description is a reasonably simplistic view of how DHCP works. It assumes a DHCP server is available on every LAN in the network (which might well be the case if you are using the DHCP server feature in a Cisco router). However, if the DHCP server is centralized somewhere in the network, you must enable the DHCP relay agent feature by configuring the LAN interface of a Cisco router to get the DHCP messages between the client and the server. The operation of the DHCP relay agent feature is shown in Figure 2-12.

Figure 2-12   *DHCP Relay Agent*

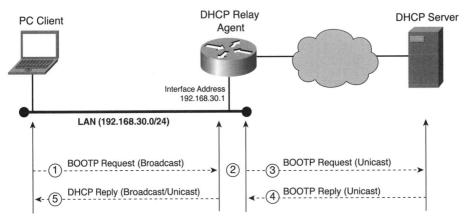

DHCP Relay operates as follows:

Step 1   All client to server messages (DHCP Discover, DHCP Request, and so on) are sent in a BOOTP Request.

Step 2   The DHCP relay agent feature is activated on the router interface via the **ip helper address** command. When the router sees a BOOTP Request that contains a DHCP message, it inserts its LAN interface address into the giaddr field of the BOOTP header, which in our example will be 192.168.30.1.

Step 3   The destination broadcast address in the original BOOTP message is replaced with the unicast IP address specified in the ip helper address command. The BOOTP request is then forwarded directly to the DHCP server as a unicast message. The DHCP server uses the giaddr field to determine the subnet pool that an address should be allocated from.

Step 4   The server to client messages are returned directly to the DHCP relay agent (router) by using the giaddr as the destination. These messages from the server, such as DHCP Offer, DHCP ACK, and so on, are carried in a BOOTP Reply.

Step 5   The relay agent receives the message and forwards the reply as a broadcast or a unicast IP packet to the client PC.

Providing Dial-In Access to an MPLS VPN

This section covers two methods of connecting switched calls to an MPLS VPN. The first method is based on VPDN and supports both analogue PSTN and ISDN calls. The second method supports only pure digital calls and is used to terminate ISDN calls directly onto a PE router.

Throughout all our remote access examples in this chapter, we use the addressing as summarized in Table 2-2.

Table 2-2   *IP Address Assignment for the SuperCom Network*

Company	Site	Subnet/Host
SuperCom	San Jose VHG/PE router (loopback 0)	194.22.15.2/32
	Management PE router (loopback 0)	194.22.15.3/32
	San Jose NAS/LAC (loopback 0)	194.22.15.4/32
	PE-CE interface addresses	192.168.2.0/24
	Management LAN	194.22.16.0/24
	RADIUS server host	194.22.16.2/32
	DHCP server host	194.22.16.3/32
	San Jose overlapping remote address pool(s)	192.168.3.0/26
	Loopback for VRF instantiation	192.168.2.100/32
FastFoods	Lyon subnet	10.2.1.0/24
	Lyon RADIUS server	10.2.1.5/32
	Lyon sales data server	10.2.1.6/32
	Fresno subnet (vending machine)	10.4.1.0/24
	Reno subnet (vending machine)	10.5.1.0/24
	Dialer for Fresno Vending	192.168.2.51/32
	Dialer for Reno Vending	192.168.2.52/32
EuroBank	San Francisco subnet	10.2.1.0/24
	Sacramento subnet (SOHO)	10.3.1.0/24
	Palo Alto (DSL CPE)	10.6.1.0/24
	Paris subnet	196.7.25.0/24
	Dialer for Modesto Branch	192.168.2.61/32
	Dialer for Laguna Branch	192.168.2.62/32

Dial-In Access via L2TP VPDN

This solution allows a service provider to offer a wholesale dial service to remote customers of an MPLS VPN. The remote clients dial a service provider POP by using the PSTN or ISDN and, after the appropriate authentication and L2TP procedures are executed, are connected to a PE router in the service provider network that provides access to the relevant VRF.

The mechanisms used to provide remote access to an MPLS VPN are based on the VPDN model. The advantage of using VPDN is to separate the remote access function from the edge function. A user can dial in to any NAS in the network and, using an L2TP tunnel, be directed to the nearest PE router that holds the appropriate VRF. Without this functionality, a VRF for every VPN that has remote access capabilities must be preinstantiated on every NAS that the user might possibly dial.

To best explain the various components and procedures, we shall use the SuperCom network shown in Figure 2-13. SuperCom can provide wholesale dial services through the NASes installed in its POPs, including the San Jose NAS shown in the diagram. The FastFoods Corporation has a requirement to provide real-time sales data to its worldwide mobile sales force from a network server that is located in FastFoods Marketing HQ in Lyon. Rather than building a private global remote access network at substantial cost, FastFoods has elected to use the SuperCom shared remote access infrastructure. This allows FastFoods to provide access to its VPN from any region worldwide where SuperCom has a POP presence. For the sake of simplifying the example, we will show the remote access process for a single remote salesperson called elvis@fastfoods.com, who is located somewhere on the U.S. West Coast and wants to access the FastFoods sales data located on a server at FastFoods European headquarters in Lyon.

Figure 2-13 *SuperCom Dial-In Using VPDN*

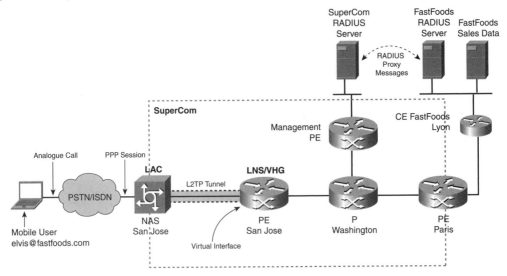

Although the remote dial-in access to an MPLS VPN follows the same procedures as a standard VPDN connection, certain parts of the process change slightly; for example, a SuperCom PE router rather than a FastFoods C router performs the LNS function. The process is summarized as follows:

- When elvis@fastfoods.com dials in using PPP, the SuperCom San Jose NAS/LAC extracts the domain name fastfoods.com, and passes it to the SuperCom RADIUS server for authentication. The SuperCom RADIUS server is reachable via the global routing table.

- If the domain name authentication succeeds, then the SuperCom RADIUS server passes back the relevant L2TP information for fastfoods.com, including the IP address of the tunnel endpoint (LNS). Note that the SuperCom RADIUS server contains domain entries rather than specific user entries; that is, it has an entry for fastfoods.com rather than one for elvis@fastfoods.com.

- The LAC builds an L2TP tunnel to the LNS. In MPLS VPN remote access terminology, the LNS can also be referred to as the *virtual home gateway (VHG)*. The term VHG refers to the fact that the LNS function is performed on a PE router rather than an LNS residing on a customer C router. In our example, this VHG/PE router is located at San Jose, and we will refer to it as the SuperCom San Jose VHG/PE router.

NOTE   You can use the terms VHG and PE/LNS interchangeably.

- The San Jose VHG/PE router must preinstantiate the FastFoods VRF that terminates the L2TP tunnel to minimize the convergence time for populating the VRF with routes.

- The San Jose VHG/PE router terminates the L2TP tunnel by using a virtual-template or a virtual-profile. (You will learn the difference later.) The SuperCom network uses virtual-profiles; therefore, it obtains the information to create a virtual interface from the SuperCom RADIUS server. This information includes items such as the VRF for the virtual interface, the interface address, and the IP address pool. The remote user accesses the VRF through an associated virtual interface.

- To obtain the relevant information to create the virtual interface, the San Jose VHG/ PE router requests authentication for elvis@fastfoods.com from the SuperCom RADIUS server. The SuperCom RADIUS server does not hold this individual user information; therefore, it must proxy the request to the relevant customer RADIUS server. In our example, this is the Lyon FastFoods RADIUS server. To achieve connectivity between the RADIUS servers, additional configuration is necessary. This is covered in a later section titled "Configuring Access Between the SuperCom and FastFoods RADIUS servers."

Configuring the SuperCom San Jose NAS/LAC

The San Jose NAS/LAC configuration is reasonably simple because the SuperCom RADIUS server provides the details that are used to create the appropriate L2TP tunnel for the dial-in user. The necessary configuration is shown in Example 2-1.

NOTE   This configuration shown here and the RADIUS attributes in the following section are not specific to MPLS VPNs but are required for any VPDN L2TP access.

Example 2-1   *San Jose NAS/LAC Configuration*

```
Hostname SanJose_NAS
!
aaa new-model
aaa authentication ppp default local group radius
aaa authorization network default local group radius
!
vpdn enable
vpdn search-order domain
!
interface Loopback0
  ip address 194.22.15.4 255.255.255.255
!
ip radius source-interface Loopback0
!
radius-server host 194.22.16.2 auth-port 1645 acct-port 1646 key a$4two
```

The **aaa** commands specify that any incoming PPP connections or network service requests (VPDN/L2TP) should be authenticated or authorized by checking the locally configured database first and then the SuperCom RADIUS server whose details are configured with the **radius-server host** command.

The **vpdn** commands enable VPDN and specify that only the domain name portion (fastfoods.com) of the incoming username (elvis@fastfoods.com) should be used when obtaining VPDN tunnel authorization from the SuperCom RADIUS server. It is also a good idea to statically configure the source address used by the router when sending RADIUS messages so that the RADIUS server can easily identify RADIUS clients. This is achieved through the **ip radius source-interface** command.

NOTE   The configuration does not rely on individual VPDN groups to be configured for each domain. The SuperCom RADIUS server provides this information, as discussed in the next section.

SuperCom RADIUS Server Attributes

The RADIUS server that SuperCom manages authenticates on the domain name associated with the remote user. Therefore, the entries in the RADIUS server consist only of domain names, not fully qualified usernames such as elvis@fastfoods.com. Each domain entry consists of a series of RADIUS attribute value (AV) pairs defining the VPDN information for that domain. This information is passed back to the LAC so that an L2TP tunnel can be built to the appropriate LNS.

NOTE	A RADIUS server does not actually distinguish between a username and a domain name; it only compares the string the RADIUS client passes to it (in our case, the LAC or LNS) in an access-request message. If the server finds an exact match for the string in its database, then AV pairs that are associated with that entry are passed back in an access-accept message. This means that the SuperCom RADIUS server is not limited to keeping information on the domain name only; it can also authenticate the fully qualified username elvis@fastfoods.com if FastFoods does not have its own RADIUS server.

The SuperCom RADIUS server attributes that are used to create an L2TP tunnel for fastfoods.com are shown in Table 2-3. The method in which the AV pairs are set or configured is beyond the scope of this book because it varies between RADIUS server implementations. The attributes shown are defined in RFC 2868, "RADIUS Attributes for Tunnel Protocol Support." The table also provides the corresponding Cisco-avpairs that were available prior to the publication of RFC 2868. The latest Cisco IOS versions accept either AV pair format.

Table 2-3   *SuperCom RADIUS Attributes*

Attribute (Type)	Value	Corresponding Cisco AV Pair
User-Name (1)	fastfoods.com	
User-Password (2)	cisco	
Tunnel-Type (64)	3 (L2TP)	vpdn: tunnel-type=l2tp
Tunnel-Medium-Type (65)	1 (IPv4)	
Tunnel-Server-Endpoint (67)	194.22.15.2 (San Jose VHG/PE)	vpdn: ip-addresses=194.22.15.2
Tunnel-Password (69)	vision	vpdn: l2tp-tunnel-password=vision
Tunnel-Client-Auth-ID (90)	SuperCom_LAC	vpdn: tunnel-id=SuperCom_LAC
Tunnel-Server-Auth-ID (91)	SuperCom_LNS	

The User-Name attribute defines the domain name that the San Jose NAS/LAC passes to the server. The password has a static value of "cisco."

NOTE A static password of "cisco" is always used in the RADIUS message when the LAC requests VPDN authorization for a domain. Therefore, all domain name entries on a RADIUS server must be configured with the password "cisco."

The other AV pairs request the San Jose NAS/LAC to build an L2TP tunnel for IPv4 packets to the destination 194.22.15.2. The local name that the San Jose NAS/LAC uses for the tunnel is "SuperCom_LAC." This name corresponds to the **terminate-from hostname** command that is configured on the San Jose VHG/PE router, which is discussed in the next section. Finally, for authentication purposes, the tunnel uses the password "vision," and the remote name expected is "SuperCom_LNS."

An alternative to using a RADIUS server for VPDN authorization is to configure a static VPDN group on the SuperCom NAS/LAC. The disadvantage of this is the increased operational overhead if there are many NAS/LACs to maintain and configure. By using a centralized RADIUS server, all VPDN configurations can be maintained in one place and used by many NAS/LACs.

Example 2-2 shows what the static VPDN configuration that corresponds to the RADIUS AV pairs in Table 2-1 looks like in Cisco IOS.

Example 2-2 *San Jose NAS/LAC VPDN Group Configuration*

```
vpdn-group 10
 request-dialin
  protocol l2tp
  domain fastfoods.com
 initiate-to ip 194.22.15.2
 local name SuperCom_LAC
 l2tp tunnel password vision
```

Configuring the SuperCom San Jose VHG/PE Router

The San Jose VHG/PE router terminates the L2TP tunnel from the San Jose NAS/LAC. The remote PPP session received through the tunnel from elvis@fastfoods.com is terminated on a virtual-access interface. The virtual-access interface is associated with the FastFoods VRF to allow elvis@fastfoods.com access to the FastFoods VPN. You can create a virtual-access interface by cloning through virtual templates or virtual-profiles.

- Virtual templates are configured for individual VPNs. Each associated virtual interface template must be configured for a specific VRF to preinstantiate the route for that VRF. Cisco IOS permits no more than 25 virtual-templates to be configured on a router; therefore, the use of virtual-templates does not scale well and is not recommended for terminating a large number of VPNs.

- Virtual-profiles are more flexible and can use a common virtual-template or an AAA (in our case, it will be RADIUS) server to provide the additional configuration details needed to create the virtual-access interface. The configuration information on the AAA server is held on a *per user* basis. Virtual-profiles simplify the configuration and provide a more scalable approach for tunnel termination because only a single virtual-template configuration is required for VPNs that terminate on the LNS.

Example 2-3 shows the necessary configuration for the San Jose VHG/PE router.

Example 2-3   *San Jose VHG/PE Router Configuration*

```
hostname SanJose_PE
!
aaa authentication ppp default local group radius
aaa authorization network default local group radius
!
virtual-profile aaa
vpdn enable
!
vpdn-group 1
 accept-dialin
  protocol l2tp
  virtual-Template 1
 terminate-from hostname SuperCom_LAC
 local name SuperCom_LNS
 l2tp tunnel password vision
!
interface virtual-Template1
 no ip address
 no peer default ip address
 ppp authentication chap callin
!
ip local pool SuperCom_Pool 192.168.3.1 192.168.3.62
ip local pool FastFoods_Pool 192.168.3.1 192.168.3.62 group VPN_FastFoods
ip local pool EuroBank_Pool 192.168.3.1 192.168.3.62 group VPN_EuroBank
!
ip radius source-interface Loopback0
!
radius-server host 194.22.16.2 auth-port 1645 acct-port 1646 key a$4two
```

The aaa configuration is identical to what the SuperCom NAS/LAC uses because both use the same SuperCom RADIUS server. The operational difference is that the San Jose NAS/LAC passes the domain name fastfoods.com to the SuperCom RADIUS server that responds directly. In contrast, the San Jose VHG/PE router passes the fully qualified username elvis@fastfoods.com to the SuperCom RADIUS server for authentication, which, in turn, proxies the message to the FastFoods RADIUS server for processing. The virtual-profile **aaa** command enables the LNS to obtain configuration information from the RADIUS server on a per-user basis that can be applied to the virtual-template. In our case, the **vpdn-group** command supplies the virtual-template number. A single VPDN group configuration is required to terminate an L2TP tunnel from any LAC that has the name

SuperCom_LAC with a password of "vision." The LAC uses the local name SuperCom_LNS for authentication, which matches the AV pair information previously provided to the SuperCom NAS/LAC in Table 2-1. The vpdn-group is associated with the generic virtual-template1. This virtual-template is used in conjunction with information received from the FastFoods RADIUS server to create the virtual-access interface for the remote user.

The San Jose VHG/PE router uses locally configured overlapping pools to provide IP addresses to remote users. The overlapping pool feature allows the same address space to be used concurrently in different VRFs by appending a group name on the **ip local pool** command. In our example, three pools have been configured to use the same address range 192.168.3.1 through 192.168.3.62:

- A SuperCom_Pool for remote users who are accessing services in the global routing table (such as best effort Internet)
- A FastFoods_Pool for remote users of the FastFoods VPN
- A EuroBank_Pool for remote users of the EuroBank VPN

NOTE   In a production network, the pools used would most likely provide registered addresses.

You can find further discussion on other addressing options in the "Advanced Features for MPLS VPN Remote Access" section.

To complete the configuration, we must preinstantiate all the VRFs to be accessed through this LNS. We cannot rely on dynamic instantiation of the VRF routing information when the first user dials in because Multiprotocol BGP might take up to 60 seconds to converge the routes for the new VRF. To avoid this delay, create and associate a loopback interface with the applicable VRF, as shown in Example 2-4.

Example 2-4   *Preinstantiation of VRFs*

```
ip vrf FastFoods
 rd 10:26
 route-target export 10:26
 route-target import 10:26
!
interface Loopback10
 ip vrf forwarding FastFoods
 ip address 192.168.2.100 255.255.255.255
```

To reduce the number of addresses required, you can use the same address 192.168.2.100 on every loopback that is required for instantiation.

NOTE	A full explanation on how routes are converged between VPN sites is provided in Chapter 12 of Cisco Press's Volume I of *MPLS and VPN Architectures*, ISBN 1587050811.

FastFoods RADIUS Server Attributes

The FastFoods RADIUS server authenticates any remote users who request access to the FastFoods VPN via a proxy request from the SuperCom RADIUS server. If authentication succeeds, an access-accept message is returned (via the SuperCom RADIUS server) that contains the RADIUS attributes required to assist in configuring the virtual-access interface in the San Jose VHG/PE router for the remote user.

NOTE	Unless the VPN customer requests SuperCom to manage its remote user lists, the SuperCom RADIUS server must have a proxy entry to a customer RADIUS server for every domain it services.

The FastFoods RADIUS server attributes for user elvis@fastfoods.com are shown in Table 2-4. All of the Cisco-avpair attributes shown here are service provider-specific, such as the pool name, loopback address, and VRF name. This information can be stored on the FastFoods RADIUS server and passed back for the user. In practice, however, this is not recommended due to the security implications of a customer being able to configure a service provider's network interfaces. It is more likely that the SuperCom RADIUS server would add the service provider-specific attributes to proxy requests, which would then be passed back with an access-accept message from the FastFoods RADIUS server. The Cisco-avpairs are shown in this table together with user-specific attributes to simplify the explanation.

Table 2-4   *User elvis@fastfoods.com RADIUS Attributes*

Attribute (Type)	Value
User-Name (1)	elvis@fastfoods.com
User-Password (2)	whatsthebuzz
Service-Type (6)	1 (Framed)
Framed-Protocol (7)	1 (PPP)
Cisco-avpair	lcp:interface-config=ip vrf forwarding FastFoods \n[1]
	ip unnumbered loopback 10 \n
	peer default ip address pool FastFoods_Pool

NOTE	The \n in the Cisco-avpair signifies an explicit carriage return. Usage will vary between RADIUS server implementations.

Based on these attributes, the SuperCom PE/LNS will create a virtual-access interface to terminate a framed PPP session. This interface will be placed in the FastFoods VRF and use the address of loopback 10, as discussed in Example 2-4. The remote user elvis@fastfoods.com will be provided with the next available address from the local address pool called FastFoods_Pool.

NOTE	It is likely that the FastFoods RADIUS server would only contain username entries such as "fred" rather than the fully qualified domain name. A proxy script on the SuperCom RADIUS server would be responsible for stripping off the domain name before proxying the request.

Configuring Access Between SuperCom and FastFoods RADIUS Servers

The FastFoods RADIUS server is only reachable via the FastFoods VRF. The SuperCom RADIUS server is connected to an interface on the Management PE router and must be reachable via the global routing table for all SuperCom routers that require RADIUS services. This is because the **radius-server host** command that is configured on the NAS and PE routers only operates in the global routing space.

Therefore, some additional configuration is required to allow the SuperCom RADIUS server to communicate with both the NAS and PE routers in the global table and the RADIUS server in the FastFoods VRF, without compromising security in the FastFoods network. This is achieved by using the MPLS VPN mechanisms of route-targets and route-maps, as shown in Figure 2-14.

The SuperCom RADIUS server should be placed in a Management VRF to isolate the SuperCom management addresses from the global table. This is done on the Management PE router shown in Figure 2-13. This allows the FastFoods RADIUS server host address to be exported to the Management VRF and the SuperCom RADIUS server host address to be exported to the FastFoods VRF. Both RADIUS servers can then communicate directly with each other. The FastFoods network remains secure because access is limited to the FastFoods RADIUS server from the Management VRF only.

Access to the SuperCom RADIUS server from the global routing table (for SuperCom routers) is achieved by placing a global static route into the Management VRF that points to the SuperCom network, as well as a static route in the global routing table that points to the SuperCom Management network.

Figure 2-14 *RADIUS Connectivity*

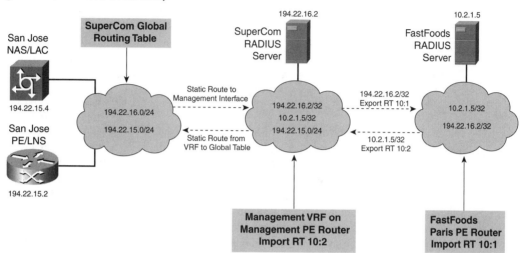

NOTE   Chapter 12 of Cisco Press's Volume I of *MPLS and VPN Architectures* provides further
detailed information on advanced scenarios such as route leaking between a VRF and the
global routing table.

Examples 2-5 and 2-6 show the relevant configurations on the Management and Paris PE
routers to accomplish proxy access.

Example 2-5 *Management PE Configuration for RADIUS Proxy*

```
hostname Management_PE
!
ip vrf SuperCom_Management
rd 10:1
export map OUT-Management-RADIUS
route-target import 10:2
!
access-list 20 permit host 194.22.16.2
!
route-map OUT-Management permit 10
 match ip address 20
 set extcommunity rt 10:1
!
ip route 194.22.16.0 255.255.255.0 Ethernet5/0
ip route vrf SuperCom_Management 194.22.15.0 255.255.255.0 POS3/0
ip route vrf SuperCom_Management 194.22.16.2 255.255.255.255 Ethernet5/0
194.22.16.2
```

The Management PE configuration has an export map defined that permits only the SuperCom RADIUS server address (194.22.16.2) to be set with the route-target 10:1. The FastFoods VRF on the Paris PE router (shown in Example 2-6) has a corresponding route-target import for 10:1. Conversely, the FastFoods VRF has a similar export map setting the route-target 10:2 for the FastFoods RADIUS server (10.2.1.5), which the Management VRF then imports. The "additive" keyword is necessary to allow the route-target 10:2 to be appended to the existing route-target 10:26. Without the "additive" keyword, the default action is to overwrite all existing route-targets.

Three static routes are defined on the Management PE router. The first static route creates a route to the Management subnet in the global routing table. The next static route creates a route to allow access to devices in the global routing table via POS3/0 (the interface that connects the Management PE to the backbone). Note that this static command does not require the "global" keyword because we are using an interface name, not a next-hop address. The last static route creates a host route to the SuperCom RADIUS server to be used to export to the FastFoods VRF. (The export route map matches on this entry.) The Paris PE router has a single static host route configured pointing to the FastFoods RADIUS server, shown in Example 2-6.

Example 2-6 *Paris PE Configuration for RADIUS Proxy*

```
hostname Paris_PE
!
ip vrf FastFoods
 rd 10:26
 export map OUT-Customer-RADIUS
 route-target export 10:26
 route-target import 10:26
 route-target import 10:1
 !
access-list 20 permit host 10.2.1.5
 !
route-map OUT-Customer-RADIUS permit 10
 match ip address 20
 set extcommunity rt 10:2 additive
 !
ip route vrf FastFoods 10.2.1.5 255.255.255.255 FastEthernet0/1 192.168.2.21
```

Example 2-7 shows the routing entries for the Management and FastFoods VRFs. As you can see, both VRFs import only the relevant host RADIUS address of 10.2.1.5 or 194.22.16.2. You can also see the static entries discussed previously.

Example 2-7 *Management and FastFoods VRF Tables*

```
Management_PE#show ip route vrf SuperCom_Management
[snip]

S    194.22.15.0/24 is directly connected, POS3/0
     10.0.0.0/32 is subnetted, 1 subnets
B       10.2.1.5 [200/0] via 194.22.15.1, 4d21h
     194.22.16.0/24 is variably subnetted, 2 subnets, 2 masks
```

Example 2-7   *Management and FastFoods VRF Tables (Continued)*

```
C        194.22.16.0/24 is directly connected, Ethernet5/0
S        194.22.16.2/32 [1/0] via 194.22.16.2, Ethernet5/0
- - - - - - - - - - - - - - - - - - - - - - - - - - - - - - - - - - - - - - - - - - - -
Paris_PE#show ip route vrf FastFoods
[snip]

     10.0.0.0/8 is variably subnetted, 2 subnets, 2 masks
S        10.2.1.0/24 [1/0] via 192.168.2.21
S        10.2.1.5/32 [1/0] via 192.168.2.21, FastEthernet0/1
     192.168.2.0/24 is variably subnetted, 2 subnets, 2 masks
B        192.168.2.100/32 [200/0] via 194.22.15.2, 00:19:03
C        192.168.2.20/30 is directly connected, FastEthernet0/1
     194.22.16.0/32 is subnetted, 1 subnets
B        194.22.16.2 [200/0] via 194.22.15.3, 00:19:33
```

The solution shown here is not without its drawbacks. For example, overlapping addresses might become an issue in the Management VRF if multiple customers' RADIUS servers were using the same address space. Some form of NAT would be necessary, which would increase the complexity and management of the solution. A new feature called *Per VRF AAA* addresses this problem by obviating the need for the service provider RADIUS to act as a proxy. It achieves this by allowing direct access to the customer's RADIUS server from the VRF. This feature is discussed in a later section.

Verifying Dial-In via VPDN Operation

Now that all the necessary components of the network have been configured for remote access, we can verify operation by examining output of various **show** commands. To provide a more complete picture of how remote access to an MPLS VPN operates, two more users have dialed into the San Jose NAS in addition to elvis@fastfoods.com. They are eric@eurobank.com and jimi@fastfoods.com. This is shown in Figure 2-15.

Figure 2-15   *Multiple VPDN Users*

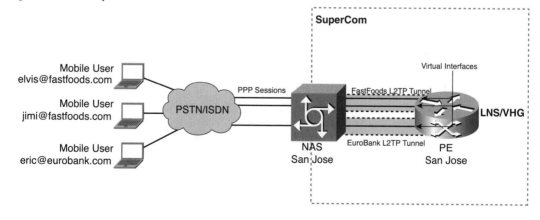

Two L2TP tunnels are created between the San Jose LAC and LNS, one for each domain (FastFoods and EuroBank). Each user has a separate PPP session activated over the appropriate tunnel, and these sessions are represented at the LNS by a virtual-access interface in the VRF.

The following debug (see Example 2-8) from the San Jose NAS shows the incoming call for elvis@fastfoods.com. After the call is connected, the San Jose NAS challenges the remote PC for the username/password. When the San Jose NAS receives this information, it extracts the domain name fastfoods.com and searches for a matching L2TP tunnel. Because no VPDN groups are explicitly configured, the SuperCom RADIUS server is queried and the relevant tunnel information is returned. A tunnel is then established to 194.22.15.2 (San Jose VHG/PE router), and the username/password of elvis@fastfoods.com is forwarded over the tunnel.

Example 2-8   *San Jose Debug*

```
%LINK-3-UPDOWN: Interface Async2, changed state to up
As2 CHAP: O CHALLENGE id 14 len 31 from "SanJose_NAS"
As2 CHAP: I RESPONSE id 14 len 39 from "elvis@fastfoods.com"
As2 VPDN: Got DNIS string 94780400
As2 VPDN: Looking for tunnel -- fastfoods.com --
As2 VPDN/RPMS/: Got tunnel info for fastfoods.com
As2 VPDN/RPMS/:    LAC SuperCom_LAC
As2 VPDN/RPMS/:    l2tp-busy-disconnect yes
As2 VPDN/RPMS/:    l2tp-tunnel-password xxxxxx
As2 VPDN/RPMS/:    IP 194.22.15.2
As2 VPDN: Share tunnel fastfoods.com IP 194.22.15.2 state established
As2 VPDN: Forward to address 194.22.15.2
As2 VPDN: Forwarding...
As2 VPDN: Bind interface direction=1
As2 VPDN: elvis@fastfoods.com is forwarded
%LINEPROTO-5-UPDOWN: Line protocol on Interface Async2, changed state
  to up
```

The San Jose debug for VPDN and virtual-template events is shown in Example 2-9. When the L2TP call is received, a virtual interface (in our case, Vi2) is cloned from the brief information that is configured in virtual-template1 (refer to Example 2-2 for details). When the username elvis@fastfoods.com is received over the L2TP tunnel, the SuperCom RADIUS server is queried for authentication and further configuration information (which is proxied to the FastFoods RADIUS server). After this information is returned, it is applied to Vi2 (Cloned from AAA - VRF, address pool, and so on) and the line protocol is changed to up.

Example 2-9   *San Jose VHG/PE-Router Debug*

```
Vi2 VTEMPLATE: ************* CLONE VACCESS2 ****************
Vi2 VTEMPLATE: Clone from virtual-Template1

default ip address
encap ppp
end
```

Example 2-9   *San Jose VHG/PE-Router Debug (Continued)*

```
VTEMPLATE: Receiving vaccess request, id 0x5B70035, result 1
Vi2 VPDN: Set to Async interface
Vi2 VPDN: Virtual interface created for elvis@fastfoods.com bandwidth 65 Kbps
Vi2 VPDN: Bind interface direction=2
2w5d: %LINK-3-UPDOWN: Interface virtual-Access2, changed state to up
VTEMPLATE: Sending vaccess request, id 0x63CDE184
VTEMPLATE: Processing vaccess requests, 1 outstanding
Vi2 VTEMPLATE: Has a new cloneblk AAA, now it has vtemplate/AAA
Vi2 VTEMPLATE: ************* CLONE VACCESS2 *****************
Vi2 VTEMPLATE: Clone from AAA

ip vrf forwarding FastFoods
ip unnumbered loopback 10
peer default ip address pool FastFoods_Pool
end

VTEMPLATE: Receiving vaccess request, id 0x63CDE184, result 1
%LINEPROTO-5-UPDOWN: Line protocol on Interface virtual-Access2,
 changed state to up
```

The following output in Example 2-10 shows the VPDN status on the San Jose NAS. Two L2TP tunnels have been created to the SuperCom_LNS with the local IDs of 28791 and 35022. The first tunnel is for FastFoods and has two PPP sessions active, whereas the second tunnel is for EuroBank with one session active. The corresponding sessions can be seen in the output from the **show vpdn session** command.

Example 2-10   *San Jose NAS VPDN Information*

```
SanJose_NAS#show vpdn tunnel

L2TP Tunnel Information Total tunnels 2 sessions 3

LocID RemID Remote Name   State  Remote Address  Port  Sessions
28791 1463  SuperCom_LNS  est    194.22.15.2     1701  2
35022 37120 SuperCom_LNS  est    194.22.15.2     1701  1

SanJose_NAS#show vpdn session

L2TP Session Information Total tunnels 2 sessions 3

LocID RemID TunID Intf  Username             State  Last Chg Fastswitch
46    46    28791 As3   jimi@fastfoods.com   est    00:14:26 enabled
49    49    28791 As2   elvis@fastfoods.com  est    00:05:13 enabled
50    50    35022 As4   eric@eurobank.com    est    00:02:04 enabled
```

The VPDN information on the San Jose VHG/PE router is shown in Example 2-11 and is similar to the LAC. Note that the interface associated with the user is a virtual-access interface and that all L2TP tunnels are terminated by using VPDN group 1 as the tunnel client name that matched the hostname "SuperCom_LAC."

Example 2-11 *San Jose VHG/PE Router VPDN Information*

```
SanJose_PE#show vpdn tunnel

L2TP Tunnel Information Total tunnels 2 sessions 3

LocID RemID Remote Name   State  Remote Address  Port  Sessions  VPDN Group
1463  28791 SuperCom_LAC  est    194.22.15.26    1701  2         1
37120 35022 SuperCom_LAC  est    194.22.15.26    1701  1         1

SanJose_PE#show vpdn sess

L2TP Session Information Total tunnels 2 sessions 3

LocID RemID TunID Intf  Username              State  Last Chg Fastswitch
46    46    1463  Vi1   jimi@fastfoods.com    est    00:36:22 enabled
49    49    1463  Vi2   elvis@fastfoods.com   est    00:27:09 enabled
50    50    37120 Vi3   eric@eurobank.com     est    00:24:01 enabled
```

If we look at the VRF information in the San Jose VHG/PE router in Example 2-12, we see
that the virtual-access interfaces have been associated with the correct VRF. The loopback
interfaces are used for preinstantiation of the VPN routes, as discussed earlier.

Example 2-12 *San Jose VHG/PE Router VRF Information*

```
SanJose_PE#show ip vrf
  Name                    Default RD        Interfaces
  EuroBank                10:27             virtual-Access3
                                            Loopback11

  FastFoods               10:26             virtual-Access1
                                            virtual-Access2
                                            Loopback10
```

In our configuration, the addresses for each of the remote access users are taken from one
of the shared pools. To achieve higher utilization of the available address space, all the
pools use the same range of 192.168.3.1–192.168.3.62. As you can see in Example 2-13,
two addresses have been used from the FastFoods_Pool, whereas one address has been used
from the EuroBank_Pool. Because these addresses are allocated to different VRFs, there is
no possibility of overlap.

Example 2-13 *San Jose VHG/PE-Router Address Pool Usage*

```
SanJose_PE#show ip local pool

Pool                     Begin         End            Free  In use
SuperCom_Pool            192.168.3.1   192.168.3.62   62    0
** pool <FastFoods_Pool> is in group <VPN_FastFoods>
FastFoods_Pool           192.168.3.1   192.168.3.62   60    2
** pool <EuroBank_Pool> is in group <VPN_EuroBank>
EuroBank_Pool            192.168.3.1   192.168.3.62   61    1
```

Examining the routing tables for FastFoods and EuroBank in Example 2-14, we can see that the host addresses have been installed as connected routes for each of the virtual-access interfaces. You can also see the loopback address used for preinstantiation of the VRFs using the address of 192.168.2.100.

Our original premise for providing remote access to FastFoods users was to provide access to the Sales Data server in Lyon (10.2.1.6). This has been achieved because the FastFoods VRF has imported the BGP route 10.2.1.0/24 from the FastFoods VRF on the Paris PE router (194.22.15.1), allowing any FastFoods remote access user who is terminating on the San Jose PE router access to the FastFoods Lyon subnet.

Example 2-14 *San Jose VHG/PE Router VRF Routing Tables*

```
SanJose_PE#show ip route vrf FastFoods
[snip]


     10.0.0.0/24 is subnetted, 1 subnets
B       10.2.1.0 [200/0] via 194.22.15.1, 02:09:57
     192.168.2.0/24 is variably subnetted, 2 subnets, 2 masks
C       192.168.2.100/32 is directly connected, Loopback10
B       192.168.2.20/30 [200/0] via 194.22.15.1, 02:09:57
     192.168.3.0/32 is subnetted, 2 subnets
C       192.168.3.2 is directly connected, virtual-Access1
C       192.168.3.1 is directly connected, virtual-Access2

SanJose_PE#show ip route vrf EuroBank
[snip]

B    196.7.25.0/24 [200/0] via 194.22.15.1, 02:14:14
     194.22.15.0/32 is subnetted, 2 subnets
B       194.22.15.3 [200/0] via 194.22.15.3, 02:14:29
B       194.22.15.1 [200/0] via 194.22.15.1, 02:13:59
     192.168.2.0/24 is variably subnetted, 2 subnets, 2 masks
C       192.168.2.100/32 is directly connected, Loopback11
B       192.168.2.24/30 [200/0] via 194.22.15.1, 02:14:14
     192.168.3.0/32 is subnetted, 1 subnets
C       192.168.3.1 is directly connected, virtual-Access3
```

Aggregating Remote User Host Addresses

The VRF routing tables in the previous example showed there was a host route installed for each remote access user. To redistribute these routes to other VPN sites across the MPLS VPN backbone, you need to configure the **redistribute connected** command configured in BGP for the VRF (under the address-family). For large-scale dial-in services, this could lead to many host routes being distributed and installed into VRFs by Multiprotocol BGP. To prevent this from happening, you should summarize the remote host addresses in the VRF to the subnet used for pool addresses by using the BGP **aggregate-address** command, as shown in Example 2-15. The summary-only keyword prevents more specific routes from being advertised. Therefore, the **redistribute connected** might be kept for other routing requirements, and any connected routes in the range 192.168.3.0/26 can be overridden by the **aggregate-address** entry.

Example 2-15 *Summarizing Pool Addresses*

```
router bgp 100
 [snip]
 !
 address-family ipv4 vrf FastFoods
 aggregate-address 192.168.3.0 255.255.255.192 summary-only
 redistribute connected
 exit-address-family
 !
 address-family ipv4 vrf EuroBank
 aggregate-address 192.168.3.0 255.255.255.192 summary-only
 redistribute connected
 exit-address-family
```

The pool addresses 192.168.3.1 to 192.168.3.62 are summarized to a single route 192.168.3.0/26, which appears in the label forwarding table (LFIB) on the San Jose VHG/ PE router as an aggregate route (see Example 2-16). Note there are two aggregates for 192.168.3.0/26, representing one for each VRF.

NOTE An entry that has an aggregate label in the forwarding table requires additional processing. First, the label is removed from the stack and a Layer 3 lookup is performed in the VRF on the underlying IP packet. If the removed label is not at the bottom of the stack (aggregates should always be at the bottom of the stack), the packet is discarded.

Example 2-16 *San Jose PE/NAS Aggregate Routes*

```
SanJose_PE#show mpls forwarding | inc 192.168.3
20     Aggregate    192.168.3.0/26[V] 0
21     Untagged     192.168.3.1/32[V] 1400      Vi2      point2point
22     Untagged     192.168.3.2/32[V] 2100      Vi1      point2point
25     Untagged     192.168.3.1/32[V] 0         Vi3      point2point
26     Aggregate    192.168.3.0/26[V] 0
```

If you look at the VRF table for FastFoods (see Example 2-17) in the Paris PE router, you can see that the host routes have been replaced with a single summarized route 192.168.3.0/26.

Example 2-17 *Paris PE-Router FastFoods VRF Table*

```
Paris_PE#show ip route vrf FastFoods
[snip]

     10.0.0.0/8 is variably subnetted, 2 subnets, 2 masks
S       10.2.1.0/24 [1/0] via 192.168.2.21
```

Example 2-17 *Paris PE-Router FastFoods VRF Table (Continued)*

```
S        10.2.1.5/32 [1/0] via 192.168.2.21, FastEthernet0/1
         192.168.2.0/24 is variably subnetted, 2 subnets, 2 masks
B        192.168.2.100/32 [200/0] via 194.22.15.2, 02:56:44
C        192.168.2.20/30 is directly connected, FastEthernet0/1
         194.22.16.0/32 is subnetted, 1 subnets
B        194.22.16.2 [200/0] via 194.22.15.3, 02:57:14
         192.168.3.0/26 is subnetted, 1 subnets
B        192.168.3.0 [200/0] via 194.22.15.2, 00:00:09
```

Dial-In Access via Direct ISDN

Direct dial-in access allows a remote user who has ISDN access to call a PE router and have that call terminate directly into the appropriate VRF. There is no L2TP tunneling necessary because the PE router performs the functions of both a PE router and a NAS. Direct ISDN dial-in is supported only with pure digital calls (not analogue calls carried within the ISDN B-channel).

Figure 2-16 shows a direct ISDN dial scenario in the SuperCom network. The San Jose NAS/PE router has a primary rate ISDN service connected; therefore, remote users who are equipped with an ISDN service can call the San Jose PE router directly. In our example, EuroBank has a small branch office located in Sacramento, which is equipped with a SOHO router that is connected to an ISDN service. This router uses dial-on-demand techniques to connect the Sacramento PCs on the 10.3.1.0/24 network to the EuroBank VPN. The link is established by using PPP, and the SOHO router is identified to the SuperCom network with the username sacramento@eurobank_SOHO. The choice of the domain name eurobank_SOHO (rather than eurobank.com) is deliberate. The rationale will be explained at the end of this section.

NOTE   The acronym *SOHO* applies to a customer network that has a small number of PCs connected, generally what you would find in a small office, home office (SOHO).

EuroBank does not have an AAA server and relies solely on SuperCom to provide all of its AAA services. Therefore, the SuperCom RADIUS server holds the entries and attributes for all remote EuroBank users (regardless of whether they are routers or single users/hosts).

As in the VPDN scenario, virtual-profiles are used to create virtual-access interfaces for incoming calls. This mechanism provides a scalable solution for terminating many different users over the same ISDN service because the configuration of the B-channel virtual-access interface is provided by the SuperCom RADIUS server based on the calling user ID.

Figure 2-16 *SuperCom Dial-In Using Direct ISDN*

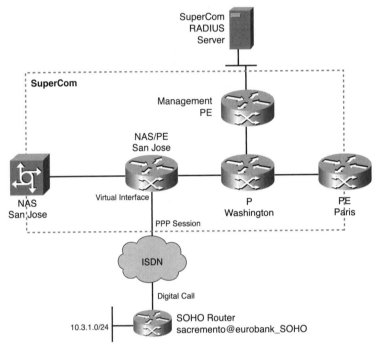

The direct dial-in ISDN process is simpler than dial-in access using VPDN; it can be summarized as follows:

1 When the Sacramento EuroBank router calls in, a PPP link is established over the ISDN B-channel.

2 The San Jose NAS/PE router obtains the username sacramento@eurobank_SOHO from the Sacramento router using CHAP, which it then forwards to the SuperCom RADIUS server for authorization.

3 If successful, the SuperCom RADIUS server passes back any configuration parameters (VRF name, address pool) that are associated with the user.

4 The San Jose NAS/PE router creates a virtual-access interface for the PPP session based on a locally configured virtual-template combined with the configuration that the SuperCom RADIUS server provides.

5 The user CHAP authentication completes and the connection is fully established within the VPN.

In the SuperCom network, the San Jose PE router also performs the LNS function to terminate L2TP tunnels from the San Jose NAS/LAC as discussed previously. To enable the

San Jose PE router to provide L2TP termination, it must have the command **vpdn enable** set. For direct dial-in ISDN calls using PPP, the LNS function is not necessary; however, this command causes interesting behavior on the San Jose PE router. When an ISDN call is received, the **vpdn enable** command causes the San Jose PE router to initially forward an access request using just the domain or DNIS name. Because the SuperCom RADIUS server has entries holding L2TP tunnel information for all domains (such as fastfoods.com and eurobank.com), there is a danger that tunnel information will be mistakenly returned to the San Jose PE router, which will then unnecessarily build an L2TP tunnel to itself. You can avoid this problem by configuring the RADIUS server to check for various attributes such as the NAS-identifier (the LAC or LNS) or the NAS-Port (an ISDN call) of the access request and providing the appropriate RADIUS response. In our example, we have opted not to rely on special RADIUS scripting procedures. Instead, we will use a different domain name to identify the direct dial-in ISDN users. Therefore, using domain "eurobank_SOHO" avoids conflict on the RADIUS server for any bona-fide eurobank.com dial-in users who are using VPDN.

Configuring the SuperCom San Jose NAS/PE Router

Example 2-18 shows the configuration for the San Jose NAS/PE router.

Example 2-18 *San Jose NAS/PE Router Configuration for Direct ISDN Dial*

```
hostname SanJose_PE
!
virtual-profile virtual-Template2
virtual-profile aaa
!
ip vrf EuroBank
 rd 10:27
 route-target export 10:27
 route-target import 10:27
!
interface Loopback11
 ip vrf forwarding EuroBank
 ip address 192.168.2.100 255.255.255.255
!
interface Serial6/0:15
 ip unnumbered Loopback0
 encapsulation ppp
 isdn switch-type primary-net5
 ppp authentication chap callin
!
interface virtual-Template2
 no ip address
 no peer default ip address
 ppp authentication chap callin
!
```

The AAA and overlapping local pool configuration is the same as for dial-in access using VPDN, as shown previously in Example 2-2. The only difference, besides the ISDN interface configuration, is the addition of a virtual-profile using virtual-template2.

NOTE   Virtual-template2 is necessary so that any incoming ISDN PPP calls have a virtual-template to which a virtual-access interface can be cloned. Virtual-template2 can also be configured with any global configuration that SuperCom might deem necessary, such as certain access-lists that would be common for all users.

The **virtual-profile aaa** command causes any additional per-user specific configurations to be retrieved from the SuperCom RADIUS server and applied to the cloned interface. Note that Loopback 11 is used to preinstantiate the EuroBank VRF.

SuperCom RADIUS Server Attributes

The RADIUS entry for the Sacramento SOHO router shown in Table 2-5 is identical to that of a single PC user except for the addition of a Framed-Route attribute, which injects a static route into the EuroBank VRF for the Sacramento LAN 10.3.1.0/24. The next-hop address for the route is then automatically set to the address selected from the local pool for the remote interface.

Table 2-5   *Sacramento Router RADIUS Attributes for Direct ISDN Dial*

Attribute (Type)	Value
User-Name (1)	sacramento@eurobank_SOHO
User-Password (2)	whatsthebuzz
Service-Type (6)	1 (Framed)
Framed-Protocol (7)	1 (PPP)
Framed-Route(22)	10.3.1.0/24
Cisco-avpair	lcp:interface-config=ip vrf forwarding EuroBank \n[1]
	ip unnumbered loopback 11 \n
	peer default ip address pool EuroBank_Pool

[1] The \n signifies an explicit carriage return that varies between server implementations.

NOTE   A new Cisco IOS feature called *Framed Route VRF aware* was necessary to support the Framed-Route attribute in the context of a VRF. This feature is available in the 12.2(8)T Release of Cisco IOS. You can also use the cisco-avpair "ip:route=10.3.1.0 255.255.255.0" in place of the Framed-Route attribute to achieve the same result.

Configuring the Sacramento SOHO Router

Example 2-19 shows the Sacramento router configuration. The **ip address negotiated** command ensures that the dialer interface receives its address from the EuroBank_Pool configured on the San Jose NAS/PE_Router. A default static route is used via interface dialer 1 to gain access to the EuroBank VPN.

Example 2-19 *Sacramento SOHO Router Configuration for Direct ISDN Dial*

```
hostname Sacramento_SOHO
!
interface BRI0/0
 no ip address
 encapsulation ppp
 dialer pool-member 5
 isdn switch-type basic-net3
!
interface Dialer1
 ip address negotiated
 encapsulation ppp
 dialer pool 5
 dialer idle-timeout 600
 dialer string 94780400
 dialer-group 1
 ppp chap hostname sacramento@eurobank_SOHO
 ppp chap password whatsthebuzz
!
ip route 0.0.0.0 0.0.0.0 Dialer1
!
dialer-list 1 protocol ip permit
```

Verifying Direct Dial-In Operation

Example 2-20 shows the routing table for the EuroBank VRF after the ISDN connection has been established from the Sacramento SOHO router. Interface Virtual-Access4 has been created in the EuroBank VRF and configured with the address 192.168.3.2 from the EuroBank local pool. (Note that Vi3 is still connected to eric@eurobank.com.) In addition, a per-user static route, denoted by the "U," for 10.3.1.0/24 has been inserted for the Sacramento LAN. This information was in the Framed-Route attribute that was returned in the access-accept message from the SuperCom RADIUS server. The Multiprotocol BGP will distribute the per-user static route to all other EuroBank VRFs assuming that redistribute static has been appropriately configured under the BGP address-family.

Example 2-20 *San Jose NAS/PE Router EuroBank VRF Routes for Direct ISDN Dial*

```
SanJose_PE#show ip route vrf EuroBank
[snip]

B    196.7.25.0/24 [200/0] via 194.22.15.1, 04:28:33
     10.0.0.0/24 is subnetted, 1 subnets
U       10.3.1.0 [1/0] via 192.168.3.2
     192.168.2.0/24 is variably subnetted, 2 subnets, 2 masks
C       192.168.2.100/32 is directly connected, Loopback11
```

continues

Example 2-20 *San Jose NAS/PE Router EuroBank VRF Routes for Direct ISDN Dial (Continued)*

```
B       192.168.2.24/30 [200/0] via 194.22.15.1, 04:28:33
        192.168.3.0/24 is variably subnetted, 3 subnets, 2 masks
C       192.168.3.1/32 is directly connected, virtual-Access3
C       192.168.3.2/32 is directly connected, virtual-Access4
B       192.168.3.0/26 [200/0] via 0.0.0.0, 00:00:54, Null0
```

Providing Dial-Out Access via LSDO

The LSDO feature is an effective and scalable method of providing dial-out services in a service provider environment. LSDO eliminates the need to configure individual dialer profiles for every outgoing destination. Instead, all the dialer profile attributes such as the dialing number, username/passwords, and PPP peer IP address are kept on an AAA server. Only a generic dialer interface needs to be configured on all service provider VHG or NAS devices. By using an AAA server, you can keep all dialer configurations at a central point and download them to any router in the service provider network that provides dial-out services.

When an interesting packet causes a dialer to be activated, the router downloads the appropriate profile from the AAA server that is then applied to the generic dialer. LSDO provides many other features such as fault tolerance, redundancy, and congestion management. You can find further detailed information on the Cisco CCO web site at www.cisco.com. This section is concerned with LSDO operation in an MPLS VPN environment through a feature enhancement called VRF-aware LDSO, which was first available in Cisco IOS version 12.2(8)T.

Figure 2-17 shows an example of LSDO operation within the SuperCom network. FastFoods has a national grid of "YummyTummy" vending machines that dispense various snacks. Normally, the vending machines are offline, and each evening FastFoods HQ queries these vending machines for stock levels and other maintenance purposes. FastFoods uses the SuperCom LSDO service to obtain a connection to each of the vending machines from within the FastFoods VPN. The step-by-step operation of the LSDO service is shown in Figure 2-17.

Our example shows a single vending machine located at the FastFoods location in Fresno, California on the subnet 10.4.1.0/24. The Fresno dial number is 99065890, and the username and password used for CHAP is "Fresno_Dialer/showmethemoney." The dialer interface that is configured on the San Jose PE router is Dialer20, and the address used for the connected route is 192.168.2.51.

The following summarizes the call flow to support LSDO for FastFoods:

Step 1   A packet arrives at the San Jose PE router bound for network 10.4.1.0/24 in the FastFoods VRF.

Figure 2-17   *LSDO Operation for FastFoods*

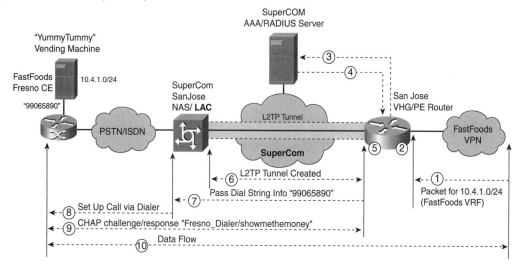

Step 2   Subnet 10.4.1.0/24 is routed to a dialer interface (in our configuration examples, Dialer20 is used) within the FastFoods VRF. This interface has been configured with "dialer aaa," which indicates that you should obtain dialer profile information from the SuperCom AAA server. A static route must be configured (we are using 192.168.2.51) pointing to interface Dialer20, and it is given the remote name "Fresno_Vending." This remote name distinguishes this route from other vending machine routes that point to the same dialer.

Step 3   The San Jose PE router issues an access-request RADIUS message to the SuperCom RADIUS server by using the username Fresno_Vending-out-FastFoods. The username uses the format "<remote name>-out-<VRF Name>." If no name has been applied to the static route, "<ip address>-out-<VRF name>" is used, where IP address is the /32 address that appears in the static route.

Step 4   The RADIUS server passes back the cisco-avpair attributes for the corresponding username entry. This consists of the dial string, username, and password for CHAP and the /32 address to be used on the dialer interface while the call is active.

Step 5   When the reply is received, a free dialer is searched for on the San Jose PE router. The dialer interface is configured with the command "dialer vpdn," which causes a vpdn-group to provide the dial-out. This vpdn-group is configured with "request-dialout."

Step 6   A virtual-access interface is created for the dial-out session, and an L2TP tunnel is created to the NAS based on the vpdn-group information. This virtual-access interface is placed inside the FastFoods VRF.

Step 7   The dial string is passed through the L2TP tunnel.

Step 8   The San Jose NAS then dials the number by using the dialer interface that is associated with the vpdn-group. This vpdn-group is configured with "accept-dialout."

Step 9   The Fresno CE router answers the call and issues a CHAP challenge. The San Jose PE router then passes the username/password it received from the RADIUS server through the PPP session.

Step 10   The call is fully connected, and data can flow in both directions.

The following sections detail the configurations that are necessary to provide the FastFoods scenario discussed in the previous steps.

Configuring the SuperCom San Jose VHG/PE Router

The San Jose PE router requires three items to be configured for LSDO: a generic dialer-interface, a vpdn-group for dial-out to the San Jose NAS, and static routes for the remote subnets that use the dialer interface.

The dialer interface configuration for Dialer20, shown in Example 2-21, is a generic config-uration that exists in the global routing table. It is not associated with a VRF, and the IP address that is allocated to it can be any value and only needs to be unique in the global table. The **dialer aaa** command causes the San Jose PE router to query the RADIUS server for dialing information. The **dialer vpdn** command allows a vpdn-group to be used for L2TP dial-out.

Example 2-21 *Dialer Interface Configuration*

```
aaa authentication ppp default local group radius
aaa authorization network default local group radius
aaa authorization configuration default group radius
!
interface Dialer20
 ip address 194.22.15.62 255.255.255.252
 encapsulation ppp
 no keepalive
 dialer in-band
 dialer aaa
 dialer vpdn
 dialer-group 2
 no peer default ip address
 no cdp enable
 ppp authentication chap callin
!
dialer-list 2 protocol ip permit
```

The existing vpdn-group 1 configuration, used in the previous VPDN dial-in examples, has been modified to allow dial-out service from the LNS (San Jose PE router) by the addition of the **request-dialout** command. The command **rotary-group 20** allows interface Dialer20 to use this vpdn-group for dial-out by initiating an L2TP connection to the San Jose LAC/NAS 194.22.15.4 (see Example 2-22).

Example 2-22 *VPDN Group Configuration for Dial-Out*

```
vpdn-group 1
 accept-dialin
  protocol l2tp
  virtual-Template 1
 request-dialout
  protocol l2tp
  rotary-group 20
 terminate-from hostname SuperCom_LAC
 initiate-to ip 194.22.15.4
 local name SuperCom_LNS
 l2tp tunnel password 7 06100632454107
 source-ip 194.22.15.2
```

Finally, you must configure some static routes in the FastFoods VRF to allow the dialer interface to function, as shown in Example 2-23. The first static route injects the interface Dialer20 into the FastFoods VRF with the next-hop of 192.168.2.51. This address must match the interface address to be downloaded from the RADIUS server for the PPP session to FastFoods Fresno. Note that the remote name Fresno_Vending has been applied to this route. This name will be used to obtain the dialing information from the RADIUS server via an access-request message. The second static route injects the actual Fresno Subnet and ensures that Dialer20 will be used, as shown in Example 2-23.

Example 2-23 *Static Routes for Dialer Interfaces*

```
ip route vrf FastFoods 192.168.2.51 255.255.255.255 Dialer20 name Fresno_Vending
ip route vrf FastFoods 10.4.1.0 255.255.255.0 192.168.2.51
```

You can use the same dialer interface within the VRF to dial other remote access sites. However, the remote name and next-hop address must be different. For example, the following configuration in Example 2-24 shows the configuration to access to the FastFoods Reno "YummyTummy" vending machine with the same interface Dialer20. (Assume that Reno is using the subnet 10.5.1.0/24.)

Example 2-24 *Additional Static Routes for Dialer Interfaces*

```
ip route vrf FastFoods 192.168.2.52 255.255.255.255 Dialer20 name Reno_Vending
ip route vrf FastFoods 10.5.1.0 255.255.255.0 192.168.2.52
```

Configuring the SuperCom San Jose LAC/NAS

Example 2-25 shows the corresponding vpdn-group used to accept the dial-out request on the San Jose LAC/NAS by using the accept-dialout service. The **dialer 2** command associates the dial-out request with interface Dialer2 which, in turn, uses the physical interface Serial0:15 to call the Fresno CE router. You might have noticed that there is no request-dialin service configured on this vpdn-group to match the accept-dialin on the San Jose PE router. This is because virtual-profiles are used on the San Jose LAC/NAS for dial-in services. (The tunnel information is downloaded from the RADIUS server, as discussed earlier in the "Dial-In Access via L2TP VPDN" section.)

Example 2-25 *San Jose LAC/NAS Configuration for LSDO*

```
vpdn-group 1
 accept-dialout
  protocol l2tp
  dialer 2
 terminate-from hostname SuperCom_LNS
 local name SuperCom_LAC
 l2tp tunnel password 7 1058000A0C181C
 source-ip 194.22.15.4
!
interface Dialer2
 ip unnumbered Loopback0
 encapsulation ppp
 dialer in-band
 dialer aaa
 dialer-group 2
 no cdp enable
 ppp authentication chap callin
!
interface Serial0:15
 no ip address
 encapsulation ppp
 dialer rotary-group 2
 isdn switch-type primary-net5
 isdn incoming-voice modem
 no cdp enable
 ppp authentication chap callin
!
dialer-list 2 protocol ip permit
```

SuperCom RADIUS Attributes

Table 2-6 lists the RADIUS attributes that will be returned to dial FastFoods Fresno. The username must match the "<remote name>-out-<VRF name>" that the San Jose PE router generates. The rest of the attributes will be applied to the dialer interface (to create a dynamic dialer map) and include the dial number, username, password, and interface address that will be applied to the virtual-access interface that is created. The "send-auth" attribute indicates that CHAP will be used for authentication.

Table 2-6   *SuperCom RADIUS Attributes for FastFoods Fresno*

Attribute (Type)	Value
User-Name (1)	"Fresno_Vending-out-FastFoods"
cisco-avpair	"outbound:dial-number=99065890"
cisco-avpair	"outbound:send-name=Fresno_Dialer"
cisco-avpair	"outbound:send-secret=showmethemoney"
cisco-avpair	"outbound:send-auth=2"
cisco-avpair	"outbound:addr=192.168.2.51"
service-type	outbound

Verifying VRF-Aware LSDO Operation

The following output in Example 2-26 shows the state of the FastFoods routing table on the San Jose VHG/PE router with no dialer interface active. You can see the two static routes that were configured previously, ultimately allowing the Fresno subnet 10.4.1.0/24 to be accessed via interface Dialer20.

Example 2-26   *FastFoods VRF with No Dialer Active*

```
SanJose_PE#show ip route vrf FastFoods
[snip]

     10.0.0.0/8 is variably subnetted, 3 subnets, 2 masks
B       10.2.1.0/24 [200/0] via 194.22.15.1, 3d20h
S       10.4.1.0/24 [1/0] via 192.168.2.51
C       10.66.162.0/23 is directly connected, Ethernet5/1
     192.168.2.0/24 is variably subnetted, 3 subnets, 2 masks
C       192.168.2.100/32 is directly connected, Loopback10
S       192.168.2.51/32 is directly connected, Dialer20
B       192.168.2.20/30 [200/0] via 194.22.15.1, 3d20h
     192.168.3.0/24 is variably subnetted, 3 subnets, 2 masks
C       192.168.3.2/32 is directly connected, virtual-Access3
C       192.168.3.1/32 is directly connected, virtual-Access1
B       192.168.3.0/26 [200/0] via 0.0.0.0, 3d19h, Null0
```

When a packet arrives at the San Jose VHG/PE router destined for 10.4.1.0/24, it is routed toward interface Dialer20. It is deemed an interesting packet because it matches the dialer-list 2 configured. Because no dial connection is active, an access-request message for dialing information is forwarded to the SuperCom RADIUS server, as shown in the following debug output (see Example 2-27). When the attributes are returned, a dynamic dialer map and an L2TP tunnel based on the vpdn-group information (using the vpdn-group with dialer rotary-group 20 configured) are created. Access to the PPP session over the dialer tunnel is via virtual-access5.

Example 2-27 *RADIUS Access-Request for LSDO*

```
RADIUS/ENCODE(00000024): acct_session_id: 44
RADIUS(00000024): sending
RADIUS: Send to unknown id 40 194.22.16.2:1645, Access-Request, len 103
RADIUS:  authenticator CD 17 02 7A B7 A5 D4 AC - 4A FB 9B 76 D4 DB 3B BA
RADIUS:  User-Name          [1]   30  "Fresno_Vending-out-FastFoods"
RADIUS:  User-Password      [2]   18  *
RADIUS:  Service-Type       [6]   6   Outbound                      [5]
RADIUS:  NAS-IP-Address     [4]   6   192.22.15.2
RADIUS:  Acct-Session-Id    [44]  10  "0000002C"
RADIUS:  Nas-Identifier     [32]  13  "SanJose_PE."

RADIUS: Received from id 40 194.22.16.2:1645, Access-Accept, len 208
RADIUS:  authenticator 52 D6 BF C7 13 10 03 B8 - 48 A5 D7 59 95 DD F5 E3
RADIUS:  Service-Type       [6]   6   Outbound                      [5]
RADIUS:  Vendor, Cisco      [26]  37
RADIUS:   Cisco AVpair      [1]   31  "outbound:dial-number=99065890"
RADIUS:  Vendor, Cisco      [26]  40
RADIUS:   Cisco AVpair      [1]   34  "outbound:send-name=Fresno_Dialer"
RADIUS:  Vendor, Cisco      [26]  43
RADIUS:   Cisco AVpair      [1]   37  "outbound:send-secret=showmethemoney"
RADIUS:  Vendor, Cisco      [26]  28
RADIUS:   Cisco AVpair      [1]   22  "outbound:send-auth=2"
RADIUS:  Vendor, Cisco      [26]  34
RADIUS:   Cisco AVpair      [1]   28  "outbound:addr=192.168.2.51"
RADIUS: Received from id 24
RADIUS/DECODE: VSA send-auth=2 maps to chap

DSES 50910: Session create
DSES 0x50910: Building dialer map
DSES 0x50910: Next hop name is Fresno_Vending
Vi5 DDR: Dialing cause ip (s=192.168.2.22, d=10.4.1.1)
Vi5 DDR: Attempting to dial 99065890
%LINK-3-UPDOWN: Interface virtual-Access5, changed state to up
Vi5 DDR: Dialer statechange to up
Vi5 DDR: Dialer call has been placed
Vi5 DDR: dialer protocol up
Vi5: Call connected, 1 packets unqueued, 0 transmitted, 1 discarded
Vi5 DDR: dialer protocol up
Vi5: Call connected, 0 packets unqueued, 0 transmitted, 0 discarded
%LINEPROTO-5-UPDOWN: Line protocol on Interface virtual-Access5, changed state to up
```

The VRF-aware dynamic dialer map is created, as shown in Example 2-28.

Example 2-28 *Dynamic Dialer Map*

```
SanJose_PE#show dialer map
Dynamic dialer map ip 192.168.2.51 vrf FastFoods name Fresno_Vending (99065890)
 on Di20
```

If you look at the FastFoods routing information after Fresno has been connected, you see that interface Virtual-Access5 has replaced interface Dialer20, and that 192.168.2.51/32 is now a connected route, as shown in Example 2-29.

Example 2-29 *FastFoods VRF with Dialer Active*

```
SanJose_PE#show ip route vrf FastFoods
[snip]

     10.0.0.0/8 is variably subnetted, 3 subnets, 2 masks
B       10.2.1.0/24 [200/0] via 194.22.15.1, 3d21h
S       10.4.1.0/24 [1/0] via 192.168.2.51
     192.168.2.0/24 is variably subnetted, 3 subnets, 2 masks
C       192.168.2.100/32 is directly connected, Loopback10
C       192.168.2.51/32 is directly connected, virtual-Access5
B       192.168.2.20/30 [200/0] via 194.22.15.1, 3d21h
     192.168.3.0/24 is variably subnetted, 3 subnets, 2 masks
C       192.168.3.2/32 is directly connected, virtual-Access3
C       192.168.3.1/32 is directly connected, virtual-Access1
B       192.168.3.0/26 [200/0] via 0.0.0.0, 3d20h, Null0
```

The VPDN tunnel information for the LNS and LAC are shown in Example 2-30. The San Jose PE router uses interface Vi5 to send and receive traffic for Fresno over the tunnel to the San Jose LAC/NAS. The San Jose LAC/NAS uses the physical interface Se0:9 to instigate the connection to Fresno.

Example 2-30 *Dialer VPDN Tunnel Information*

```
SanJose_PE#show vpdn
[snip]
LocID RemID Remote Name   State  Remote Address  Port  Sessions VPDN Group
32199 38359 SuperCom_LAC  est    194.22.15.4     1701  1        1

LocID RemID TunID Intf          Username               State  Last Chg Fastswitch
53    178   32199 Vi5           Fresno_Vending         est    00:00:24 enabled
-------------------------------------------------------------------------------
SanJose_NAS#show vpdn
LocID RemID Remote Name   State  Remote Address  Port  Sessions
38359 32199 SuperCom_LNS  est    194.22.15.2     1701  1

LocID RemID TunID Intf          Username               State  Last Chg Fastswitch
178   53    38359 Se0:9                                est    00:00:30 enabled
```

VRF Static Route Download from an AAA Server

In our LSDO example, the static routes were configured manually in the San Jose PE router to provide reachability to the FastFoods remote LAN subnets. An alternative to configuring the static VRF routes explicitly on the San Jose PE router is to automatically download them from the SuperCom RADIUS server. This is achieved through the AAA route download feature in Cisco IOS. The advantage of this feature is that you can manage static routes to remote sites from a central location and then download these routes to specific routers that are providing dial-out services for VPN customers. This provides a scalable solution for managing a large number of remote routes as well as shifting dial-out load to other remote-access servers by simply reconfiguring the RADIUS server and reloading the routes to another router.

You can enable the static route download feature on the San Jose PE router using the following global command:

```
aaa route download [time] [authorization method-list]
```

If a method-list is not specified, then the default AAA server configured is used. The routes are downloaded periodically from the AAA server. The time parameter is optional and specifies the interval to download new routes from the RADIUS server; by default, this is set to 720 minutes.

After this command is configured, the San Jose PE router immediately issues a series of RADIUS access-request messages for static routes. The username/key supplied in each RADIUS request message consists of the router hostname plus an incrementing index in the form <hostname>-n. For example, the San Jose PE router uses the following usernames to download routes from the RADIUS server:

   SanJose_PE-1, SanJose_PE-2 … SanJose_PE-n

The RADIUS access-request messages continue until the RADIUS server issues an access-reject due to the username/key not existing. The incorporation of the hostname in the request message means that the RADIUS server can download specific static routes to particular routers. By supplying an index to the hostname, the static routes can be logically grouped, for example, by VRF. In this way, you can achieve a scalable method of static route distribution.

In our example, we will configure the SuperCom RADIUS server to download static routes for both FastFoods and EuroBank, replacing the manual method of configuring routes directly into the router. EuroBank has been included to show how routes can be downloaded on a per-VRF basis based on the <hostname>-n username.

Table 2-7 shows the RADIUS entries and attributes for the EuroBank and FastFoods static routes. Note that the static routes are specified by using the cisco-avpair "ip:route" attribute, which now supports VRFs as part of the VRF-aware Framed-Route feature that is available in Cisco IOS 12.2(8)T onward. All FastFoods routes are grouped under the username SanJose_PE-1, whereas all EuroBank routes are grouped under the username SanJose_PE-2. (We are showing two EuroBank branches located at Modesto and Laguna in California.) The routes configured consist of the connected route for the dialer interface at each remote site, plus the corresponding LAN subnet pointing to the connected route. Enabling these routes to be downloaded into other PE routers would require a separate username entry corresponding to the target router's hostname.

Table 2-7   *Static Route Download Attributes for FastFoods and EuroBank*

Attribute (Type)	Value
User-Name (1)	"SanJose_PE-1" ← FastFoods Entry
User-Password (2)	"cisco"

Table 2-7   *Static Route Download Attributes for FastFoods and EuroBank (Continued)*

Attribute (Type)	Value
Cisco-avpair	"ip:route=vrf FastFoods 192.168.2.51 255.255.255.255 dialer20 name Fresno_Vending"
	"ip:route=vrf FastFoods 192.168.2.52 255.255.255.255 dialer20 name Reno_Vending"
	"ip:route=vrf FastFoods 10.4.1.0 255.255.255.0 192.168.2.51"
	"ip:route=vrf FastFoods 10.5.1.0 255.255.255.0 192.168.2.52"
User-Name (1)	"SanJose_PE-2" ← EuroBank Entry
User-Password (2)	"cisco"
Cisco-avpair	"ip:route=vrf EuroBank 192.168.2.61 255.255.255.255 dialer20 name Modesto_Branch"
	"ip:route=vrf EuroBank 192.168.2.62 255.255.255.255 dialer20 name Laguna_Branch"
	"ip:route=vrf EuroBank 196.7.28.0 255.255.255.0 192.168.2.61"
	"ip:route=vrf EuroBank 196.7.30.0 255.255.255.0 192.168.2.62"

The debug output in Example 2-31 shows how static routes are downloaded for FastFoods and EuroBank VRFs. The routes have been grouped by VRF on the RADIUS server so that the first request (SanJose_PE-1) passes back all the static routes for FastFoods and the second request (SanJose_PE-2) passes back all the static routes for EuroBank. The third request (SanJose_PE-3) is rejected because there are no more routes to download.

Example 2-31   *Static Route Download Debug*

```
RADIUS(00000000): Send to unknown id 21646/8 194.22.16.2 1645, Access-Request, len 87
RADIUS:  User-Name          [1]   14  "SanJose_PE-1"
RADIUS:  User-Password      [2]   18  *
RADIUS:  Service-Type       [6]   6   Outbound              [5]
RADIUS:  NAS-IP-Address     [4]   6   194.22.15.2
RADIUS:  Acct-Session-Id    [44]  10  "00000000"
RADIUS:  Nas-Identifier     [32]  13  "SanJose_PE."
RADIUS: Received from id 21646/8 192.22.16.2 1645, Access-Accept, len 326
RADIUS:  Vendor, Cisco      [26]  88
RADIUS:     Cisco AVpair    [1]   82  "ip:route=vrf FastFoods 192.168.2.51
 255.255.255.255 dialer20 name Fresno_Vending"
RADIUS:  Vendor, Cisco      [26]  86
RADIUS:     Cisco AVpair    [1]   80  "ip:route=vrf FastFoods 192.168.2.52
 255.255.255.255 dialer20 name Reno_Vending"
RADIUS:  Vendor, Cisco      [26]  66
RADIUS:     Cisco AVpair    [1]   60  "ip:route=vrf FastFoods 10.4.1.0
 255.255.255.0 192.168.2.51"
RADIUS:  Vendor, Cisco      [26]  66
RADIUS:     Cisco AVpair    [1]   60  "ip:route=vrf FastFoods 10.5.1.0
```

continues

Example 2-31 *Static Route Download Debug (Continued)*

```
   255.255.255.0 192.168.2.52"
RADIUS(00000000): Send to unknown id 21646/9 194.22.16.2 1645,
  Access-Request, len 87
RADIUS:  User-Name          [1]    14   "SanJose_PE-2"
RADIUS:  User-Password      [2]    18   *
RADIUS:  Service-Type       [6]    6    Outbound                   [5]
RADIUS:  NAS-IP-Address     [4]    6    194.22.15.2
RADIUS:  Acct-Session-Id    [44]   10   "00000000"
RADIUS:  Nas-Identifier     [32]   13   "SanJose_PE."
RADIUS: Received from id 21646/9 194.22.16.2 1645, Access-Accept, len 327
RADIUS:  Vendor, Cisco      [26]   87
RADIUS:   Cisco AVpair      [1]    81   "ip:route=vrf EuroBank 192.168.2.61
  255.255.255.255 dialer20 name Modesto_Branch"
RADIUS:  Vendor, Cisco      [26]   86
RADIUS:   Cisco AVpair      [1]    80   "ip:route=vrf EuroBank 192.168.2.62
  255.255.255.255 dialer20 name Laguna_Branch"
RADIUS:  Vendor, Cisco      [26]   67
RADIUS:   Cisco AVpair      [1]    61   "ip:route=vrf EuroBank 196.7.28.0
  255.255.255.0 192.168.2.61"
RADIUS:  Vendor, Cisco      [26]   67
RADIUS:   Cisco AVpair      [1]    61   "ip:route=vrf EuroBank 196.7.30.0
  255.255.255.0 192.168.2.62"
RADIUS(00000000): Send to unknown id 21646/10 194.22.16.2 1645, Access-Request,
  len 87
RADIUS:   authenticator 5D 95 36 F8 0F 84 37 F6 - 90 23 71 0C 8D 5D 00 71
RADIUS:  User-Name          [1]    14   "SanJose_PE-3"
RADIUS:  User-Password      [2]    18   *
RADIUS:  Service-Type       [6]    6    Outbound                   [5]
RADIUS:  NAS-IP-Address     [4]    6    194.22.15.2
RADIUS:  Acct-Session-Id    [44]   10   "00000000"
RADIUS:  Nas-Identifier     [32]   13   "SanJose_PE."
RADIUS: Received from id 21646/10 194.22.16.2 1645, Access-Reject, len 35
```

The output in Example 2-32 verifies the static routes that have been downloaded from the SuperCom Radius server.

Example 2-32 *Verifying Downloaded Static Routes*

```
SanJose_PE#show ip route static download
Connectivity: A - Active, I - Inactive

A    192.168.2.61 255.255.255.255 Dialer20 name Modesto_Branch
A    192.168.2.62 255.255.255.255 Dialer20 name Laguna_Branch
A    196.7.28.0 255.255.255.0 192.168.2.61
A    196.7.30.0 255.255.255.0 192.168.2.62
A    10.4.1.0 255.255.255.0 192.168.2.51
A    10.5.1.0 255.255.255.0 192.168.2.52
A    192.168.2.51 255.255.255.255 Dialer20 name Fresno_Vending
A    192.168.2.52 255.255.255.255 Dialer20 name Reno_Vending
```

The previous output does not show in which VRFs these downloaded routes have been placed; however, you can easily confirm this by viewing the routing tables of each VRF, as shown in Example 2-33. Downloaded static routes are indicated in the routing table by the code P rather than the customary code S.

Example 2-33 *Verifying Static Routes in VRFs*

```
SanJose_PE#show ip route vrf FastFoods | inc P.*
Codes: C - connected, S - static, I - IGRP, R - RIP, M - mobile, B - BGP
       D - EIGRP, EX - EIGRP external, O - OSPF, IA - OSPF inter area
       N1 - OSPF NSSA external type 1, N2 - OSPF NSSA external type 2
       E1 - OSPF external type 1, E2 - OSPF external type 2, E - EGP
       P - periodic downloaded static route
P       10.5.1.0/24 [1/0] via 192.168.2.52
P       10.4.1.0/24 [1/0] via 192.168.2.51
P       192.168.2.51/32 is directly connected, Dialer20
P       192.168.2.52/32 is directly connected, Dialer20

SanJose_PE#show ip route vrf EuroBank | inc P.*
Codes: C - connected, S - static, I - IGRP, R - RIP, M - mobile, B - BGP
       D - EIGRP, EX - EIGRP external, O - OSPF, IA - OSPF inter area
       N1 - OSPF NSSA external type 1, N2 - OSPF NSSA external type 2
       E1 - OSPF external type 1, E2 - OSPF external type 2, E - EGP
       P - periodic downloaded static route
P     196.7.28.0/24 [1/0] via 192.168.2.61
P     196.7.30.0/24 [1/0] via 192.168.2.62
P       192.168.2.62 is directly connected, Dialer20
P       192.168.2.61 is directly connected, Dialer20
```

Providing Dial-Out Access Without LSDO (Direct ISDN)

Sometimes the VRF-aware LSDO solution might not be applicable. This occurs when there is direct ISDN dial-out from the VHG or when the number of dial-out customers is small and contained to a single LAC/LNS pair (therefore, not many routers need to be configured). The L2TP tunnels for dial-out can be statically configured.

NOTE If VRF-aware LSDO was not used, then a dialer profile configuration for each remote destination is required on every VHG or NAS (for direct ISDN) that provided dial-out services. In a large network, this would involve a considerable amount of operational overhead.

The static dialer profile configuration (no AAA servers are used) is shown in Example 2-34. This configuration applies to dial-out via a statically configured L2TP tunnel. Note that the changes only involve the configuration on the San Jose PE router.

Example 2-34 *Dialer Profile Configuration Without LSDO*

```
interface Dialer20
 ip vrf forwarding FastFoods
 ip unnumbered Loopback10
 encapsulation ppp
 no keepalive
 dialer pool 20
 dialer remote-name Fresno_Vending
 dialer string 99065890
 dialer vpdn
 dialer-group 2
 peer default ip address 192.168.2.51
 no cdp enable
 ppp authentication chap callin
 ppp chap hostname Fresno_Dialer
 ppp chap password 0 showmethemoney
!
ip route vrf FastFoods 10.4.1.0 255.255.255.0 192.168.2.51
ip route vrf FastFoods 192.168.2.51 255.255.255.255 Dialer20 permanent
!
vpdn-group 1
 accept-dialin
  protocol l2tp
  virtual-Template 1
 request-dialout
  protocol l2tp
  pool-member 20
 terminate-from hostname SuperCom_LAC
 initiate-to ip 194.22.15.4
 local name SuperCom_LNS
 l2tp tunnel password 7 06100632454107
 source-ip 194.22.15.2
```

In the case of direct dial ISDN, the vpdn-group configuration in the previous example would not apply, and the **dialer vpdn** command must be removed from interface dialer 20. For direct dial ISDN in the SuperCom network, all that would be necessary on the San Jose VHG/PE router would be to add the ISDN interface to the dial-out pool, as shown in Example 2-35.

Example 2-35 *ISDN Dial-Out Pool*

```
!
interface Serial6/0:15
 ip unnumbered Loopback0
 encapsulation ppp
 dialer pool-member 20
 isdn switch-type primary-net5
 no cdp enable
 ppp authentication chap callin
end
```

Providing Dial Backup for MPLS VPN Access

Dial backup protection for a primary CE router/PE router link can be provided easily by using either of the dial-in architectures (VPDN or Direct ISDN) that were previously discussed. The primary and backup links normally reside on the same CE router. Consider the scenario shown in Figure 2-18. The EuroBank San Francisco CE router has a primary connection terminating on the San Jose PE router. The primary link is protected by a backup interface that can use either VPDN (L2TP) or direct ISDN dial to establish a backup link to the EuroBank VRF.

If the primary link fails, the backup interface, which is a dialer interface, automatically calls the San Jose LAC/NAC (using an analogue or digital call). The procedures followed are identical to those for VPDN or direct dial-in ISDN access.

Figure 2-18 *Dial Backup for FastFoods San Jose*

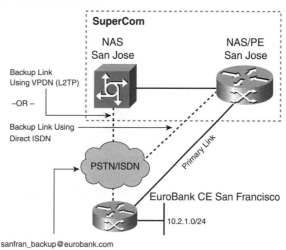

Example 2-36 shows the common configuration and RADIUS attributes for providing a backup link (in our example, interface Dialer2) to EuroBank San Francisco by using the **backup interface** command. See Table 2-8 for the corresponding list of RADIUS attributes on the SuperCom RADIUS Server.

Example 2-36 *EuroBank San Francisco CE Router Configuration for Backup*

```
interface Serial0/0
 backup interface Dialer2
 ip address 192.168.2.25 255.255.255.252
 !
interface Dialer2
 ip address negotiated
 encapsulation ppp
 dialer pool 5
 dialer idle-timeout 600
```

continues

Example 2-36 *EuroBank San Francisco CE Router Configuration for Backup (Continued)*

```
 dialer string 94780400
 dialer-group 1
 ppp chap hostname sanfran_backup@eurobank.com
 ppp chap password 0 heyiamup
 !
dialer-list 1 protocol ip permit
```

Table 2-8 *San Francisco Router RADIUS Attributes for Backup*

Attribute (Type)	Value
User-Name (1)	"sanfran_backup@eurobank.com"
User-Password (2)	"heyiamup"
Service-Type (6)	1 (Framed)
Framed-Protocol (7)	1 (PPP)

You might have noticed that these configurations are similar to the EuroBank Sacramento SOHO router used in the Direct ISDN dial-in scenario. However, the difference in the rest of the configuration depends on whether static routing or dynamic routing is used.

If static routing is used over the backup link, the configuration at the CE router contains two default routes (shown in Example 2-37): one pointing to the primary interface and the other pointing to the backup interface (with a higher metric). The RADIUS attributes used (see Table 2-9) insert a static Framed-Route using the framed route VRF-aware feature into the EuroBank VRF for the San Francisco LAN via the backup link. If the primary interface fails on the San Francisco CE router, the dialer backup interface and the corresponding static route become active.

Example 2-37 *Backup Static Routes*

```
ip route 0.0.0.0 0.0.0.0 192.168.2.26
ip route 0.0.0.0 0.0.0.0 dialer 2 230
```

Table 2-9 *Additional RADIUS Attributes for Backup Static Routing*

Attribute (Type)	Value
Framed-Route(22)	10.2.1.0/24
cisco-avpair	"lcp:interface-config=ip vrf forwarding EuroBank \n ip unnumbered loopback 11 \n peer default ip address pool EuroBank_Pool"

For dynamic routing, configure the dialer interface and the virtual-access interface with static IP addresses (those that are not obtained from a pool). You do not need to use the

RADIUS Framed-Route attribute (see Table 2-10). Example 2-38 uses the Routing Information Protocol (RIP) as the routing protocol, and the addresses used at each end of the
backup link come from the 192.168.2.0/24 subnet, which happens to be the same range that
the primary link uses. If a different subnet is used for the backup link, a corresponding RIP
network statement for that subnet is necessary.

Example 2-38 *Dynamic Routing Using RIP*

```
! San Francisco CE router
!
router rip
 version 2
 redistribute connected
 network 192.168.2.0
-----------------------------------------------
!San Jose PE router
router rip
!
 address-family ipv4 vrf EuroBank
 version 2
 redistribute bgp 100 metric 10
 redistribute static
 network 192.168.2.0
 no auto-summary
 exit-address-family
```

Table 2-10   *Additional RADIUS Attributes for Backup Dynamic Routing*

Attribute (Type)	Value
cisco-avpair	"lcp:interface-config=ip vrf forwarding EuroBank \n
	ip address 192.168.2.41 255.255.255.252"

Providing DSL Access to an MPLS VPN

The DSL technology provides high-speed network access over a pair of copper wires,
which essentially is the local loop from the telephone company central office (CO) to
residential or business premises. A modulation technology called *Discrete Multitone*
(DMT) allows the transmission of high-speed data over the copper pair. It is not within the
scope of this book to explain the details of DSL operation; however, the aspects that relate to
successful operation within an MPLS VPN network are covered in the following sections.

DSL has the following basic components:

- At the customer end, there is a customer premises equipment (CPE), which can be a
  device, such as a router (preferably Cisco). Alternatively, it can be a device that is
  capable of bridging client PCs, which do not need routing capability. It can also be a
  directly connected client PC that uses a DSL adapter card and special software.

NOTE   On the physical layer, there will also be a plain old telephone service (POTS) filter or splitter on the customer premises to allow simultaneous use of a phone and DSL device on the same pair of wires.

- The subscriber line is terminated at another large-scale splitter at the CO to separate the voice calls from the DSL data connection. The DSL data connection is terminated at a digital subscriber line access multiplexer (DSLAM), whose function is to provide high-density termination of all the copper pairs feeding into it. The DSLAM connects to an aggregation device by using ATM.

- The aggregation device is a router that provides the higher-level protocol termination from the ATM connection. Each customer DSL connection is terminated on separate ATM PVCs.

DSL uses ATM as its basic transport mechanism. You can use various encapsulation methods depending on the application that is required. All the encapsulations use ATM adaptation layer 5 (AAL5) to segment the data into ATM cells and RFC 1483 to allow the transport of multiple protocols over the same ATM PVC. RFC 1483 comes in two variants. The first method allows multiple protocols to be carried over the same PVC. In Cisco IOS, this is configured using the aal5snap keyword. The second method does higher layer protocol multiplexing implicitly by PVC (that is, one protocol per PVC).

NOTE   RFC 1483 has been obsoleted by RFC 2684. However, the overwhelming practice is to still refer to the standard as RFC 1483, which implies the latest iteration.

The possible encapsulation methods are shown in Figure 2-19.

Figure 2-19   *DSL Encapsulation Formats*

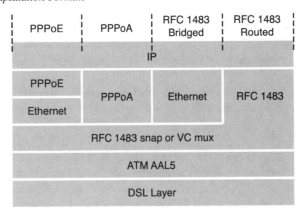

Each of these encapsulation methods and their operation within an MPLS VPN network for remote access are discussed in the following sections.

DSL Access by Using RFC 1483 Routed Encapsulation

This connection method is particularly straightforward and consists of an ATM PVC between the DSL CPE and the PE router, as shown in Figure 2-20 for a EuroBank DSL CPE connection.

Figure 2-20 *DSL RFC 1483 Routed*

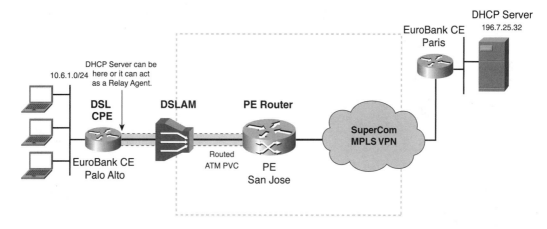

A static (or unnumbered) IP address is configured at both ends of the link, and the ATM subinterface at the PE router end is placed into a statically configured VRF. No remote user authorization and authentication is necessary in this scenario. From an MPLS perspective, there is no difference between this configuration and any other permanent circuit connection, such as Frame Relay, Packet Over SONET (POS), or leased line. Because the DSL CPE is a router, it can be configured with dynamic routing to the PE router if required and act as a DHCP server to its locally connected devices. If address management were required to be coordinated from a EuroBank central location, then a DHCP server could be located elsewhere in the EuroBank VPN, such as Paris in our example. Therefore, the DSL CPE would act as a DHCP relay agent to the Paris DHCP server. Note that this DHCP server would only support EuroBank DHCP requests.

RFC 1483 routed is most suited for remote office applications rather than residential users. The following configuration (see Example 2-39) shows how to place an RFC 1483 routed DSL CPE into the EuroBank VRF.

Example 2-39 *San Jose PE Router Configuration RFC 1483 Routed*

```
interface ATM2/0.1 point-to-point
 ip vrf forwarding EuroBank
 ip address 192.168.2.74 255.255.255.252
 pvc 1/32
  ubr 256
  encapsulation aal5snap
```

DSL Access Using RFC 1483 Bridged Encapsulation

In this access scenario, all traffic between the DSL CPE and the PE router is bridged and no routing occurs. The traffic is carried on the ATM PVC within an RFC 1483 bridged packet, which includes the Layer 2 information (Ethernet addresses and so on). From the perspective of the San Jose PE router, shown in Figure 2-21, the ATM subinterface appears as a LAN interface. This is accomplished by configuring route-bridge encapsulation (RBE) on the subinterface.

Figure 2-21 *DSL RFC 1483 Bridged*

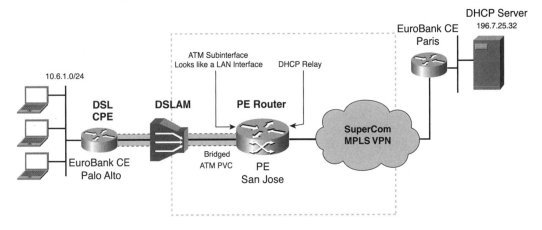

Because the DSL CPE has no routing functionality, it cannot act as a DHCP server. Therefore, if DHCP is required, then a remote EuroBank DHCP server must provide it. In our example, the San Jose PE router acts as the relay agent to the Paris EuroBank DHCP server.

Configuring the San Jose PE Router

Example 2-40 shows the configuration for RBE on the San Jose PE router. Because the subinterface ATM2/0.1 acts as a LAN interface in RBE, the San Jose router (10.6.1.1/32) appears as the gateway for the EuroBank Palo Alto subnet 10.6.1.0/24. The San Jose PE router relays any DHCP requests in the normal manner to 196.7.25.32, using the **ip helper-address global** command.

Example 2-40 *San Jose PE Router Configuration for RFC 1483 Bridged*

```
interface ATM2/0.1 point-to-point
 ip vrf forwarding EuroBank
 ip address 10.6.1.1 255.255.255.0
 ip helper-address global 196.7.25.32
 no ip mroute-cache
 atm route-bridged ip
 pvc 1/32
  ubr 256
  encapsulation aal5snap
```

Configuring the Palo Alto DSL CPE

The DSL CPE configuration is basic and only requires bridging to be configured, as shown in Example 2-41.

Example 2-41 *Palo Alto DSL CPE Configuration for RFC 1483 Bridged*

```
interface Ethernet0
 no ip address
 no ip directed-broadcast
 bridge-group 1
!
interface ATM0
 no ip address
 no ip directed-broadcast
 no ip mroute-cache
 no atm ilmi-keepalive
 pvc 1/32
  ubr 256
  encapsulation aal5snap
  bridge-group 1
!
bridge 1 protocol ieee
```

The disadvantage of this solution is that DSL customers must have a DHCP server that is available within their own Intranet because the DSL CPE is not capable of providing the IP addresses. This might not be desirable for the customer if he does not have the operational and support infrastructure to manage and maintain his own DHCP server(s). A new feature called DHCP Relay – MPLS VPN support is available from Cisco IOS 12.2(4)B and 12.2(8)T; it allows the DHCP server to exist outside of the VRF, either in the global routing table or another VRF. A DHCP server that is enabled with this feature is able to support overlapping addresses; therefore, a single server might provide addresses to many VRFs. This means that the service provider could provide a centralized DHCP server to support all remote VPN customers. This feature and its applicability to the RFC 1483 bridged scenario are discussed in detail in the earlier section, "Advanced Features for MPLS VPN Remote Access."

DSL Access Using PPP Over ATM

In the PPP over ATM (PPPoA) scenario shown in Figure 2-22, the Palo Alto DSL CPE has routing functionality and uses PPP to connect to the San Jose PE router. The PPP session runs over the ATM PVC between the DSL CPE and the PE router; therefore, it is called PPP over ATM, or PPPoA. The locally connected PCs can either be statically configured with IP addresses or request them from a DHCP server that is configured on either the DSL CPE or a remote server in the EuroBank intranet.

Figure 2-22 *DSL PPPoA*

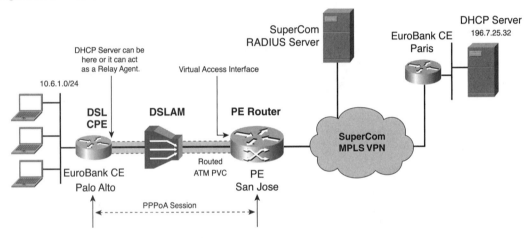

The advantage of using PPPoA in a DSL access scenario is that you can perform a single authentication and accounting instance on the DSL connection for all PCs behind the DSL CPE. The PCs can obtain their addresses from a local DHCP pool that is configured on the DSL CPE or from a customer DHCP server.

NOTE   The steps for establishing the PPPoA session are identical to those explained in the "Dial-In Access via Direct ISDN" section.

When the PPP call is received, a virtual-access interface is cloned from a virtual-template for the PPP session. The RADIUS server authenticates the PPP session and supplies additional configuration information for the virtual-access interface. You can obtain addressing for the PPP session in several ways, including the RADIUS server, a local IP pool, or an on-demand address pool, which is described in the "Advanced Features for MPLS VPN Remote Access" section.

Configuring the San Jose PE Router

Example 2-42 shows the configuration that is necessary on the San Jose PE router to terminate a PPPoA session. As with all PPP terminations that are accessing a VPN, scalability is achieved via the combination of virtual-profiles supported by a RADIUS server. This technique has been explained in detail in the earlier section, "Providing Dial-In Access to an MPLS VPN." The virtual-template1 has been associated with the PPP ATM PVC that is connecting to the DSL CPE using the **encapsulation aal5mux ppp** command. When a PPP connection is received on PVC 1/32, virtual-template1 is used to clone a virtual access interface with additional configuration information being supplied by the SuperCom RADIUS server.

Example 2-42 *San Jose PE Router Configuration for PPPoA*

```
hostname SanJose_PE
!
aaa authentication ppp default local group radius
aaa authorization network default local group radius
!
virtual-profile aaa
!
interface ATM2/0.1 point-to-point
 pvc 1/32
  ubr 256
  encapsulation aal5mux ppp virtual-Template1
 !
interface virtual-Template1
 no ip address
 no peer default ip address
 no keepalive
 ppp authentication chap callin
!
ip radius source-interface Loopback0
!
radius-server host 194.22.16.2 auth-port 1645 acct-port 1646 key a$4two
```

Note that virtual-template1 is the same one we used to terminate L2TP VPDN sessions from the San Jose LAC/NAS described in the "Dial-In Access via L2TP VPDN" section.

Configuring the EuroBank Palo Alto DSL CPE

Example 2-43 shows the PPPoA configuration for the DSL CPE. You might notice that it is similar in many respects to the configuration used in the EuroBank Sacramento SOHO router shown previously in Example 2-19. The only difference is that an ATM PVC is used rather than an ISDN channel. The SuperCom RADIUS server will use the username paloalto@eurobank_dsl to authenticate and download the appropriate per-user configuration.

Example 2-43 *Palo Alto DSL CPE for PPPoA Configuration*

```
interface ATM0
 no ip address
 no ip redirects
 no atm ilmi-keepalive
 pvc 1/32
  ubr 256
  encapsulation aal5mux ppp dialer
  dialer pool-member 1
 !
 dsl operating-mode auto
!
interface Dialer1
 ip address negotiated
 no ip redirects
 encapsulation ppp
 dialer pool 1
 dialer-group 1
 no cdp enable
 ppp chap hostname paloalto@eurobank_DSL
 ppp chap password atwistedpair
!
ip route 0.0.0.0 0.0.0.0 Dialer1
!
dialer-list 1 protocol ip permit
```

SuperCom RADIUS Server Attributes

The RADIUS entry for the Palo Alto DSL router shown in Table 2-11 is straightforward and almost identical to the attributes used for any other direct dial-in PPP router. In our configuration, the PPP address is obtained from the local pool defined for EuroBank on the San Jose PE router. A VRF-aware Framed-Route 10.6.1.0/24 is injected into the EuroBank VRF to provide reachability to the Palo Alto LAN. Loopback 11 is the interface used to preinstantiate the EuroBank VRF.

Table 2-11 *Palo Alto RADIUS Attributes for PPPoA*

Attribute (Type)	Value
User-Name (1)	paloalto@eurobank_DSL
User-Password (2)	atiwstedpair
Service-Type (6)	1 (Framed)
Framed-Protocol (7)	1 (PPP)
Framed-Route (22)	10.6.1.0/24
Cisco-avpair	lcp:interface-config=ip vrf forwarding EuroBank \n[1] ip unnumbered loopback 11 \n peer default ip address pool EuroBank_Pool

[1] The \n signifies an explicit carriage return; this varies between server implementations.

Verifying PPPoA Operation

Because the PPPoA operation is similar to what you have already read in Direct ISDN access, there is no real value in showing information such as routing table and debugs again; the outputs are also similar. The main differences are that the username and framed route injected are different, and we are connecting using an ATM PVC. The output shown in Example 2-44 confirms that the San Jose PE router has terminated the Palo Alto PPPoA session on virtual-access5. As you can see, "jimi" and "eric" are also logged on via an L2TP VPDN session from the San Jose LAC/NAS. The address 192.168.3.2 has been allocated from the EuroBank local address pool, which is why it appears to be the same one "jimi" is using that was allocated from the FastFoods local pool using the overlapping address pool feature.

Example 2-44 *PPPoA DSL and VPDN User Information*

```
SanJose_PE#show user
    Line       User        Host(s)              Idle        Location
*   0 con 0                idle                 00:00:00

    Interface  User                   Mode      Idle        Peer Address
    Vi3        eric@eurobank.com      PPPoVPDN  00:45:11 192.168.3.3
    Vi5        paloalto@eurobank_     PPPoATM   00:00:07 192.168.3.2
    Vi6        jimi@fastfoods.com     PPPoVPDN  00:51:06 192.168.3.2
```

Closer inspection of the virtual access interface, shown in Example 2-45, confirms that it has been cloned from virtual-template1 via a PPPoA session using additional configuration provided by the AAA (RADIUS) server and that it is in the EuroBank VRF.

Example 2-45 *PPPoA Virtual-Access Interface*

```
SanJose_PE#show interface vi5
virtual-Access5 is up, line protocol is up
  Hardware is Virtual Access interface
  Interface is unnumbered. Using address of Loopback11 (192.168.2.100)
  MTU 1500 bytes, BW 100000 Kbit, DLY 100000 usec,
     reliability 255/255, txload 1/255, rxload 1/255
  Encapsulation PPP, LCP Open
  Open: IPCP
  PPPoATM vaccess, cloned from AAA, virtual-Template1
  [snip]

SanJose_PE#show ip vrf EuroBank
  Name                        Default RD        Interfaces
  EuroBank                    10:27             virtual-Access3
                                                virtual-Access5
                                                Loopback11
```

DSL Access Using PPP over Ethernet

In the PPP over Ethernet (PPPoE) scenario shown in Figure 2-23, the Palo Alto DSL CPE is connected to the San Jose PE router by using a simple bridged connection much like the

RFC 1483 bridged scenario. PPPoE sessions are initiated directly from the PC clients with PPPoE software installed and bridged over the ATM PVC via encapsulated Ethernet-bridged frames. Therefore, the San Jose PE Router has a virtual-access interface for each PC client, as opposed to a single interface like in the PPPoA scenario. The advantage of PPPoE is that software resides on the client PCs; therefore, DSL CPE only needs to have basic bridging capabilities, and no routing functions are necessary, which keeps the hardware costs down. Because each PC runs its own PPP session, authentication and accounting information can be tracked on a per-user basis.

A DHCP function is not necessary because the SuperCom RADIUS server provides each PC with an IP address for its PPP session. Authentication and virtual-access creation and configuration are performed by using the same procedures as explained in the earlier section, "Dial-In Access via Direct ISDN."

Figure 2-23   *DSL PPPoE*

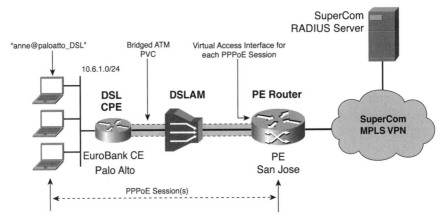

Configuring the SuperCom PE Router

The VPDN code in Cisco IOS processes PPPoE. Therefore, you must define a VPDN group to terminate all PPPoE connections that arrive at the San Jose PE router, as shown in Example 2-46. The VPDN group supplies the virtual-template to be used to clone a virtual-access interface for the PPP session. The linkage between the ATM PVC and the VPDN group is accomplished by using the **protocol pppoe** command on both the ATM interface and vpdn-group configuration.

Example 2-46   *San Jose PE Router Configuration for PPPoE*

```
aaa authentication ppp default local group radius
aaa authorization network default local group radius
!
virtual-profile aaa
!
interface ATM2/0.1 point-to-point
```

Example 2-46 *San Jose PE Router Configuration for PPPoE (Continued)*

```
 pvc 1/32
  ubr 256
  encapsulation aal5snap
  protocol pppoe
  !
 vpdn-group 4
  accept-dialin
   protocol pppoe
   virtual-Template 1
  !
 interface virtual-Template1
  no ip address
  no peer default ip address
  no keepalive
  ppp authentication chap callin
  !
 ip radius source-interface Loopback0
  !
 radius-server host 194.22.16.2 auth-port 1645 acct-port 1646 key a$4two
```

Configuring the Palo Alto DSL CPE

The DSL CPE only requires a bridging configuration and is identical to the configuration shown in the RFC1483 bridged section in Example 2-41.

SuperCom RADIUS Server Attributes

The RADIUS attributes for "anne" allow access to the EuroBank VRF and provide an address out of the EuroBank local address pool. Table 2-12 lists these attributes and their respective values.

Table 2-12 *User anne@eurobank_DSL RADIUS Attributes*

Attribute (Type)	Value
User-Name (1)	"anne@eurobank_DSL"
User-Password (2)	"irisheyes"
Service-Type (6)	1 (Framed)
Framed-Protocol (7)	1 (PPP)
Cisco-avpair	"lcp:interface-config=ip vrf forwarding EuroBank \n[1]
	ip unnumbered loopback 11 \n
	peer default ip address pool EuroBank_Pool"

[1] The \n signifies an explicit carriage return; usage varies between RADIUS servers.

Verifying PPPoE Operation

In our example, remote user anne@paloalto_DSL has connected via the PPPoE client in her PC to the San Jose PE router. When the PPP session is established, her virtual-access interface is placed into the EuroBank VRF.

A PPPoE frame contains one of two ethertypes:

- 0x8863 -PPPoE control packet, which manages the PPPoE session
- 0x8864 -PPPoE data packet, which carries the actual PPP packet

Two sessions exist for any PPPoE client connection. The first is a VPDN L2TP-like session for the PPPoE tunnel, and the second is for the actual PPP session that is carried within the PPPoE frame. These two sessions correspond to the two Ethertypes in the frame.

As mentioned previously, the VPDN code processes the PPPoE connection. Therefore, if we display the VPDN PPPoE tunnel information as shown in Example 2-47, we can see the Ethernet endpoints connected over the ATM PVC. The remote MAC address 0090.a9fd.249e is the network interface card on "anne's" PC. The MAC address 0004.6d7f.6038 is that used on the ATM interface at the San Jose PE Router.

Example 2-47 *VPDN Session Information for the PPPoE Client*

```
SanJose_PE#show vpdn | begin PPPoE
PPPoE Tunnel and Session Information Total tunnels 1 sessions 1

PPPoE Session Information
UID     SID     RemMAC          OIntf           Intf      Session
                LocMAC                          VASt      state
58      3       0090.a9fd.249e  ATM2/0.1        Vi5       CNCT_PTA
                0004.6d7f.6038  VP/VC:  1/32    UP
```

You can view the actual PPP session for "anne" by displaying the active users on the San Jose PE router shown in Example 2-48. The address 192.168.3.5 has been allocated from the EuroBank local pool. Meanwhile, L2TP VPDN users "eric" and "jimi" are still connected. They must be hard workers to be logged in for so long!

Example 2-48 *PPPoE DSL and VPDN User Information*

```
SanJose_PE#show user
[snip]
Interface    User                  Mode       Idle        Peer Address
Vi3          eric@eurobank.com     PPPoVPDN   14:12:23 192.168.3.3
Vi7          anne@eurobank_palo    PPPoE      00:03:14 192.168.3.5
Vi6          jimi@fastfoods.com    PPPoVPDN   14:18:18 192.168.3.2
```

In Example 2-49, the PPP session has been terminated on virtual-access7, cloned from virtual-template1 as per the vpdn-group 4 configuration in Example 2-46.

Example 2-49 *PPPoE Virtual-Access Interface*

```
SanJose_PE#show interface vi7
virtual-Access7 is up, line protocol is up
  Hardware is Virtual Access interface
  Interface is unnumbered. Using address of Loopback11 (192.168.2.100)
  MTU 1492 bytes, BW 100000 Kbit, DLY 100000 usec,
    reliability 255/255, txload 1/255, rxload 1/255
  Encapsulation PPP, LCP Open
  Open: IPCP
  PPPoE vaccess, cloned from AAA, virtual-Template1
  Bound to ATM2/0.1 VCD: 1, VPI: 1, VCI: 32, loopback not set
  [snip]

SanJose_PE#show ip vrf EuroBank
  Name                           Default RD          Interfaces
  EuroBank                       10:27               virtual-Access3
                                                     virtual-Access7
                                                     Loopback11
```

DSL Access Using PPPoX and VPDN (L2TP)

All the DSL scenarios discussed so far have terminated directly on a PE router. However, you can separate the DSL PPP termination function from the PE router function by using the L2TP VPDN architecture, as discussed in the earlier section, "Dial-In Access via Direct ISDN." L2TP VPDN provides the scalability required for large-scale DSL to MPLS VPN terminations. Figure 2-24 shows the EuroBank Palo Alto DSL PE router using PPPoX and L2TP to access the San Jose PE router. The LAC function in this case is most likely a Cisco 6400 universal access concentrator.

For the purposes of simplifying Figure 2-24, we have shown the Palo Alto CPE capable of operating in either mode: PPPoE where the CPE acts as a bridge, or PPPoA where the CPE acts as a router.

Figure 2-24 *PPPoX Using VPDN (L2TP)*

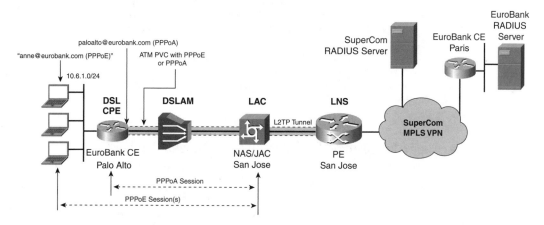

If the CPE were configured to support PPPoE, the following call processing would occur:

Step 1   The user anne@eurobank.com initiates a PPPoE session from her PC.

Step 2   The PPP packet encapsulated in an Ethernet frame is transported over the ATM PVC by using RFC 1483 bridged mode.

Step 3   When the NAS (most likely a 6400 universal access concentrator) receives the initial packet, it looks for a VPDN group that has the **protocol pppoe** command configured.

Step 4   The VPDN group points to a virtual-template that you can use to clone a virtual-access interface for the PPP session. This virtual-access interface acts as the output interface to the L2TP tunnel, which is created in the next steps.

Step 5   The NAS or universal access concentrator challenges the PPPoE client for a username password. Because the vpdn is configured, the domain name eurobank.com is used to search for a VPDN group or query to the SuperCom RADIUS server for L2TP tunnel information.

Step 6   An L2TP tunnel is then built to the LNS.

Step 7   The LNS receives the full username anne@eurobank.com through the tunnel and authenticates it using the appropriate RADIUS server (either the customer's or the service provider's).

Step 8   The information returned from the RADIUS server is then used to configure a virtual-access interface and provide an IP address to the PPPoE client.

If the CPE is configured for PPPoA, the following call processing occurs:

Step 1   The DSL CPE initiates a PPPoA call.

Step 2   The PPP packet is carried directly in RFC 1483 encapsulation.

Step 3   The NAS/universal access concentrator receives the packet and creates a virtual-access interface from the virtual-template defined on the PVC configuration. This virtual access interface is used as the output interface to the L2TP tunnel, to be created in the next steps.

Step 4   From this point, the steps are the same as from Step 5 in the PPPoE scenario.

Configuring the SuperCom San Jose NAS/Universal Access Concentrator

Example 2-50 shows the necessary VPDN configuration for the San Jose NAS/universal access concentrator. VPDN-group 1 is used to terminate any incoming PPPoE sessions. VPDN-group 10 is used to create an L2TP tunnel to the San Jose VHG/PE router for any PPPoX users who have the domain "eurobank.com."

NOTE   We could have just as easily retrieved the vpdn-group 10 configuration from the SuperCom RADIUS server instead of statically configuring it, in the same manner that we have done in the Dial In using VPDN (L2TP) scenario covered at the beginning of this chapter. If a Cisco 6400 universal access concentrator is being used as the LAC, then Cisco IOS 12.2(3)B onward must be used to support retrieving L2TP tunnel information from the RADIUS server.

However, because we have explicitly defined the vpdn-group for the tunnel, no RADIUS server configuration was necessary.

Example 2-50   *San Jose NAS/Universal Access Concentrator VPDN Configuration*

```
vpdn enable
vpdn search-order domain
!
vpdn-group 1
 accept-dialin
  protocol pppoe
  virtual-Template 1
!
vpdn-group 10
 request-dialin
  protocol l2tp
  domain eurobank.com
 initiate-to ip 194.22.15.2
 local name SuperCom_LAC
 l2tp tunnel password vision
```

Example 2-51 shows the interface configuration to terminate the PPPoX sessions. ATM0/0/0.2 uses PVC 1/32 to terminate any PPPoE clients that are connected via a bridged CPE. It uses the PPPoE vpdn-group (as described in Step 3 on the previous page) to find virtual-template1 so that a virtual-access interface can be cloned. ATM0/0/0.3 uses PVC 1/33 to connect to a CPE that is configured for PPPoA. It directly uses virtual-template1 to clone a virtual-access template. In both cases, the virtual-access template that is created will be used as the output interface from the L2TP tunnel (going to the San Jose PE router).

Example 2-51   *San Jose NAS/Universal Access Concentrator PPPoX Interface Configuration*

```
!
interface ATM0/0/0.2 point-to-point
 Description Termination for PPPoE clients from PVC 1/32
 no ip route-cache
 no ip mroute-cache
 pvc 1/32
  encapsulation aal5snap
  protocol pppoe
!
```

continues

Example 2-51 *San Jose NAS/Universal Access Concentrator PPPoX Interface Configuration (Continued)*

```
interface ATM0/0/0.3 point-to-point
 Description Termination for PPPoA DSL CPE from PVC 1/33
 no ip route-cache
 no ip mroute-cache
 pvc 1/33
   encapsulation aal5mux ppp virtual-Template1
!
interface virtual-Template1
 no ip address
 no keepalive
 no peer default ip address
 ppp authentication chap callin
```

It is not necessary to show the San Jose PE router configuration or per-user RADIUS attributes because these are the same as has been discussed in previous scenarios.

Verifying PPPoX and VPDN Operation

The output in Example 2-52 shows the VPDN session information for the user "anne" who has connected to the San Jose NAS/universal access concentrator by using PPPoE. (Assume that the Palo Alto CPE has been configured appropriately.) Virtual-access2 has been created to terminate the PPPoE and provide an output interface to the L2TP tunnel that has been created to 194.22.15.2 (San Jose PE router).

Example 2-52 *PPPoE and L2TP Session Information*

```
SanJose_UAC#show vpdn

L2TP Tunnel and Session Information Total tunnels 1 sessions 1

LocID RemID Remote Name   State  Remote Address  Port  Sessions
27748 34770 SuperCom_LNS  est    194.22.15.2     1701  1

LocID RemID TunID Intf      Username       State  Last Chg Fastswitch
24    41    27748 Vi2       anne@eurobank  est    00:15:54 enabled

%No active L2F tunnels

PPPoE Tunnel and Session Information Total tunnels 1 sessions 1

PPPoE Tunnel Information

Session count: 1

PPPoE Session Information
SID       RemMAC         LocMAC        Intf   VASt   OIntf       VP/VC
1         0004.27fd.249e 0004.c12b.b807 Vi2   UP     ATM0/0/0.2  1/32

SanJose_UAC#show user
   Line       User      Host(s)          Idle       Location
*  0 con 0              idle             00:00:00
   Vi2        anne@eurob Virtual PPP (PPPoE ) 00:17:30
```

The Palo Alto DSL CPE has now been reconfigured to operate in PPPoA mode. The output in Example 2-53 shows the session and user information. The PPPoA session has been terminated on virtual-access1 and an L2TP session has been created to the San Jose PE router.

Example 2-53 *PPPoA and L2TP Session Information*

```
SanJose_UAC#show vpdn

L2TP Tunnel and Session Information Total tunnels 1 sessions 1

LocID RemID Remote Name   State  Remote Address  Port  Sessions
26460 4452  SuperCom_LNS  est    194.22.15.2     1701  1

LocID RemID TunID Intf       Username      State  Last Chg Fastswitch
26    65    26460 Vi1        paloalto@euro est    00:05:22 enabled

SanJose_UAC#show user
    Line       User    Host(s)            Idle        Location
*   0 con 0            idle               00:00:00
    Vi1        paloalto@e Virtual PPP (ATM   ) 00:04:10
```

Providing Cable Access to an MPLS VPN

The Data-over-Cable Service Interface Specification (DOCSIS) is a standard that allows data traffic to be carried over a cable network that is primarily used for delivering television channels. Data is transmitted by using radio frequency (RF) signals over the cable system. Two-way communication is achieved by providing a "downstream" carrier signal from the cable network to the customer and an "upstream" carrier signal from the customer to the cable network. Cable modems are devices at the customer premises that convert a digital data stream to an RF signal (upstream) and RF back to digital data (downstream). At the head end of the cable network, a cable modem termination system (CMTS) performs the corresponding RF to data operation for many customers (many modems).

Normally, several hundred users can share a single 6-MHz downstream channel and one or more upstream channels. The downstream channel takes the place of a single television transmission channel.

In a DOCSIS 1.0-compliant hybrid fiber-coaxial (HFC) network (or just cable for short), the physical cable interface from a head end router can have many branches, each terminating at a cable modem. Access to an MPLS VPN is achieved through a cable subinterface that has a VRF statically configured on it. Version 1.0 of the DOCSIS specification uses a Service ID (SID) to identify a particular cable modem and all the devices (PCs) behind it. Traffic from the same SID always terminates on the same subinterface at the cable head end PE router; therefore, all CPEs that are connected to the same cable modem are in the same VPN.

Figure 2-25 shows a cable access scenario in the SuperCom network. Both our customers, EuroBank and FastFoods, have cable users connected to their VPNs. The SuperCom San Jose PE router has been upgraded to offer cable services and physically terminates the cable on interface Cable 3/0. The EuroBank and FastFoods cable modems logically terminate on separate subinterfaces of Cable 3/0. Table 2-13 shows the various address assignments to be used in our cable example.

Figure 2-25 *Cable Access to SuperCom MPLS VPN*

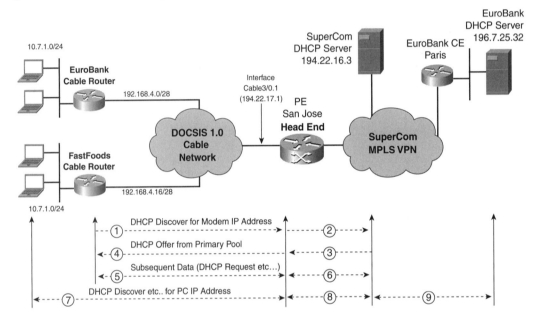

Table 2-13 *IP Address Assignment for SuperCom Cable Access*

Company	Site	Subnet/Host
SuperCom	Default/Management interface (Cable 3/0.1)	194.22.17.0/32
	SuperCom DHCP server host	194.22.16.3/32
EuroBank	Host subnet	10.7.1.0/24
	Cable modem subnet (Cable 3/0.5)	192.168.4.0/28
	EuroBank DHCP server	196.7.25.32/32
FastFoods	Host subnet	10.7.1.0/24
	Cable modem subnet (Cable 3/0.6)	192.168.4.16/28

Each cable subinterface on the San Jose head end PE router is configured with the following:

- A VRF name—EuroBank or FastFoods.

- A primary address — 192.168.4.1/28 for EuroBank and 192.168.4.17/28 for FastFoods. The primary address subnet allocates IP addresses by the SuperCom DHCP server for all cable modems that will be part of that VRF. For example, all EuroBank cable modems (assuming there is more than one) that connect to the San Jose head end PE router are allocated an address from 192.168.4.0/28.

- A secondary address — 10.7.1.1/24. Both FastFoods and EuroBank use the same subnet for their cable users, but there is no overlap because the subnet is in different VRFs. The secondary address subnet is used to satisfy DHCP requests from CPE (PCs) hosts that are connected to the cable modems. Either the SuperCom DHCP server or the customer DHCP server can supply these addresses. In either case, the server must be reachable within the VRF. You can achieve this through the use of static routes or a management extranet, which was discussed earlier in the "Dial-In Access via L2TP VPDN" section.

- A DHCP helper address for cable modem address requests and another helper address for PC host address requests. (They can be the same server address.)

In our example, the SuperCom DHCP server supplies all cable modem IP addresses. (The server has a DHCP scope configured for 192.168.4.0/28 and 192.168.4.16/28.) The EuroBank PC users obtain their addresses directly from the EuroBank DHCP server located in Paris, whereas the FastFoods PC users receive their addresses from the SuperCom RADIUS server.

Referring to Figure 2-25, the steps for obtaining cable connectivity are as follows:

Step 1   When the EuroBank or FastFoods cable modem is powered up, it issues a DHCP Discover for an IP address.

Step 2   At this point, the San Jose head end PE router cannot determine which subinterface (hence VRF) this cable modem is associated with. In this case, it uses information from the first subinterface that is configured on Cable 3/0 as its default. It relays the request by using the helper address (for cable modems) that is defined on Cable 3/0.1 with the *giaddr* set to 194.22.17.1. The helper address in this case is the SuperCom DHCP server 194.22.16.3.

NOTE   Remember from our previous discussions on DHCP that the *giaddr* is used in the relayed packet to indicate the source of the relay and the subnet for the address that is being requested.

Step 3   When the SuperCom DHCP server receives the request, it uses the *giaddr* and the MAC address of the cable modem to determine which scope to provide an address from. The modem MAC address must have previously been provisioned in the DHCP server.

Step 4   The DHCP server returns an address out of the appropriate pool (192.168.4.0/28 or 192.168.4.16/28) for the EuroBank or FastFoods modem in a DHCP Offer message.

Step 5   Any subsequent communication from the modem such as a DHCP Request or DHCP Renew are sent directly to the SuperCom DHCP server.

Step 6   When the San Jose head end PE router receives these messages from the cable network, it can determine the correct subinterface to associate the packet with (through the SID) and hence the VRF. This means that the SuperCom DHCP server must be reachable within the VRF.

Step 7   The PC clients issue a DHCP Discover to obtain an IP address.

Step 8   The PC request is relayed to the helper address that is defined on the subinterface for hosts. The *giaddr* is set to the secondary address of the interface. (Remember: The primary address that is configured is for modems, and the secondary address is used for client PCs.) Depending on the value of the helper address, the packet is relayed to the SuperCom DHCP server or the customer's DHCP server. If the DHCP request came from a FastFoods user, the packet is relayed to the SuperCom DHCP server to obtain an address.

Step 9   If the DHCP request came from a EuroBank user, the request is relayed to the EuroBank DHCP server to obtain an address for the PC.

NOTE   There is no user authorization and authentication necessary in the cable access solution. The cable subinterfaces cannot be dynamically configured. All the appropriate configurations must be in place before the first cable modem is connected.

Configuring the SuperCom Head End PE Router

Example 2-54 shows the PE router configuration to provide cable access to the EuroBank and FastFoods VPN.

Example 2-54 *San Jose PE Router Configuration for Cable Access*

```
ip dhcp relay information option
!
interface Cable3/0.1
 description Non-VPN and modems
 ip address 194.22.17.1 255.255.255.0
```

Example 2-54 *San Jose PE Router Configuration for Cable Access (Continued)*

```
 cable dhcp-giaddr policy
 cable helper-address 194.22.16.3
 !
interface Cable3/0.5
 description EuroBank Cable Network
 ip vrf forwarding EuroBank
 ip address 10.7.1.1 255.255.255.0 secondary
 ip address 192.168.4.1 255.255.255.240
 cable dhcp-giaddr policy
 cable helper-address 194.22.16.3 cable-modem
 cable helper-address 196.7.25.32 hosts
 !
interface Cable3/0.6
 description FastFoods Cable Network
 ip vrf forwarding FastFoods
 ip address 10.7.1.1 255.255.255.0 secondary
 ip address 192.168.4.17 255.255.255.240
 cable dhcp-giaddr policy
 cable helper-address 194.22.16.3
 !
 ip route 192.168.4.0 255.255.255.240 Cable3/0.5
 ip route 192.168.4.16 255.255.255.240 Cable3/0.6
 ip route 10.7.1.1 255.255.255.0 Cable3/0.6
 ip route vrf EuroBank 194.22.16.3 255.255.255.255 FastEthernet2/0 194.22.16.3 global
 ip route vrf FastFoods 194.22.16.3 255.255.255.255 FastEthernet2/0 194.22.16.3
 global
```

The **ip dhcp relay information option** command inserts additional information (circuit identifier and the remote ID) into the relayed packet that the DHCP server can use for additional processing. Interface Cable 3/0.1 is used to initially relay the DHCP Discover message to the SuperCom DHCP server by using the helper address 194.22.16.3. Because this interface is not associated with a VRF, all non-VPN cable modems and host PCs also use it.

The **cable dhcp-giaddr policy** command that appears under all the subinterfaces directs the router to use the primary or secondary address in the *giaddr* depending on whether it is a cable modem or host PC address request.

The subinterfaces Cable 3/0.5 and Cable 3/0.6 have primary and secondary addresses defined to allow connectivity to both cable modems and host PCs. Because EuroBank uses the SuperCom DHCP server for its cable modem addresses and its own DHCP server to allocate PC addresses, there are two corresponding helper addresses configured for cable modem or hosts. FastFoods relies on SuperCom to provide all addresses; therefore there is only a single helper address needed for both types of requests. These helper addresses are specified by using the **cable helper-address** command.

In our cable example, we have opted to use static routes to allow the appropriate connectivity between the cable subnets and the SuperCom DHCP server. However, in practice, it might be more secure to place the SuperCom DHCP server into its own management VRF, as discussed previously in the "Dial-In Access via L2TP VPDN" section.

NOTE   In our example, we have had to inject the RFC 1918 private subnet 10.7.1.0/24 into the global table to provide the SuperCom DHCP server access to the FastFoods subnet. In practice, this is not recommended because of the possibility of overlapping addresses. You should use registered customer addresses in the global space if possible.

Verifying Cable Operation

The debug output in Example 2-55 was generated from a DHCP Discover due to the initialization of the FastFoods cable modem. When the DHCP Discover message is received (in a BOOTP Request), it is forwarded to 194.22.16.3 (SuperCom DHCP) with the *giaddr* of 194.22.17.1. The DHCP Offer is then forwarded back (in a BOOTP Reply). When the DHCP Request is received from the cable modem (to confirm use of the address allocated), the *giaddr* used is 192.168.4.17, which is that of the FastFoods subinterface. (The router now knows the association between the cable modem and the subinterface.)

Example 2-55   *Debug of FastFoods Modem Address Reques*

```
DHCPD: adding relay information option.
DHCPD: setting giaddr to 194.22.17.1.
DHCPD: BOOTREQUEST from 0100.02fd.fa0d.77 forwarded to 194.22.16.3.
DHCPD: forwarding BOOTREPLY to client 0002.fdfa.0d77.
DHCPD: validating relay information option.
DHCPD: broadcasting BOOTREPLY to client 0002.fdfa.0d77.
DHCPD: adding relay information option.
DHCPD: setting giaddr to 192.168.4.17.
DHCPD: BOOTREQUEST from 0100.02fd.fa0d.77 forwarded to 194.22.16.3.
DHCPD: forwarding BOOTREPLY to client 0002.fdfa.0d77.
DHCPD: validating relay information option.
DHCPD: broadcasting BOOTREPLY to client 0002.fdfa.0d77.?
```

The output in Example 2-56 confirms the addresses that have been allocated for the EuroBank and FastFoods cable modems. Each modem has been allocated an address within its respective VRFs using the subnet that is defined on the primary address.

Example 2-56   *Cable Modem Address Allocation*

```
SanJose_PE#show cable modem
Interface    Prim Online   Timing Rec     QoS CPE IP address      MAC address
             Sid  State    Offset Power
Cable3/0/U1  1    online   2812   -0.50   5   0   192.168.4.18    0002.fdfa.0d77
Cable3/0/U0  2    online   2812    0.25   5   0   192.168.4.4     0003.e350.92e9

SanJose_PE#show ip vrf int
Interface           IP-Address      VRF                         Protocol
Cable3/0.5          192.168.4.1     EuroBank                    up
Cable3/0.6          192.168.4.17    FastFoods                   up
```

DHCP requests for PC clients are relayed as per normal operation; the only difference is that the secondary address is used as the *giaddr.*

Advanced Features for MPLS VPN Remote Access

The previous sections have covered basic integration of remote access technologies (dial-up, DSL, and cable) into the MPLS VPN environment. This section covers some advanced Cisco IOS features that you can use with remote access and includes the following:

- On-demand address pools (ODAPs)
- Per-VRF AAA
- DHCP relay — VPN support

ODAPs

In most dial-up scenarios, the dial-in server supplies an IP address to the dial-in user (or router). You can allocate the IP addresses to PPP sessions by using a variety of methods:

- Statically configured using the RADIUS Framed-IP-address attribute.

- Local address pools that can be either overlapping or nonoverlapping. Overlapping/nonoverlapping local pools are implemented and maintained locally on the router. Overlapping local pools have been used throughout the SuperCom examples.

- Addresses can also be provided from overlapping pools that the RADIUS server manages. If overlapping pools are configured on a RADIUS server, authentication and accounting must be configured on the same server.

- An address pool that a DHCP server manages. The DHCP server only maintains a common pool from which addresses are dynamically assigned upon request. This method does not provide the scalability of overlapping pools.

To supplement the existing address allocation methods, *ODAPs* were introduced in IOS 12.2(8)T. Using ODAPs allows an address pool to expand and contract based on address usage. Each ODAP is associated with a VRF and is initially populated with one or more subnets that a RADIUS or DHCP server provides.

If the allocation of addresses from a pool reaches a preset high utilization mark, additional subnets are leased from the RADIUS or DHCP server to satisfy demand. Conversely, if utilization falls below a certain level, subnets are handed back to the RADIUS or DHCP server that provided the lease. Each time a subnet is leased, a corresponding summarized route is inserted into the VRF that is then removed when the lease is returned to the RADIUS or DHCP server.

A separate ODAP is configured for each VRF that requires address assignment services on a router. Both PPP and normal DHCP client requests can be serviced from the same pool.

NOTE	The RADIUS or DHCP server that is used in the network must support the leasing and returning of IP subnets on a per-VRF basis. ODAPs are supported in Cisco Access Registrar from V1.7 onward.

Figure 2-26 illustrates how ODAPs would work in the SuperCom network to provide addresses for FastFoods from the San Jose PE router.

Figure 2-26   *SuperCom ODAP for FastFoods*

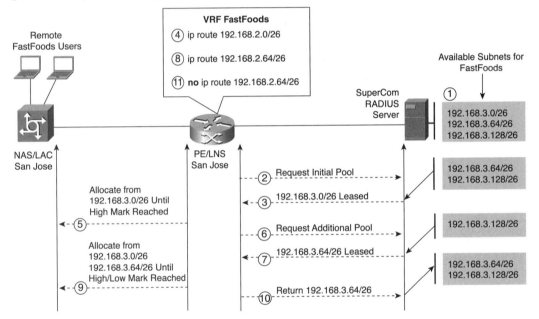

The following describes the operational steps for ODAP:

Step 1   The SuperCom RADIUS server has been allocated three /26 address blocks starting at 192.168.3.0 to support requests from the FastFoods ODAP. Note that these address blocks do not have to be contiguous or unique. The same address blocks can be allocated to other pools in different VRFs. (The way the RADIUS server implements this varies between products and is not within the scope of this chapter; however, Cisco Access Registrar is recommended.)

Step 2   On startup, the San Jose PE router requests a subnet to populate its ODAP for FastFoods. It does this through a RADIUS access-request message with the NAS-Identifier attribute set to "odap-dhcp" to allow the

RADIUS server to distinguish it from a normal user authentication request. The User-Name attribute contains the VRF that the ODAP subnet is being requested for.

Step 3 The RADIUS server responds with the first available subnet from its resource pool. In this case, this is 192.168.3.0/26, which provides 62 useable addresses for PPP clients.

Step 4 A route is automatically placed into the FastFoods VRF for 192.168.2.0/26. Multiprotocol BGP distributes this throughout the FastFoods VPN.

Step 5 At this point, addresses can be allocated from the ODAP pool to any PPP client requests (could be from the NAS/LAC or direct ISDN) until the high utilization mark is reached.

Step 6 Assuming the high mark is reached, the San Jose PE router requests another address pool. The size of the pool it requests is configurable.

Step 7 The next available subnet 192.168.3.64/26 is then passed back and added to the ODAP for FastFoods, leaving one subnet available in the RADIUS server. If no subnets are available, the RADUS server responds with an access-reject message.

Step 8 A corresponding route for 192.168.3.64/26 is placed into the FastFoods VRF.

Step 9 Addresses are then allocated from the expanded ODAP by using an available pool of 124 addresses until the low or high utilization mark is reached. Note that the utilization marks are a percentage of the *total current pool size*. If possible, addresses are allocated from the first leased subnet. Therefore, over time, the last leased has addresses returned to it as PPP sessions terminate.

Step 10 Assuming that the low utilization mark has been reached, the last leased subnet (192.168.3.64/26) is released back to the RADIUS server if there are no active addresses currently being leased from it.

Step 11 When the subnet is returned to the RADIUS server, the corresponding route is removed from the FastFoods VRF.

Configuring the SuperCom San Jose PE Router

Example 2-57 shows the configuration that is necessary to enable ODAP for the FastFoods VRF.

Example 2-57   *San Jose PE Router Configuration for ODAP*

```
aaa authentication ppp default local group radius
aaa authorization network default local group radius
aaa authorization configuration default group radius

ip address-pool dhcp-pool

ip dhcp pool FastFoods_ODAP
   vrf FastFoods
   utilization mark high 80
   utilization mark low 25
   origin aaa subnet size initial /26 autogrow /26
!
radius-server host 194.22.16.2 auth-port 1645 acct-port 1646 key a$4two
radius-server attribute 32 include-in-access-req
radius-server attribute 44 include-in-access-req
radius-server vsa send authentication
```

The **aaa authorization configuration** command allows the San Jose PE router to configure the ODAP with subnets received from the SuperCom RADIUS server. The command **ip address-pool dhcp-pool** enables ODAP as the global address mechanism for PPP sessions that terminate in a VRF; however, this default can be overridden at the interface level.

The ODAP is configured with the **ip dhcp pool** command for each VRF that requires it—in our case, for FastFoods. The high and low utilizations are specified as a percentage (80% and 25%) of the total number of addresses in the pool (could be multiple subnets). The **origin** command activates the ODAP for the FastFoods VRF. In our example, we obtain subnets from the AAA server, which is the SuperCom RADIUS server. The initial subnet requested is a /26 in size; thereafter, if expansion of the pool is necessary, the requested subnets are also /26.

When requesting a subnet, the RADIUS access-request message must contain the NAS-Port identifier ("odap-dhcp") and an accounting session-id attribute so that the RADIUS server can distinguish different subnet requests. This is achieved by allowing the RADIUS attributes 32 and 44 to be included in the message. In addition, the **radius-server vsa send authentication** command allows the PE router to include cisco-avpairs in the request—in particular, a "pool-mask" indicating the size of subnet required.

RADIUS Attributes

The RADIUS attributes remain relatively unchanged from previous examples except that the peer default address pool used is the DHCP-pool for ODAP rather than a locally configured pool (see Table 2-14). This is achieved by using the interface command **peer default ip address dhcp-pool.**

Table 2-14   *User Attributes for ODAP*

Attribute (Type)	Value
User-Name (1)	elvis@fastfoods.com
User-Password (2)	whatsthebuzz
Service-Type (6)	1 (Framed)
Framed-Protocol (7)	1 (PPP)
Cisco-avpair	lcp:interface-config=ip vrf forwarding FastFoods \n[1] ip unnumbered loopback 10 \n peer default ip address dhcp-pool

[1] The \n signifies an explicit carriage return. Usage varies between RADIUS server implementations.

NOTE   Because the global default on the San Jose PE router was set to ODAP with the **ip address-pool dhcp-pool** command, it is not necessary to enter a peer default command in the interface config.

Verifying ODAP Operation

The San Jose PE router and the SuperCom RADIUS server have had ODAP configured for both the FastFoods and EuroBank VRFs. The output in Example 2-58 shows the RADIUS debug messages from the San Jose PE router requesting an initial subnet for FastFoods. As you can see, the User-Name attribute consists of the VRF name. The cisco-avpair consists of the pool-mask indicating that a /26 subnet is required. The NAS-identifier indicates to the RADIUS server that this is an ODAP request. The response from the SuperCom RADIUS server is subnet 192.168.3.0/26, which is used to initially configure the ODAP. The procedure is the same for the EuroBank VRF.

Example 2-58   *ODAP RADIUS Access Request and Accept Messages*

```
RADIUS(00000000): Send to unknown id 21645/68 194.22.16.2:1645, Access-Request,
  len 136
[snip]
RADIUS:  User-Name          [1]   11   "FastFoods"
RADIUS:  User-Password      [2]   18   *
RADIUS:  Vendor, Cisco      [26]  33
RADIUS:   Cisco AVpair      [1]   27   "pool-mask=255.255.255.192"
RADIUS:  Acct-Session-Id    [44]  10   "00000038"
RADIUS:  Nas-Identifier     [32]  11   "odap-dhcp"
RADIUS:  Vendor, Cisco      [26]  15
RADIUS:   cisco-nas-port    [2]   9    "Port 56"
RADIUS:  NAS-Port           [5]   6    60000
RADIUS:  NAS-IP-Address     [4]   6    194.22.15.2
RADIUS:  Service-Type       [6]   6    Outbound            [5]
```

continues

Example 2-58 *ODAP RADIUS Access Request and Accept Messages (Continued)*

```
RADIUS: Received from id 21645/68 194.22.16.2:1645, Access-Accept, len 126
[snip]
RADIUS:  Termination-Action  [29]  6   1
RADIUS:  Vendor, Cisco        [26]  29
RADIUS:   Cisco AVpair        [1]   23  "pool-addr=192.168.3.0"
RADIUS:  Vendor, Cisco        [26]  33
RADIUS:   Cisco AVpair        [1]   27  "pool-mask=255.255.255.192"
```

The three remote users from our VPDN dial-in scenario, elvis@fastfoods.com, jimi@fastfoods.com, and eric@eurobank.com, have dialed in again, but this time they have received addresses for their PPP sessions from the ODAPs that are associated with their VRFs. For the sake of example, the FastFoods ODAP has had its high/low utilization marks set to 3% and 2% respectively to force expansion of the pool with just two users. Example 2-59 shows the ODAP status for the FastFoods and EuroBank VRFs.

Example 2-59 *FastFoods and EuroBank ODAPs*

```
SanJose_PE#show ip dhcp pool

Pool FastFoods_ODAP :
 Utilization mark (high/low)    : 3 / 2
 Subnet size (first/next)       : 26 / 26 (autogrow)
 VRF name                       : FastFoods
 Total addresses                : 124
 Leased addresses               : 2
 Pending event                  : none
 2 subnets are currently in the pool :
 Current index      IP address range                      Leased addresses
 192.168.3.3        192.168.3.1    - 192.168.3.62         2
 192.168.3.65       192.168.3.65   - 192.168.3.126        0

Pool EuroBank_ODAP :
 Utilization mark (high/low)    : 80 / 25
 Subnet size (first/next)       : 26 / 26 (autogrow)
 VRF name                       : EuroBank
 Total addresses                : 62
 Leased addresses               : 1
 Pending event                  : none
 1 subnet is currently in the pool :
 Current index      IP address range                      Leased addresses
 192.168.3.2        192.168.3.1    - 192.168.3.62         1
```

Both ODAPs have received an initial subnet allocation of 192.168.3.0/26.

NOTE   There is no restriction on what subnets can be used. Our example uses the same subnet range for both VRFs to show the overlapping pool capability of ODAP.

Two addresses have been leased from FastFoods_ODAP (for "elvis" and "jimi") from the first available subnet. Because the high utilization mark has been exceeded, the FastFoods_ODAP has requested an expansion with the extra subnet 192.168.3.64/26 being provided from the SuperCom RADIUS server. The EuroBank_ODAP has leased one address to "eric."

Example 2-60 shows the routing tables for both VRFs. You can see the connected routes to the virtual-access interfaces for each user. Also, note the static routes that have been injected for each of the ODAP subnets pointing to null0. In this case, the BGP **aggregate-address** command, as discussed previously, is not necessary. However, to achieve proper summarization, the connected routes must not be redistributed into Multiprotocol BGP.

Example 2-60 *FastFoods and EuroBank Routing Table with ODAP*

```
SanJose_PE#show ip route vrf FastFoods
[snip]

     10.0.0.0/24 is subnetted, 1 subnets
B        10.2.1.0 [200/0] via 194.22.15.1, 2d02h
     192.168.2.0/24 is variably subnetted, 2 subnets, 2 masks
C        192.168.2.100/32 is directly connected, Loopback10
B        192.168.2.20/30 [200/0] via 194.22.15.1, 2d02h
     192.168.3.0/24 is variably subnetted, 4 subnets, 2 masks
S        192.168.3.64/26 [1/0] via 0.0.0.0, Null0
C        192.168.3.2/32 is directly connected, virtual-Access5
C        192.168.3.1/32 is directly connected, virtual-Access4
S        192.168.3.0/26 [1/0] via 0.0.0.0, Null0

SanJose_PE#show ip route vrf EuroBank
[snip]

B    196.7.25.0/24 [200/0] via 194.22.15.1, 2d02h
     192.168.2.0/24 is variably subnetted, 2 subnets, 2 masks
C        192.168.2.100/32 is directly connected, Loopback11
B        192.168.2.24/30 [200/0] via 194.22.15.1, 2d02h
     192.168.3.0/24 is variably subnetted, 2 subnets, 2 masks
C        192.168.3.1/32 is directly connected, virtual-Access3
S        192.168.3.0/26 [1/0] via 0.0.0.0, Null0
```

Per VRF AAA

So far in this chapter, the SuperCom RADIUS server has authenticated user PPP sessions that terminate on the San Jose PE router. In the FastFoods case, the RADIUS access-requests were proxied to the FastFoods RADIUS server at Lyon where the actual user information was stored. As has been discussed previously, this requires that a route be available between the two RADIUS servers to allow them to communicate. It also involves a series of configuration steps to import and export routes between the Management VRF, customer VRF, and global routing table. Such configurations, although quite common in MPLS VPN networks, can be prone to error and security issues.

You can eliminate the requirement of a RADIUS proxy for remote access by using a new feature call per-VRF AAA. This feature allows direct access to a customer RADIUS server from within the VRF for user authentication. The advantage of this is that a service provider RADIUS server is not required, nor are complex Intranet configurations for proxy RADIUS access. Because only one RADIUS server is required, a failure point is removed and access-request response time is improved.

The initial implementation of per-VRF AAA requires that you define a virtual-template for each VRF that contains a customer RADIUS server. Apart from the VRF name and interface addressing method, the virtual-template supplies the relevant configurations that define the access to the customer RADIUS server. A per-VRF virtual-template is required because the VHG/PE router forwards only a single access-request containing the username@domainname and password (received through the L2TP tunnel). Therefore, the VHG/PE router must know the VRF and RADIUS server for a domain before the PPP session is established so that the received username@domainname and password can be forwarded to the correct customer RADIUS server.

NOTE   Future enhancements to the per-VRF AAA feature plan to allow the service provider RADIUS server to dynamically provide the customer RADIUS information (as well as the VRF, interface addressing, and so on). Therefore, future versions will have three RADIUS requests: one from the LAC to the SP RADIUS server for tunnel information, one for the LNS to SP RADIUS server for VPN and Customer RADIUS information, and one from the LNS to Customer RADIUS server to authenticate the customer.

Figure 2-27 shows the per-VRF AAA in the SuperCom network for FastFoods.

Essentially, remote access is the same as the VPDN scenario described previously, except that configuration information for the virtual-access interface is obtained from a specific virtual-template for FastFoods. This virtual-template is associated with a vpdn-group that is configured to terminate FastFoods users only. You do this by using a different hostname in the vpdn-group configuration. When the San Jose NAS/LAC receives a call for elvis@fastfoods.com, it creates the L2TP tunnel as normal, but instead of using SuperCom_LAC as the L2TP client name, a different LAC client name is used to identify FastFoods (in our case, it is FastFoods_LAC). The SuperCom RADIUS server (which is not shown) supplies this information. When the San Jose VHG/PE router receives the L2TP request, it searches for a VPDN-group that matches the LAC client name (in the terminate-from host command) and then uses the associated virtual-template. The virtual-template provides the information that allows the San Jose VHG/PE router direct access to the FastFoods RADIUS server with the FastFoods VRF so that elvis@fastfoods.com can be authenticated.

Figure 2-27 *Per-VRF AAA VPDN Access*

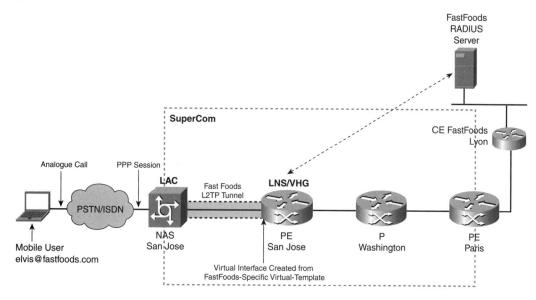

The SuperCom LAC/NAS configuration remains the same as the VPDN scenario. However, the configuration changes required for per-VRF AAA for other components are shown in the following sections.

Configuring the SuperCom San Jose PE Router

The San Jose VHG/PE router requires several configuration changes. First, you must configure an AAA server group that defines the details of the FastFoods RADIUS server. The configuration for the FastFoods RADIUS server is shown in Example 2-61. To support the possibility of overlapping addresses of customer RADIUS servers when there are multiple VRFs using the per-VRF AAA feature, a new command **server-private** has been defined under the server group. This allow RADIUS servers that have the same IP address to be defined but associated with a different VRF. The server group also associates the VRF where the private RADIUS server is located. In our example, the FastFoods VRF uses the RADIUS server 10.2.1.5 located at Lyon, which is directly reachable in the VRF routing table. In addition, you must configure a method list for authentication and authorization for the FastFoods server group. The virtual-template for FastFoods uses these method lists.

Example 2-61 *Configuring the FastFoods RADIUS Server Group*

```
aaa group server radius SG_FastFoods
 server-private 10.2.1.5 auth-port 1645 acct-port 1646 key Two4a$
 ip vrf forwarding FastFoods
 !
aaa authentication ppp FastFoods_List group SG_FastFoods
aaa authorization network FastFoods_List group SG_FastFoods
```

Next, you must define RADIUS-specific commands for the VRF, as shown in Example 2-62. In our case, the FastFoods RADIUS server contains unqualified usernames (no "@fastfoods.com"); therefore, the first command strips off the domain name for any access-requests in the FastFoods VRF. The second command provides a source address in the VRF that allows the FastFoods RADIUS server to reach the San Jose PE router.

Example 2-62 *FastFoods RADIUS-Specific Commands for per-VRF AAA*

```
radius-server domain-stripping vrf FastFoods
!
ip radius source-interface lo10 vrf FastFoods
```

Finally, the FastFoods-specific vpdn-group and virtual-template are configured, as shown in Example 2-63. Note the hostname for the vpdn-group matches the tunnel client name attribute from the SuperCom RADIUS server FastFoods domain entry. Any FastFoods PPP sessions that are established over the L2TP tunnel for this vpdn-group use the virtual-template3. The virtual template defines all the relevant information to create a virtual-access interface in the FastFoods VRF, including which AAA method list to use for FastFoods users. The FastFoods_List causes the access-request message to be sent to the FastFoods RADIUS server 10.2.1.5 with a source address of 192.168.2.100 (loopback 10).

Example 2-63 *VPDN and Virtual Template Configuration for per-VRF AAA*

```
vpdn-group 2
 accept-dialin
  protocol l2tp
  virtual-Template 3
 terminate-from hostname FastFoods_LAC
 local name SuperCom_LNS
 l2tp tunnel password vision
!
interface virtual-Template3
 ip vrf forwarding FastFoods
 ip unnumbered Loopback10
 peer default ip address dhcp-pool
 ppp authentication chap FastFoods_List
 ppp authorization FastFoods_List
```

SuperCom RADIUS Server Attributes

The only attribute that changes for the FastFoods domain entry is the name of the Tunnel client, which is FastFoods_LAC (see Table 2-15).

Table 2-15 *SuperCom RADIUS Attributes for per-VRF AAA*

Attribute (Type)	Value
User-Name (1)	fastfoods.com
User-Password (2)	cisco
Tunnel-Type (64)	3 (L2TP)

Table 2-15   *SuperCom RADIUS Attributes for per-VRF AAA (Continued)*

Attribute (Type)	Value
Tunnel-Medium-Type (65)	1 (IPv4)
Tunnel-Server-Endpoint (67)	194.22.15.2 (San Jose VHG/PE)
Tunnel-Password (69)	vision
Tunnel-Client-Auth-ID (90)	FastFoods_LAC
Tunnel-Server-Auth-ID (91)	SuperCom_LNS

Verifying per-VRF AAA Operation

Now that per-VRF AAA has been configured for FastFoods, when elvis@fastfoods.com and jimi@fastfoods.com dial in again, they are associated with vpdn-group 2. This is because the tunnel client name FastFoods_LAC was provided with the L2TP tunnel request from the San Jose LAC/NAS. All other non-FastFoods users such as EuroBank user "eric" still use vpdn-group 1 with the SuperCom RADIUS server providing most of the interface configurations. You can verify this by examining the VPDN information on the San Jose VHG/PE router, as shown in Example 2-64.

Example 2-64   *Verifying VPDN Connection Information*

```
SanJose_PE#show vpdn

L2TP Tunnel and Session Information Total tunnels 2 sessions 3

LocID RemID Remote Name   State  Remote Address  Port  Sessions VPDN Group
36418 11895 SuperCom_LAC  est    194.22.15.26    1701  1        1

LocID RemID TunID Intf        Username              State  Last Chg
14    54    36418 Vi6         eric@eurobank.com     est    2d08h

LocID RemID Remote Name   State  Remote Address  Port  Sessions VPDN Group
47519 24880 FastFoods_LAC est    194.22.15.26    1701  2        2

LocID RemID TunID Intf        Username              State  Last Chg
20    60    47519 Vi4         elvis@fastfoods.com   est    00:00:56
21    61    47519 Vi5         jimi@fastfoods.com    est    00:00:08
```

The RADIUS debug output in Example 2-65 shows the access-request message for user "elvis" being sent directly to the FastFoods RADIUS server 10.2.1.5 by using the RADIUS source address (NAS –IP-Address) of 192.168.2.100, which is loopback 10. (Use for preinstantiation of the FastFoods VRF.) Note that the domain name has been stripped off the username.

Example 2-65 *Access-Request DEBUG for per-VRF AAA*

```
RADIUS(00000036): Send to unknown id 1645/24 10.2.1.5:1645, Access-Request, len 82
RADIUS:  authenticator 39 FA 82 72 D4 E1 72 92 - EA 1A DA 33 48 6E 5A A0
RADIUS:  Framed-Protocol      [7]   6   PPP                     [1]
RADIUS:  User-Name            [1]   6   "elvis"
RADIUS:  CHAP-Password        [3]   19  *
RADIUS:  NAS-Port-Type        [61]  6   Virtual                 [5]
RADIUS:  Service-Type         [6]   6   Framed                  [2]
RADIUS:  NAS-IP-Address       [4]   6   192.168.2.100
RADIUS:  Nas-Identifier       [32]  13  "SanJose_PE."
RADIUS: Received from id 1645/24 10.2.1.5:1645, Access-Accept, len 20
RADIUS:  authenticator 14 A1 41 83 94 A9 60 29 - 52 C8 47 16 72 E2 46 3A
RADIUS(00000036): Received from id 1645/24
2d08h: %LINK-3-UPDOWN: Interface virtual-Access4, changed state to up
```

Examining the characteristics of the virtual-access4 interface for elvis@fastfoods.com, you can see that it was cloned from virtual-template3, as defined in vpdn-group 2 (see Example 2-66).

Example 2-66 *Virtual-Access Interfaces*

```
SanJose_PE#show interface virtual-access 4
virtual-Access3 is up, line protocol is up
  Hardware is Virtual Access interface
  Interface is unnumbered. Using address of Loopback10 (192.168.2.100)
  MTU 1500 bytes, BW 256 Kbit, DLY 100000 usec,
     reliability 255/255, txload 1/255, rxload 1/255
  Encapsulation PPP, LCP Open
  Open: IPCP
  PPPoVPDN vaccess, cloned from virtual-Template3
  Protocol l2tp, tunnel id 25317, session id 12, loopback not set
  [snip]
```

DHCP Relay: VPN Support

This feature provides VRF-aware support for DHCP Relay and allows a single DHCP server to support DHCP clients in different VRFs, which might have overlapping address spaces. The DHCP server can be located in the global table, allowing the service provider to offer DHCP services, a local VRF (that is, the one the client resides in), or a remote VRF (that is, an extranet VPN).

NOTE   The DHCP server must have the capability to support overlapping address pools for this feature to work.

This feature allows a DHCP relay agent to provide additional information in the DHCP request to allow the DHCP server to identify the correct VPN namespace for IP address assignment or policy application. This additional information is provided by using the

DHCP Relay Agent Information option, known as Option 82. The relay agent uses Option 82 to convey information in the form of suboptions. For DHCP VPN-related activities, the suboptions used are as follows:

- **VPN-ID**—The relay agent uses this suboption to convey to the DHCP server the VPN that the DHCP request is associated with. The relay agent also uses VPN-ID to identify for the VRF any replies from the DHCP server. The identifier can consist of either the VRF name or the VPN ID as defined in RFC 2685.

NOTE   Configuration of a VPN ID for a VPN is optional. You can still use the VRF name to identify configured VPNs in the router. The VRF name is not affected by the VPN ID configuration. The identification mechanisms are independent of each other.

- **Subnet-selection**—This suboption identifies the IP subnet in the VRF that the request originated from. In normal relay agent processing, the subnet is derived from the gateway address (*giaddr*) of the relay agent. The DHCP server also uses the *giaddr* to communicate with the relay agent. However, when relaying a request from a VRF, the *giaddr* is the address configured on the VRF interface, which might not be visible to the DHCP server. Therefore, the subnet-selection suboption allows separation of the client subnet from the address used to communicate with the DHCP server. This will be explained in the example provided later in this section.

- **Server-ID-override**—After a client has been allocated an IP address, it sends renew or release packets directly to the DHCP server. However, the DHCP server might not be directly reachable from the client VRF. (It might be in the global table.) The Server-ID-override suboption is used to change the IP address of the DHCP server in reply packets to the VRF interface address of the relay agent. The relay agent inserts its VRF interface address into this suboption when it first relays the request. When the reply is returned, the value of this field is then copied to the DHCP server address option; therefore, the client is "tricked" into sending its renew/release packets directly to the relay agent.

NOTE   The DHCP server must also support DHCP Option 82 as well as provide a mechanism to manage overlapping addresses from different name spaces. This capability is available in Version 5.5 of the Cisco Network Registrar.

Figure 2-28 shows VPN-aware DHCP Relay operation for the EuroBank Palo Alto CPE that is connected to the SuperCom network by using DSL. In this scenario, the CPE is connected by using RFC 1483 bridged, and the VRF ATM interface at the San Jose PE router is configured with route bridge encapsulation (RBE). Therefore, it behaves as if it were a LAN interface. The DHCP server is located in the SuperCom global routing table, which does not have direct reachability to the 10.6.1.0/24 subnet of EuroBank Palo Alto.

Figure 2-28   *VPN-Aware DHCP Relay Operation*

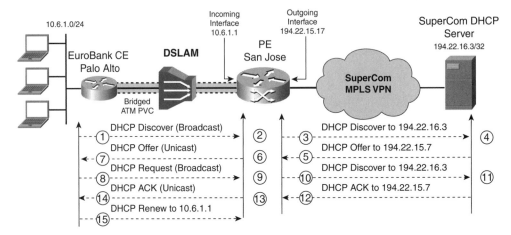

The DHCP relay operation can be summarized in the following steps:

Step 1   A client on the Palo Alto subnet 10.6.1.0/24 requests an address by broadcasting a DHCP Discover message. This message contains information such as the MAC address and hostname. This is carried in a bridged packet toward the San Jose PE router.

Step 2   The San Jose PE router acting as the relay agent receives the packet. Before forwarding it to the SuperCom DHCP server, the San Jose PE router adds the relay agent information (Option 82) as follows: VPN-ID = "EuroBank", Subnet-Selection = "10.6.1.0/24", Server-ID-Override = "10.6.1.1." The *giaddr* field is set to 194.22.15.17, which is the outgoing interface address in the global routing table that is reachable from the SuperCom DHCP server.

Step 3   The relay agent unicasts the DHCP Discover message toward the SuperCom DHCP server 194.22.16.3.

Step 4   The DHCP server receives the packet and uses the VPN-ID and Subnet-Selection suboptions to allocate an address from the correct VPN namespace.

Step 5   The DHCP server sends the DHCP offer back to the San Jose PE router by using the value of the giaddr field, which was 194.22.15.17.

Step 6   The relay agent removes the Option 82 information.

Step 7   The DHCP Offer is unicast (using the MAC address) to the requesting client.

Step 8   The client then confirms its received address by broadcasting a DHCP Request toward the relay agent.

Step 9   The San Jose PE router then adds the option 82 information.

Step 10   The DHCP Request message is then relayed to the SuperCom DHCP server.

Step 11   The DHCP server then formally allocates the address, using the Option 82 information to access the correct namespace.

Step 12   A DHCP Acknowledge is then forwarded to the San Jose PE router.

Step 13   The San Jose PE router receives the DHCP Ack message and changes the DHCP server ID to the address in the Server-ID-Override, which is 10.6.1.1.

Step 14   The acknowledge is then forwarded directly to the DHCP client.

Step 15   Any subsequent renew or release messages are sent directly to 10.6.1.1. When the San Jose PE router receives these messages, it adds the Option 82 information and relays the packet toward the SuperCom DHCP server.

Configuring the San Jose PE Router

The only configuration changes that are necessary apply to the San Jose PE router. Several commands have been introduced or modified to support the DHCP Relay—VPN Support feature and are shown in the following configuration (see Example 2-67), which applies to the DSL RFC1483 scenario discussed previously.

The command **ip dhcp relay information option vpn** inserts the DHCP Relay Agent Information option (Option 82) into any DHCP requests that the San Jose PE router receives. In particular, the vpn keyword ensures that the three VPN-related suboptions—VPN-ID, Subnet-Selection, and Server-ID-Override—are added.

NOTE   Option 82 can also be used to convey suboptions that are unrelated to VPNs, such as the circuit identifier suboption and the remote ID suboption used in cable access.

Example 2-67 *DHCP Relay Configuration*

```
ip dhcp relay information option vpn
!
ip vrf EuroBank
 rd 10:27
 vpn id ACDE48:27
 route-target export 10:27
 route-target import 10:27
```

continues

Example 2-67   *DHCP Relay Configuration (Continued)*

```
!
interface ATM2/0.1 point-to-point
 description RBE connection to Palo Alto DSL CPE
 ip vrf forwarding EuroBank
 ip address 10.6.1.1 255.255.255.0
 ip helper-address global 194.22.16.3
 no ip mroute-cache
 atm route-bridged ip
 pvc 1/32
  ubr 256
  encapsulation aal5snap
 !
```

The **vpn id** command under the VRF configuration allows a unique ID that is distinct from the VRF name to be allocated. The VPN ID is specified in the format defined by RFC 2685 and consists of the following elements:

- An Organizational Unique Identifier (OUI) that consists of a three-octet hex number. The IEEE Registration Authority assigns OUIs to any company that manufactures components under the ISO/IEC 8802 standard. The OUI generates universal LAN MAC addresses and protocol identifiers for use in local and metropolitan-area network (MAN) applications. For example, an OUI for Cisco Systems is 00-03-6B (hex).

- A VPN index, consisting of a four-octet hex number, which identifies the VPN within the company.

Our example used ACDE48 as the OUI, which is defined by the IEEE to represent private use. The VPN index used is the same as the unique identifier used in the Route-Distinguisher.

The ip helper address has been modified to support a DHCP server address that is reachable in the global routing table, another VRF, or the local VRF. It now takes the form ip helper-address [vrf *name* | global] *address*. If neither VRF nor global keywords are used, the DHCP address must be reachable in the local VRF.

Our example uses the SuperCom DHCP server, which is reachable on the management LAN in the global routing table.

Verifying VPN-Aware DHCP Relay Operation

The output shown in Example 2-68 is a debug of DHCP activity on the San Jose PE router when a client on the Palo Alto LAN requests a DHCP address. The first section shows the DHCP Discover being received with the *giaddr* initially being set to 10.6.1.1 (the incoming interface address). The Option 82 information is added, and the *giaddr* is then overwritten with the outgoing global interface address on the San Jose PE router (the interface that is used to reach the DHCP server). The next sections show the BOOTREPLY from the DHCP server (containing the DHCP Offer), followed by the DHCP Request from the client and then another BOOTREPLY (containing the DHCP Ack).

Example 2-68 *VPN-Aware DHCP Relay Debug Output*

```
DHCPD: DHCPDISCOVER received from client 0100.0347.bb2f.12 on interface ATM2/0.1.
DHCPD: there is no address pool for 10.6.1.1.
DHCPD: setting giaddr to 10.6.1.1.
DHCPD: adding relay information option.
DHCPD: VPN id =ACDE48:27
DHCPD: Selected subnet=10.6.1.0
DHCPD: Server-id-override=10.6.1.1
DHCPD: giaddr changed to 194.22.15.17
DHCPD: BOOTREQUEST from 0100.0347.bb2f.12 forwarded to 194.22.16.3.

DHCPD: forwarding BOOTREPLY to client 0003.47bb.2f12.
DHCPD: Vrf name from sub-option = EuroBank
DHCPD: Forwarding reply on numbered intf
DHCPD: creating ARP entry (10.6.1.2, 0003.47bb.2f12).
DHCPD: unicasting BOOTREPLY to client 0003.47bb.2f12 (10.6.1.2).

DHCPD: DHCPREQUEST received from client 0100.0347.bb2f.12.
DHCPD: setting giaddr to 10.6.1.1.
DHCPD: adding relay information option.
DHCPD: VPN id =ACDE48:27
DHCPD: Selected subnet=10.6.1.0
DHCPD: Server-id-override=10.6.1.1
DHCPD: giaddr changed to 192.22.15.17
DHCPD: BOOTREQUEST from 0100.0347.bb2f.12 forwarded to 192.22.16.3.

DHCPD: forwarding BOOTREPLY to client 0003.47bb.2f12.
DHCPD: Vrf name from sub-option = EuroBank
DHCPD: Forwarding reply on numbered intf
DHCPD: creating ARP entry (10.6.1.2, 0003.47bb.2f12).
DHCPD: unicasting BOOTREPLY to client 0003.47bb.2f12 (10.6.1.2).
```

Summary

Remote access to an MPLS VPN supports many different access technologies. These include PSTN and ISDN dial-in and dial-out, all DSL encapsulation modes, and cable access using a DOCSIS-1.0 compliant network. By centralizing configuration and addressing functions on service provider or customer AAA/DHCP servers, a highly scalable remote access solution can be built. In addition, many features have been introduced or enhanced in Cisco IOS to provide VRF-aware support, including ODAPs, per-VRF AAA, DHCP Relay—VPN Support, and VPN-ID among others. The use of these features and the architectures described throughout this chapter allows a service provider to build a single remote access infrastructure that many customers can share. Remote access to an MPLS VPN allows a customer to obviate the need to build, manage, and maintain his own remote access infrastructure, lowering costs and improving coverage. Service providers can generate new revenue streams by assuming responsibility of remote access provisioning on behalf of the customer.

CHAPTER 3

PE-CE Routing Protocol Enhancements and Advanced Features

The initial implementation of the Cisco Systems Inc. Multiprotocol Label Switching (MPLS) virtual private network (VPN) architecture provided support for several, but not all, routing protocols between the provider edge (PE) routers and customer edge (CE) routers. This initial support included Border Gateway Protocol (BGP-4), static routing, Routing Information Protocol (RIP) version 2 and Open Shortest Path First (OSPF), each of which was described in detail in the first volume of this book. Deployment experience has shown that the majority of services have been provisioned using either static routing or BGP-4. However, this combination is changing as MPLS technology has gained more acceptance among a diverse mix of end customers. Many of these customers have more complex routing topologies that are best served through more integration with the customer Interior Gateway Protocol (IGP).

Because of this change, several enhancements have been added to the support of the OSPF protocol, and the ability to run either Enhanced Interior Gateway Routing Protocol (EIGRP) or Integrated Intermediate-System to Intermediate-System (IS-IS) has been added to the list of PE-CE protocols. This chapter describes the enhancements made to the OSPF protocol. It also provides a detailed look at how EIGRP and IS-IS have been implemented and how each is configured at the PE routers.

NOTE	As with all other PE-CE routing protocols, when introducing EIGRP or IS-IS between the service provider and the VPN customer, no additional protocol changes are required at the CE routers. They can continue to run standard IOS images.

Throughout this chapter, we will refer to the sample service provider topology, as shown in Figure 3-1. All relevant IP address ranges for the service provider backbone and attached VPN customers are shown in Table 3-1.

Figure 3-1   *Sample Service Provider Topology*

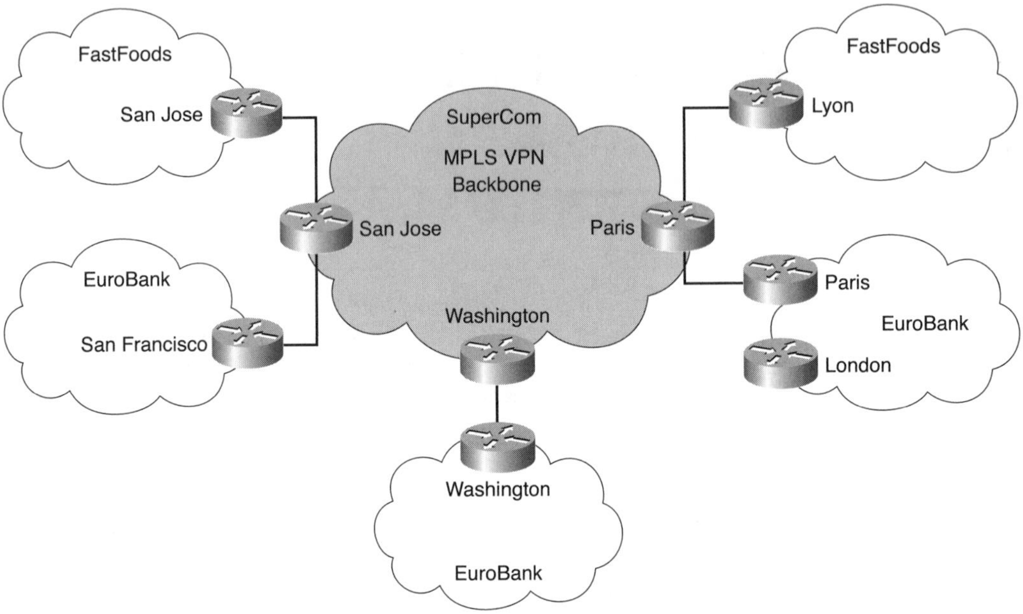

Table 3-1   *IP Address Assignment for SuperCom Backbone*

Company	Site	Subnet
FastFoods	San Jose	195.12.2.0/24
	Lyon	10.2.1.0/24
EuroBank	San Francisco	10.2.1.0/24
	London	196.7.24.0/24
	Paris	196.7.25.0/24
	Washington	196.7.26.0/24
SuperCom	Paris (Loopback 0)	194.22.15.1/32
	San Jose (Loopback 0)	194.22.15.2/32
	Washington (Loopback 0)	194.22.15.3/32
	PE-CE Interface Addresses	192.168.2.0/24

PE-CE Connectivity: OSPF

The use of OSPF for PE-CE connectivity was extensively covered in Volume 1 of this publication. However, various enhancements have been made since Volume 1 was first published that increase the viability of deploying this particular routing protocol. Therefore, it is useful to provide a quick review of how OSPF is used in this environment and then describe the enhancements that have been applied to the architecture.

Before diving into the details of these enhancements, it is perhaps helpful to review why OSPF might be chosen as the routing protocol on the PE-CE link. It is clear that OSPF is a complex routing protocol that might not suit all environments. Indeed, it is probably fair to say that OSPF might only be desirable for VPN customers who want to retain OSPF within each of their sites, either during a migration or on a permanent basis.

There are many reasons why customers might want to retain their OSPF configurations, although the most common reasons are as follows:

- Prevention of a large number of external routes within the OSPF topology
- Provision of a more flexible topology that is able to support backdoor connectivity between customer sites
- Avoidance of having to redistribute OSPF information into other protocols such as BGP-4 or RIP version 2 at the CE routers
- Avoidance of having to learn/support another routing protocol such as BGP-4 at the network edge

---

NOTE   Redistribution is a mechanism that allows a router to move routes from one protocol (or static entry) in its routing table to another routing protocol. The desire to restrict the amount of redistribution can be extremely important in a normal OSPF environment. This is because a route that is redistributed into OSPF will appear as an external OSPF route within the topology. The OSPF protocol dictates that external routes be flooded across the whole OSPF domain, which increases the overhead of the protocol as well as the CPU load on all routers that are participating in the OSPF domain.

Certain OSPF area types, such as *stub* or *totally stubby*, can be deployed so that external routes are not sent into the area. However, this can have the drawback of suboptimal routing because the area does not have the full topology information in which to make a decision on the best exit point toward the OSPF backbone for a particular external route.

Due to the tight integration of OSPF with Multiprotocol BGP used in the MPLS VPN backbone, the use of OSPF does not necessitate the generation of external routes when redistributing between VPN sites and Multiprotocol BGP. Using OSPF as the PE-CE routing protocol is better from the customer's perspective than redistribution from BGP into OSPF at the customer site.

OSPF PE-CE Connectivity Requirements

To facilitate the multitude of possible OSPF topologies and to provide connectivity between VPN sites that run the OSPF protocol, an additional level of routing hierarchy, referred to as the *MPLS VPN Superbackbone*, is required. This additional level of hierarchy is necessary so that VPN sites can run independent OSPF processes and learn routes from other VPN sites without the necessity of a direct adjacency with those sites.

The OSPF protocol already provides two levels of hierarchy: the backbone (area 0) and nonbackbone areas that have to be directly attached to the backbone. The third level of hierarchy, which the MPLS VPN architecture provides, exists above the normal backbone area (if it exists). To help illustrate this point, Figure 3-2 shows how a particular VPN client might attach to an MPLS VPN environment.

Figure 3-2   *OSPF Client Connectivity to an MPLS VPN Backbone*

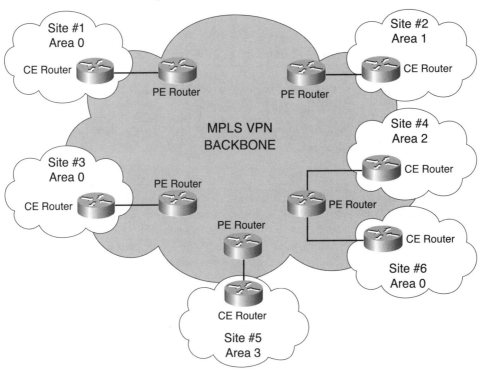

There are a couple of interesting observations that you can make from Figure 3-2. The first is that multiple OSPF backbone areas (Area 0) are possible within the same VPN customer environment. Each site can choose to run an independent backbone area, or multiple sites can act collectively as one backbone area through the use of *sham-links*.

NOTE   Sham-links are discussed in more detail in the section titled "VPN Client Backdoor Links" later in this chapter.

When backbone areas are used within a VPN customer topology, the only caveat to be aware of is that any site configured to run an OSPF backbone area must be attached directly with the MPLS VPN Superbackbone, either through a direct link or a virtual link. This is mandatory because the PE routers always act as Area Border Routers (ABRs) and need to be able to exchange intra-area information with other ABR or backbone area routers.

The second interesting observation is that you can have a complete OSPF domain, with backbone and nonbackbone areas, attached to a single Virtual Routing & Forwarding instance (VRF) at the PE router. This is possible because the PE router acts as an ABR and presents all OSPF areas behind the MPLS VPN backbone as nonbackbone areas to the local OSPF domain.

NOTE   If multiple areas are attached to the same VRF, then the backbone area must exist within the VRF. This is necessary to provide connectivity between these nonbackbone areas. Assigning a loopback interface to the VRF and placing this loopback within the backbone area can achieve it.

Basic OSPF Operation Between PE and CE Routers

In *MPLS and VPN Architectures,* (Volume I), Chapter 9, "MPLS/VPN Architecture Overview," several steps were highlighted that are necessary when you are initially provisioning a new VPN customer. With the exception of Step 4, we will not expand on these further within this chapter. However, it is important to understand that these steps are the basic building blocks of the VPN and are required regardless of the PE-CE protocol that will be used for the VPN customer:

1 Define and configure the VRFs.

2 Define and configure the route distinguishers.

3 Define and configure the import and export policies.

4 Configure the PE-CE links.

5 Associate the CE interfaces to the previously defined VRFs.

6 Configure Multiprotocol BGP.

7 Mutually redistribute (except in the case of BGP on the PE-CE links) routes between Multiprotocol BGP and the routing protocol on the PE-CE links.

Although each OSPF interface is associated with a particular VRF, it is necessary to provide a mechanism whereby the PE router is able to distinguish which routes belong to which VRFs, and to understand which interfaces belong to which OSPF processes. To achieve this aim, a separate OSPF process is necessary for each VRF that will receive VPN routes via OSPF.

Due to the complexity of OSPF and the associated topology database, the option to use different routing contexts (as with BGP-4 and RIP version 2, for example) is not currently available in Cisco IOS. Therefore, a different OSPF process (with a different *process-id*) is required per VRF. Future IOS releases will provide content support.

Figure 3-3 shows the separation of each OSPF process and its association with a particular VRF.

Figure 3-3 *OSPF Process Separation and Association with VRFs*

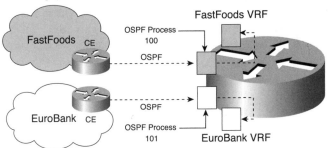

The separation of different VRFs into independent OSPF processes is achieved using an extension to the **router ospf** command, as illustrated in Example 3-1.

Example 3-1 *Separation of VRFs into Different OSPF Processes*

```
router OSPF <OSPF Process ID> VRF <vrf-name>
```

The PE router from Figure 3-3 is configured to support the attachment of the EuroBank and FastFoods VPN customers by using the **router OSPF** command, as shown in Example 3-2.

Example 3-2 *Use of Router OSPF Command for Multiple OSPF Processes*

```
router ospf 100 vrf FastFoods
 network 192.168.2.16 0.0.0.3 area 1
!
router ospf 101 vrf EuroBank
 network 192.168.2.12 0.0.0.3 area 1
```

Selection of the OSPF process-id for each VPN client is important because it determines how routes received from CE routers at this site are advertised into the OSPF topology of other sites. By default, the process-id must be the same on all PE routers; otherwise, the OSPF routes transported across the MPLS VPN backbone will be inserted as external routes (type 5 LSAs) in the local OSPF domain, instead of interarea (type 3 LSAs) routes. This process is described in more detail in the later section "Controlling LSA Type Generation at PE Routers." You can control the process through the use of a *domain-id*.

NOTE   Using the same process-id for a given VPN can be problematic because more than one VRF might want to use the same process-id on the PE router. This is not possible; therefore, the domain-id becomes an important tool.

NOTE   The OSPF process-id was not taken into account in early Cisco IOS implementations of OSPF on the PE-CE links, and all intra-area OSPF routes were advertised as interarea routes into the OSPF topology database at other PE routers. The process-id value became important only with the introduction of support for OSPF domains in IOS releases 12.1(4.4)T, 12.1(4.4), and 12.0(16.3)ST. Take special care when upgrading your IOS software to a release that supports OSPF domains inside an MPLS VPN; the upgrade might break your customer's OSPF routing due to the different method of PE router link-state advertisement (LSA) generation.

The last step within the provisioning process of an OSPF VPN customer is to make sure that locally received OSPF routes are redistributed into Multiprotocol BGP and that remote OSPF routes are redistributed into the local OSPF process from Multiprotocol BGP. The necessary configuration steps for the EuroBank VPN customer are shown in Example 3-3.

Example 3-3   *Redistribution for OSPF VPN Customers*

```
interface Serial0/0/0
 description ** interface to EuroBank VPN
 ip vrf forwarding EuroBank
 ip address 192.168.2.14 255.255.255.252
!
router ospf 101 vrf EuroBank
 network 192.168.2.12 0.0.0.3 area 1
 redistribute bgp 10 subnets metric 20
!
router bgp 10
 !
 address-family ipv4 vrf EuroBank
 redistribute ospf 101 match internal external 1 external 2
 no auto-summary
 no synchronization
 exit-address-family
```

NOTE   It is mandatory to use the subnets option when you are redistributing BGP into OSPF; otherwise, Cisco IOS redistributes only the major networks and supernets. It is also mandatory to use the **match** command when you are redistributing from OSPF into BGP; otherwise, only the internal OSPF routes are redistributed into BGP.

Changing the OSPF router-id

Each router within an OSPF network needs to hold a unique identifier within the OSPF domain. This identifier is used so that a router can recognize self-originated LSAs and so that other routers can know during routing calculation which router originated a particular LSA. The LSA common header has a field known as the *Advertising Router*, and this is set to the originating router's *router-id*.

The router-id that is used for the VRF OSPF process within a Cisco router is selected from the highest loopback address available within the VRF, or if no loopback interface exists, it is selected from the highest interface address. This might be problematic if the interface address selected for the router-id goes down, as a change of router-id is forced, and the OSPF process on the router must restart. The restart of an OSPF process requires rebuilding of its OSPF adjacencies, resynchronization of the OSPF topology databases, and a full SPF run on all routers in all OSPF areas in which the affected router participates. This can cause significant instability within the OSPF domain. Because of this, it is recommended that you set the router-id to a fixed interface address, such as a loopback interface. You can do this by using the **router-id** command within the OSPF process configuration, as shown in Example 3-4.

Example 3-4   *Setting VRF OSPF router-id*

```
SanJose(config)# router ospf 101 vrf EuroBank
SanJose(config-router)# router-id a.b.c.d
```

NOTE   It is possible to use the same IP address for the loopback interfaces within multiple VRFs. However, even if OSPF processes are in different VRFs, they cannot have the same router-id. In this case, only one of the VRF OSPF processes will use the loopback address as its router-id; the other processes will use the highest interface address within their respective VRFs. Use of the **router-id** command can make this selection more deterministic; therefore, it is useful to assign a loopback with a unique address to each VRF OSPF process within the VRF.

Monitoring OSPF Running Inside a VRF

After all the necessary configuration steps have been completed, the **show ip ospf** command can be used to view any OSPF processes that have been created. Example 3-5 shows the OSPF process that was created in Example 3-2 for the EuroBank VPN.

Example 3-5   *show ip ospf Command Output Highlighting OSPF Process Creation*

```
SanJose# show ip ospf

Routing Process "ospf 101" with ID 192.168.2.14 and Domain ID 0.0.0.101
 Supports only single TOS(TOS0) routes
 Supports opaque LSA
 Connected to MPLS VPN Superbackbone
 It is an area border router
 SPF schedule delay 5 secs, Hold time between two SPFs 10 secs
 Minimum LSA interval 5 secs. Minimum LSA arrival 1 secs
 Number of external LSA 3. Checksum Sum 0x209BC
 Number of opaque AS LSA 0. Checksum Sum 0x0
 Number of DCbitless external and opaque AS LSA 0
 Number of DoNotAge external and opaque AS LSA 0
 Number of areas in this router is 1. 1 normal 0 stub 0 nssa
 External flood list length 0
    Area 1
        Number of interfaces in this area is 1
        Area has no authentication
        SPF algorithm executed 6 times
        Area ranges are
        Number of LSA 14. Checksum Sum 0x9BE51
        Number of opaque link LSA 0. Checksum Sum 0x0
        Number of DCbitless LSA 0
        Number of indication LSA 0
        Number of DoNotAge LSA 0
        Flood list length 0
```

The output from Example 3-5 shows that the EuroBank site from Example 3-2 has been connected to the MPLS VPN Superbackbone and that the PE router is acting as an ABR for the exchange of routing information between EuroBank sites. The number of interfaces that are attached to this particular OSPF process and their relevant area information are also shown.

After the OSPF processes for any attached VPN clients have been created, it is possible to start learning routes from the attached sites, as illustrated in Example 3-6.

Example 3-6   *Route Population of OSPF VRFs*

```
SanJose# show ip route vrf EuroBank
Codes: C - connected, S - static, I - IGRP, R - RIP, M - mobile, B -
       D - EIGRP, EX - EIGRP external, O - OSPF, IA - OSPF inter are
       N1 - OSPF NSSA external type 1, N2 - OSPF NSSA external type
       E1 - OSPF external type 1, E2 - OSPF external type 2, E - EGP
       i - IS-IS, L1 - IS-IS level-1, L2 - IS-IS level-2, ia - IS-IS
       * - candidate default, U - per-user static route, o - ODR
       P - periodic downloaded static route

Gateway of last resort is not set

     10.0.0.0/30 is subnetted, 1 subnets
O       10.2.1.40/30 [110/74] via 192.168.2.13, 00:00:17, Serial0/0/0
C    192.168.2.12/30 is directly connected, Serial0/0/0
```

NOTE	Cisco IOS uses a structure called a *Protocol Descriptor Block (PDB)* to hold information about each routing process configured on the router. Each router can hold a maximum of 32 PDBs.
	At the time of writing this chapter, each VRF OSPF process required the use of a separate PDB; therefore, there is a limitation on the number of VRF OSPF processes that can be run on each PE router. Because the MPLS VPN backbone typically requires four PDBs (backbone IGP, BGP-4, static, and connected), each PE router can support up to 28 separate OSPF processes. If further processes are required, then further PE routers must be deployed.
	In future versions of IOS, this restriction will be removed by allowing multiple VRFs to share the same process through use of the routing context mechanism.

NOTE	You can obtain the number of PDBs that are currently allocated on a Cisco router by using the **show ip protocol summary** command.

BGP Extended Community Attributes for OSPF Routes

Multiprotocol BGP (as defined in RFC 2858) is used within an MPLS VPN environment to distribute VPN routing information among PE routers. When OSPF is used on the PE-CE links, there are several things that need to be carried within the Multiprotocol BGP update to allow a receiving PE router to correctly process the incoming VPN routing information.

The MPLS VPN architecture relies on the import and export of routes based on route-target values to build the VPN structure. In addition to the route-target values, Multiprotocol BGP updates that carry OSPF routes need some additional information to facilitate seamless propagation of OSPF information among customer sites. This information indicates to the receiving PE router what type of OSPF route is contained within the update and what type of LSA should be generated or flooded toward the CE router.

The MPLS VPN architecture makes use of the BGP extended community attribute to convey the type of OSPF route contained within the Multiprotocol BGP update. The format of this attribute is provided in Figure 3-4. This attribute *must* be present within the Multiprotocol BGP update when carrying OSPF routes.

Figure 3-4   *Format of the Extended Community Attribute for OSPF*

The first two octets of the attribute define the BGP extended community type, and this is encoded with type 0x0306. The next four octets define the OSPF area where the prefix resides. (This value is set to 0 for autonomous system External routes.) The next octet defines the OSPF *route-type*. The last octet is used as an optional field, which currently indicates the external metric type.

Several 1-octet route-types are defined. They are generated based on the OSPF LSA type:

- Type 1 and 2 intra-area route (router and network LSAs): route-type 2
- Type 3 summary route (network-summary LSA): route-type 3
- Type 5 autonomous system external route (autonomous system-external LSA): route-type 5
- Type 7 not-so-stubby-area (NSSA): route-type 7
- Sham-link endpoint addresses: route-type 129

Example 3-7 shows the Multiprotocol BGP update that is generated for the 192.168.2.12/30 subnet from Example 3-2, as well as the associated extended community attributes for the route.

Example 3-7   *Multiprotocol BGP Update Showing OSPF Route-Type*

```
SanJose# show ip bgp vpnv4 all 192.168.2.12

BGP routing table entry for 100:251:192.168.2.12/30, version 194
Paths: (1 available, best #1, table EuroBank)
  Advertised to non peer-group peers:
  194.22.15.1 194.22.15.3
  Local
    0.0.0.0 from 0.0.0.0 (194.22.15.2)
      Origin incomplete, metric 0, localpref 100, weight 32768,
      valid, sourced, best
        Extended Community: RT:1:793 OSPF DOMAIN ID:0.0.0.101 OSPF
    RT:1:2:0
```

Using the format of the extended community attribute as shown in Figure 3-4, you can see that the OSPF route-type is set to a value of OSPF RT:1:2:0. The update is from area 1, and it is a Type 2 intra-area route. The last field, which is set to 0, indicates that the prefix is neither a metric Type 1 nor Type 2 external route.

Controlling LSA Type Generation at PE Routers

When Cisco first introduced the ability to run OSPF on the PE-CE links, only the route-type within the Multiprotocol BGP update was taken into consideration when generating LSAs at the PE routers. This meant that all intersite routes were injected as Type 3 LSAs into the attached VPN sites, unless the route-type was set to external, meaning that the original route was redistributed into OSPF from another source.

In most cases, VPN customers run a single OSPF process before migrating to a solution that utilizes the MPLS VPN architecture. For such customers, internal OSPF routes appear as internal routes in other sites, resulting in the desired behavior. Some customers, however, run multiple OSPF processes, perhaps linked with a non-OSPF backbone. For these customers, the default MPLS VPN behavior changes what was previously an external OSPF route into an internal OSPF route. This significantly changes the routing behavior, especially if stub areas are used, because intersite routes are now advertised into the area.

To rectify such issues, the implementation of an OSPF domain-id is required so that the MPLS VPN backbone can identify distinct OSPF domains inside each VPN network that is running OSPF across the PE-CE links. For each OSPF route, the receiving PE router needs to identify the OSPF domain to which the route belongs so that the correct LSA type is generated into any relevant attached VPN sites. The format of the domain-id is shown in Figure 3-5.

When the PE router redistributes intersite OSPF routes that originated in a different OSPF domain, it always uses Type 5 LSAs. Within the same OSPF domain, the PE router uses Type 3 LSAs for internal OSPF routes and Type 5 LSAs for external OSPF routes.

Figure 3-5   *Domain-id Extended Community Format*

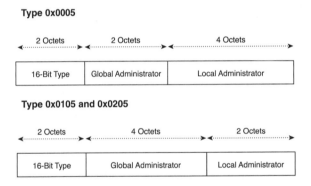

NOTE   The type field of the domain-id extended community attribute can be 0x0005, 0x0105, or 0x0205. In the Cisco Systems Inc. implementation, the type field that is used currently is 0x0005, although the format of the global and local administrator fields is as defined for type 0x0105 and 0x0205. (The global administrator field is four octets and carries the domain-id, and the local administrator field is two octets and is ignored.) For example, if the process-id of a particular VPN customer is 101, then the domain-id extended community attribute is encoded as 00 05 00 00 00 65 xx xx (where xx xx is the local administrator field and is ignored).

NOTE   With the introduction of OSPF domain support, each VPN site must use the same OSPF domain-id unless it is desirable for intersite routes to be viewed as *external* within the OSPF process. The default domain-id is the same as the OSPF process-id, although using the **domain-id <ip-address>** configuration command might change this. You can view the current domain-id value in the output of the **show ip ospf** command.

Prevention of Routing Loops Between OSPF Sites

In many deployment scenarios, it is necessary to provide dual attachment for customer sites to different PE routers, or perhaps have more than one connection from the customer site to the same PE router at the service provider location. This implies that the same set of routes can be advertised into a customer site from multiple points, potentially resulting in the creation of routing loops. To overcome the potential for routing loops, a *down bit* within the options field of the generic OSPF header is used, as illustrated in Figure 3-6.

Figure 3-6   *OSPF Header Showing Options Field and Down Bit*

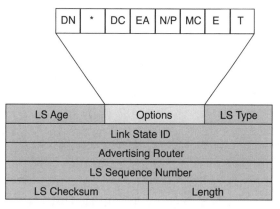

The down bit is set only when a PE router generates a Type 3 summary LSA into an attached site of a particular VPN. After receiving an LSA with the down bit set, a PE router is able to determine that it should ignore the LSA during SPF computation and not redistribute the route into Multiprotocol BGP.

You can easily inspect the value of the down bit within the OSPF database with the **show ip ospf** command, as shown in Example 3-8.

Example 3-8 *Examination of the LSA to Check Down Bit Setting*

```
SanJose# show ip ospf data summary 10.3.1.15

          OSPF Router with ID (192.168.1.12) (Process ID 101)

                  Summary Net Link States (Area 1)

  LS age: 401
  Options: (No TOS-capability, DC, Downward)
  LS Type: Summary Links(Network)
  Link State ID: 10.3.1.15 (summary Network Number)
  Advertising Router: 192.168.1.12
  LS Seq Number: 80000001
  Checksum: 0xC886
  Length: 28
  Network Mask: /32
        TOS: 0   Metric: 65
```

Type 5 and Type 7 LSAs also require some kind of mechanism that will prevent them from continually being advertised around the backbone network and between VPN sites. To facilitate this requirement, the originating PE router sets an external route tag—the *domain-tag*—within the Type 5 or Type 7 LSA. If a PE router receives an LSA that contains the same tag as the locally configured tag, then the PE router knows that another PE router generated this route and the LSA is ignored. The format of the 32-bit domain-tag can be seen in Figure 3-7.

Figure 3-7 *Domain-Tag Format*

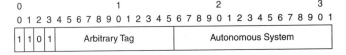

By default, the top 4 bits of the tag are always set to 1101, and the lowest 16 bits are set to the autonomous system number of the MPLS VPN backbone. You can change this default value by using the **domain-tag <32-bit value>** command within the OSPF process configuration.

Example 3-9 shows the external route tag setting for a particular Type 5 LSA. In this example, the External route tag value of 3489661143 equates to 11010000000000000000000011010111 in binary. This shows that the top 4 bits are set to 1101 and the bottom 16 bits are set to the MPLS VPN backbone autonomous system number of 215.

Example 3-9   *External Route Tag Example*

```
SanJose# show ip ospf data external

              OSPF Router with ID (192.168.2.16) (Process ID 100)

              Type-5 AS External Link States

  LS age: 1040
  Options: (No TOS-capability, DC)
  LS Type: AS External Link
  Link State ID: 192.168.2.16 (External Network Number)
  Advertising Router: 10.2.1.49
  LS Seq Number: 8000002B
  Checksum: 0xF59E
  Length: 36
  Network Mask: /32
        Metric Type: 2 (Larger than any link state path)
        TOS: 0
        Metric: 1
        Forward Address: 0.0.0.0
        External Route Tag: 3489661143
```

VPN Client Backdoor Links

When connecting VPN sites that run the OSPF protocol, you might assume that the data path between the two sites is only available across the MPLS VPN backbone. This might not necessarily be the case, and many large VPNs today provide a backup path between sites. These paths are referred to as *backdoor links*, and they present a problem that must be addressed so that routing can be influenced based on policy. The presence of backdoor links is the major reason that OSPF might be desirable on the PE-CE links; the use of other protocols cannot achieve the desired connectivity goals.

Figure 3-8 shows a sample network that has backdoor links between customer sites. The EuroBank VPN sites are attached to the MPLS VPN backbone, but the customer has also deployed direct links between the sites. Because these links are to be used only for backup purposes, the traffic should flow across the MPLS backbone if possible.

The backup links in the EuroBank network pose an interesting OSPF problem. All EuroBank sites are in the same OSPF area; therefore, the full connectivity within each site is advertised to all other sites. Route selection rules in OSPF dictate that the intra-area routes are preferred over the interarea routes, which means that all traffic between the sites will follow the intra-area path via the backdoor links. In other words, the EuroBank sites will never use the MPLS backbone for intersite traffic, unless, of course, the backdoor links become unavailable. Even worse, the PE routers will ignore the Multiprotocol BGP routes that they receive from other PE routers because they have an intra-area OSPF route advertised to them from the CE routers. Example 3-10 shows the selection of the backdoor path to reach the EuroBank Paris CE router from the San Jose PE router.

Figure 3-8 *OSPF Backdoor Links*

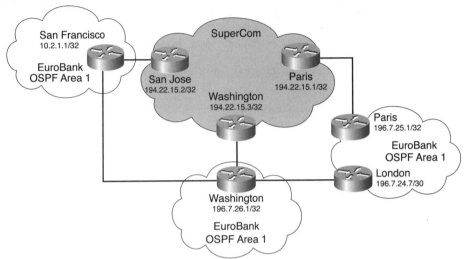

Example 3-10 *Backdoor Link Selection Example*

```
SanJose# show ip bgp v a 196.7.25.1
BGP routing table entry for 100:251:196.7.25.1/32, version 58
Paths: (3 available, best #2)
  Advertised to non peer-group peers:
  194.22.15.1 194.22.15.3
  Local
    194.22.15.3 (metric 30) from 194.22.15.3 (194.22.15.3)
      Origin incomplete, metric 22, localpref 100, valid, internal
      Extended Community: RT:1:793 OSPF DOMAIN ID:0.0.0.101 OSPF
      RT:1:2:0 OSPF 2
  Local
    192.168.2.13 from 0.0.0.0 (194.22.15.2)
      Origin incomplete, metric 86, localpref 100, weight 32768,
      valid, sourced, best
      Extended Community: RT:1:793 OSPF DOMAIN ID:0.0.0.101 OSPF
      RT:1:2:0 OSPF 2
  Local
    194.22.15.1 (metric 30) from 194.22.15.1 (194.22.15.1)
      Origin incomplete, metric 11, localpref 100, valid, internal
      Extended Community: RT:1:793 OSPF DOMAIN ID:0.0.0.101 OSPF
      RT:1:2:0 OSPF 2

SanJose# show ip route vrf EuroBank 196.7.25.1
Routing entry for 196.7.25.1/32
  Known via "ospf 101", distance 110, metric 86, type intra area
  Redistributing via bgp 215
  Advertised by bgp 215
  Last update from 192.168.2.13 on Serial0/0/0, 00:00:17 ago
  Routing Descriptor Blocks:
  * 192.168.2.13, from 192.168.2.14, 00:00:17 ago, via Serial0/0/0
      Route metric is 86, traffic share count is 1
```

Using this example, you can see that the 196.7.25.1/32 prefix (which is the loopback address of the EuroBank Paris CE router) is learned via Multiprotocol BGP from the Paris and Washington PE routers and is inserted locally into Multiprotocol BGP at the San Jose PE router. The locally generated route is considered the best path within Multiprotocol BGP. However, examination of the EuroBank VRF routing table shows that the selected path is learned via OSPF with a next-hop of 192.168.2.13, which is the EuroBank San Francisco CE router.

This seemingly illogical route selection is made because the intra-area path is preferred over the interarea path generated by the San Jose PE router. In addition, OSPF has a lower administrative distance than Internal BGP. This clearly shows that the MPLS VPN backbone will not be used for any intersite traffic, which will be carried exclusively by the backdoor links between the EuroBank sites. This default behavior is acceptable if the purpose of the connectivity into the MPLS VPN backbone is for backup purposes only. However, because this is generally not the case, the default behavior is not normally acceptable. To overcome this issue, an extra (logical) intra-area link between the PE routers is introduced to the topology. This link, known as a sham-link, is established between the VRF loopback interfaces in the PE routers, and it is treated as an OSPF demand circuit that has no periodic flooding across the link.

OSPF PE-CE Sham-Link Support

The sham-link provides virtual intra-area connectivity across the MPLS VPN Super-backbone so that traffic can be attracted to the backbone rather than taking the backdoor link between sites. As previously stated, this logical link runs within VRFs of the same VPN between PE routers. An OSPF adjacency is created and database exchange (for the particular OSPF process) occurs across the link. This means that the PE router can flood Type 1 and Type 2 LSAs between sites across the MPLS VPN backbone, thereby creating the desired intra-area connectivity.

With a sham-link configured between PE routers, if the PE router receives an update via Multiprotocol BGP for a particular prefix, it will prefer the intra-area path for the same prefix, which is still learned across the sham-link. Therefore, the traffic will flow across the MPLS VPN backbone.

In our example topology of Figure 3-8, the EuroBank customer has backdoor links between most of its sites; therefore, sham-links are necessary to prevent intersite traffic from crossing the backdoor links. Because backdoor links exist between the San Francisco and Washington CE routers and the Washington and London CE routers, you should deploy sham-links between the PE routers to which the CE routers attach. In our example, this means that a sham-link is required between the San Jose and Washington PE routers and the Washington and Paris PE routers. Figure 3-9 shows the use of the sham-link function-ality, but only between the San Jose and Washington PE routers for ease of illustration.

Figure 3-9   *OSPF Sham-Link Deployment*

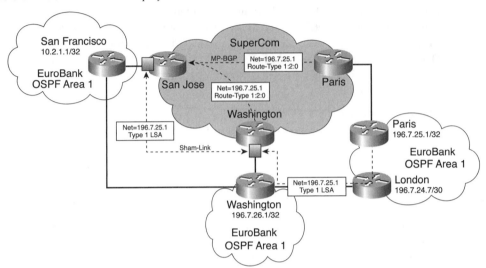

Creation of sham-links for the EuroBank customer results in two separate sham-links: one between the San Jose PE router and Washington PE router, and another between the Washington PE router and the Paris PE router. It is worth noting that no sham-link exists between the Paris PE router and the San Jose PE router. The reason for this is that no backdoor link exists between the EuroBank San Francisco and Paris sites; therefore, a sham-link is not strictly required. In practice, it might be easier from a provisioning and network management point of view to configure a sham-link between these two sites, thereby creating a full mesh of sham-links for this VPN. This results in several unnecessary sham-links, but it does relieve the service provider from the burden of understanding which VPN site has backdoor links with which other VPN sites.

NOTE   A sham-link is required between any two sites that share a backdoor link. If no backdoor link exists between the sites, then a sham-link is not required. If the MPLS VPN backbone is to be used for connectivity, then the OSPF cost of the sham-link must be better than any other path via the backdoor links between the VPN sites.

OSPF Sham-Link Configuration

A separate loopback interface inside the VRF is required for each VRF that is to be connected to other PE routers using sham-links. This loopback interface is used as an endpoint address for the sham-link. The same loopback interface in a VRF can be used to terminate any number of sham links. (There is no requirement for a different loopback address per sham-link within the same VRF.) This loopback address should not be redistributed into Multiprotocol BGP because the sham-link endpoint address is distributed between PE routers using the OSPF extended community attribute with *route-type* 129. Example 3-11 shows the configuration necessary for the creation of a sham-link between the San Jose and Washington PE routers from Figure 3-9.

Example 3-11   *OSPF Sham-Link Configuration*

```
hostname SanJose
!
interface loopback 1
 description ** interface for sham-link to Washington
 ip vrf forwarding EuroBank
 ip address 10.2.1.2 255.255.255.255
!
router ospf 101 vrf EuroBank
 area 1 sham-link 10.2.1.2 196.7.26.2 cost 40

hostname Washington
!
interface loopback 1
 description ** interface for sham-link to San Jose
 ip vrf forwarding EuroBank
 ip address 196.7.26.2 255.255.255.255
!
router ospf 101 vrf EuroBank
 area 1 sham-link 196.7.26.2 10.2.1.2 cost 40
```

The **area** command is used to create the sham-link, and the source and destination loopback interfaces identify the two endpoints of the sham-link. An OSPF cost must be associated with the sham-link so that shortest path first (SPF) can use it to calculate the shortest path. If the cost of the sham-link is better than any backdoor link between sites, then intersite traffic flows across the MPLS VPN backbone. If the cost is higher than the backdoor link path, then intersite traffic flows across the backdoor link. This behavior provides flexibility within the OSPF topology. You can manipulate traffic flow based on administrator-controlled policy (OSPF costs) rather than on the intra-area versus interarea rule.

The **show ip ospf sham-link** command shown in Example 3-12 can now be used to check that the sham-link from Example 3-11 has been successfully created.

Example 3-12   *show ip ospf sham-link Command Output*

```
SanJose# show ip ospf sham-link

Sham Link OSPF_SL0 to address 196.7.26.2 is up
Area 1 source address 10.2.1.2
  Run as demand circuit
  DoNotAge LSA allowed. Cost of using 40 State POINT_TO_POINT,
  Timer intervals configured, Hello 10, Dead 40, Wait 40,
    Hello due in 00:00:04
    Adjacency State FULL (Hello suppressed)
```

continues

Example 3-12 *show ip ospf sham-link Command Output (Continued)*

```
Index 2/2, retransmission queue length 4, number of
retransmission 0
First 0x63311F3C(205)/0x63311FE4(59) Next
0x63311F3C(205)/0x63311FE4(59)
Last retransmission scan length is 0, maximum is 0
Last retransmission scan time is 0 msec, maximum is 0 msec
Link State retransmission due in 360 msec
```

The output from the previous example confirms that the sham-link is active and that it runs as a demand circuit. (No period flooding occurs across the link, and hellos are suppressed.) The newly created sham-link is advertised within the PE routers Type 1 LSA as an unnumbered point-to-point connection between two PE routers. This is illustrated in Example 3-13.

Example 3-13 *Sham-Link Representation Within the OSPF Database*

```
SanJose# show ip ospf data router 10.2.1.2

            OSPF Router with ID (10.2.1.2) (Process ID 101)

            Router Link States (Area 1)

  LS age: 527
  Options: (No TOS-capability, DC)
  LS Type: Router Links
  Link State ID: 10.2.1.2
  Advertising Router: 10.2.1.2
  LS Seq Number: 8000001F
  Checksum: 0x4CEB
  Length: 60
  Area Border Router
  AS Boundary Router
  Number of Links: 3

    Link connected to: another Router (point-to-point)
     (Link ID) Neighboring Router ID: 196.7.26.2
     (Link Data) Router Interface address: 0.0.0.18
      Number of TOS metrics: 0
       TOS 0 Metrics: 1
```

PE-CE Connectivity: Integrated IS-IS

Now that the enhancements to the OSPF protocol have been covered, it is time to introduce the first new protocol to be added to the list of PE-CE protocols: IS-IS. Although IS-IS is not expected to be one of the more widely deployed protocols for this type of connectivity due to its limited deployment within Enterprise networks, its availability as a PE-CE protocol might still be important in certain scenarios. For example, a VPN client might be running IS-IS on the internal network and might want to maintain the IS-IS topology when moving to an MPLS VPN environment. The primary reasons for this are similar to those discussed within the OSPF section:

- Avoidance of having to redistribute IS-IS information into other protocols such as BGP-4 or RIP version 2 at the CE routers

- Avoidance of having to learn/support another routing protocol such as BGP-4 at the network edge

Support for IS-IS is also important for the migration of an ISP, which uses IS-IS as its routing protocol toward the MPLS VPN backbone, such as in the Carrier's Carrier architecture. This architecture is explained in more detail in Chapter 6, "Large-Scale Routing and Multiple Service Provider Connectivity."

IS-IS PE-CE Connectivity Requirements

IS-IS, like OSPF, is a link-state routing protocol, and it is widely adopted within the service provider community. The technical details of how IS-IS operates are outside the scope of this publication. Readers who require this level of detail should refer to the Cisco Press book *IS-IS Network Design Solutions*, written by Abe Martey.

As with the OSPF protocol, IS-IS can split a routing domain into a series of areas where interarea connectivity is achieved by interconnection across a Level 2 backbone, partially overlaying the individual Level 1 areas. In general, small IS-IS topologies are built within a single area, and this area includes all the routers within the routing domain. As the network increases in size, it is split into a Level 2 backbone and a number of Level 1 areas. Routers establish Level 1 adjacencies to perform routing within a local area (intra-area routing) and Level 2 adjacencies to perform routing between Level 1 areas (interarea routing).

The IS-IS Level 2 backbone is created through the connection of all Level 2 routers from all areas, and local areas attach to the backbone via a Level 1-2 router. Within a local area, all routers know how to reach all other routers within the area, but they know nothing about routers in other areas.

The default behavior of a Cisco router for the first IS-IS process to be created is to act as a Level 1-2 router. This is basically a combination of Level 1 and Level 2. (The router establishes both Level 1 and Level 2 adjacencies and maintains two separate databases: one for the local Level 1 area and another for the Level 2 backbone.) You can configure the router to act as a Level 1 (intra-area) router only, as both a Level 1 router and a Level 2 (interarea) router (the default), or as an interarea router only. Because of this range of options, various combinations for connectivity can be established.

With the introduction of an MPLS VPN backbone between VPN sites, an additional Level of routing hierarchy (referred to as Level 3) above Level 2 has been added (similar to OSPF). This additional level is required so that VPN sites can run independent IS-IS processes and learn routes from other VPN sites without maintaining a direct adjacency with those sites. With this additional level, the routing hierarchy changes from Level 1/Level 2/Level 1 to Level 1/Level 2/Level 3/ Level 2/Level 1. This gives various connectivity options between the PE routers and CE routers.

To help you understand how IS-IS might be deployed, we'll assume that EuroBank has decided to migrate its internal network to the IS-IS protocol and run Level 1-2 everywhere. FastFoods also runs IS-IS and attaches to the SuperCom MPLS VPN backbone, but it only runs Level 2. This connectivity can be seen in Figure 3-10.

Figure 3-10 *IS-IS PE-CE Connectivity Options*

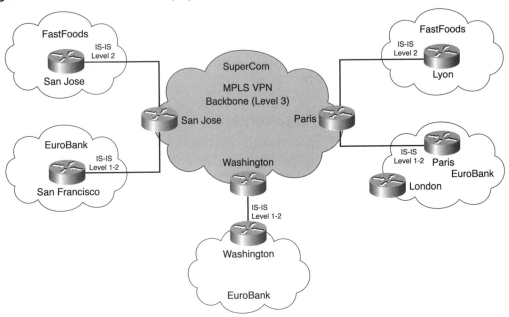

A VPN site can attach to the MPLS VPN backbone by using Level 1, Level 1-2, or Level 2 modes of operation. You will learn about each of these options and how they affect the routing between sites in the next sections.

Separation of IS-IS VPN Routing Information

As with all PE-CE connectivity options, the PE router needs to be able to provide separation between VPN clients. Separation of forwarding information is achieved through the use of VRFs. However, separation at the routing protocol level is also needed so that the PE router can identify which routing updates belong to which clients. IS-IS uses the same mechanism as the OSPF protocol (as shown in Figure 3-3)—that is, a separate process is required for each IS-IS VPN client. To support this mechanism, an extension to the **router isis** command has been provided, as shown in Example 3-14.

Example 3-14 *Extension to router isis Command*

```
SanJose(config)# router isis <tag> VRF vrf-name
```

The <tag> option within the **router isis** command allows a tag to be allocated that can be used to reference the particular IS-IS process. This is necessary when you are assigning interfaces to the process using the **ip router isis** command. Example 3-15 shows the necessary configuration to create the EuroBank and FastFoods IS-IS processes and to assign the relevant interfaces to these processes on the San Jose PE router.

Example 3-15 *Configuration of IS-IS Process on PE Routers*

```
hostname SanJose
!
ip vrf EuroBank
 rd 100:251
 route-target export 1:793
 route-target import 1:793
!
ip vrf FastFoods
 rd 100:269
 route-target export 1:821
 route-target import 1:821
!
interface Serial 3/0/0
 description ** interface to EuroBank San Francisco CE-router
 ip vrf forwarding EuroBank
 ip address 192.168.2.14 255.255.255.252
 ip router isis EuroBank
!
interface Serial 3/0/1
 description ** interface to FastFoods San Jose CE-router
 ip vrf forwarding FastFoods
 ip address 192.168.2.17 255.255.255.252
 ip router isis FastFoods
!
router isis EuroBank vrf EuroBank
 net 47.1234.0000.0000.0020.00
 metric-style wide
!
router isis FastFoods vrf FastFoods
 net 47.3456.0000.0001.0020.00
 metric-style wide
```

After all of the IS-IS processes have been created and the relevant interfaces have been associated with customer VRFs, the PE router can form a routing adjacency with the attached CE routers for the purposes of exchanging routing information.

Propagation of IS-IS Routes Within Multiprotocol BGP

After all of the relevant IP prefix information has been collected from the attached VPN site, it is necessary to distribute this to other PE routers within the network so that full connectivity can be provided to the VPN customer. This, as with all other PE-CE routing protocols other than BGP-4, requires redistribution from the VRF into Multiprotocol BGP. It is achieved by using the **redistribute** command within the BGP process. An example of this redistribution for the EuroBank VPN is given in Example 3-16, which shows that both Level 1 and Level 2 routes should be redistributed from the VRF. The IS-IS cost is automatically transferred into the BGP MED attribute during the redistribution process.

Example 3-16 *Redistribution of IS-IS Routes into Multiprotocol BGP*

```
router bgp 10
 !
 address-family ipv4 vrf EuroBank
 redistribute isis EuroBank vrf EuroBank level-1-2
 no auto-summary
 no synchronization
 exit-address-family
 !
```

NOTE   To get locally connected interfaces that are within the VRF into Multiprotocol BGP, it is necessary to configure **redistribute connected** within the BGP address family for that VRF.

After the VPN prefix information has been imported into any receiving VRFs at remote PE routers, you must apply redistribution once again so that the information can be advertised to any attached CE routers that reside within the VPN. Example 3-17 shows the necessary configuration for this redistribution within the EuroBank VPN.

Example 3-17 *Redistribution from VRF into IS-IS Process*

```
router isis EuroBank vrf EuroBank
 net 47.1234.0000.0000.0020.00
 redistribute bgp 10 metric transparent level-1-2
 metric-style wide
```

NOTE   The transparent keyword within the configuration of the previous example tells the PE router to redistribute the IS-IS routes with the metric carried in the MED attribute of the Multiprotocol BGP route. If the metric is non-zero, then the same metric is used within the IS-IS LSP. If the metric is zero, then the default IS-IS metric is used.

With the Level 1-2 keyword configured on the **redistribute bgp** command, the Multiprotocol BGP routes are redistributed as external IS-IS routes into Level 1 and Level 2 IS-IS topology databases.

After the redistribution has been configured within the relevant IS-IS routing process, any routes that were learned via Multiprotocol BGP and were installed within the VRF are advertised toward the relevant CE routers.

Leve1 1-2 PE Router to CE Router Connectivity

Now that you have learned the basic configuration steps for implementing IS-IS as a PE-CE routing protocol, you can move on to how different topologies are deployed.

The first type of IS-IS connectivity to consider is Level 1-2. This is the default mode on a Cisco router, and the EuroBank VPN is using this mode of operation for all its internal connectivity. Because this is the default, no additional configuration is necessary from that which was configured in Example 3-15. Therefore, within the EuroBank VPN, the San Francisco, Washington, Paris, and London CE routers, and the IS-IS processes that are associated with this VPN on the SuperCom PE routers, are all using is-type Level 1-2, as illustrated in Figure 3-11.

Figure 3-11 *EuroBank Level 1-2 IS-IS Topology*

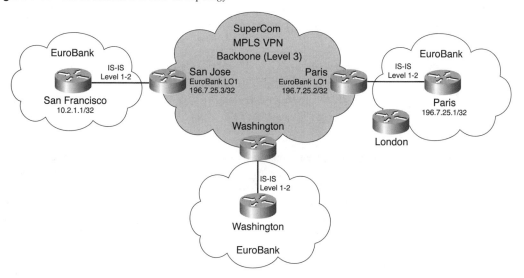

You can view the topology of the routers within the EuroBank VPN by using the **show isis topology** command. You can view the adjacency formation by using the **show clns neighbors** command, as shown in Examples 3-18 and 3-19. These examples show only the local site connectivity on the San Jose PE router because no routes at this point have been distributed between EuroBank sites across the MPLS VPN backbone.

Example 3-18 *show isis Topology Output for EuroBank VPN*

```
SanJose# show isis topology

Area EuroBank:
IS-IS paths to level-1 routers
System Id          Metric  Next-Hop         Interface   SNPA
SanFrancisco       10      San Francisco    Se3/0/0     *HDLC*
SanJose            --

IS-IS paths to level-2 routers
System Id          Metric  Next-Hop         Interface   SNPA
SanFrancisco       10      San Francisco    Se3/0/0     *HDLC*
SanJose            --
```

Example 3-19 *show clns neighbors output*

```
SanJose# show clns neighbors

Area EuroBank:
System Id     Interface   SNPA        State  Holdtime  Type Protocol
SanFrancisco  Se3/0/0     *HDLC*      Up     26        L1L2 IS-IS

SanJose# show clns neighbors detail

Area EuroBank:
System Id     Interface   SNPA        State  Holdtime  Type Protocol
SanFrancisco  Se3/0/0     *HDLC*      Up     28        L1L2 IS-IS
  Area Address(es): 47.1234
  IP Address(es):  192.168.2.13*
  Uptime: 00:00:36
```

At this stage of the deployment, the San Francisco EuroBank CE router should see all
routers within its local site in addition to the San Jose PE router. Because both the PE router
and the CE router are running Level 1-2, all routes that are reachable within the site should
be seen both within the Level 1 and Level 2 link-state database. Example 3-20 confirms this
and shows that the San Francisco CE router has Level 1 and Level 2 link-state packets
(LSPs) from the San Jose PE router.

Example 3-20 *Level 1-2 Database for EuroBank CE Router*

```
SanFrancisco# show isis database detail

IS-IS Level-1 Link State Database:
LSPID                LSP Seq Num    LSP Checksum  LSP Holdtime  ATT/P/OL
SanFrancisco.00-00 * 0x00000004     0x85CB        942           1/0/0
  Area Address: 47.1234
  NLPID:        0xCC
  Hostname: SanFrancisco
  IP Address:   10.2.1.1
  Metric: 10         IP 192.168.2.12/30
  Metric: 0          IP 10.2.1.1/32
```

Example 3-20 *Level 1-2 Database for EuroBank CE Router (Continued)*

```
   Metric: 10        IS-Extended SanJose.00
SanJose.00-00           0x00000003   0xBE4C        1065          1/0/0
   Area Address: 47.1234
   NLPID:       0xCC
   Hostname: SanJose
   IP Address:   196.7.25.3
   Metric: 10        IP 192.168.2.12/30
   Metric: 0         IP 196.7.25.3/32
   Metric: 10        IS-Extended SanFrancisco.00
IS-IS Level-2 Link State Database:
LSPID             LSP Seq Num  LSP Checksum  LSP Holdtime  ATT/P/OL
SanFrancisco.00-00 * 0x00000002   0xDC7E        925          0/0/0
   Area Address: 47.1234
   NLPID:       0xCC
   Hostname: SanFrancisco
   IP Address:   10.2.1.1
   Metric: 10        IS-Extended SanJose.00
   Metric: 0         IP 10.2.1.1/32
   Metric: 10        IP 192.168.2.12/30
SanJose.00-00           0x00000004   0x050A        1058          0/0/0
   Area Address: 47.1234
   NLPID:       0xCC
   Hostname: SanJose
   IP Address:   196.7.25.3
   Metric: 10        IS-Extended SanFrancisco.00
   Metric: 0         IP 196.7.25.3/32
   Metric: 10        IP 10.2.1.1/32
   Metric: 10        IP 192.168.2.12/30
```

IS-IS always prefers intra-area routes to interarea routes. This means that in our example, the EuroBank San Francisco CE router will select any Level 1 routes over Level 2 routes learned from the San Jose PE router. The previous example showed that the only route reachable at the San Jose PE router is 196.7.25.3/32, and this was advertised both at Level 1 and Level 2. Example 3-21 shows that the San Francisco CE router has selected the Level 1 path for this particular prefix.

Example 3-21 *San Francisco CE Router Level 1-2 Route Selection*

```
SanFrancisco# show ip route
Codes: C - connected, S - static, I - IGRP, R - RIP, M - mobile, B - BGP
       D - EIGRP, EX - EIGRP external, O - OSPF, IA - OSPF inter area
       N1 - OSPF NSSA external type 1, N2 - OSPF NSSA external type 2
       E1 - OSPF external type 1, E2 - OSPF external type 2, E - EGP
       i - IS-IS, L1 - IS-IS level-1, L2 - IS-IS level-2, ia - IS-IS inter area
       * - candidate default, U - per-user static route, o - ODR
       P - periodic downloaded static route

Gateway of last resort is not set
```

continues

Example 3-21 *San Francisco CE Router Level 1-2 Route Selection (Continued)*

```
          196.7.25.0/32 is subnetted, 1 subnets
 i L1     196.7.25.3 [115/10] via 192.168.2.14, Serial1/0
          10.0.0.0/32 is subnetted, 1 subnets
 C        10.2.1.1 is directly connected, Loopback0
          192.168.2.0/30 is subnetted, 1 subnets
 C        192.168.2.12 is directly connected, Serial1/0
```

Now that all the local site routes have been learned, you must redistribute them from within
the VRF into Multiprotocol BGP so that other PE routers can import them. An example of
how to configure this redistribution was shown earlier. After the redistribution has been
completed, any routes that are learned from the San Francisco CE router or locally attached
VRF interfaces that are associated with the EuroBank IS-IS process are carried within
Multiprotocol BGP (see Example 3-22). This example also shows the output of **debug isis
vrf**, which can be used to confirm that the routes are passed to Level 3 (MPLS VPN
backbone) and advertised by Multiprotocol BGP.

Example 3-22 *IS-IS Routes Carried Within Multiprotocol BGP*

```
SanJose# show ip bgp vpnv4 vrf EuroBank
BGP table version is 54, local router ID is 194.22.15.2
Status codes: s suppressed, d damped, h history, * valid, > best, i - internal
Origin codes: i - IGP, e - EGP, ? - incomplete

   Network          Next Hop          Metric LocPrf Weight Path
Route Distinguisher: 100:251 (default for vrf EuroBank)
*> 10.2.1.1/32      192.168.2.13           10        32768 ?
*> 192.168.2.12/30  0.0.0.0                 0        32768 ?


SanJose# show ip bgp vpnv4 vrf EuroBank 10.2.1.1
BGP routing table entry for 100:251:10.2.1.1/32, version 54
Paths: (1 available, best #1, table EuroBank)
Advertised to non peer-group peers:
192.168.1.14 194.22.15.3
Local
192.168.2.13 from 0.0.0.0 (194.22.15.2)
Origin incomplete, metric 10, localpref 100, weight 32768, valid, sourced, best
Extended Community: RT:1:793


SanJose# debug isis vrf

5d22h: ISIS-VRF: EuroBank:Adv(ISIS=>BGP VPN) 10.2.1.1/32, L3
5d22h: ISIS-VRF: EuroBank:Adv(ISIS=>BGP VPN) 192.168.2.12/30, L3
```

It is also necessary to redistribute any remote EuroBank routes into the local site at the PE
router. Example 3-23 shows some debugging output that confirms successful redistribution
of Multiprotocol BGP routes into Level 1 and Level 2 IS-IS topology databases, and also
the San Francisco CE router's routing table after this redistribution has been performed at
the San Jose PE router.

Example 3-23 *San Francisco CE Router After Redistribution*

```
SanJose# debug isis vrf

5d22h: ISIS-VRF: EuroBank:Learn(ISIS<=BGP VPN) 196.7.25.1/32, adv L1
5d22h: ISIS-VRF: EuroBank:Learn(ISIS<=BGP VPN) 196.7.25.2/32, adv L1
5d22h: ISIS-VRF: EuroBank:Learn(ISIS<=BGP VPN) 192.168.2.24/30, adv L1
5d22h: ISIS-VRF: EuroBank:Learn(ISIS<=BGP VPN) 196.7.25.1/32, adv L2
5d22h: ISIS-VRF: EuroBank:Learn(ISIS<=BGP VPN) 196.7.25.2/32, adv L2
5d22h: ISIS-VRF: EuroBank:Learn(ISIS<=BGP VPN) 192.168.2.24/30, adv L2

San Francisco# show ip route
Codes: C - connected, S - static, I - IGRP, R - RIP, M - mobile, B - BGP
       D - EIGRP, EX - EIGRP external, O - OSPF, IA - OSPF inter area
       N1 - OSPF NSSA external type 1, N2 - OSPF NSSA external type 2
       E1 - OSPF external type 1, E2 - OSPF external type 2, E - EGP
       i - IS-IS, L1 - IS-IS level-1, L2 - IS-IS level-2, ia - IS-IS inter area
       * - candidate default, U - per-user static route, o - ODR
       P - periodic downloaded static route

Gateway of last resort is not set

     196.7.25.0/32 is subnetted, 3 subnets
i L2    196.7.25.2 [115/20] via 192.168.2.14, Serial1/0
i L1    196.7.25.3 [115/10] via 192.168.2.14, Serial1/0
i L2    196.7.25.1 [115/20] via 192.168.2.14, Serial1/0
     10.0.0.0/32 is subnetted, 1 subnets
C       10.2.1.1 is directly connected, Loopback0
     192.168.2.0/30 is subnetted, 2 subnets
C       192.168.2.12 is directly connected, Serial1/0
i L2    192.168.2.24 [115/20] via 192.168.2.14, Serial1/0
```

As you can see, the San Francisco CE router learned routes from remote EuroBank sites. All of these routes are seen as Level 2 routes within the routing table instead of Level 1 routes. That is because the PE router acts as a Level 2 router into the backbone; therefore, any routes that are reachable across the backbone are seen as Level 2. But what if the San Francisco CE router were running in Level 1 mode only? Example 3-24 shows the routing table of the San Francisco CE router after changing it to Level 1 only.

Example 3-24 *San Francisco CE Router Level 1 Only Routing Table*

```
SanFrancisco(config)#router isis EuroBank
SanFrancisco(config-router)#is-type level-1

SanFrancisco# show ip route
Codes: C - connected, S - static, I - IGRP, R - RIP, M - mobile, B - BGP
       D - EIGRP, EX - EIGRP external, O - OSPF, IA - OSPF inter area
       N1 - OSPF NSSA external type 1, N2 - OSPF NSSA external type 2
       E1 - OSPF external type 1, E2 - OSPF external type 2, E - EGP
       i - IS-IS, L1 - IS-IS level-1, L2 - IS-IS level-2, ia - IS-IS inter area
       * - candidate default, U - per-user static route, o - ODR
       P - periodic downloaded static route
```

continues

Example 3-24 *San Francisco CE Router Level 1 Only Routing Table (Continued)*

```
Gateway of last resort is 192.168.2.14 to network 0.0.0.0

      196.7.25.0/32 is subnetted, 3 subnets
i ia    196.7.25.2 [115/20] via 192.168.2.14, Serial1/0
i L1    196.7.25.3 [115/10] via 192.168.2.14, Serial1/0
i ia    196.7.25.1 [115/20] via 192.168.2.14, Serial1/0
      10.0.0.0/32 is subnetted, 1 subnets
C        10.2.1.1 is directly connected, Loopback0
      192.168.2.0/30 is subnetted, 2 subnets
C        192.168.2.12 is directly connected, Serial1/0
i ia    192.168.2.24 [115/20] via 192.168.2.14, Serial1/0
i*L1 0.0.0.0/0 [115/10] via 192.168.2.14, Serial1/0
```

The output from Example 3-24 highlights a couple of interesting points. The first thing to notice is that the routes from other EuroBank sites are no longer Level 2 but *ia* (IS-IS interarea). This is because the CE router no longer holds a Level 2 database; it sees any routes that are not within the local site as interarea routes that are reachable via the PE router. These interarea routes are available due to a process known as *route leaking*, which will be discussed later in this chapter.

The second observation is that a default route that is pointing toward the PE router has been installed in the CE router's routing table. The Level 1 router uses this default route to indicate how to exit the area to reach destinations that are not local to the area.

Level 2 PE Router to CE Router Connectivity

Our second example concentrates on the FastFoods VPN, which has sites in San Jose and Lyon, France, as illustrated in Figure 3-12. This type of connectivity requires some additional configuration from that in Example 3-15 because the default IS type needs to be changed to Level 2 only. This can be achieved by using the **is-type level-2-only** command within the IS-IS process configuration.

Figure 3-12 *FastFoods Level 2 IS-IS Topology*

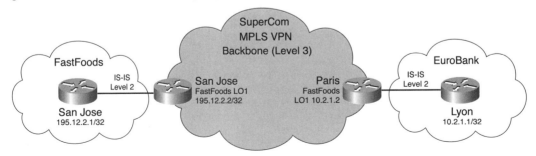

As in the Level 1-2 example, you can view the topology of the routers within the FastFoods San Jose site by using the **show isis topology** command. You can view the adjacency formation by using the **show clns neighbors** command, as shown in Example 3-25.

Example 3-25 *FastFoods Level 2 IS-IS Topology*

```
SanJosePE# show isis topology

Area FastFoods:

IS-IS paths to level-2 routers
System Id           Metric  Next-Hop           Interface  SNPA
SanJoseCE           10      SanJoseCE          Se3/0/1    *HDLC*
SanJosePE           - -

SanJosePE# show clns neighbor
Area FastFoods:
System Id       Interface  SNPA       State  Holdtime  Type Protocol
SanJoseCE       Se3/0/1    *HDLC*     Up     27        L2   IS-IS

SanJosePE# show clns neighbor detail
Area FastFoods:
System Id       Interface  SNPA       State  Holdtime  Type Protocol
SanJoseCE       Se3/0/1    *HDLC*     Up     29        L2   IS-IS
  Area Address(es): 47.3456
  IP Address(es):  192.168.2.18*
  Uptime: 00:37:57
```

The FastFoods VPN only has a Level 2 database. Example 3-26 shows the IS-IS database information for the San Jose CE router, as well as its routing table built from this database. This output shows all the local prefix information, but it does not include remote FastFoods site routes because redistribution to/from the MPLS/VPN backbone has yet to be configured.

Example 3-26 *FastFood Level 2 IS-IS Database*

```
SanJoseCE# show isis database detail

IS-IS Level-2 Link State Database:
LSPID               LSP Seq Num    LSP Checksum  LSP Holdtime    ATT/P/OL
SanJoseCE.00-00   * 0x0000000E     0xBDBD        487             0/0/0
  Area Address: 47.3456
  NLPID:        0xCC
  Hostname: SanJoseCE
  IP Address:   195.12.2.1
  Metric: 10         IS-Extended SanJosePE.00
  Metric: 0          IP 195.12.2.1/32
  Metric: 10         IP 192.168.2.16/30
SanJosePE.00-00     0x0000000E     0x34C8        727             0/0/0
  Area Address: 47.0001.0194
  Area Address: 47.3456
  NLPID:        0xCC
  Hostname: SanJosePE
  IP Address:   195.12.2.2
```

continues

Example 3-26 *FastFood Level 2 IS-IS Database (Continued)*

```
   Metric: 10        IS-Extended SanJoseCE.00
   Metric: 0         IP 195.12.2.2/32
   Metric: 10        IP 192.168.2.16/30

SanJoseCE# show ip route
Codes: C - connected, S - static, I - IGRP, R - RIP, M - mobile, B - BGP
       D - EIGRP, EX - EIGRP external, O - OSPF, IA - OSPF inter area
       N1 - OSPF NSSA external type 1, N2 - OSPF NSSA external type 2
       E1 - OSPF external type 1, E2 - OSPF external type 2, E - EGP
       i - IS-IS, L1 - IS-IS level-1, L2 - IS-IS level-2, ia - IS-IS inter area
       * - candidate default, U - per-user static route, o - ODR
       P - periodic downloaded static route

Gateway of last resort is not set

     195.12.2.0/32 is subnetted, 2 subnets
C       195.12.2.1 is directly connected, Loopback0
i L2    195.12.2.2 [115/10] via 192.168.2.17, Serial1/1
     192.168.2.0/30 is subnetted, 1 subnets
C       192.168.2.16 is directly connected, Serial1/1
```

For the San Jose CE router to learn routes from other FastFoods sites, redistribution from IS-IS to Multiprotocol BGP and from Multiprotocol BGP to IS-IS must be configured at the San Jose PE router. After this redistribution has been completed and all relevant routes have been distributed between the San Jose and Paris PE routers, the San Jose CE router can see all remote sites via a Level 2 route, as shown in Example 3-27.

Example 3-27 *San Jose CE Router Routing Table After Redistribution*

```
SanJoseCE# show ip route
Codes: C - connected, S - static, I - IGRP, R - RIP, M - mobile, B - BGP
       D - EIGRP, EX - EIGRP external, O - OSPF, IA - OSPF inter area
       N1 - OSPF NSSA external type 1, N2 - OSPF NSSA external type 2
       E1 - OSPF external type 1, E2 - OSPF external type 2, E - EGP
       i - IS-IS, L1 - IS-IS level-1, L2 - IS-IS level-2, ia - IS-IS inter area
       * - candidate default, U - per-user static route, o - ODR
       P - periodic downloaded static route

Gateway of last resort is not set

     10.0.0.0/32 is subnetted, 2 subnets
i L2    10.2.1.1 [115/20] via 192.168.2.17, Serial1/1
i L2    10.2.1.2 [115/20] via 192.168.2.17, Serial1/1
     195.12.2.0/32 is subnetted, 2 subnets
C       195.12.2.1 is directly connected, Loopback0
i L2    195.12.2.2 [115/10] via 192.168.2.17, Serial1/1
     192.168.2.0/30 is subnetted, 2 subnets
i L2    192.168.2.28 [115/20] via 192.168.2.17, Serial1/1
C       192.168.2.16 is directly connected, Serial1/1
```

Level 1 Only PE Router to CE Router Connectivity

In our final connectivity example, the EuroBank VPN has decided that Level 2 connectivity is not required; therefore it has reconfigured its routers from Level 1-2 to Level 1 by using the **is-type level-1** command within the IS-IS process configuration. The new topology is shown in Figure 3-13 and Example 3-28.

Figure 3-13 *EuroBank Level 1 IS-IS Topology*

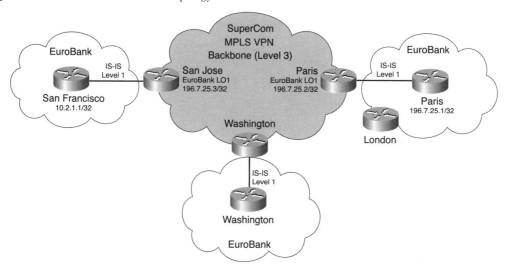

Example 3-28 *EuroBank Level 1 IS-IS Topology*

```
SanJose# show isis topology

Area EuroBank:
IS-IS paths to level-1 routers
System Id              Metric  Next-Hop            Interface   SNPA
vxr18                  10      vxr18               Se3/0/0     *HDLC*
7500-20                -


SanJose# show clns neighbor detail

Area EuroBank:
System Id      Interface  SNPA       State  Holdtime  Type Protocol
SanFrancisco   Se3/0/0    *HDLC*     Up     26        L1   IS-IS
  Area Address(es): 47.1234
  IP Address(es):  192.168.2.13*
  Uptime: 00:06:59
```

Because there is no Level 2 database, only a Level 1 adjacency exists between the PE router and CE router. Example 3-29 shows the IS-IS database information for the San Francisco

CE router. This output shows all the local prefix information and, because there are no changes to the redistribution (as already provided in earlier examples), or how routes are treated within Multiprotocol BGP, all the remote EuroBank routes as well.

Example 3-29 *San Francisco CE Routers Level 1 Database*

```
SanFrancisco# show isis database detail

IS-IS Level-1 Link State Database:
LSPID                    LSP Seq Num   LSP Checksum  LSP Holdtime   ATT/P/OL
SanFrancisco.00-00 * 0x00000041    0x011D        516            0/0/0
  Area Address: 47.1234
  NLPID:        0xCC
  Hostname: SanFrancisco
  IP Address:   10.2.1.1
  Metric: 10        IP 192.168.2.12/30
  Metric: 0         IP 10.2.1.1/32
  Metric: 10        IS-Extended SanJose.00
SanJose.00-00        0x00000003   0xFF24        610            0/0/0
  Area Address: 47.1234
  NLPID:        0xCC
  Hostname: SanJose
  IP Address:   196.7.25.3
  Metric: 10        IP 192.168.2.12/30
  Metric: 0         IP 196.7.25.3/32
  Metric: 10        IS-Extended SanFrancisco.00
  Metric: 10        IP-Interarea 196.7.25.2/32
  Metric: 10        IP-Interarea 196.7.25.1/32
  Metric: 10        IP-Interarea 192.168.2.24/30
```

The San Francisco CE router routing table in Example 3-30 shows that all routes are seen as interarea via the PE router. This is no different from the Level 1-2 example earlier in this section. This means that the PE router can be Level 1 or Level 2, and the only difference from the CE router's perspective is that no default route via the PE router exists within the routing table. This is because the PE router has no Level 2 neighbors and decides that there is no Level 2 exit point within the CE router's local area. No gateway of last resort is set.

Example 3-30 *San Francisco CE Routers Routing Table*

```
SanFrancisco# show ip route
Codes: C - connected, S - static, I - IGRP, R - RIP, M - mobile, B - BGP
       D - EIGRP, EX - EIGRP external, O - OSPF, IA - OSPF inter area
       N1 - OSPF NSSA external type 1, N2 - OSPF NSSA external type 2
       E1 - OSPF external type 1, E2 - OSPF external type 2, E - EGP
       i - IS-IS, L1 - IS-IS level-1, L2 - IS-IS level-2, ia - IS-IS inter area
       * - candidate default, U - per-user static route, o - ODR
       P - periodic downloaded static route

Gateway of last resort is not set

     196.7.25.0/32 is subnetted, 3 subnets
i ia    196.7.25.2 [115/20] via 192.168.2.14, Serial1/0
i L1    196.7.25.3 [115/10] via 192.168.2.14, Serial1/0
i ia    196.7.25.1 [115/20] via 192.168.2.14, Serial1/0
```

Example 3-30 *San Francisco CE Routers Routing Table (Continued)*

```
         10.0.0.0/32 is subnetted, 1 subnets
C        10.2.1.1 is directly connected, Loopback0
         192.168.2.0/30 is subnetted, 2 subnets
C        192.168.2.12 is directly connected, Serial1/0
i ia     192.168.2.24 [115/20] via 192.168.2.14, Serial1/0
```

Prevention of Routing Loops Between IS-IS Sites

All routes that are redistributed from a customer VRF into the PE-CE IS-IS process are seen as *IP-interarea* routes. This process is known as *route leaking* and is defined in RFC 2966, "Domain-Wide Prefix Distribution with Two-Level IS-IS."

RFC 2966 defines an *up/down* bit that indicates whether a particular route has been leaked from Level 2 into Level 1. If the up/down bit is set to 0, then the route was originated within that Level 1 area. If the up/down bit is set to 1, then the route has been redistributed into the area from Level 2. This means that any route with the down bit set will always be leaked downward (such as from Level 2 to Level 1) and never upward (such as from Level 1 to Level 2).

In a normal IS-IS deployment, the up/down bit is used to prevent routing information and forwarding loops. This is achieved by making sure that any L1/L2 router does not readvertise into Level 2 any Level 1 routes that have the up/down bit set.

Within an MPLS VPN environment, the bit is set when redistributing a route from a higher level to a lower level (such as from the MPLS VPN backbone into Level 2 or Level 1, or from Level 2 to Level 1). The up/down bit is checked when redistributing a route from a lower level to a higher level also (such as from Level 2 or Level 1 into the MPLS VPN backbone, or from Level 1 into Level 2). If the bit is set, then the redistribution does not occur and Multiprotocol BGP does not advertise the route.

Figure 3-14 provides an illustration of how the up/down bit is used for loop prevention.

Figure 3-14 *Up/Down Bit: Prevention of Loops*

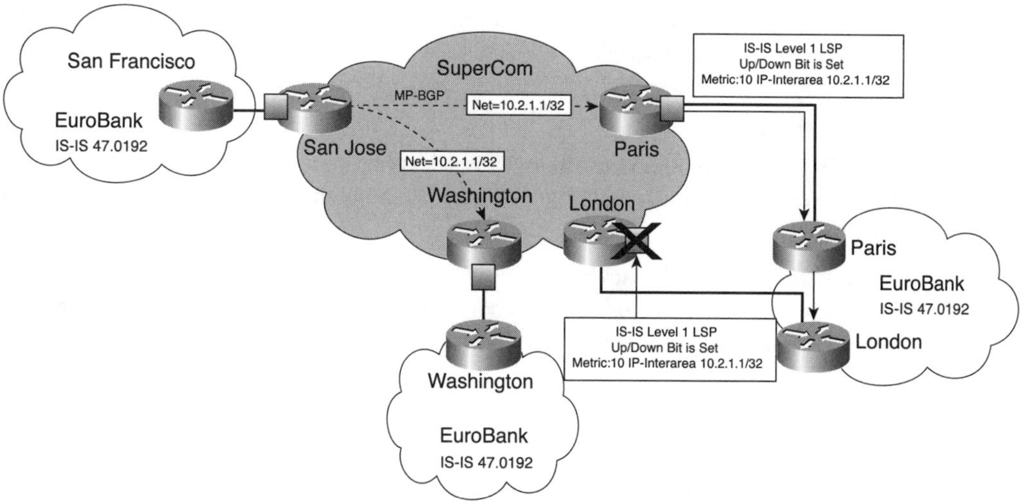

PE-CE Connectivity: EIGRP

The last protocol to review in this chapter is EIGRP. This protocol, described in depth in the *EIGRP Network Design Solutions* book by Cisco Press (ISBN 1-57870-165-1), has been widely adopted within the Enterprise space, and a large percentage of Enterprise networks rely on EIGRP for their connectivity requirements. Therefore, it is important to provide support for EIGRP within the MPLS VPN architecture, specifically for PE-CE connectivity.

EIGRP PE-CE Connectivity Requirements

As with all other PE-CE routing protocols, the MPLS VPN backbone within an EIGRP environment must be transparent. The backbone should also integrate with existing EIGRP route selection rules to ensure that the intersite traffic flow is affected only by configured routing policy. To achieve this when running EIGRP on the PE-CE links, the VPN routes are carried between sites and injected into receiving sites as internal EIGRP routes, with their original metrics unaltered. As with a regular multiprocess EIGRP setup, the exception to this behavior is when the originating site belongs to a different EIGRP autonomous system, or if the route originated from within a different routing protocol. This scenario is described in more detail later in this section.

Throughout this section, we'll use the EuroBank network, which is now running EIGRP as its internal routing protocol. EuroBank has chosen to run two EIGRP processes in its network: one for its U.S. sites (autonomous system 21) and one for its international sites (autonomous system 22). Figure 3-15 illustrates the EIGRP setup in the EuroBank network and its connectivity to the MPLS VPN backbone.

NOTE   Although it is not common, there are many valid reasons why someone would want to run several EIGRP processes in the network. Please refer to the *EIGRP Network Design Solutions* book for more details.

Figure 3-15 shows that the EuroBank VPN client has three sites; two are within autonomous system 21 (namely San Francisco and Washington), and one is within autonomous system 22 (Paris).

Because the MPLS VPN backbone is transparent to the EIGRP protocol, no EIGRP adjacencies are formed across the backbone, and no EIGRP updates or queries are sent between PE routers, resulting in better scalability of the overall EIGRP network.

Figure 3-15 *EIGRP PE-CE Connectivity Example*

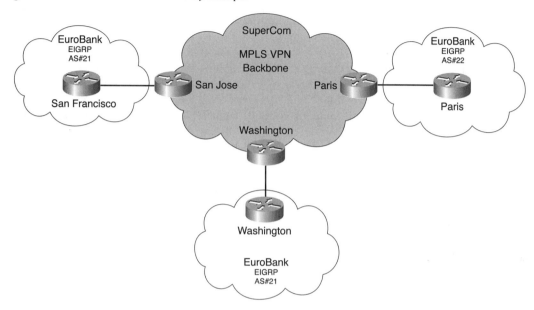

Separation of EIGRP VPN Routing Information

As with all other PE-CE routing protocols, it is necessary to provide separation of routing information among different VPNs. Unlike the other protocols that have been described within this chapter, EIGRP makes use of routing contexts to provide separation. Routing contexts were described in detail in Volume 1 of *MPLS and VPN Architectures* (ISBN 1-58705-081-1), Chapter 9, "MPLS/VPN Architecture Overview."

Example 3-31 shows an EIGRP process that is created for the default global routing table and specific contexts that are then created for individual VRFs via the use of address-families within the main process.

Example 3-31 *Creation of EIGRP Routing Contexts*

```
SanJose# conf t
Enter configuration commands, one per line.  End with CNTL/Z.
SanJose(config)#router eigrp 1
SanJose(config-router)#address-family ipv4 vrf EuroBank
SanJose(config-router-af)#
```

After the relevant EIGRP VRF routing context has been created, you must configure the autonomous system number of the attached VPN site. You can achieve this by using the **autonomous-system** command, as shown in Example 3-32.

Example 3-32 *Creation of VRF-Specific Autonomous System Number*

```
SanJose(config-router-af)#autonomous-system 21
```

NOTE In traditional EIGRP configuration, the EIGRP process number had to be equal to the EIGRP autonomous system number. When configuring the EIGRP as the PE-CE routing protocol, each instance of the EIGRP protocol could use an autonomous system number (configured with the **autonomous-system** command) that was different from the EIGRP process number.

The final configuration step within the EIGRP VRF is to specify a list of networks for the routing process. You use the **network** command to achieve this. Example 3-33 shows the necessary commands for the San Francisco EuroBank site that is attached to the San Jose PE router.

Example 3-33 *Specification of Networks Within the EIGRP Process*

```
router eigrp 1
 !
 address-family ipv4 vrf EuroBank
 network 10.2.1.0 0.0.0.255
 network 192.168.2.12 0.0.0.3
 no auto-summary
 autonomous-system 21
 exit-address-family
 !
```

NOTE Example 3-33 shows that automatic summarization has been disabled through use of the **no auto-summary** command. The default EIGRP behavior is that automatic summarization is enabled. Automatic summarization might cause undesirable results in an MPLS VPN environment because a site would receive the same summary from multiple other sites and would therefore not be able to determine which site to use for a more specific route.

After the PE-CE link configuration has been successfully completed, an EIGRP neighborship relationship should exist between the PE router and CE router. You can see this by using the **show ip eigrp vrf <vrf-name> neighbor** command, as shown in Example 3-34. A summary of the topology can also be viewed by using the **show ip eigrp vrf <vrf-name> topology summary** command.

Example 3-34 *Use of the show ip eigrp vrf neighbor Command*

```
SanJose# show ip eigrp vrf EuroBank neighbor
IP-EIGRP neighbors for process 21
H   Address          Interface      Hold Uptime    SRTT   RTO  Q  Seq Type
                                    (sec)          (ms)        Cnt Num
0   192.168.2.13    Se3/0/0        10 00:41:58    1      200  0  3


SanJose# show ip eigrp vrf EuroBank topology summary
IP-EIGRP Topology Table for AS(21)/ID(192.168.2.14) Routing Table: EuroBank Head
  serial 1, next serial 5
2 routes, 0 pending replies, 0 dummies
IP-EIGRP(1) enabled on 1 interfaces, neighbors present on 1 interfaces
Quiescent interfaces:  Se3/0/0
```

At this point in the configuration, routes from the attached VPN site should be available at the PE router and should be installed within the local VRF routing table, as shown in Example 3-35.

Example 3-35 *EIGRP Routes Within VRF Routing Table*

```
SanJose# show ip route vrf EuroBank

Routing Table: EuroBank
Codes: C - connected, S - static, I - IGRP, R - RIP, M - mobile, B - BGP
       D - EIGRP, EX - EIGRP external, O - OSPF, IA - OSPF inter area
       N1 - OSPF NSSA external type 1, N2 - OSPF NSSA external type 2
       E1 - OSPF external type 1, E2 - OSPF external type 2, E - EGP
       i - IS-IS, L1 - IS-IS level-1, L2 - IS-IS level-2, ia - IS-IS inter area
       * - candidate default, U - per-user static route, o - ODR

Gateway of last resort is not set

     10.0.0.0/32 is subnetted, 1 subnets
D       10.2.1.1 [90/2297856] via 192.168.2.13, 00:19:50, Serial3/0/0
     192.168.2.0/30 is subnetted, 1 subnets
C       192.168.2.12 is directly connected, Serial3/0/0
```

Example 3-35 shows that the 10.2.1.1/32 subnet, which is reachable at the EuroBank San Francisco CE router, is now available within the EuroBank VRF on the San Jose PE router.

Propagation of EIGRP Routes Within Multiprotocol BGP

After all the VPN site routes have been successfully received into the relevant VRF at the PE router, you must redistribute them from the VRF into Multiprotocol BGP so that other PE routers can have access to these routes. You can achieve this by using the **redistribute** command within the BGP address-family configuration, as shown in Example 3-36.

Example 3-36 *Redistribution of EIGRP Routes into Multiprotocol BGP*

```
router bgp 10
 !
 address-family ipv4 vrf EuroBank
 redistribute eigrp 21
 no auto-summary
 no synchronization
 exit-address-family
 !
```

Example 3-37 confirms that the local EIGRP routes within the EuroBank VRF have been successfully redistributed into Multiprotocol BGP. The example shows the details for the loopback0 interface on the San Francisco CE router.

Example 3-37 *Confirmation of Successful Redistribution into Multiprotocol BGP*

```
SanJose# show ip bgp v vrf EuroBank 10.2.1.1
BGP routing table entry for 100:251:10.2.1.1/32, version 8
Paths: (1 available, best #1, table EuroBank)
  Advertised to non peer-group peers:
  192.168.1.14 194.22.15.3
  Local
    192.168.2.13 from 0.0.0.0 (194.22.15.2)
      Origin incomplete, metric 2297856, localpref 100, weight 32768,
      valid, sourced, best
      Extended Community: RT:1:793 0x8800:32768:0 0x8801:21:640000
      0x8802:65281:1657856 0x8803:65281:1500
```

Similarly to the OSPF and IS-IS case, a number of additional extended BGP communities (which you can see in the previous example) are used to propagate EIGRP metric and other route attributes with the Multiprotocol BGP update. The exact format of these BGP communities is described in the following section.

BGP Extended Community Attributes for EIGRP Routes

To provide a fully transparent transport of EIGRP routing information across the MPLS VPN backbone, six new extended BGP communities are defined to carry the EIGRP metric information across the Multiprotocol BGP backbone. These communities can propagate EIGRP autonomous system numbers, all five EIGRP metrics (bandwidth, delay, load, reliability, and MTU), and other attributes that are propagated in EIGRP updates for routes that are redistributed in EIGRP. Some examples of additional attributes include the administrator-defined tag, originating routing protocol, autonomous system number, and the route metric in the originating routing protocol. Table 3-2 shows the format of each of these attributes.

Table 3-2   *EIGRP Extended Community Attributes*

EIGRP Attributes Appended	
Type 0x8800	
Usage	EIGRP route metric information appended
Values	Flags + tag
EIGRP Metric Information	
Type 0x8801	
Usage	EIGRP route metric information appended
Values	Autonomous system + delay
Type 0x8802	
Usage	EIGRP route metric information
Values	Reliability + hop + BW
Type 0x8803	
Usage	EIGRP route metric information
Values	Reserve + load + MTU
EIGRP External Information	
Type 0x8804	
Usage	EIGRP External route information
Values	Remote autonomous system + remote ID
Type 0x8805	
Usage	EIGRP External route information
Values	Remote protocol + remote metric

The *EIGRP External Information* Extended Community attributes carry the original protocol that the route was learned from. Several values are assigned to each of the relevant protocols, and these are shown in Table 3-3.

Table 3-3 *EIGRP External Information Protocol Values*

Protocol	Value
IGRP	1
EIGRP	2
Static	3
RIP	4
Hello	5
OSPF	6
IS-IS	7
EGP	8
BGP	9
IDRP	10

EIGRP-VRF Route Types

As the last step in achieving end-to-end EIGRP connectivity across the MPLS VPN backbone, the routes received by a PE router through Multiprotocol BGP must be redistributed into EIGRP and propagated to the CE routers. The **redistribute** command is used inside the VRF address family in the EIGRP process, as shown in Example 3-38. It is also highly recommended that you disable EIGRP's automatic route summarization with the **no auto-summary** command; otherwise, the routes that are transported across the Multiprotocol BGP backbone might be unintentionally summarized.

Example 3-38 *Redistribution of MP-BGP Routes into EIGRP*

```
router eigrp 1
 !
 address-family ipv4 vrf EuroBank
 redistribute bgp 10
 no auto-summary
```

The extended BGP communities that were attached to the Multiprotocol BGP route when the original EIGRP route was inserted into Multiprotocol BGP are used to ensure that the MPLS VPN backbone is transparent to EIGRP and that all EIGRP metric information is preserved between sites. If the backbone were not transparent, then all intersite routes would be seen as external within the EIGRP topology. That is undesirable from a routing policy point of view.

The first decision that the PE router must make is whether to insert the redistributed route into the EIGRP topology table as an internal or external route. If the route were not redistributed into BGP from an EIGRP process (the EIGRP-specific extended BGP communities are not attached to the route), or if the route were redistributed from an EIGRP process with a different autonomous system number (the EIGRP autonomous system number that is configured in the VRF differs from the autonomous system number carried in the EIGRP Metric Information community), the route would be inserted into EIGRP as an external route. Otherwise, it would be inserted as an internal EIGRP route.

The origin of the route also influences the rules that a receiving PE router follows for the generation of the EIGRP metrics:

- In the case of non-EIGRP routes, the PE router generates an External EIGRP route by using the default EIGRP metric. If no default metric exists, then the PE router does not generate a route toward the CE router.

- In the case of EIGRP routes that originate within the same autonomous system, the PE router generates an Internal EIGRP route by using the metrics contained within the Extended Community attributes.

- In the case of EIGRP routes that originate within a different autonomous system, the PE router generates an External EIGRP route by using the default metric. If the default metric does not exist, the route is *not* advertised toward the CE by using the Extended Community attribute information.

Summary

With the introduction of EIGRP and IS-IS protocols on the PE-CE links, Cisco Systems Inc. is now able to support all modern IP routing protocols within an MPLS VPN environment.

In addition to this, support for the OSPF protocol has been further enhanced so that the presence of backdoor backup links between customer sites no longer causes undesired effects. This is achieved through the use of sham-links that are configured between PE routers to which the customer sites that have backdoor links are connected, and the creation of routing adjacencies across these links.

The introduction of these new routing protocols is essential for the continued adoption of the MPLS VPN architecture and so that more complex customer routing topologies can be supported and migrated toward this type of solution.

CHAPTER 4

Virtual Router Connectivity

The individual components of the Multiprotocol Label Switching (MPLS) virtual private network (VPN) architecture offer network designers additional service capabilities beyond those originally envisioned in the MPLS VPN architecture. This chapter focuses on the virtual routing and forwarding (VRF) table capabilities built into Cisco IOS, such as the ability to do the following:

- Use the VRF functionality without using MPLS label imposition or Multiprotocol Border Gateway Protocol (BGP) extensions. (This is sometimes referred to as *VRF-lite* or *multi-VRF* functionality.)

- Build complex routing scenarios without being directly connected to the MPLS VPN backbone via a provider edge (PE) router

- Perform network address translation (NAT) from multiple independent private address spaces into a single global address space within an individual router. (This functionality is called provider edge router NAT, or PE-NAT.)

- Connect multiple VPN customers to the same router interface by using the VRF selection based on source IP address feature.

Apart from the obvious uses in a test lab setup in which a single router can mimic a large number of independent devices, the multi-VRF functionality is commonly implemented in scenarios when several independent VPNs need to be connected to a single customer edge (CE) router. The traditional MPLS VPN architecture would require the conversion of such a CE router into a provider edge (PE) router. However, the CE router might be unable to run the full MPLS VPN functionality, usually due to memory or CPU limitations. Even if the CE router is capable of performing this functionality, the service provider might object to a customer router participating in the MPLS VPN backbone, or the end customer might require a more flexible topology so that it can isolate its internal VPNs.

Configuring Virtual Routers on CE Routers

Consider, for example, the EuroBank VPN network introduced in the previous chapters, which contains four sites (San Francisco, Washington, London, and Paris). Each site has a single CE router that participates in a simple VPN. Three of these sites are connected to the PE routers in San Jose, Washington, and Paris, and the London site is connected to the Paris site.

<table>
<tr><td>NOTE</td><td>If you are not yet familiar with the SuperCom/EuroBank case study, you can find the detailed setup used in this case study in Chapters 2, "Remote Access to an MPLS VPN," and 3, "PE-CE Routing Protocol Enhancements and Advanced Features."</td></tr>
</table>

Now imagine that the EuroBank would like to introduce a level of separation between different departments within the organization. (For example, the trading floor in each site should be completely isolated from retail banking.)

<table>
<tr><td>NOTE</td><td>Isolation among departments or related companies is a common requirement in today's world of mergers, spin-offs, and acquisitions. For example, a company that is preparing to spin off one of its operations might start this process by isolating the relevant departments from the rest of the company. The request for interdepartment isolation could also be for security reasons. For example, a company that is developing highly secretive products as well as consumer goods would need to isolate the two production lines to maintain a level of confidentiality.</td></tr>
</table>

Due to the separation of the Trading and Retail departments, EuroBank is introducing a new addressing scheme, which is outlined in Table 4-1. This scheme adds addressing space for loopback interfaces on the CE routers, which was not required previously.

Table 4-1 *New EuroBank IP Address Assignment*

Department	Site	Subnet
EuroBank Trading	San Francisco	10.2.1.0/25
	London	196.7.24.0/25
	Paris	196.7.25.0/25
	Washington	196.7.26.0/25
EuroBank Retail	San Francisco	10.2.1.128/25
	London	196.7.24.128/25
	Paris	196.7.25.128/25
	Washington	196.7.26.125/25
Loopback interfaces for EuroBank CE routers	San Francisco	196.7.1.1/32
	London	196.7.1.4/32
	Paris	196.7.1.3/32
	Washington	196.7.1.2/32

To achieve its goal of organizational separation, EuroBank effectively needs to divide its intranet VPN into two independent department VPNs. EuroBank could implement this requirement in a number of ways:

- Use access lists to build a complex peer-to-peer VPN on top of the existing VPN network.

NOTE   Refer to Chapter 8 of *MPLS and VPN Architectures* (Volume I) (1-58705-081-1, Cisco Press, 2002) for more details on how to use access lists to build peer-to-peer VPNs.

- Deploy two CE routers in each site with two links going into the MPLS VPN backbone. Each CE router would then serve one of the VPNs, as shown in Figure 4-1.

Figure 4-1   *Two CE Routers per EuroBank Site*

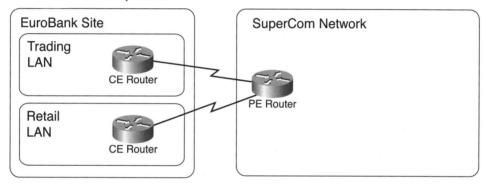

- Turn the CE routers into PE routers and extend the MPLS VPN backbone to each individual site, as shown in Figure 4-2. The service provider might want to retain the full control of the PE routers and might not accept PE routers being installed on a customer site. In addition, the existing CE routers might need to be replaced with higher capacity devices (having more memory and faster CPU) to support the full load imposed on them by being part of the MPLS VPN backbone.

Figure 4-2   *PE Router on the EuroBank Site*

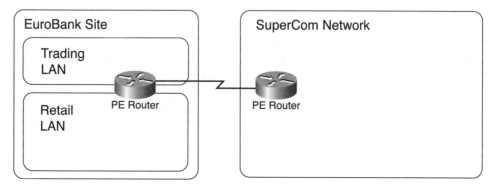

- Build a hierarchical VPN using the carrier's carrier model, which is described in detail in Chapter 6, "Large-Scale Routing and Multiple Service Provider Connectivity."

The easiest scenario to implement from the previous list would be the scenario in which two CE routers are deployed on each site. Unfortunately, this scenario involves higher acquisition costs (two CE routers need to be deployed) and operational costs (two links going into the MPLS VPN backbone).

In addition to the previous options, the multi-VRF functionality offers EuroBank another very cost-effective option. The CE router could have two independent routing entities, each one performing IP routing for one of the VPN customers, as illustrated in Figure 4-3.

Figure 4-3 *Separation of the Trading and Retail Sites in a Single CE Router*

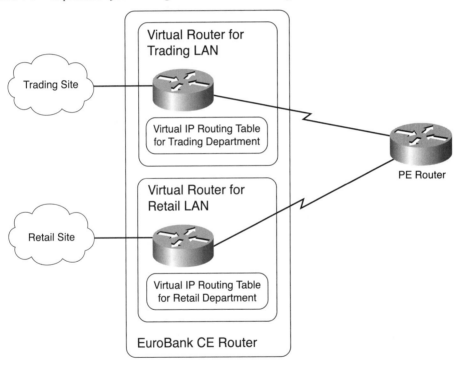

Each VPN customer (Retail and Trading) would have its own IP address space, IP routing table, and IP routing process. (Routing Information Protocol, or RIP, is used in this example.) Each department could even have additional routers in its site. These routers would participate in their own routing domain exchanging routing protocol data (in our case RIP updates) with the relevant routing instance in the CE router, which is similar to the setup in Figure 4-4.

Figure 4-4   *CE Router Separation of Complex Sites*

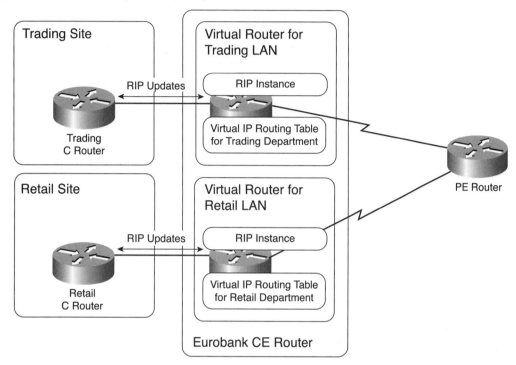

Figure 4-4 depicts an efficient use of multi-VRF functionality, which enables EuroBank to reduce its acquisition costs compared to other implementation options by not having to deploy multiple CE routers. However, the operational costs remain the same because the CE router still needs two separate links to the PE router (one for each VPN customer). More creativity is needed to reduce the operational costs:

- Frame Relay encapsulation can be deployed on the point-to-point serial links and Frame Relay subinterfaces can be used to emulate the two links. This approach can be used on any fixed serial link, including channelized interfaces, high-speed serial links, and optical links.

- VLAN encapsulation can be deployed if the PE-CE connection is implemented with Ethernet-type technology.

- IP tunnels can be configured between PE and CE routers to emulate two independent point-to-point links regardless of the underlying transport technology. Tunnels should generally be avoided due to the security reasons discussed in the "Linking the Virtual Router with the MPLS VPN Backbone" section later in this chapter, as well as for performance reasons and issues such as fragmentation of IP packets that are close to the maximum MTU size.

Assuming that EuroBank can use the Frame Relay approach, the configuration of the CE router becomes fairly simple, as demonstrated in the multi-VRF configuration of the San Francisco CE router displayed in Example 4-1.

Example 4-1 *San Francisco CE Router Configuration*

```
hostname SanFrancisco
!
ip subnet-zero
ip cef
!
ip vrf Retail
 rd 1:2
!
ip vrf Trading
 rd 1:1
!
interface Loopback0
 ip address 196.7.1.1 255.255.255.255
 no ip directed-broadcast
!
interface Ethernet0/0
 ip vrf forwarding Trading
 ip address 10.2.1.1 255.255.255.128
 no ip directed-broadcast
!
interface Ethernet0/1
 ip vrf forwarding Retail
 ip address 10.2.1.129 255.255.255.128
 no ip directed-broadcast
!
interface Serial0/0
 no ip address
 encapsulation frame-relay
!
interface Serial0/0.313 point-to-point
 description *** Link to PE_SanJose ***
 ip vrf forwarding Trading
 ip address 192.168.2.13 255.255.255.252
 frame-relay interface-dlci 313
!
interface Serial0/0.613 point-to-point
 description *** Second link to PE_SanJose ***
 ip vrf forwarding Retail
 ip address 192.168.2.17 255.255.255.252
 frame-relay interface-dlci 613
!
router rip
 version 2
 no auto-summary
 !
 address-family ipv4 vrf Trading
 version 2
 network 10.0.0.0
```

Example 4-1   *San Francisco CE Router Configuration (Continued)*

```
network 192.168.2.0
no auto-summary
exit-address-family
!
address-family ipv4 vrf Retail
version 2
network 10.0.0.0
network 192.168.2.0
no auto-summary
exit-address-family
```

The router configuration in Example 4-1 looks like a typical PE router configuration:

- Two virtual routing and forwarding tables (Trading and Retail) are defined for two VPN customers.

- A global loopback interface is configured.

NOTE   It is always advisable to configure at least one interface with an IP address that belongs to the router's global IP routing table; otherwise, a number of router functions that require a valid global IP address might not work. For example, if you want to use the BGP routing protocol for the VRF routing, the BGP process would not start because as it cannot assign a router ID.

- Individual local-area network (LAN) and wide-area network (WAN) interfaces are assigned to VRFs.

- Two instances of RIP routing are configured—one for each VRF.

The configuration also contains a number of significant differences from the usual PE router configuration:

- MPLS is not configured and no labels are assigned to the VRF routes.

- Multiprotocol BGP routing is not configured.

- There is no redistribution between the PE-CE routing protocol and Multiprotocol BGP.

- The incoming interface at the CE router is associated with a VRF, as is the CE router to PE router link. A normal PE router does not associate upstream links with a particular VRF.

The configuration on all the other PE routers and CE routers has to be modified to support the needs of the two EuroBank VPNs. The configuration from the San Jose PE router is included in Example 4-2.

Example 4-2   *Configuration of the San Jose PE Router*

```
hostname PE_SanJose
!
!
ip vrf EuroBank_Retail
 rd 10:2512
 route-target export 10:2512
 route-target import 10:2512
!
ip vrf EuroBank_Trading
 rd 10:2511
 route-target export 10:2511
 route-target import 10:2511
!
interface Serial0/0.331 point-to-point
 description *** Link to EuroBank San Francisco ***
 ip vrf forwarding EuroBank_Trading
 ip address 192.168.2.14 255.255.255.252
 frame-relay interface-dlci 331
!
interface Serial0/0.631 point-to-point
 description *** Second Link to EuroBank San Francisco ***
 ip vrf forwarding EuroBank_Retail
 ip address 192.168.2.18 255.255.255.252
 frame-relay interface-dlci 631
!
router rip
 version 2
 !
 address-family ipv4 vrf EuroBank_Trading
 version 2
 redistribute bgp 10 metric transparent
 network 192.168.2.0
 no auto-summary
!
 address-family ipv4 vrf EuroBank_Retail
 version 2
 redistribute bgp 10 metric transparent
 network 192.168.2.0
 no auto-summary
 !
router bgp 10
 address-family ipv4 vrf EuroBank_Trading
 redistribute rip
 !
 address-family ipv4 vrf EuroBank_Retail
 redistribute rip
```

If you inspect the routing tables of the San Francisco CE router (displayed in Example 4-3), you can see that the global routing table contains only a single loopback interface, whereas the individual VRF routing tables possess the relevant routing information for the Trading and Retail groups of EuroBank.

Example 4-3   *IP Routing Tables on the San Francisco Router*

```
SanFrancisco#show ip route
Codes: C - connected, S - static, I - IGRP, R - RIP, B - BGP
       D - EIGRP, EX - EIGRP external, O - OSPF, IA - OSPF inter area
       N1 - OSPF NSSA external type 1, N2 - OSPF NSSA external type 2
       E1 - OSPF external type 1, E2 - OSPF external type 2, E - EGP
       * - candidate default, U - per-user static route, o - ODR

Gateway of last resort is not set

     196.7.1.0 255.255.255.255 is subnetted, 1 subnets
C       196.7.1.1 is directly connected, Loopback0

SanFrancisco#show ip route vrf Trading

Routing Table: Trading
Codes: C - connected, S - static, I - IGRP, R - RIP, B - BGP
       D - EIGRP, EX - EIGRP external, O - OSPF, IA - OSPF inter area
       N1 - OSPF NSSA external type 1, N2 - OSPF NSSA external type 2
       E1 - OSPF external type 1, E2 - OSPF external type 2, E - EGP
       * - candidate default, U - per-user static route, o - ODR

Gateway of last resort is not set

     196.7.25.0 255.255.255.128 is subnetted, 1 subnets
R       196.7.25.0 [120/2] via 192.168.2.14, 00:00:06, Serial0/0.313
     196.7.24.0 255.255.255.128 is subnetted, 1 subnets
R       196.7.24.0 [120/3] via 192.168.2.14, 00:00:06, Serial0/0.313
     196.7.26.0 255.255.255.128 is subnetted, 1 subnets
R       196.7.26.0 [120/2] via 192.168.2.14, 00:00:06, Serial0/0.313
     10.0.0.0 255.255.255.128 is subnetted, 1 subnets
C       10.2.1.0 is directly connected, Ethernet0/0
     192.168.2.0 255.255.255.252 is subnetted, 4 subnets
R       192.168.2.40 [120/1] via 192.168.2.14, 00:00:07, Serial0/0.313
R       192.168.2.32 [120/1] via 192.168.2.14, 00:00:07, Serial0/0.313
R       192.168.2.48 [120/2] via 192.168.2.14, 00:00:07, Serial0/0.313
C       192.168.2.12 is directly connected, Serial0/0.313

SanFrancisco#show ip route vrf Retail

Routing Table: Retail
Codes: C - connected, S - static, I - IGRP, R - RIP, B - BGP
       D - EIGRP, EX - EIGRP external, O - OSPF, IA - OSPF inter area
       N1 - OSPF NSSA external type 1, N2 - OSPF NSSA external type 2
       E1 - OSPF external type 1, E2 - OSPF external type 2, E - EGP
       * - candidate default, U - per-user static route, o - ODR

Gateway of last resort is not set

     196.7.25.0 255.255.255.128 is subnetted, 1 subnets
R       196.7.25.128 [120/2] via 192.168.2.18, 00:00:20, Serial0/0.613
     196.7.24.0 255.255.255.128 is subnetted, 1 subnets
R       196.7.24.128 [120/3] via 192.168.2.18, 00:00:20, Serial0/0.613
```

continues

Example 4-3   *IP Routing Tables on the San Francisco Router (Continued)*

```
      196.7.26.0 255.255.255.128 is subnetted, 1 subnets
R        196.7.26.128 [120/2] via 192.168.2.18, 00:00:20, Serial0/0.613
      10.0.0.0 255.255.255.128 is subnetted, 1 subnets
C        10.2.1.128 is directly connected, Ethernet0/1
      192.168.2.0 255.255.255.252 is subnetted, 4 subnets
R        192.168.2.44 [120/1] via 192.168.2.18, 00:00:20, Serial0/0.613
R        192.168.2.36 [120/1] via 192.168.2.18, 00:00:20, Serial0/0.613
R        192.168.2.52 [120/2] via 192.168.2.18, 00:00:20, Serial0/0.613
C        192.168.2.16 is directly connected, Serial0/0.613
```

Running OSPF in Virtual Router Scenarios

The previous example used RIP within the customer VPN for a simple reason: RIP is the simplest routing protocol to use in the multi-VRF scenarios. Using routing protocols with loop prevention mechanisms, such as Open Shortest Path First (OSPF) or Intermediate System-to-Intermediate System (IS-IS), requires additional configuration steps. The moment you configure the OSPF or IS-IS routing process and associate it with a VRF, the router starts behaving like a PE router and performs the loop prevention actions based on the setting of the *down* bit in OSPF or the *up/down* bit in IS-IS, as discussed in Chapter 3.

Assume that OSPF is introduced as the routing protocol in the trading department for EuroBank sites San Francisco and Washington, as shown in Figure 4-5.

Figure 4-5   *OSPF in EuroBank Network*

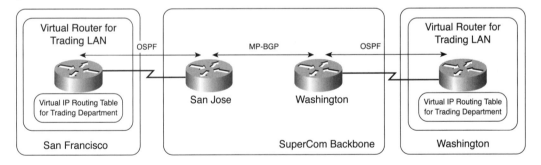

The relevant configuration of the San Francisco CE router is shown in Example 4-4.

Example 4-4   *OSPF Configuration on the San Francisco CE Router*

```
router ospf 1 vrf Trading
 log-adjacency-changes
 network 0.0.0.0 255.255.255.255 area 0
```

With OSPF running inside a VRF, the CE router in San Francisco rejects all OSPF routes from sites that are not connected to the San Jose PE router. These routes would be received across the MPLS VPN backbone by the San Jose PE router and propagated to the San Francisco CE router through OSPF with the down bit set, as shown in Figure 4-6.

Figure 4-6   *OSPF Update Propagation in EuroBank Network*

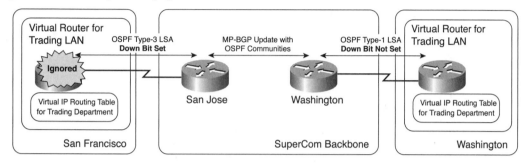

The following sequence of events occurs when a route from the EuroBank Washington site is propagated through the MPLS VPN backbone toward the San Francisco CE router:

1 The OSPF process that is running in a VRF at the Washington CE router sends a type 1 (router) link-state advertisement (LSA) to the Washington PE router.

2 The Washington PE router redistributes the OSPF route into Multiprotocol BGP and appends OSPF-specific extended BGP communities to the route.

3 The San Jose PE router receives the Multiprotocol BGP route from the Washington PE router with OSPF-specific extended BGP communities.

4 The San Jose PE router redistributes the Multiprotocol BGP route into OSPF and sends it as a type 3 (summary) LSA toward the San Francisco CE router, with the down bit set in the LSA.

5 The San Francisco CE router acts as a PE router because the OSPF process is configured in the context of a VRF; therefore, the CE router receives but ignores the LSA because the LSA has the down bit set. As a result, the route announced in the LSA is not installed in the VRF routing table, and the destinations in Washington are not reachable from San Francisco.

You can verify this process by inspecting the VRF IP routing table on the San Francisco CE router. The only entries in the IP routing table are the OSPF external routes that originate from the Paris and London sites, as shown in Example 4-5. (PE routers do not set the down bit on these routes because the routes do not originate in an OSPF process and consequently do not carry OSPF communities in the Multiprotocol BGP update.)

Example 4-5 *IP Routing Table in VRF Trading*

```
SanFrancisco#show ip route vrf Trading

Routing Table: Trading
Codes: C - connected, S - static, I - IGRP, R - RIP, B - BGP
       D - EIGRP, EX - EIGRP external, O - OSPF, IA - OSPF inter area
       N1 - OSPF NSSA external type 1, N2 - OSPF NSSA external type 2
       E1 - OSPF external type 1, E2 - OSPF external type 2, E - EGP
       * - candidate default, U - per-user static route, o - ODR

Gateway of last resort is not set

     196.7.25.0 255.255.255.128 is subnetted, 1 subnets
O E2    196.7.25.0 [110/1] via 192.168.2.14, 00:02:39, Serial0/0.313
     196.7.24.0 255.255.255.128 is subnetted, 1 subnets
O E2    196.7.24.0 [110/2] via 192.168.2.14, 00:02:39, Serial0/0.313
     10.0.0.0 255.255.255.128 is subnetted, 1 subnets
C       10.2.1.0 is directly connected, Ethernet0/0
     192.168.2.0 255.255.255.252 is subnetted, 3 subnets
O E2    192.168.2.40 [110/1] via 192.168.2.14, 00:02:39, Serial0/0.313
O E2    192.168.2.48 [110/1] via 192.168.2.14, 00:02:39, Serial0/0.313
C       192.168.2.12 is directly connected, Serial0/0.313
```

Detailed investigation of the topology database of the OSPF process associated with the Trading VRF in the San Francisco router (shown in Example 4-6) shows the actual source of the problem. The LSA associated with the Washington subnets has the down bit set; therefore the San Francisco CE router ignores it and does not set the routing bit. The result is that the OSPF process will not transfer this subnet into the IP routing table even if the LSA would be considered and used in the SPF algorithm.

Example 4-6 *OSPF LSA for Washington Subnet in Trading OSPF Process*

```
SanFrancisco#show ip ospf 1 database summary 196.7.26.0

            OSPF Router with ID (192.168.2.13) (Process ID 1)

                Summary Net Link States (Area 0)

  LS age: 298
  Options: (No TOS-capability, DC, Downward)
  LS Type: Summary Links(Network)
  Link State ID: 196.7.26.0 (summary Network Number)
  Advertising Router: 192.168.2.14
  LS Seq Number: 80000002
  Checksum: 0xA87
  Length: 28
  Network Mask: 255.255.255.128
        TOS: 0  Metric: 74
```

To support the multi-VRF functionality in combination with OSPF, you must use a new command that disables the down bit check within the VRF-specific OSPF process and is described in Table 4-2.

Table 4-2   *Configuring OSPF with Multi-VRF*

Command Syntax	Description
capability vrf-lite	To suppress the PE-specific checks on a router when the OSPF process is associated with the VRF, use the **capability vrf-lite** command in router configuration mode. To restore the checks, use the no form of this command.

After configuring the **capability vrf-lite** command in each OSPF process on the San Francisco CE router (as shown in Example 4-7), the LSAs received from the San Jose PE router are installed in the VRF routing table (see Example 4-8) and the routing bit is set on these LSAs in the OSPF topology database (see Example 4-9).

Example 4-7   *Correct OSPF Configuration on the San Francisco CE Router*

```
router ospf 1 vrf Trading
 log-adjacency-changes
 capability vrf-lite
 network 0.0.0.0 255.255.255.255 area 0
```

Example 4-8   *VRF Routing Table on the San Francisco CE Router*

```
SanFrancisco#show ip route vrf Trading

Routing Table: Trading
Codes: C - connected, S - static, I - IGRP, R - RIP, B - BGP
       D - EIGRP, EX - EIGRP external, O - OSPF, IA - OSPF inter area
       N1 - OSPF NSSA external type 1, N2 - OSPF NSSA external type 2
       E1 - OSPF external type 1, E2 - OSPF external type 2, E - EGP
       * - candidate default, U - per-user static route, o - ODR

Gateway of last resort is not set

     196.7.25.0 255.255.255.128 is subnetted, 1 subnets
O E2    196.7.25.0 [110/1] via 192.168.2.14, 00:00:07, Serial0/0.313
     196.7.24.0 255.255.255.128 is subnetted, 1 subnets
O E2    196.7.24.0 [110/1] via 192.168.2.14, 00:00:07, Serial0/0.313
     196.7.26.0 255.255.255.128 is subnetted, 1 subnets
O IA    196.7.26.0 [110/138] via 192.168.2.14, 00:00:07, Serial0/0.313
     10.0.0.0 255.255.255.128 is subnetted, 1 subnets
C       10.2.1.0 is directly connected, Ethernet0/0
     192.168.2.0 255.255.255.252 is subnetted, 4 subnets
O E2    192.168.2.40 [110/1] via 192.168.2.14, 00:00:08, Serial0/0.313
O IA    192.168.2.32 [110/65] via 192.168.2.14, 00:00:08, Serial0/0.313
O E2    192.168.2.48 [110/1] via 192.168.2.14, 00:00:08, Serial0/0.313
C       192.168.2.12 is directly connected, Serial0/0.313
```

Example 4-9 *LSA with Down Bit Set Is Used for IP Routing*

```
SanFrancisco#show ip ospf 1 data summary 196.7.26.0

              OSPF Router with ID (192.168.2.13) (Process ID 1)

                 Summary Net Link States (Area 0)

  Routing Bit Set on this LSA
  LS age: 1964
  Options: (No TOS-capability, DC, Downward)
  LS Type: Summary Links(Network)
  Link State ID: 196.7.26.0 (summary Network Number)
  Advertising Router: 192.168.2.14
  LS Seq Number: 80000008
  Checksum: 0xFD8D
  Length: 28
  Network Mask: 255.255.255.128
        TOS: 0  Metric: 74
```

Running BGP in Virtual Router Scenarios

Running BGP in a multi-VRF scenario should be relatively straightforward in most cases. The BGP implementation in Cisco IOS provides a rich set of features, including **ignore-as** and **as-override** functionality that enable the PE router to cope with most BGP designs.

NOTE   The use of BGP in complex MPLS VPN routing scenarios is described in Chapter 11, "Provider Edge (PE) to Customer Edge (CE) Connectivity Options," of *MPLS and VPN Architectures* (Volume I).

The only potential problem might arise from the design requirement that a CE router serving multiple VPN customers must use different autonomous system numbers in each VRF. Assume that EuroBank wants to change the PE-CE routing protocol on the Paris CE router from RIP to BGP and that it requires autonomous system 65100 to be used for the Trading VPN and autonomous system 65200 to be used for the Retail VPN, as shown in Figure 4-7. This requirement cannot be easily implemented because Cisco IOS supports only a single BGP process with a single autonomous system number on any router.

This requirement can be partially solved by using the **local-as** feature that allows a BGP router to present itself as being in a different autonomous system on a per-neighbor basis. The relevant IP routing configuration of the Paris CE router is shown in Example 4-10.

Figure 4-7   *CE Router with Two Different BGP Autonomous Systems*

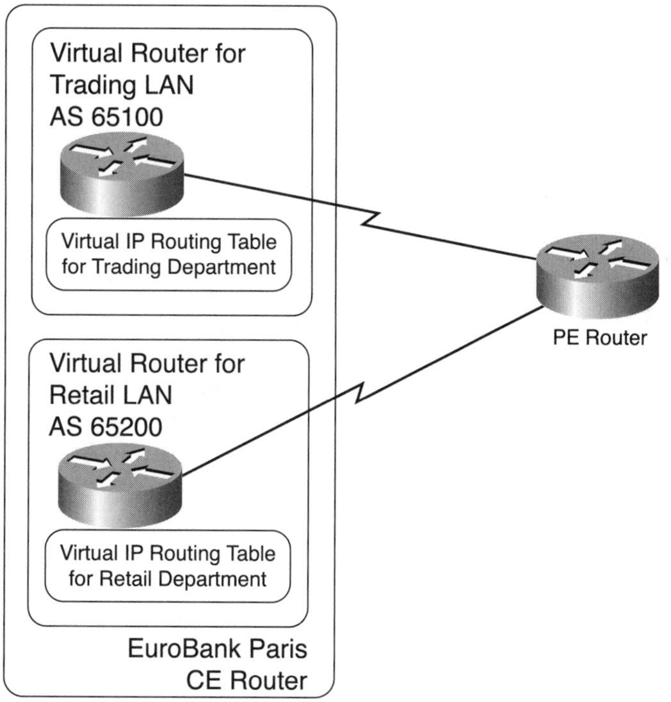

NOTE	The EuroBank design introduces a third autonomous system (65001) to be used on the Paris CE router. If you tried to reuse autonomous system 65100 or autonomous system 65200 as the router's BGP autonomous system number, the autonomous system path would indicate that destinations in one VPN are reachable through the other VPN because the router's autonomous system number is always inserted in the autonomous system path.

Example 4-10 *IP Routing Configuration of the Paris CE Router*

```
router rip
 version 2
 !
 address-family ipv4 vrf Trading
 redistribute bgp 65001 metric transparent
 !
 address-family ipv4 vrf Retail
 redistribute bgp 65001 metric transparent
 !
router bgp 65001
 !
```

continues

Example 4-10 *IP Routing Configuration of the Paris CE Router (Continued)*

```
address-family ipv4 vrf Trading
redistribute rip
neighbor 192.168.2.42 remote-as 10
neighbor 192.168.2.42 local-as 65100
!
address-family ipv4 vrf Retail
redistribute rip
neighbor 192.168.2.46 remote-as 10
neighbor 192.168.2.46 local-as 65200
```

The **local-as** feature permits the BGP session to be established because the BGP autonomous system numbers exchanged in the BGP open messages match the autonomous system numbers expected by the remote BGP peer. The BGP updates sent from the CE router to the PE router, however, contain two autonomous system numbers prepended to the autonomous system path: the autonomous system number configured in the BGP routing process and the autonomous system number configured with the **local-as** command. The resulting BGP table on the Paris PE router is shown in Example 4-11.

Example 4-11 *Multiprotocol BGP Table on PE_Paris*

```
PE_Paris#show ip bgp vpnv4 all regexp 65...
BGP table version is 88, local router ID is 194.22.15.1
Status codes: s suppressed, d damped, h history, * valid, > best, i - internal,
    S Stale
Origin codes: i - IGP, e - EGP, ? - incomplete

   Network          Next Hop         Metric LocPrf Weight Path
Route Distinguisher: 10:2511 (default for vrf EuroBank_Trading)
*> 192.168.2.40/30  192.168.2.41          0             0 65100 65001 ?
*> 192.168.2.48/30  192.168.2.41          0             0 65100 65001 ?
*> 196.7.24.0/25    192.168.2.41          1             0 65100 65001 ?
*> 196.7.25.0/25    192.168.2.41          0             0 65100 65001 ?
Route Distinguisher: 10:2512 (default for vrf EuroBank_Retail)
*> 192.168.2.44/30  192.168.2.45          0             0 65200 65001 ?
*> 192.168.2.52/30  192.168.2.45          0             0 65200 65001 ?
*> 196.7.24.128/25  192.168.2.45          1             0 65200 65001 ?
*> 196.7.25.128/25  192.168.2.45          0             0 65200 65001 ?
```

Similarly, the CE router prepends the autonomous system number configured with the **neighbor local-as** command to all incoming BGP updates, as shown in Example 4-12.

Example 4-12 *Local Autonomous System Number Prepended to Incoming BGP Updates*

```
Paris#show ip bgp vpnv4 vrf Trading
BGP table version is 56, local router ID is 192.168.252.2
Status codes: s suppressed, d damped, h history, * valid, > best, i -internal,
    S Stale
Origin codes: i - IGP, e - EGP, ? - incomplete
```

Example 4-12 *Local Autonomous System Number Prepended to Incoming BGP Updates (Continued)*

```
     Network          Next Hop          Metric LocPrf Weight Path
   Route Distinguisher: 1:1 (default for vrf Trading)
   *> 192.168.2.12/30  192.168.2.42                        0 65100 10 ?
   *> 192.168.2.32/30  192.168.2.42                        0 65100 10 ?
   *> 192.168.2.40/30  0.0.0.0              0          32768 ?
   *> 192.168.2.48/30  0.0.0.0              0          32768 ?
   *> 196.7.24.0/25    192.168.2.50         1          32768 ?
   *> 196.7.25.0/25    0.0.0.0              0          32768 ?
   *> 196.7.26.0/25    192.168.2.42                        0 65100 10 ?
```

The presence of an extra autonomous system number in the autonomous system path might interfere with the BGP loop prevention code in other C routers. These routers would reject the incoming BGP update if the autonomous system number that is configured with the **neighbor local-as** command on the CE router equals their BGP autonomous system number, as demonstrated in Figure 4-8.

Figure 4-8 *BGP Update Ignored Due to Extra Autonomous System Number in the Autonomous System Path*

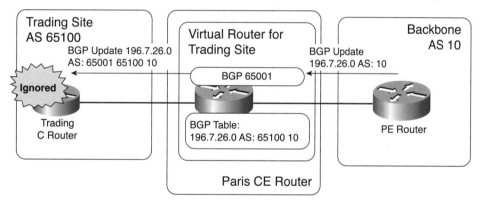

The following sequence of events occurs in Figure 4-8:

1 The PE router sends a VPN prefix to the CE router through BGP. Because the prefix was redistributed into BGP on another PE router, the autonomous system path contains only the provider's autonomous system number (10).

2 A virtual autonomous system number is inserted into the autonomous system path due to the behavior of the **neighbor local-as** command before the BGP prefix is inserted into the BGP table on a Paris CE router. Therefore, the BGP entry in the Paris CE router contains autonomous system path 65100 10.

3 The BGP prefix is propagated to a C router in the Paris Trading site. The real autonomous system number of the Paris CE router is prepended to the autonomous system path, resulting in an autonomous system path of 65001 65100 10.

4 The Paris trading C router rejects the BGP update because the BGP update contains its own autonomous system number (65100).

This issue was solved in Cisco IOS release 12.2T and 12.0ST with an additional option of the **neighbor local-as** command described in Table 4-3.

Table 4-3 *Disabling Prepending of **neighbor local-as** Autonomous System Number on Incoming BGP Updates*

Command Syntax	Description
neighbor *ip-address* **local**-as *as-number* [**no-prepend**]	Configures the router not to prepend the local autonomous system number to routes that are received from external peers.

The **no-prepend** option of the **neighbor local-as** command prevents the BGP router with **neighbor local-as** configured on a BGP neighbor from prepending the **neighbor local-as** autonomous system number to incoming BGP updates. The usage of this command on the Paris CE router (the configuration is shown in Example 4-13) results in the desired BGP routing table, which is displayed in Example 4-14.

Example 4-13 *Disabling Local Autonomous System Prepending on Incoming BGP Updates*

```
router bgp 65001
!
 address-family ipv4 vrf Trading
 neighbor 192.168.2.42 local-as 65100 no-prepend
!
 address-family ipv4 vrf Retail
 neighbor 192.168.2.46 local-as 65200 no-prepend
```

Example 4-14 *VRF BGP Routes on the Paris CE Router*

```
Paris#show ip bgp vpnv4 all
BGP table version is 75, local router ID is 192.168.252.2
Status codes: s suppressed, d damped, h history, * valid, > best, i - internal,
              S Stale
Origin codes: i - IGP, e - EGP, ? - incomplete

   Network          Next Hop            Metric LocPrf Weight Path
Route Distinguisher: 1:1 (default for vrf Trading)
*> 10.2.1.0/25      192.168.2.42                          0 10 ?
*> 192.168.2.12/30  192.168.2.42                          0 10 ?
*> 192.168.2.32/30  192.168.2.42                          0 10 ?
*> 192.168.2.40/30  0.0.0.0                  0        32768 ?
*> 192.168.2.48/30  0.0.0.0                  0        32768 ?
*> 196.7.24.0/25    192.168.2.50             1        32768 ?
*> 196.7.25.0/25    0.0.0.0                  0        32768 ?
*> 196.7.26.0/25    192.168.2.42                          0 10 ?
Route Distinguisher: 1:2 (default for vrf Retail)
*> 10.2.1.129/32    192.168.2.46                          0 10 ?
*> 192.168.2.16/30  192.168.2.46                          0 10 ?
*> 192.168.2.36/30  192.168.2.46                          0 10 ?
*> 192.168.2.44/30  0.0.0.0                  0        32768 ?
*> 192.168.2.52/30  0.0.0.0                  0        32768 ?
*> 196.7.24.128/25  192.168.2.54             1        32768 ?
*> 196.7.25.128/25  0.0.0.0                  0        32768 ?
*> 196.7.26.129/32  192.168.2.46                          0 10 ?
```

Complex Virtual Router Setups

The multi-VRF examples introduced so far have implemented simple VPN topologies where the individual VPNs and associated VRFs were completely isolated. By using additional MPLS VPN-related Cisco IOS features, you can extend these scenarios to more complex topologies implemented within a single CE router, while remaining isolated from the complexities of the MPLS VPN backbone.

Consider another request of the EuroBank customer, which is illustrated in Figure 4-9. The trading floor and retail banking in the San Francisco site must be clearly separated, but they require access to a common file server that is located at the same site. This server must not be reachable by trading or retail employees located at other sites.

Figure 4-9 *San Francisco Connectivity Requirements*

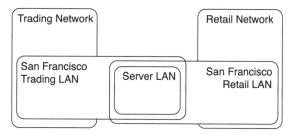

The connectivity requirements are easily implemented with the overlapping VPN topology introduced in Chapter 12, "Advanced MPLS/VPN Topologies" of *MPLS and VPN Architectures* (Volume I). The initial approach to the San Francisco CE router configuration would involve configuring three VRFs with appropriate route distinguishers and route targets, as shown in Example 4-15.

Example 4-15 *Overlapping VPN Configuration on the San Francisco CE Router*

```
ip vrf CommonServer
 rd 1:3
 route-target export 1:3
 route-target import 1:3
 route-target import 1:1
 route-target import 1:2
!
ip vrf Retail
 rd 1:2
 route-target export 1:2
 route-target import 1:3
 route-target import 1:2
!
ip vrf Trading
 rd 1:1
 route-target export 1:1
 route-target import 1:3
 route-target import 1:1
```

After properly configuring all the VRFs and the route targets, you would probably be surprised to learn that the routes are not propagated between VRFs—a result of the fact that the inter-VRF route import and export works only through Multiprotocol BGP. To enable the route propagation between these VRFs, you must configure the BGP routing process on the CE router and redistribute the VRF routes into the per-VRF BGP address family. You must perform these configuration steps even though BGP is not used for peering sessions or for advertisement of routes to other routers.

NOTE   Configuration of a VPNv4 address family is not required because the CE router does not peer with VPNv4 BGP neighbors.

When this redistribution is configured (shown in Example 4-16), the routes are imported into the desired VRFs, as Example 4-17 demonstrates.

Example 4-16 *BGP Configuration on the San Francisco CE Router*

```
router bgp 65002
 address-family ipv4 vrf Trading
 redistribute connected
 !
 address-family ipv4 vrf Retail
 redistribute connected
 !
 address-family ipv4 vrf CommonServer
 redistribute connected
```

Example 4-17 *VRF Routing Table on the San Francisco CE Router*

```
SanFrancisco#show ip route vrf CommonServer

Routing Table: CommonServer
Codes: C - connected, S - static, I - IGRP, R - RIP, B - BGP
       D - EIGRP, EX - EIGRP external, O - OSPF, IA - OSPF inter area
       N1 - OSPF NSSA external type 1, N2 - OSPF NSSA external type 2
       E1 - OSPF external type 1, E2 - OSPF external type 2, E - EGP
       * - candidate default, U - per-user static route, o - ODR

Gateway of last resort is not set

Gateway of last resort is not set

     10.0.0.0/8 is variably subnetted, 3 subnets, 2 masks
B       10.2.1.0/25 is directly connected, 00:07:41, Ethernet0/0
C       10.2.2.0/24 is directly connected, Ethernet0/2
B       10.2.1.128/25 is directly connected, 00:07:41, Ethernet0/1
     192.168.2.0/30 is subnetted, 2 subnets
B       192.168.2.12 is directly connected, 00:07:41, Serial0/0.313
B       192.168.2.16 is directly connected, 00:07:41, Serial0/0.613
```

NOTE   The configuration in Example 4-16 covers a simple setup with no C routers; therefore, the
redistribution of connected routes into Multiprotocol BGP satisfies the design
requirements. If the trading or retail site would contain additional C routers, the routing
protocol used with these C routers would have to be redistributed into Multiprotocol BGP.

More in-depth exploration of the data structures on the San Francisco CE router reveals that
the behavior of the San Francisco CE router more closely mimics the behavior of a PE
router even though it remains a standalone multi-VRF device:

- There are multiple instances of the same BGP route with different route
  distinguishers, as shown in Example 4-18. (Local copies of the BGP route with route
  distinguishers equal to the VRF route distinguishers are generated automatically
  during the import process.)

Example 4-18 *Multiprotocol BGP Table on the San Francisco CE Router*

```
SanFrancisco#show ip bgp vpnv4 all
BGP table version is 17, local router ID is 196.7.1.1
Status codes: s suppressed, d damped, h history, * valid, > best, i - internal,
              S Stale
Origin codes: i - IGP, e - EGP, ? - incomplete

   Network          Next Hop            Metric LocPrf Weight Path
Route Distinguisher: 1:1 (default for vrf Trading)
*> 10.2.1.0/25      0.0.0.0                  0         32768 ?
*> 10.2.2.0/24      0.0.0.0                  0         32768 ?
*> 192.168.2.12/30  0.0.0.0                  0         32768 ?
Route Distinguisher: 1:2 (default for vrf Retail)
*> 10.2.1.128/25    0.0.0.0                  0         32768 ?
*> 10.2.2.0/24      0.0.0.0                  0         32768 ?
*> 192.168.2.16/30  0.0.0.0                  0         32768 ?
Route Distinguisher: 1:3 (default for vrf CommonServer)
*> 10.2.1.0/25      0.0.0.0                  0         32768 ?
*> 10.2.1.128/25    0.0.0.0                  0         32768 ?
*> 10.2.2.0/24      0.0.0.0                  0         32768 ?
*> 192.168.2.12/30  0.0.0.0                  0         32768 ?
*> 192.168.2.16/30  0.0.0.0                  0         32768 ?
```

- Labels are allocated to the VRF routes (see Example 4-19) even though MPLS is not
  configured on an interface and no Multiprotocol BGP neighbors are configured.

Example 4-19 *MPLS Forwarding Table on the San Francisco Router*

```
SanFrancisco#show mpls forwarding-table
Local  Outgoing    Prefix           Bytes Tag  Outgoing    Next Hop
tag    tag or VC   or Tunnel Id     switched   interface
16     Aggregate   10.2.1.0/25[V]   0
17     Aggregate   192.168.2.12/30[V]    \
```

continues

Example 4-19 *MPLS Forwarding Table on the San Francisco Router (Continued)*

```
                                    0
   18    Aggregate   10.2.1.128/25[V]   0
   19    Aggregate   192.168.2.16/30[V]    \
                                    0
   20    Aggregate   10.2.2.0/24[V]    0
```

Linking the Virtual Router with the MPLS VPN Backbone

The configuration examples in the previous section used the simplest possible connectivity between the multi-VRF CE router and the PE router: Frame Relay subinterfaces. This connectivity type or other connectivity types where you could configure subinterfaces on the same physical interface (such as VLAN-based Ethernet, Fast Ethernet, or Gigabit Ethernet connectivity) are highly recommended because they are simple to configure and produce almost no undesired side effects (apart from the IP quality of service, or QoS, configuration that might be more complex than an equivalent connection on a point-to-point link). There are, however, several new access technologies, such as cable networks, that do not allow you to configure multiple subinterfaces between a pair of routers. In these scenarios, generic routing encapsulation (GRE) tunnels can be used to establish multiple virtual links between the adjacent routers.

GRE Refresher

The GRE technology is used in Cisco IOS to tunnel a variety of different protocols across a generic IP backbone. GRE tunnels are configured as regular tunnel interfaces in Cisco IOS and are established between two IP addresses: *tunnel source* and *tunnel destination*. After the tunnel is configured and operational, it behaves exactly like a point-to-point link from the routing perspective. Routing protocols (or static routing) are run over the tunnel, routes are exchanged and installed in the IP routing table, and the traffic can start to flow over the tunnel.

When the tunnel interface appears as the next-hop interface in the IP routing and forwarding tables, packets can be routed into the tunnel. These packets are encapsulated in another IP datagram with the source and destination address set to the configured tunnel source and destination. The IP protocol type in the IP header is set to 47 to indicate that the IP datagram carries a GRE-encapsulated packet.

The packets with IP protocol type 47 received by a router are processed as follows:

- The IP source address is compared to the tunnel destination that is configured on tunnel interfaces to find the corresponding tunnel interface.

- After the tunnel interface is found, the tunnel key (if it is configured) is compared to the corresponding value in the IP datagram. If the values do not match, the packet is dropped.

NOTE	The tunnel key does not significantly increase the security of the tunneled data because it is a simple clear-text value (similar to an SNMP community string). The tunnel key should be used primarily to prevent configuration mismatches.

- The packet is processed as if it arrived through the point-to-point link (tunnel interface).

GRE Tunnels in the MPLS VPN Architecture

The GRE tunnels can be freely combined with the MPLS VPN architecture as long as you maintain the following rules:

- A tunnel interface can be configured to belong to a VRF. Such a tunnel can then be used to establish intra-VRF connectivity across an IP backbone. In this case, the backbone would not necessarily require MPLS to be enabled nor would it require the full feature set of an MPLS VPN deployment. The same concept can be applied to establish multiple logical links over a single physical link between a PE router and a CE router.

- Tunnel interfaces can be used to link PE routers, without the requirement of running LDP within the backbone network. In this case, labeled VPN packets are encapsulated within a GRE datagrams rather than being labeled with an IGP label derived from LDP. However, you usually still have to run LDP between the tunnel endpoints to ensure that an LDP implicit-null label is assigned to the Multiprotocol BGP next-hop.

- In most IOS releases, although the tunnel interface can be configured as a VRF interface, the tunnel endpoints (tunnel source and tunnel destination addresses) must be reachable in the global IP address space by the routers that terminate the GRE tunnels. This essentially means that GRE tunnel encapsulation code is not VRF-aware. In this case, the Global IP routing table forwards the IP datagrams that carry the tunneled traffic. In addition, IP datagrams that carry tunneled traffic must be received over a global interface.

NOTE	With a sophisticated configuration relying on VRF routes where global next-hops and global routes point to VRF interfaces, you can configure the router such that the GRE-encapsulated traffic can be received over a VRF interface. Such a configuration is complex and should be avoided.

- The restrictions that are described in the previous bullet have been removed in the IOS 12.0S release, which supports VRF-based tunnel interfaces. In this IOS release, the tunnel endpoints can belong to a VRF and the GRE-encapsulated traffic can be received over an interface that belongs to the same VRF.

These rules (particularly the requirement that the GRE endpoints must be in global IP space) also explain why the use of GRE tunnels to link the PE routers with the CE routers is discouraged from a security perspective:

- If the service provider is running a secure IP backbone, where all customer traffic is carried in the VPNs, the backbone is exposed to traffic from a CE router, which has to be received over a global interface.

- If the service provider is running a public Internet in the global IP address space of its MPLS VPN backbone, the CE router becomes exposed to the Internet.

NOTE   Using GRE tunnels has other drawbacks. For example, the encapsulated traffic cannot be load-shared based on source and destination IP address. Furthermore, the additional IP header that is needed for GRE encapsulation reduces the usable payload size, sometimes resulting in the need to fragment transported IP datagrams, which might result in reduced forwarding performance of the router that is performing the fragmentation or reassembly.

You can avoid both security risks by deploying proper IP access lists on PE routers or CE routers, but these access lists require additional mandatory configuration operations in the provisioning process. Alternatively, you could deploy VRF-aware GRE tunnels if the IOS release you are using in your network supports them.

NOTE   Throughout the configuration examples in the remainder of this chapter, GRE tunnels based on global IP addresses will be used to reduce the complexity of the examples and to ensure that you can successfully use the examples with any IOS release that supports MPLS VPN functionality.

Using GRE Tunnels to Link Multi-VRF CE Routers to the MPLS VPN Backbone

Based on the information in the previous two sections, it should be easy to deploy several point-to-point virtual links between the CE router and the PE router by using the setup shown in Figure 4-10.

Keep the following guidelines in mind when using this design:

- One global loopback interface needs to be configured as tunnel source/destination on the CE router and PE router for each parallel link.

Figure 4-10   *Virtual VRF Interfaces Implemented with PE-CE GRE Tunnels*

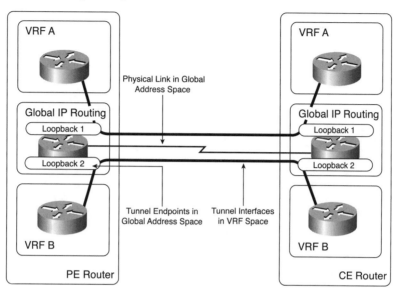

NOTE	You can use the same loopback interface on the PE router for tunnel links to multiple CE routers, but the parallel tunnels terminated at the same remote router must have distinct source addresses to enable proper assignment of incoming tunneled traffic to the tunnel interface.

- The PE-CE link needs to be in global IP address space; that is, a VRF is not configured at the PE router end. Global routing (either static routing or a dynamic routing protocol) must be established across this link to propagate the tunnel source and destination addresses between the PE router and the CE router. BGP is the recommended routing protocol in designs based on dynamic routing because of its security features.

- Incoming access lists should be configured on both the PE router and CE router. These access lists should permit only the tunneled traffic between the tunnel source and the destination addresses and the routing protocol updates (if a dynamic routing protocol is used between the PE router and the CE router).

- Individual tunnel interfaces are configured (one per VRF) and assigned to their respective VRF. VRF IP addresses are configured on the tunnel interfaces, and VRF routing protocols are configured to run over the tunnel interfaces.

Alternatively, you can implement a virtual link for one VRF (VRF B in Figure 4-11) over a physical link that belongs to another VRF (VRF A in Figure 4-11) by using VRF-aware GRE tunnels.

Figure 4-11   *VRF-Aware GRE Tunnel Established Between the PE Router and the CE Router*

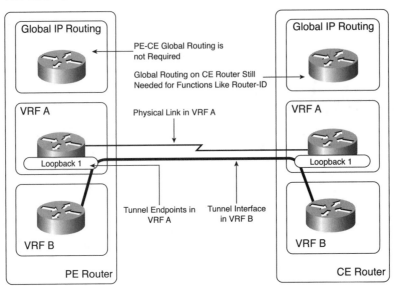

Keep the following guidelines in mind when you are implementing this design:

- One VRF loopback interface needs to be configured as the tunnel source/destination on the CE router and PE router for each parallel tunnel link. Similarly to the previous case, the same loopback interface can be used for multiple tunnel endpoints as long as these tunnels terminate at different remote routers.

- The PE-CE link needs to be in the same VRF as the VRF loopback interface that is acting as the tunnel endpoint.

- Individual tunnel interfaces are configured (one per VRF) and assigned to their respective VRF. VRF IP addresses are configured on the tunnel interfaces and VRF routing protocols are configured to run over the tunnel interfaces.

From the service provider's perspective, most of the security restrictions are removed by using this setup. However, from the customer's perspective, it is still possible that a malicious user who belongs to Site A (VRF A) could insert GRE packets that are destined for the PE router and spoof traffic that is supposedly originating in VRF B. To remove this potential security hole, you can use a more complex, but also more secure, design in which the PE-CE link belongs to a dedicated VRF on the PE router (to remove security issues on the PE router side) and to the global IP address space on the CE router (to remove security issues on the CE router side). Such a design is presented in Figure 4-12.

Figure 4-12 *More Secure PE-CE Tunnel Design*

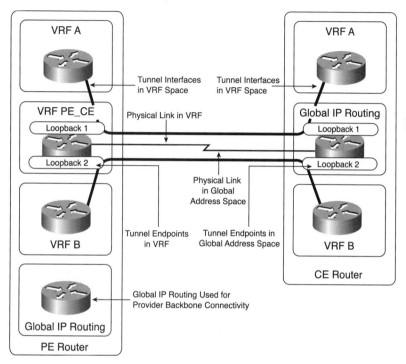

As you can see from the discussions in this section, deployment of GRE tunnels between PE routers and CE routers is complex; therefore, you should always try to implement a simple solution, be it using Frame Relay encapsulation in a WAN environment or VLAN encapsulation in a LAN environment.

Deploying GRE Tunnels to Support Multi-VRF in EuroBank's European Sites

Each EuroBank site must have two logical connections to the adjacent PE router to support the separation of the Trading and Retail departments. This requirement is easy to implement in the U.S. sites (San Francisco and Washington) by using additional Frame Relay data-link connection identifiers (DLCIs) between the CE routers and the PE routers. Assume that cost considerations prevent the use of the same strategy in Europe; EuroBank would like to retain a single DLCI between its Paris CE router and the Paris PE router as well as a single DLCI between the EuroBank Paris site (Paris CE router) and the EuroBank London site (London C router). Working together with the SuperCom service provider, EuroBank decided to implement the multi-VRF concept in combination with tunnel interfaces throughout Europe, as shown in Figure 4-13. In addition, EuroBank will use GRE tunnels based on global IP routing. (Tunnel endpoints are in global IP address space on PE routers and CE routers.)

Figure 4-13   *Tunnel Interfaces That Link CE Router VRFs in Europe*

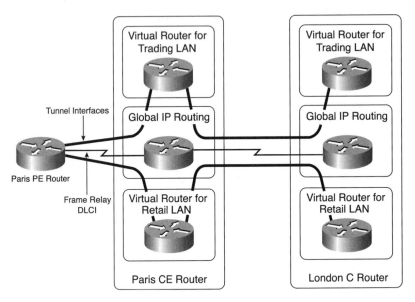

Perform the following steps to implement the required design:

Step 1   Configure loopback interfaces on the PE router and the CE router in Paris.

Step 2   Configure tunnel interfaces between the Paris PE router and the Paris CE router as well as between the Paris CE router and the London C router.

Step 3   Configure the WAN link. The WAN links that link the PE routers and CE routers must be in the global IP routing table on both ends.

Step 4   Advertise loopback interface addresses between the tunnel endpoints.

Step 5   Place tunnel interfaces in the target VRFs.

Step 6   Perform the remainder of the VRF configuration. (Configure VRF interfaces and VRF routing protocols.)

The following sections explain each step in more detail.

Configuring Loopback Interfaces

Loopback interfaces must be configured on a PE router and a CE router in Paris, as shown in Example 4-20. Loopback interfaces must also be configured in the London C router.

Example 4-20 *Loopback Interface Configuration*

```
PE_Paris(config)#
interface Loopback2511
 ip address 192.168.251.1 255.255.255.255
 no ip directed-broadcast
!
interface Loopback2512
 ip address 192.168.251.2 255.255.255.255
 no ip directed-broadcast

CE_Paris(config)#
interface Loopback1
 ip address 192.168.252.1 255.255.255.255
 no ip directed-broadcast
!
interface Loopback2
 ip address 192.168.252.2 255.255.255.255
 no ip directed-broadcast

C_London(config)#
interface Loopback1
 ip address 192.168.252.11 255.255.255.255
 no ip directed-broadcast
!
interface Loopback2
 ip address 192.168.252.12 255.255.255.255
 no ip directed-broadcast
```

Configuring Tunnel Interfaces

Tunnel interfaces must be configured between the Paris PE router and the Paris CE router as well as between the Paris CE router and the London C router, as shown in Example 4-21.

Example 4-21 *Tunnel Interface Configuration*

```
PE_Paris(config)#
interface Tunnel2511
 description *** Trading tunnel to CE Paris ***
 tunnel source Loopback2511
 tunnel destination 192.168.252.1
 tunnel key 2511
!
interface Tunnel2512
 description *** Retail tunnel to CE Paris ***
 tunnel source Loopback2512
 tunnel destination 192.168.252.2
 tunnel key 2512
```

continues

Example 4-21 *Tunnel Interface Configuration (Continued)*

```
CE_Paris(config)#
interface Tunnel1
 description *** Trading tunnel to PE Paris ***
 tunnel source Loopback1
 tunnel destination 192.168.251.1
 tunnel key 2511
!
interface Tunnel2
 description *** Retail tunnel to PE Paris ***
 tunnel source Loopback2
 tunnel destination 192.168.251.2
 tunnel key 2512
!
interface Tunnel11
 description *** Trading tunnel to London ***
 tunnel source Loopback1
 tunnel destination 192.168.252.11
 tunnel key 2511
!
interface Tunnel12
 description *** Retail tunnel to London ***
 tunnel source Loopback2
 tunnel destination 192.168.252.12
 tunnel key 2512

C_London(config)#
interface Tunnel1
 description *** Trading tunnel to Paris ***
 tunnel source Loopback1
 tunnel destination 192.168.252.1
 tunnel key 2511
!
interface Tunnel2
 description *** Trading tunnel to Paris ***
 tunnel source Loopback2
 tunnel destination 192.168.252.2
 tunnel key 2512
```

NOTE As specified in the design rules, the parallel tunnel interfaces between a pair of routers must use different tunnel source and destination IP addresses. Conversely, the tunnel interfaces going to different routers (for example, tunnel interfaces on the Paris CE router) could use the same tunnel source IP address.

Configure the WAN Links

The link between the Paris PE router and the Paris CE router must be in the global IP routing table on the PE router. Similarly, the links from the Paris CE router to the Paris PE router and London C router must be in the global IP routing table on the Paris CE router, as shown in Example 4-22.

Example 4-22 *WAN Interface Configuration*

```
PE_Paris(config)#
interface Serial0/0.641 point-to-point
 description *** Link to EuroBank Paris ***
 ip address 192.168.2.26 255.255.255.252
 no ip directed-broadcast
 frame-relay interface-dlci 641

CE_Paris(config)#
interface Serial0/0.1 point-to-point
 description *** Link to London ***
 ip address 192.168.2.29 255.255.255.252
 no ip directed-broadcast
 frame-relay interface-dlci 274
!
interface Serial0/0.614 point-to-point
 description *** Link to PE_Paris ***
 ip address 192.168.2.25 255.255.255.252
 no ip directed-broadcast
 frame-relay interface-dlci 614
```

Advertise the Loopback Interfaces

Loopback interface addresses must be advertised between the tunnel endpoints. BGP is deployed between the PE router and the CE router, and RIP is used internally in the EuroBank network, as shown in Example 4-23. Note that the CE router is configured as a global BGP neighbor on the PE router.

Example 4-23 *Global IP Routing Supporting Tunnel Interfaces*

```
PE_Paris(config)#
router bgp 10
 network 192.168.251.1 mask 255.255.255.255
 network 192.168.251.2 mask 255.255.255.255
 neighbor 192.168.2.25 remote-as 65001
 neighbor 192.168.2.25 route-map NoAdvertise in
 neighbor 192.168.2.25 filter-list 1 out
!
ip as-path access-list 1 permit ^$
!
route-map NoAdvertise permit 10
 set community no-advertise

CE_Paris(config)#
router rip
 version 2
 network 192.168.2.0
 network 192.168.252.0
 no auto-summary
```

continues

Example 4-23 *Global IP Routing Supporting Tunnel Interfaces (Continued)*

```
!
router bgp 65001
 network 192.168.252.1 mask 255.255.255.255
 network 192.168.252.2 mask 255.255.255.255
 neighbor 192.168.2.26 remote-as 10
```

```
C_London(config)#
router rip
 version 2
 network 192.168.2.0
 network 192.168.252.0
 no auto-summary
```

The previous examples also include a number of additional measures introduced in the global BGP routing configuration between the PE router and the CE router to ensure security and stability of the design:

- The CE router advertises only its own loopback interfaces in BGP, and not the other subnets from the customer network (C-network).

- The PE router sets the **no-advertise** community on updates received from the CE router to prevent them from being propagated further into the service provider network (P-network).

- The PE router filters outgoing updates toward the CE router with a filter list to prevent memory and CPU overload on the CE router.

Place Tunnel Interfaces into the Target VRFs

Tunnel interfaces are placed in the target VRFs, as shown in Example 4-24.

Example 4-24 *VRF Interface Configuration*

```
PE_Paris(config)#
interface Tunnel2511
 ip vrf forwarding EuroBank_Trading
 ip address 192.168.2.42 255.255.255.252
!
interface Tunnel2512
 ip vrf forwarding EuroBank_Retail
 ip address 192.168.2.46 255.255.255.252
```

```
CE_Paris(config)#
interface Tunnel1
 ip vrf forwarding Trading
 ip address 192.168.2.41 255.255.255.252
!
interface Tunnel2
 ip vrf forwarding Retail
 ip address 192.168.2.45 255.255.255.252
!
```

Example 4-24 *VRF Interface Configuration (Continued)*

```
interface Tunnel11
 ip vrf forwarding Trading
 ip address 192.168.2.49 255.255.255.252
!
interface Tunnel12
 ip vrf forwarding Retail
 ip address 192.168.2.53 255.255.255.252

C_London(config)#
interface Tunnel1
 ip vrf forwarding Trading
 ip address 192.168.2.50 255.255.255.252
!
interface Tunnel2
 ip vrf forwarding Retail
 ip address 192.168.2.54 255.255.255.252
```

Remaining VRF Configuration

The VRFs need to be configured, with their respective VRF routing protocols, and the LAN interfaces in Paris and London need to be assigned to these VRFs. BGP is deployed between the PE router and the CE router in Paris, and RIP is used between the Paris CE router and the London C router. The VRF IP routing configurations are included next. (Please refer to the "Running BGP in Virtual Router Scenarios" earlier in this chapter for a detailed description of the BGP configuration used in Example 4-25.)

Example 4-25 *VRF IP Routing Configuration*

```
PE_Paris(config)#
router bgp 10
 address-family ipv4 vrf EuroBank_Trading
 neighbor 192.168.2.41 remote-as 65100
!
 address-family ipv4 vrf EuroBank_Retail
 neighbor 192.168.2.45 remote-as 65200

Paris(config)#
router rip
 address-family ipv4 vrf Trading
 version 2
 redistribute bgp 65001 metric transparent
 network 192.168.2.0
 network 196.7.25.0
!
 address-family ipv4 vrf Retail
 version 2
 redistribute bgp 65001 metric transparent
 network 192.168.2.0
 network 196.7.25.0
!
```

continues

Example 4-25 *VRF IP Routing Configuration (Continued)*

```
router bgp 65001
 address-family ipv4 vrf Trading
 redistribute rip
 neighbor 192.168.2.42 remote-as 10
 neighbor 192.168.2.42 local-as 65100 no-prepend
 !
 address-family ipv4 vrf Retail
 redistribute rip
 neighbor 192.168.2.46 remote-as 10
 neighbor 192.168.2.46 local-as 65200 no-prepend

London(config)#
router rip
 address-family ipv4 vrf Trading
 version 2
 network 192.168.2.0
 network 196.7.24.0
 !
 address-family ipv4 vrf Retail
 version 2
 network 192.168.2.0
 network 196.7.24.0
```

After you have completed all these configuration steps, you can verify proper operation of this design by inspecting the VRF IP routing table on the London C router, which is shown in Example 4-26.

Example 4-26 *VRF IP Routing Tables on the London C Router*

```
London#show ip route vrf Trading
Routing Table: Trading
Codes: C - connected, S - static, I - IGRP, R - RIP, B - BGP
       D - EIGRP, EX - EIGRP external, O - OSPF, IA - OSPF inter area
       N1 - OSPF NSSA external type 1, N2 - OSPF NSSA external type 2
       E1 - OSPF external type 1, E2 - OSPF external type 2, E - EGP
       * - candidate default, U - per-user static route, o - ODR

Gateway of last resort is not set

     196.7.25.0 255.255.255.128 is subnetted, 1 subnets
R       196.7.25.0 [120/1] via 192.168.2.49, 00:00:03, Tunnel1
     196.7.24.0 255.255.255.128 is subnetted, 1 subnets
C       196.7.24.0 is directly connected, Ethernet0/0
     196.7.26.0 255.255.255.128 is subnetted, 1 subnets
R       196.7.26.0 [120/1] via 192.168.2.49, 00:00:03, Tunnel1
     10.0.0.0 255.255.255.128 is subnetted, 1 subnets
R       10.2.1.0 [120/1] via 192.168.2.49, 00:00:03, Tunnel1
     192.168.2.0 255.255.255.252 is subnetted, 4 subnets
R       192.168.2.40 [120/1] via 192.168.2.49, 00:00:03, Tunnel1
R       192.168.2.32 [120/1] via 192.168.2.49, 00:00:03, Tunnel1
C       192.168.2.48 is directly connected, Tunnel1
R       192.168.2.12 [120/1] via 192.168.2.49, 00:00:05, Tunnel1
```

Example 4-26 *VRF IP Routing Tables on the London C Router (Continued)*

```
London#show ip route vrf Retail

Routing Table: Retail
Codes: C - connected, S - static, I - IGRP, R - RIP, B - BGP
       D - EIGRP, EX - EIGRP external, O - OSPF, IA - OSPF inter area
       N1 - OSPF NSSA external type 1, N2 - OSPF NSSA external type 2
       E1 - OSPF external type 1, E2 - OSPF external type 2, E - EGP
       * - candidate default, U - per-user static route, o - ODR

Gateway of last resort is not set

     196.7.25.0 255.255.255.128 is subnetted, 1 subnets
R       196.7.25.128 [120/1] via 192.168.2.53, 00:00:10, Tunnel2
     196.7.24.0 255.255.255.128 is subnetted, 1 subnets
C       196.7.24.128 is directly connected, Loopback1001
     196.7.26.0 255.255.255.255 is subnetted, 1 subnets
R       196.7.26.129 [120/1] via 192.168.2.53, 00:00:10, Tunnel2
     10.0.0.0 255.255.255.255 is subnetted, 1 subnets
R       10.2.1.129 [120/1] via 192.168.2.53, 00:00:10, Tunnel2
     192.168.2.0 255.255.255.252 is subnetted, 4 subnets
R       192.168.2.44 [120/1] via 192.168.2.53, 00:00:11, Tunnel2
R       192.168.2.36 [120/1] via 192.168.2.53, 00:00:11, Tunnel2
C       192.168.2.52 is directly connected, Tunnel2
R       192.168.2.16 [120/1] via 192.168.2.53, 00:00:12, Tunnel2
```

VRF Selection Based on Source IP Address

In the traditional implementation of the MPLS VPN architecture in Cisco IOS, each physical or logical interface was associated with one VRF table, resulting in a one-VPN-per-interface design limitation. Service providers that wanted to offer access to different VPN networks (or different upstream ISPs) to many customers who were connected to a shared media (cable or Ethernet infrastructure) first encountered this limitation.

In situations in which more than one VPN customer had to be connected to a single physical interface, the following solutions were available:

- VPN customers who were connected to a LAN interface were split into multiple virtual LANs (VLAN), each VLAN subinterface belonging to a different VRF. This approach could separate the Trading and Retail LANs in the EuroBank network if the EuroBank CE routers had only one LAN interface.

- Subinterfaces were also used (if available) for multiple VPN customers who were connected to the same WAN interface. This approach worked if the WAN technology that was deployed in the network supported subinterfaces. For example, Frame Relay and ATM supported subinterfaces based on Frame Relay DLCI or ATM virtual circuits (VCs).

- In some scenarios, GRE tunnels could be used to create logical interfaces.

- PPP-over-Ethernet (PPPoE) could be deployed between the VPN customers (even individual workstations) and the PE routers to separate the VPN customers into different VPNs.

All the designs presented in the previous bulleted list use the one-interface-per-customer paradigm and thus share a common scalability problem: The number of customers that a single PE router can support is limited by the number of interfaces that the Cisco IOS supports.

A new functionality, VRF selection based on source IP address, was introduced in Cisco IOS release 12.0S to circumvent the one-VPN-per-interface design rule and associated scalability issues. With this functionality, the VPN packet forwarding is performed as follows:

- If the VRF selection feature is enabled on an interface, a lookup is performed on the source IP address in the VRF selection table to determine the VRF to which the sending IP host belongs.

- After the target VRF is found, the VRF Cisco Express Forwarding (CEF) table lookup is performed on the destination IP address to find the next-hop and associated MPLS label stack.

- Global CEF table lookup is performed on the destination IP address if the VRF selection lookup fails. (The source IP address is not associated with a VRF.)

The three simple configuration commands in Table 4-4 are associated with this functionality.

Table 4-4   *Configuring VRF Selection Based on Source IP Address*

Command Syntax	Description
vrf selection source *address mask* **vrf** *name*	This global command populates the VRF selection table. A single (global) per-router VRF selection table is supported in IOS release 12.0S.
ip vrf select source	This interface-level command enables the VRF selection lookup for packets that are received through the specified interface. The **ip vrf select source** and **ip vrf forwarding** commands are mutually exclusive. If the VRF Selection feature is configured on an interface, you cannot configure VRFs (using the **ip vrf forwarding** command) on the same interface.
ip vrf receive *vrf-name*	This interface-level command enables redistribution of the IP prefix configured on the specified interface into the specified VRF routing table. The detailed usage guidelines of this command are covered later in this section.

VRF Selection in the EuroBank Network

The VRF selection functionality can be applied in those EuroBank sites that must support two VPNs per site (Trading and Retail VPN) but are not implemented with a VLAN-supporting technology, as shown in Figure 4-14. For example, these sites could have been implemented with 10BASE-T Ethernet, shared 100BASE-T Ethernet, or Token Ring.

Figure 4-14 *Two Sites Connected to the Same Physical Interface*

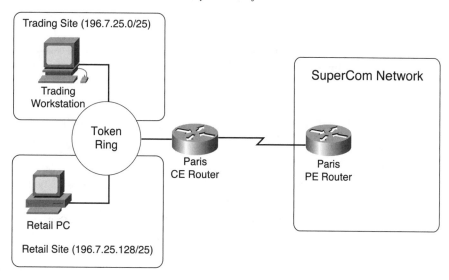

The LAN functionality that is deployed in the Paris site prohibits the use of the VLAN subinterface on the Paris CE router. The only way to separate the Trading hosts from the Retail hosts is to use the VRF selection functionality, resulting in a configuration that is similar to the one in Example 4-27. (The configuration in the example includes only the VRF selection-specific configuration commands. The rest of the configuration is similar to the one in Example 4-1.)

Example 4-27 *VRF Selection on the Paris CE Router*

```
vrf selection source 196.7.25.0 255.255.255.128 vrf Trading
vrf selection source 196.7.25.128 255.255.255.128 vrf Retail
!
interface TokenRing 0/0
 ip vrf select source
 ip address 196.7.25.1 255.255.255.0
```

NOTE   Security is a major issue when deploying the VRF selection functionality. Because the Trading and Retail workstations in Paris reside on the same shared LAN segment, each user can observe the traffic of the other department. It is also easy for an intruder to break into a workstation from another VPN and gain unauthorized access into that VPN.

Designing the Return Path for the VPN Traffic

With the configuration from Example 4-27, the IP packets sent from workstations that are attached to the Paris LAN are forwarded to appropriate VPNs and eventually reach the desired VPN destinations. However, the Paris LAN interface belongs to the global IP routing table of the Paris CE router (the interface is not in a VRF); therefore, its IP subnet is not automatically propagated into the VRF routing tables for the Trading and Retail VPN. Consequently, the VPN IP hosts in other sites cannot return the traffic to Paris IP hosts.

You can use two designs to establish the return path for the VPN traffic:

- The whole IP prefix that is assigned to an interface with VRF selection is inserted into the VRF routing tables.

- Parts of the IP address space assigned to the interface are inserted into the appropriate VRF table.

You can use the **ip vrf receive** command if you want to transfer the IP prefix assigned to the interface on which you've configured the VRF selection to the VRF routing tables. With this command, you can specify which VRF routing table shall receive the global IP prefix assigned to the interface on which you use the command. The IP prefix appears in the VRF routing table as a connected interface and must be redistributed into Multiprotocol BGP like any other directly connected VRF subnet.

In the EuroBank example, the commands to use are shown in Example 4-28.

Example 4-28 *Insertion of Interface-Wide IP Prefix into the VRF Tables*

```
interface TokenRing 0/0
 ip vrf receive Trading
 ip vrf receive Retail
```

The **ip vrf receive** command in Example 4-28 inserts the IP prefix 196.7.25.1/24 that covers hosts belonging to the Trading and Retail sites into both the Trading and Retail VRF table. As a result, hosts from other Trading sites can access Retail hosts in the Paris site, and hosts from other Retail sites can access the Trading hosts in Paris. The undesired inter-VPN communication can be performed only in one direction (other sites to Paris hosts), but many denial-of-service attacks need only one-way communication. The design from Example 4-28 should not be used in security-conscious environments.

A more secure approach to the return-traffic design involves VRF static routes pointing to the global interface:

- For every VRF that is associated with an interface through the VRF selection functionality, configure a VRF static route covering only the IP address space assigned to that VRF with the **vrf selection** command. The static route should point to the directly connected interface, as shown in Example 4-29.

Example 4-29 *Secure VPN Return Traffic Design*

```
ip route vrf Trading 196.7.25.0 255.255.255.128 TokenRing 0/0
ip route vrf Retail 196.7.25.128 255.255.255.128 TokenRing 0/0
```

- Redistribute the VRF static routes into Multiprotocol BGP to propagate them to other PE routers.

With this approach, each VRF table receives only the IP prefix associated with the hosts in its VPN, preventing undesired intersite inter-VPN traffic. The base problem of the VRF selection functionality still remains, though: The users from different VPNs that are attached to the same physical shared media can still communicate with each other.

Performing NAT in a Virtual Router Environment

NAT in conjunction with private IP addresses (as defined in RFC 1918) was initially introduced as a temporary measure to ensure continuous growth of the Internet while IPv6 was developing. As with many temporary measures, it was widely accepted and further extended in the Cisco IOS implementation to include port address translation (PAT) and two-way NAT. Today, NAT is used as one of the primary means of connecting enterprise networks to the Internet. It is also commonly deployed in scenarios in which networks that are using overlapping or private IP address spaces need to be interconnected.

In the MPLS VPN environment, NAT is generally implemented in three scenarios:

- When the service provider wants to offer Internet access to its customers who use private IP addresses, at least one device between the end user and the Internet has to perform the NAT function. Traditionally, this task was left to the CE devices because NAT within the VRF was not supported. The typical setup together with sample CE router configuration is shown in Figure 4-15 and Example 4-30.

Figure 4-15   *CE Router NAT on Internet Interface*

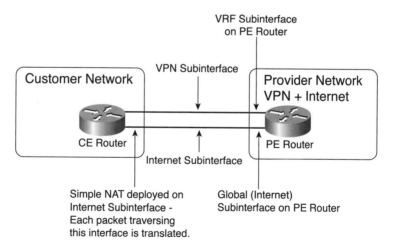

NOTE The setup in Figure 4-15 is based on the design where two separate subinterfaces are used for VPN and Internet connectivity. Similar, although more complex, setup could be used for other types of VPN connectivity.

Example 4-30 *Simple NAT Performed Toward Internet*

```
!
! Define a separate subinterface for Internet access. This is the
! NAT outside interface
!
interface Serial0.2 point-to-point
 description *** Link to public Internet ***
 ip address 194.22.18.1 255.255.255.252
 ip nat outside
 frame-relay interface-dlci 200
!
! All other interfaces are NAT inside interfaces
!
interface Ethernet0
 ip nat inside
!
! Define Overload NAT translation using IP address of outside interface
!
ip nat inside source list 1 interface Serial0.2 overload
!
! All packets going to Internet are translated
!
access-list 1 permit any
```

- When the service provider wants to offer common services to a number of its customers, the customers have to use coordinated IP addresses to be able to access the common servers. This requirement either triggers the need for renumbering customer networks or the need for a NAT function performed inside the customer address space. The NAT could be performed at individual CE routers. The typical setup together with sample configuration is shown in Figure 4-16 and Example 4-31.

Example 4-31 *Complex NAT Toward Common Server Performed on the CE Router*

```
!
! Define a loopback interface with coordinate IP address
!
interface Loopback0
 ip address 194.22.18.1 255.255.255.255
!
! WAN interface toward PE router is NAT outside interface
!
interface Serial0
 ip nat outside
```

Example 4-31   *Complex NAT Toward Common Server Performed on the CE Router (Continued)*

```
!
! LAN interface is NAT inside interface
!
interface Ethernet0
 ip nat inside
!
! Only packets toward common server are translated
!
route-map Translate
 match ip address 101
!
access-list 101 permit ip any host 194.22.16.1
!
! Define a route-map controlled overload NAT translation
! using IP address of the loopback interface
!
ip nat inside source route-map Translate interface Loopback0 overload
```

Figure 4-16   *Complex CE Router NAT on VPN Interface*

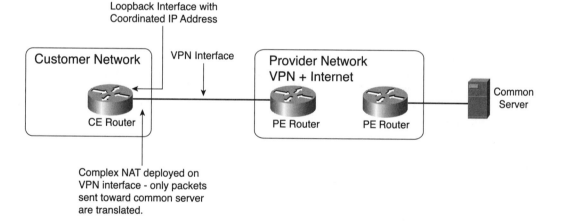

- Instead of performing NAT within customer address space on each CE router, the service provider could deploy a bank of NAT devices (one per customer) on a central location, preferably close to the common servers. A sample setup for three customer VPNs is displayed in Figure 4-17.

Figure 4-17 *Centralized Per-VPN NAT*

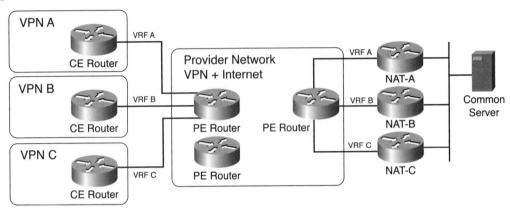

In all cases, the service provisioning is simpler and more controlled if the service provider can perform the VRF-aware NAT functionality in the PE routers. This feature, called PE-NAT, was introduced in Cisco IOS release 12.2T and will be described in this section together with a refresher on NAT configuration and operation.

NOTE The NAT functionality of Cisco IOS and related configuration commands is also briefly covered in Chapter 1 of *Enhanced IP Services for Cisco Networks* from Cisco Press. For an in-depth description of NAT in Cisco IOS and detailed configuration guidelines, which are beyond the scope of this book, please refer to the Cisco IOS documentation available on www.cisco.com.

NAT Refresher

The basic NAT functionality is best explained in its simplest application: enabling a network that has private IP addresses (shown in Figure 4-18) to communicate with the public Internet.

In this scenario, the NAT device performs the following functions:

- When an IP packet is received from the inside interface, the source IP address is replaced with a global IP address, the IP checksum of the IP packet is recomputed, and the packet is forwarded toward its final destination. The global IP address that corresponds to the source IP address is stored in a *translation table*.

- When an IP packet is received from the outside interface, the destination IP address is compared to the addresses in the translation table. If there is a match, the destination global IP address is replaced with the private IP address and the packet is forwarded toward a host in the inside of the network.

Figure 4-18   *Basic NAT Functionality*

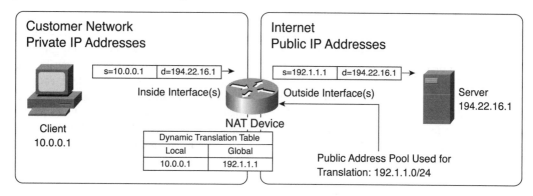

The global IP addresses used to replace the private IP addresses could be statically mapped to the private IP addresses (*static NAT*). This setup is commonly used to ensure that servers (such as web hosts and e-mail servers) with private IP addresses are always reachable from the global Internet through the same public IP address, as shown in Figure 4-19.

Figure 4-19   *Static NAT Used to Access Servers in Private IP Address Space*

Logical Topology

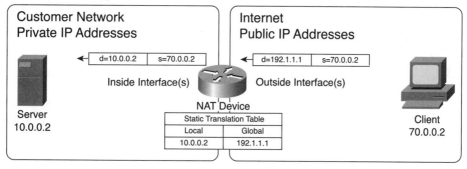

Client View

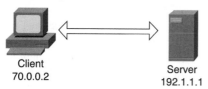

Alternatively, you can define a pool of global IP addresses (*NAT pool*) that are shared between all users in the private network and allocated on-demand. Cisco IOS also provides a rich set of configuration commands with which you can decide on a packet-per-packet basis whether the source IP address should be translated.

Basic NAT performs translation based on the IP address only, which means that it requires a distinct global IP address for every user who is simultaneously accessing the global Internet from the private network. Typically, such a user would only open a few TCP or UDP sessions at a time. However, the TCP or UDP protocol permits a single IP address to open more than 65 thousand sessions. This capability enhanced the operation of NAT by allowing the introduction of PAT, which is also called *overload NAT*. PAT allows multiple private IP addresses to be mapped to one global IP address (see Figure 4-20). The NAT device performs TCP and UDP port translation together with the IP address translation.

Figure 4-20 *PAT*

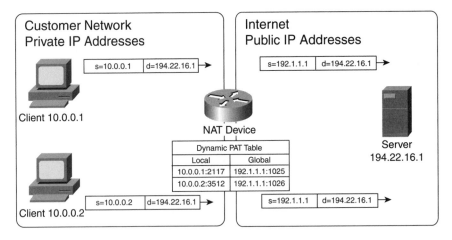

NOTE   The basic NAT functionality can support any protocol that is running on top of IP. PAT works only for applications that are running on top of TCP or UDP.

Configuring NAT on a PE Router

The PE-NAT implementation in Cisco IOS extends the existing NAT functionality to include VRF-aware NAT. The VRF-aware NAT supports most of the NAT functionality in IOS (static and dynamic NAT translations, PAT translation, overlapped translations, use of route maps to select IP packets to be translated, and so on). In the first PE-NAT release, the NAT translation can be performed within a single VRF (not VRF-to-VRF) or between a VRF and the global IP routing table.

Any VRF or global interface can be an inside or an outside interface. Furthermore, an interface that is connecting a PE router to the network core (MPLS-enabled interface of the PE router) can be configured as the inside interface, and NAT can be applied to all MPLS-encapsulated VPN packets received through that interface (giving the network designers an option to perform NAT in a single point in the network).

The NAT configuration commands were changed only slightly; the **vrf** option was added to the **inside source** and **outside source** NAT commands, as shown in Table 4-5.

Table 4-5   *Configuring VRF-Aware NAT on PE Routers*

Command Syntax	Description
ip nat inside source {**list** {*access-list-number*	*name*} **pool** *name* [**overload**]	**static** *local-ip global-ip*} **vrf** *name*	To enable NAT of the inside source address within a VRF, use the **ip nat inside source vrf** global configuration command.
ip nat outside source {**list** {*access-list-number*	*name*} **pool** *name*	**static** *global-ip local-ip*} **vrf** *name*	To enable NAT of the outside source address within a VRF, use the **ip nat outside source vrf** global configuration command.
ip nat inside destination list {*access-list-number*	*name*} **pool** *name* **vrf** *name*	To enable NAT of the inside destination address within a VRF, use the **ip nat inside destination vrf** global configuration command.

In the following two sections, we discuss how to use the modified NAT commands to implement two common deployment scenarios in an MPLS VPN network:

- Using PE-NAT to allow users who have overlapping addresses access to common services

- Using PE-NAT to give users who have private IP addresses access to the Internet

Using PE-NAT to Access Common Services

In this scenario, the SuperCom service provider would like to offer common services that are co-located with the Washington PE router, as shown in Figure 4-21. A number of services can be implemented with this approach, including Voice over IP (VoIP) gateways, web hosting, e-mail hosting, hosting of other applications, or common DNS.

Figure 4-21 *Common Services in SuperCom Network*

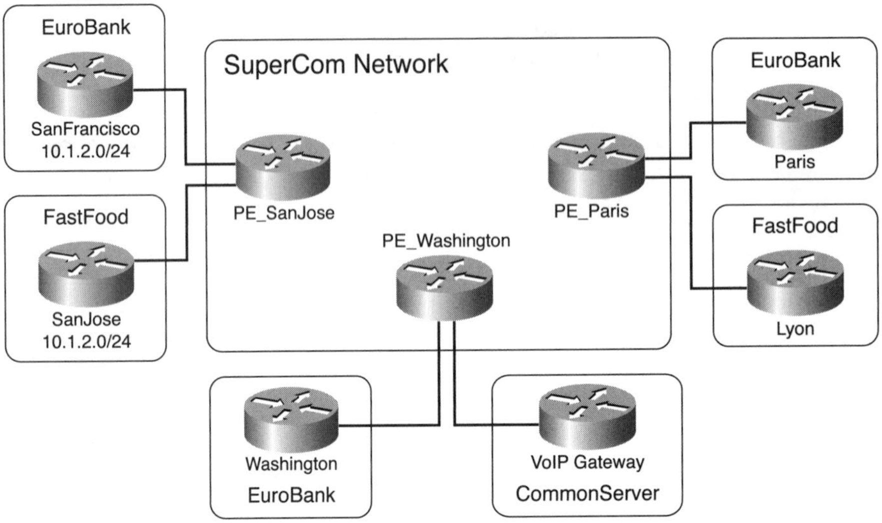

As always, the communication between the end users and the common server that is located in Washington will only be successful if the users can reach the common server IP subnet and vice versa. It's easy to ensure that the users can reach the common server by using the overlapping VPN topology described in Chapter 12, "Advanced MPLS/VPN Topologies" of *MPLS and VPN Architectures* (Volume I). The communication from the common server to the end users is more problematic. In this case, the end users in EuroBank San Francisco and FastFoods San Jose use overlapping IP addresses; therefore, there is no unique return path from the Washington-based server to these users.

The SuperCom designers can use several different approaches to solve this problem:

- Deploy standard NAT on all the CE routers that are accessing the common server. With this approach, a small portion of global IP address space would be assigned to each customer site; even a single IP address would be enough in most cases. The CE router would then use the overload NAT to map source IP addresses of packets sent toward the common service to an allocated global IP address, as shown in Figure 4-22. (See Example 4-31 earlier in this section for a CE router NAT sample configuration.)

- Deploy PE-NAT on the Washington PE router to perform the NAT operation at a central service point. With this approach, SuperCom can also minimize the use of public IP addresses because all MPLS VPN users can use the same NAT address pool, as shown in Figure 4-23. Furthermore, with careful design, the NAT address pool can use private IP addresses, saving on public address space.

Figure 4-22   *Complex NAT Performed on a CE Router*

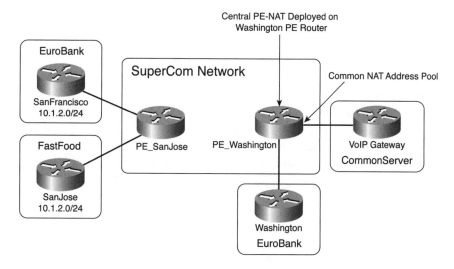

Figure 4-23   *PE-NAT Deployed in SuperCom Network*

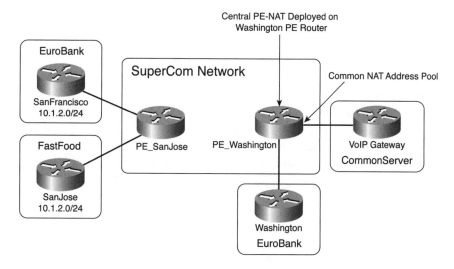

NOTE   To minimize the complexity, the diagrams throughout the rest of this section will only include Washington and San Jose PE routers and connected CE routers.

The SuperCom designers decided to deploy a centralized PE-NAT solution by using the addressing scheme displayed in Table 4-6.

Table 4-6 *Common Server Address Assignment*

Description	IP Prefix
Common server subnet	194.22.16.0/24
PE router address	194.22.16.1
VoIP gateway	194.22.16.2
Outside NAT pool	172.16.0.0/22

The PE-NAT limitation (NAT is only performed inside a single VRF) requires careful design on the Washington PE router that includes the following components:

- A dedicated VRF is created for the common server.
- A NAT pool is established in the Washington PE router, and the routing between the common server and the NAT pool is configured in the common server VRF.
- For all customers who are accessing the common server, customer VRFs are configured on the Washington PE router, and the route toward the common server is inserted into the customer VRF.
- VRF-aware NAT is configured on the Washington PE router.

Each one of these components is discussed in a separate subsection that follows.

Common Server VRF Configuration

A VRF must be created on the Washington PE router to isolate the common server from the global IP address space in which the Internet service is offered, as shown in Example 4-32. In environments that have more relaxed security requirements, the common server might also reside in global IP address space. Contrary to the overlapping VPN topology, no route leakage between this VRF and the customer VRFs is defined.

Example 4-32 *CommonServer VRF Definition*

```
ip vrf CommonServer
 rd 100:100
 route-target export 100:100
 route-target import 100:100
 !
interface FastEthernet3/0
 ip vrf forwarding CommonServer
 ip address 194.22.16.1 255.255.255.0
```

NAT Pool and Related IP Routing Configuration

A single NAT pool is defined to cover the needs of all customers who are accessing the common server. The corresponding configuration commands are shown in Example 4-33.

Example 4-33 *NAT Pool Definition*

```
ip nat pool Common 172.16.0.0 172.16.3.255 netmask 255.255.252.0
```

An IP route that covers the NAT pool is defined in the CommonServer VRF to enable the routing of return packets from the common server toward the PE router with the commands in Example 4-34. You can announce this route to the common server through a PE-CE routing protocol, or you can use static or default routing on the common server.

Example 4-34 *IP Routing from the Common Server to the IP NAT Pool*

```
ip route vrf CommonServer 172.16.0.0 255.255.252.0 Null0
!
router rip
 version 2
!
 address-family ipv4 vrf CommonServer
 version 2
 redistribute static
 network 194.22.16.0
```

The IP route toward the NAT pool is propagated toward the common server (see Example 4-35); therefore, the NAT pool from which the translated return addresses will come is reachable from the common server.

Example 4-35 *IP Routing on the Common Server*

```
CommonServer#show ip route
Codes: C - connected, S - static, I - IGRP, R - RIP, B - BGP
       D - EIGRP, EX - EIGRP external, O - OSPF, IA - OSPF inter area
       N1 - OSPF NSSA external type 1, N2 - OSPF NSSA external type 2
       E1 - OSPF external type 1, E2 - OSPF external type 2, E - EGP
       * - candidate default, U - per-user static route, o - ODR
       P - periodic downloaded static route

Gateway of last resort is not set

     172.16.0.0 255.255.252.0 is subnetted, 1 subnets
R       172.16.0.0 [120/1] via 194.22.16.1, 00:00:01, FastEthernet0/0
C    194.22.16.0 255.255.255.0 is directly connected, FastEthernet0/0
```

NOTE   It is unnecessary to redistribute routes from the CommonServer VRF into Multiprotocol BGP. The CommonServer VRF is completely isolated from the rest of the MPLS VPN network (similar to the VRF-lite configuration discussed previously in this chapter).

Customer VRF Configuration

The current PE-NAT implementation works only inside a single VRF. Due to this requirement, you need to define a VRF on the Washington PE router for every customer who accesses the common server so that the NAT function will be performed inside the customer VRF.

The EuroBank VRF is already defined in the Washington PE router. You must create the FastFoods VRF, as shown in Example 4-36.

Example 4-36 *Customer VRF Definition*

```
ip vrf FastFoods
 rd 100:252
 route-target export 100:252
 route-target import 100:252
```

You must define a static route toward the common server in every customer VRF on the Washington PE router to ensure that (from the PE router's perspective) NAT will always be performed inside the customer VRF. You must redistribute this static route into Multiprotocol BGP and any relevant PE-CE routing protocol to enable connectivity from CE routers to the central server. Both configuration steps are illustrated in Example 4-37.

NOTE   No interfaces are placed in VRFs of customers who do not connect directly to the Washington PE router.

Example 4-37 *IP Routing from Customers to the Common Server*

```
ip route vrf EuroBank 194.22.16.0 255.255.255.0 FastEthernet3/0 194.22.16.2
ip route vrf FastFoods 194.22.16.0 255.255.255.0 FastEthernet3/0 194.22.16.2
!
router bgp 10
 address-family ipv4 vrf FastFoods
 redistribute static
!
 address-family ipv4 vrf EuroBank
 redistribute static
!
router rip
 address-family ipv4 vrf EuroBank
 redistribute static
```

After these configuration steps, the route toward the common server is inserted into the EuroBank and FastFoods VRFs on the Washington PE router (see Example 4-38). This route is propagated to other PE routers and to the CE routers (see Example 4-39). Therefore, the common server is reachable from all customer sites.

Example 4-38 *Route Toward the Common Server in the EuroBank and FastFood VRF on the Washington PE Router*

```
PE_Washington#sh ip route vrf EuroBank 194.22.16.0
Routing entry for 194.22.16.0 255.255.255.0
  Known via "static", distance 1, metric 0
  Redistributing via bgp 10
  Advertised by bgp 10
  Routing Descriptor Blocks:
  * 194.22.16.2, via FastEthernet3/0
      Route metric is 0, traffic share count is 1

PE_Washington#show ip route vrf FastFood 194.22.16.0
Routing entry for 194.22.16.0 255.255.255.0
  Known via "static", distance 1, metric 0
  Redistributing via bgp 10
  Advertised by bgp 10
  Routing Descriptor Blocks:
  * 194.22.16.2, via FastEthernet3/0
      Route metric is 0, traffic share count is 1
```

Example 4-39 *Route Toward the Common Server in the San Jose PE Router and Connected CE Routers*

```
PE_SanJose#show ip route vrf FastFood 194.22.16.0
Routing entry for 194.22.16.0/24
  Known via "bgp 10", distance 200, metric 0, type internal
  Redistributing via rip
  Advertised by rip metric transparent
  Last update from 194.22.15.3 00:06:42 ago
  Routing Descriptor Blocks:
  * 194.22.15.3 (Default-IP-Routing-Table), from 194.22.15.3
      Route metric is 0, traffic share count is 1
      AS Hops 0

SanJose#show ip route 194.22.16.0
Routing entry for 194.22.16.0 255.255.255.0
  Known via "rip", distance 120, metric 1
  Redistributing via rip
  Last update from 192.168.2.18 on Serial0.236, 00:00:19 ago
  Routing Descriptor Blocks:
  * 192.168.2.18, from 192.168.2.18, 00:00:19 ago, via Serial0.236
      Route metric is 1, traffic share count is 1

SanFrancisco#show ip route 194.22.16.0
Routing entry for 194.22.16.0/24
  Known via "rip", distance 120, metric 1
  Redistributing via rip
  Last update from 192.168.2.14 on Serial0.313, 00:00:03 ago
  Routing Descriptor Blocks:
  * 192.168.2.14, from 192.168.2.14, 00:00:03 ago, via Serial0.313
      Route metric is 1, traffic share count is 1
```

NAT Configuration on the Washington PE Router

With the IP routing in place, NAT is configured with the following steps:

- The interface that connects the common server to the Washington PE router is configured as an outside NAT interface with the commands in Example 4-40.

Example 4-40 *Outside NAT Interface Configuration*

```
interface FastEthernet3/0
 ip nat outside
```

- A single route map is defined to match packets that are exchanged between the customers and the common server. A sample route map configuration is shown in Example 4-41.

Example 4-41 *Route Map and Access List Used in NAT Definitions*

```
ip access-list extended CommonNAT
 permit ip any 194.22.16.0 0.0.0.255
!
route-map CommonNAT permit 10
 match ip address CommonNAT
```

NOTE Performing NAT based on a route map is strongly advised in complex NAT scenarios because Cisco IOS creates extended translation entries when a route map is used with the **ip nat** command.

- The interfaces that connect CE routers to the Washington PE router are configured as inside NAT interfaces with the **ip nat inside** command, as shown in Example 4-42.

Example 4-42 *Interfaces Toward CE Routers Are Configured as NAT Inside Interfaces*

```
interface Serial6/3.312 point-to-point
 description *** Link to EuroBank Washington ***
 ip nat inside
```

- Inside source NAT translation is configured for the EuroBank and FastFoods VRF with commands shown in Example 4-43.

Example 4-43 *Per-VRF Inside Source IP Address Translation Definition*

```
ip nat inside source route-map CommonNAT pool Common vrf EuroBank
ip nat inside source route-map CommonNAT pool Common vrf FastFoods
```

After these configuration steps, PE-NAT is fully operational, *but only for customer sites that are attached directly to the Washington PE router.* For example, the Washington CE router can access the common server, but the San Francisco CE router cannot because the packets sent from it toward the common server are not forwarded from an inside NAT interface to an outside NAT interface from the perspective of the Washington PE router. To enable NAT functionality for remote sites, you must define all the core interfaces (interfaces that link PE routers with P routers and other PE routers) as inside interfaces, which is shown in Example 4-44.

Example 4-44 *Interfaces Toward Network Core Are Configured as NAT Inside Interfaces*

```
interface Serial6/0
  description *** Link to PE_SanJose ***
  ip nat inside
```

Testing the proper PE-NAT configuration is simple; a Telnet session is opened from a CE router toward the common server, and the NAT translation entries are examined on the PE router. Example 4-45 shows two translation entries: one for the Washington CE router in the EuroBank VRF and the other one for the San Jose CE router in the FastFoods VRF. Opening a few Telnet sessions from CE routers to the common server results in NAT translations shown in Example 4-45.

Example 4-45 *NAT Translations on the PE Router*

```
PE_Washington#show ip nat translations verbose
Pro Inside global     Inside local     Outside local     Outside global
tcp 172.16.0.1:11007   192.168.2.17:11007 194.22.16.2:23     194.22.16.2:23
    create 00:00:24, use 00:00:24, left 23:59:35, Map-Id(In): 4,
    flags:
extended, use_count: 0, VRF : FastFood
tcp 172.16.0.2:11012   192.168.2.33:11012 194.22.16.2:23     194.22.16.2:23
    create 00:00:08, use 00:00:08, left 23:59:51, Map-Id(In): 5,
    flags:
extended, use_count: 0, VRF : EuroBank
```

Using PE-NAT for Shared Firewalls

You can use NAT functionality that is similar to the one deployed in the previous scenario to give MPLS VPN customers who have private IP addresses access to the Internet through a shared PE-NAT device. The corresponding topology of the SuperCom network is shown in Figure 4-24.

In this setup, the Washington PE router is directly connected to an Internet gateway router through a LAN connection. Internet access that is implemented through packet leaking between VRFs and global IP routing (described in more detail in Chapter 13, "Advanced MPLS/VPN Topics" of the *MPLS and VPN Architecture* (Volume I) book will be used in this scenario.

Figure 4-24 *Internet Access with Shared PE-NAT*

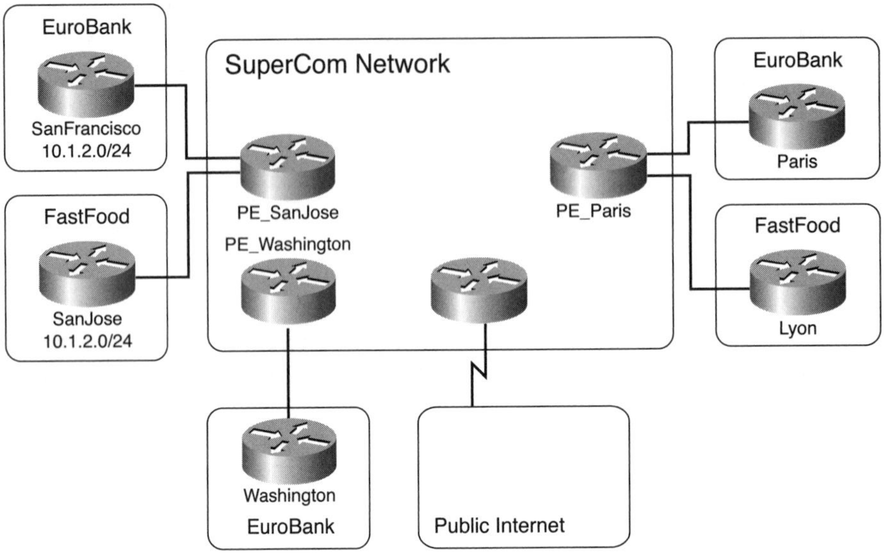

NOTE In this particular setup, it would be even simpler to use an Internet-in-a-VPN approach and employ the same design that was used for common server access in the previous section. The only difference in the configuration would be that the per-VRF static route toward the common server (as configured in the previous section) would be replaced by a per-VRF default route.

The design used to implement PE-NAT between a VRF and the global IP routing table is similar to the inter-VRF design and has the same limitations of PE-NAT. (NAT is only performed inside a single VRF.)

Step 1 The interface toward the Internet gateway is placed in the global IP routing table, as shown in Example 4-46.

Example 4-46 *Internet Gateway Interface Configuration*

```
interface FastEthernet3/0
 ip address 194.22.16.1 255.255.255.0
```

Step 2   A single NAT pool is defined with the command in Example 4-47 to cover the needs of all customers who are accessing the Internet. A subset of the subnet defined on the Washington PE router, the Internet gateway link is used to simplify IP routing.

Example 4-47 *NAT Pool Definition*

```
ip nat pool Common 194.22.16.16 194.22.16.31 netmask 255.255.255.240
```

Step 3   A global IP route covering the NAT pool is defined with the command in Example 4-48 to ensure that the Washington PE router will perform proxy-ARP when the Internet gateway forwards return traffic toward IP addresses in the NAT pool.

Example 4-48 *Global IP Routing to IP NAT Pool*

```
ip route 194.22.16.16 255.255.255.240 Null0
```

Step 4   A VRF is defined for every customer who accesses the common server. (The EuroBank VRF is already defined in the Washington PE router, but the FastFood VRF must be created, as shown in Example 4-49.)

Example 4-49 *Customer VRF Definition*

```
ip vrf FastFood
 rd 100:252
 route-target export 100:252
 route-target import 100:252
```

Step 5   A default route with the Internet gateway as the global next-hop is defined in every customer VRF on the Washington PE router to ensure that (from the PE router's perspective) NAT will be performed inside a single VRF. This default route must be redistributed into Multiprotocol BGP and any relevant PE-CE routing protocol, as shown in Example 4-50.

Example 4-50 *Default IP Routing from Customers to the Internet Gateway*

```
ip route vrf EuroBank 0.0.0.0 0.0.0.0 194.22.16.2 global
ip route vrf FastFood 0.0.0.0 0.0.0.0 194.22.16.2 global
!
router bgp 10
 address-family ipv4 vrf FastFood
 redistribute static
 default-information originate
!
 address-family ipv4 vrf EuroBank
 redistribute static
 default-information originate
!
router rip
 address-family ipv4 vrf EuroBank
 redistribute static
```

After these configuration steps have been completed, the default IP route toward the Internet gateway is inserted into the EuroBank and FastFood VRFs on the Washington PE router (see Example 4-51). This route is propagated to other PE routers and to the CE routers (see Example 4-52 and Example 4-53). Therefore, the Internet gateway is reachable from all customer sites.

Example 4-51 *Default Route in the EuroBank VRF on the Washington PE Router*

```
PE_Washington#show ip route vrf EuroBank 0.0.0.0
Routing entry for 0.0.0.0 0.0.0.0, supernet
  Known via "static", distance 1, metric 0, candidate default path
  Redistributing via rip, bgp 10
  Advertised by rip
               bgp 10
  Routing Descriptor Blocks:
  * 194.22.16.2 (Default-IP-Routing-Table)
      Route metric is 0, traffic share count is 1
```

Example 4-52 *Default Route in the EuroBank VRF in the San Jose PE Router*

```
PE_SanJose#show ip route vrf EuroBank 0.0.0.0
Routing entry for 0.0.0.0 0.0.0.0, supernet
  Known via "bgp 10", distance 200, metric 0, candidate default path, type internal
  Redistributing via rip
  Advertised by rip metric transparent
  Last update from 194.22.15.3 00:54:22 ago
  Routing Descriptor Blocks:
  * 194.22.15.3 (Default-IP-Routing-Table), from 194.22.15.3
      Route metric is 0, traffic share count is 1
      AS Hops 0
```

Example 4-53 *Default Route in the San Francisco Router*

```
SanFrancisco#show ip route 0.0.0.0
Routing entry for 0.0.0.0/0, supernet
  Known via "rip", distance 120, metric 1, candidate default path
  Redistributing via rip
  Last update from 192.168.2.14 on Serial0.313, 00:00:27 ago
  Routing Descriptor Blocks:
  * 192.168.2.14, from 192.168.2.14, 00:00:27 ago, via Serial0.313
      Route metric is 1, traffic share count is 1
```

You do not need to propagate an IP route toward the NAT pool to the Internet gateway because the addresses in the NAT pool belong to a subnet that is directly connected to the Internet gateway. The Internet gateway relies on the Washington PE router to perform proxy-ARP.

With IP routing in place, NAT is configured with the following steps:

Step 1   The interface that connects the common server to the Washington
PE router is configured as an outside NAT interface with commands from
Example 4-54. The interfaces that connect CE routers to the Washington PE
router as well as core interfaces are configured as inside NAT interfaces.

Example 4-54 *NAT Interface Assignments*

```
interface FastEthernet3/0
 description *** Link toward Internet gateway ***
 ip nat outside
!
interface Serial6/0
 description *** Link to PE_SanJose ***
 ip nat inside
!
interface Serial6/3.312 point-to-point
 description *** Link to EuroBank Washington ***
 ip nat inside
```

Step 2   A single **route-map** is defined to match all packets that are exchanged
between the customers and the Internet gateway with the command in
Example 4-55.

Example 4-55 *Route Map and Access List Used in NAT Definitions*

```
route-map CommonNAT permit 10
```

Step 3   Inside source overload NAT translation is configured for the EuroBank
and FastFood VRFs with the commands in Example 4-56.

Example 4-56 *Per-VRF Inside Source IP Address Translation Definition*

```
ip nat inside source route-map CommonNAT pool Common vrf EuroBank overload
ip nat inside source route-map CommonNAT pool Common vrf FastFood overload
```

Similarly to the previous scenario, testing the proper PE-NAT configuration is simple: A Telnet
session is opened from a CE router toward an Internet destination, and the NAT translation
entries are examined on the PE router. Example 4-57 shows several translation entries from
different VRFs, all of them using the same global IP address from the common NAT pool.

Example 4-57 *NAT Translations on the PE Router*

```
PE_Washington#show ip nat translations verbose
Pro Inside global      Inside local      Outside local      Outside global
tcp 194.22.16.17:11008 192.168.2.17:11008 15.0.0.1:23        15.0.0.1:23
    create 00:00:34, use 00:00:34, left 23:59:25, Map-Id(In): 4,
    flags:
extended, timing-out, use_count: 0, VRF : FastFood
tcp 194.22.16.17:11009 192.168.2.17:11009 15.0.0.1:23        15.0.0.1:23
```

continues

Example 4-57 *NAT Translations on the PE Router (Continued)*

```
        create 00:00:32, use 00:00:06, left 23:59:53, Map-Id(In): 4,
        flags:
  extended, use_count: 0, VRF : FastFood
  tcp 194.22.16.17:11269 192.168.2.33:11269 15.0.0.1:23       15.0.0.1:23
        create 00:00:09, use 00:00:09, left 23:59:50, Map-Id(In): 6,
        flags:
  extended, use_count: 0, VRF : EuroBank
```

Summary

This chapter discussed how MPLS VPN technology can help you design sophisticated networks without deploying the full MPLS VPN functionality. You can use multiple routing tables in a single CE router to separate multiple co-located VPNs without deploying an on-site PE router.

These routing tables behave almost as independent routers and have to be linked with a PE router through independent physical or logical interfaces. The independent logical interfaces are simplest to create on physical media that support subinterfaces (Frame Relay, ATM, or switched Ethernet). If, however, you cannot use one of these physical media, you can still implement logical interfaces with GRE tunnels, although tunnels will make your network more complex and slightly less secure because the CE router must have access to the global IP routing table of the adjacent PE router. In the access layer (such as LAN interfaces of the CE routers), you can also use the VRF selection based on source IP address if the access layer technology does not permit you to separate the VPN users into virtual groups (such as virtual LANs).

Another functionality that is closely related to MPLS VPN is the ability to perform VRF-aware NAT. This functionality, usually deployed in a PE router, gives the service providers scalable means of implementing centralized controlled NAT solutions in scenarios where they previously had to potentially deploy distributed NAT on every CE router.

The VRF-aware NAT functionality is usually deployed on a PE router, although it would be completely feasible to use the identical functionality in a multi-VRF CE router to implement multiple independent NAT instances in the same physical device.

PART III

Advanced Deployment Scenarios

CHAPTER 5

Protecting the MPLS-VPN Backbone

When the subject of security in a Multiprotocol Label Switching (MPLS) virtual private network (VPN) backbone is discussed, comparisons are inevitably made with VPNs that are delivered via Frame Relay or Asynchronous Transfer Mode (ATM) services. This most likely stems from the fact that before the existence of MPLS VPN technology, VPNs were delivered by using Layer 2 point-to-point connections such as ATM or Frame Relay permanent virtual circuits (PVCs). In the case of pre-MPLS Layer 3 service provider networks, generic routing encapsulation (GRE) or IP Security (IPSec) tunnels were the VPN provisioning mechanism. In any event, the primary responsibility of the service provider was to provide an end-to-end connection as a conduit through their core network; Layer 3 customer information was transported transparently. The service provider did not participate or have visibility of the customer network.

In contrast, an MPLS VPN service provider maintains instances of the customer's routing table in each PE router to which a customer site is connected and consequently has visibility of the customer network topology. Any customer who is migrating a site from a Layer 2 ATM/Frame Relay-provisioned network to an MPLS VPN would naturally expect to receive the same or a better level of security that he had previously received; therefore, a comparison of MPLS VPNs versus Layer 2 services would be warranted.

An independent study on this subject by Miercom, a third-party testing facility in Princeton Junction, New Jersey, concluded that MPLS VPN networks "met or exceeded all of the security characteristics of a comparable Layer 2-based VPN such as Frame Relay or ATM." The study tested various security aspects of an MPLS VPN network against the comparable features in an ATM and Frame Relay network. The basic security items compared were as follows:

- Address and routing separation in the MPLS VPN architecture is equivalent to Layer 2 models.

- An MPLS VPN service provider core network is invisible to a customer network, as is a customer network to the core network.

- An MPLS VPN network is as resistant to Denial of Service (DoS) attacks as a Layer 2 network.

The inherent security capabilities of an MPLS VPN that provide a favorable comparison to Layer 2 networks are discussed in the following sections.

<table>
<tr><td>NOTE</td><td>Readers who want to do further reading on Frame Relay/ATM security comparisons to MPLS VPNs can obtain the Miercom report from www.miercom.com. A Cisco whitepaper entitled "Security of the MPLS Architecture" is also highly recommended and can be obtained from http://cisco.com/warp/public/cc/pd/iosw/prodlit/mxinf_ds.htm. Similar information on MPLS VPN security can also be found in draft-behringer-mpls-security.</td></tr>
</table>

This chapter does not attempt to make comparisons to Layer 2-based services but instead focuses on the security capabilities available in the MPLS VPN architecture and provides practical examples and steps that a service provider can take to increase the security of an MPLS VPN backbone and any attached VPN sites.

<table>
<tr><td>NOTE</td><td>This chapter does not deal with the aspects of securing an individual Cisco router. Readers who want to learn more about securing Cisco routers are recommended to download the "Securing a Cisco Router" whitepaper from http://www.cisco.com/warp/public/707/21.pdf</td></tr>
</table>

Inherent Security Capabilities

An MPLS VPN service offering allows a service provider to utilize its Layer 3 backbone to provide a common infrastructure that customers can share, supporting the paradigm of "Build Once and Sell Many." To facilitate such a service, the service provider must rely on the inherent security capabilities that were built into MPLS from day one of its inception. These capabilities have been previously explained in Volume 1 of *MPLS and VPN Architectures*; however, it is appropriate to revisit some of them so that we can evaluate MPLS from a security perspective. These inherent security capabilities can be categorized as follows:

- Address space and routing separation
- No visibility of the core network
- Resistance to label spoofing

Address Space Separation

Those familiar with the MPLS architecture will know that the address space separation is one of the basic capabilities afforded by an MPLS VPN. The address space of different VPNs, each possibly consisting of many customer sites, is entirely independent. All customers who are connected to an MPLS VPN network can use the whole range of IP addresses—either public or private IP addresses as defined by RFC 1918—and successfully operate their Intranet VPNs, without interference from other VPNs or traffic in the core network. The core addressing range is also separated from each customer address space, allowing the service provider to build its core, if necessary, from the RFC 1918 address range.

Address separation is achieved through the use of different virtual routing/forwarding (VRF) instances on the PE router for each customer or group of customer sites connected to that PE router. Each VRF is populated with routes from either the CE router or other VRFs within the network. Routes from CE routers are learned through static routing or dynamic routing protocols, which are VRF context aware. Therefore, the routing protocol will update routes only within that VRF instance. Routes from other VRFs (located on local or remote provider edge, or PE, routers) are obtained via Multiprotocol Border Gateway Protocol (BGP). The decision of which routes to import, which in turn forms the VPN (intranet or extranet), is determined by the route targets (BGP extended community attributes) that are associated with that VRF.

Multiprotocol BGP is not VPN aware; its primary function in an MPLS VPN backbone is to distribute customer routes between PE routers. The standard BGP path selection applies when selecting the best route, regardless of whether it is an Internet route or a VPN route. Therefore, to ensure uniqueness of customer routes carried across the backbone, a 64-bit route distinguisher is prepended to all VPN routes, forming a VPNv4 address. The route distinguisher guarantees address separation when VPN routes are carried across the core.

The circuit addresses that are used between a PE router and a CE router are a potential area where overlapping addressing can occur. This is possible when the service provider is assigning circuit addresses from an RFC 1918 block to a customer who is also using an address block from RFC 1918 for his private network. The issue here is that if the service provider is tasked with assigning circuit addresses from RFC 1918, the address assignment policy used might not necessarily be compatible with the address assignment policy that the customer is using to allocate private addresses for his subnets. In this case, overlapping addresses could occur. This problem can be avoided by either allowing the customer to assign circuit addresses or having the service provider assign circuit addresses out of a registered address pool. The problem with allowing the customer to assign addresses is that PE-CE circuit addresses between customer VRFs might not be unique. Therefore, if the service provider were providing management of the PE-CE circuits, an overlap of addresses could occur in the management VRF. The use of registered addresses by the service provider might not be practical for those providers who do not have a large enough block available.

NOTE   The IP address assignment of the PE-CE circuits and the problems that have been discussed are described in detail in draft-guichard-PE-CE-addr, which you can find at http://www.ietf.org/internet-drafts/. This draft proposes a solution to assist service providers with their address assignment by allocating a unique private address range for exclusive use by MPLS VPN providers with no possibility of overlap with RFC 1918 customer networks.

Although the MPLS VPN architecture provides address separation, it does not intrinsically guarantee that the routes the CE router or a remote VRF inject into the VRF are valid. A bogus CE router could be introduced that injects spoofed routes, or a configuration error by the service provider could introduce routes into the VRF that are not part of that VPN, compromising security. However, you can take various steps to mitigate or minimize the possibility of such breaches. These precautions are discussed in the following sections. The next sections also discuss several Internet Engineering Task Force (IETF) drafts that address the area of CE-to-CE authentication in an effort to eliminate security problems due to service provider configuration errors.

No Visibility of the Core Network

Unless specifically configured by the service provider, the core network infrastructure including addressing and topology is not visible to a customer VPN. Likewise, the customer VPN information is not necessarily visible to the core network. This is because Multiprotocol BGP transfers VPN information between PE routers, and labels perform the forwarding function in the core of the network. Customer VPN routes that originate from another PE router across the core network will be associated with the BGP next-hop address of the originating PE router. The BGP next-hop address of the PE router is not visible or reachable in the customer address space, even though it is the BGP next-hop address that is used to forward customer VPN traffic in the network core.

To illustrate this point, we will use the SuperCom network shown in Figure 5-1 and examine the VPN routes in the FastFoods network contained in the San Jose PE router.

Figure 5-1   *SuperCom Network*

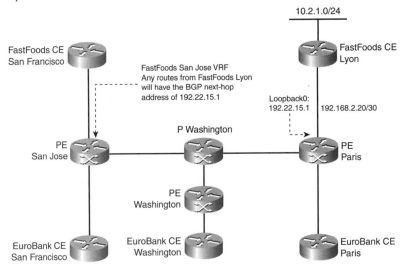

The FastFoods VRF in the San Jose PE router has several VPN routing entries, as shown in Example 5-1. Some of these entries originated from the FastFoods Lyon site (10.2.1.0/24, 192.168.2.20/30) that is connected to the Paris PE router. Therefore, all routes from FastFoods Lyon will have the BGP next-hop address of 194.22.15.1, which is the Paris PE router in the SuperCom network.

Example 5-1   *Inability to Access BGP Next-Hop PE Router from a VRF*

```
SanJose_PE#show ip route vrf FastFoods
[snip]
     10.0.0.0/24 is subnetted, 1 subnets
B       10.2.1.0 [200/0] via 194.22.15.1, 02:00:02
S     195.12.2.0/24 [1/0] via 192.168.2.17
     192.168.2.0/30 is subnetted, 2 subnets
C       192.168.2.16 is directly connected, Serial5/0
B       192.168.2.20 [200/0] via 194.22.15.1, 01:59:47
SanJose_PE#ping vrf FastFoods 194.22.15.1

Type escape sequence to abort.
Sending 5, 100-byte ICMP Echos to 192.22.15.1, timeout is 2 seconds:
.....
Success rate is 0 percent (0/5)
```

A ping of the address 194.22.15.1 in Example 5-1 shows that is not reachable from the FastFoods VRF even though it appears as the BGP next-hop in the FastFoods routing table on the PE router.

When a customer VPN packet is sent to its destination VRF, the MPLS label associated with the PE router BGP next-hop is used to forward the packet in the core network. After labels have been distributed for routes in the core (we can selectively choose which routes get a label), the P and PE routers can begin to forward datagrams based on attached MPLS labels only. The routers in the P-network only need to know the egress interface and outgoing label for the incoming labelled packet to allow forwarding. No visibility is required of customer routes or even the customer VPN label that is hidden further in the label stack. Therefore, in its simplest form, the core network only really needs to know about the PE router BGP addresses in its Interior Gateway Protocol (IGP) to forward customer VPN datagrams.

Although the core addressing is not visible to the customer network, the same cannot be guaranteed for the subnet used for PE-CE circuit addressing. Visibility of PE router circuit information might allow the C-network to intrude or perform DoS attacks on the PE router. Using unnumbered interfaces on the PE-CE circuit might initially provide a simple deterrent by hiding the address used at the PE end, but you could easily discover this by using **traceroute**. In the case of a managed CE router service, where the customer does not have access to the CE router, the PE-CE circuit address could be filtered to prevent it from being redistributed into the customer network. In addition, various inbound filters can be applied at the PE router to restrict CE router access. The various techniques available are explained in a later section.

One method of potentially revealing addresses in the core topology from a VPN is through the use of the **traceroute** command. The information that is passed back by **traceroute** is read-only. Therefore, even though circuit addresses on core routers are visible, there is no way to reach those routers from a VPN. Addresses in the core network can be hidden from view in a VPN by configuring the **no mpls ip propagate-ttl forwarded** command on the PE router. When a **traceroute** is issued from a VRF with this command enabled, no core addresses are returned; however, the address of the egress PE-circuit that is connected to the CE router *is* visible. The **no mpls ip propagate-ttl forwarded** command is discussed in detail in Chapter 13 of Volume 1 of *MPLS and VPN Architectures*.

Resistance to Label Spoofing

In MPLS VPN operation, labels are allocated to an IP route by the downstream router (the next-hop router in the direction of the destination). *Label spoofing* is the ability of the upstream router to replace or insert a label into a packet that was not originally allocated by the downstream router. Therefore, if the downstream router were allowed to receive a tampered packet, it would either send it to an incorrect destination or drop it if there were no corresponding output label. Although it is possible to spoof a destination or source IP address in an IP network, label spoofing is not possible in an MPLS network.

A Cisco router does not accept labeled packets on an interface that is not enabled for label switching. Label switching should not be enabled on the PE router interface that leads to the CE router (unless the Carrier Supporting Carrier service is used); therefore, any labeled packets that arrive at a PE router from a CE router are dropped. In this case, label spoofing is not possible. The CE router can spoof the source or destination IP address before the packet gets to the PE router, but this would only affect the customer's own VPN due to the address separation capability of MPLS VPN. In essence, the customers would be spoofing themselves.

Label spoofing might be possible in the P-network if an unauthorized P router is somehow attached. However, by using the LDP protocol for label distribution in combination with message digest 5 (MD5) authentication, the possibility of this scenario will be substantially mitigated. MD5 authentication is explained later in the section titled "Neighbor Authentication."

Carrier Supporting Carrier

Labels are accepted from a CE router in the case of Carrier Supporting Carrier (CsC). The CsC architecture is detailed in Chapter 6, "Large-Scale Routing and Multiple Service Provider Connectivity." In this case, the CE router imposes labels for IGP routes in the customer carrier VPN; therefore, you might think it would be possible to spoof labels. However, there are several security mechanisms in the PE router that prevent this from occurring:

- The PE router controls which labels the CsC CE router uses for any routes it learns from remote PE routers.

- The PE router keeps track of which label bindings have been advertised to which interface.

- When a packet is received from a CsC CE router, the label is examined and verified that it has one of the values assigned to routes in the same VRF as the interface. If it is not, then the packet is dropped.

Assume in Figure 5-2 that CsC is enabled between the Paris PE router and the EuroBank Paris CE router. The Paris PE router has advertised the VRF route 196.7.26.0/24 to the EuroBank CE router along with the associated label 27. The value of this label binding is confirmed in the two **show** commands in Example 5-2. The first command shows the label binding for the prefix, whereas the second command shows the label forwarding entry (LFIB) that will be used. Notice that the forwarding entry also has an identifier "VPN Route" indicating that label 27 is allocated within the EuroBank VRF.

When the Paris PE router receives a packet from EuroBank with label 27, the VPN route identifier in the LFIB is compared to the VRF (if any) that is defined on the incoming interface. If they do not match, the packet is dropped; otherwise, the packet is forwarded.

Figure 5-2 *Prevention of Label Spoofing in CsC*

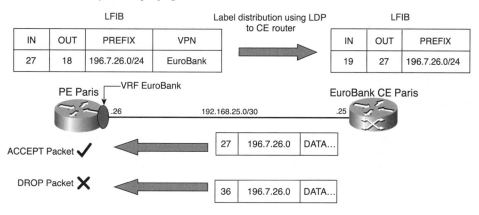

Example 5-2 *Label Binding*

```
Paris_PE#show mpls ldp binding vrf EuroBank 196.7.26.0 255.255.255.0 detail
  196.7.26.0/24, rev 15
        local binding:  label: 27
          Advertised to:
          192.168.2.25:0
        remote binding: lsr: 192.168.2.25:0, label: 19

Paris_PE#show mpls forwarding label 27 detail
Local  Outgoing     Prefix                Bytes tag  Outgoing   Next Hop
```

continues

Example 5-2 *Label Binding (Continued)*

```
tag    tag or VC    or Tunnel Id         switched    interface
27     18           196.7.26.0/24[V]  0             Se4/0       point2point
       MAC/Encaps=4/12, MRU=1496, Tag Stack{18 22}
       0F008847 0001200000016000
       VPN route: EuroBank
       No output feature configured
     Per-packet load-sharing
```

Static Labels

Static labels is a new feature available from Cisco IOS 12.0(23)S onward. This feature allows static bindings to be configured between labels and IPv4 prefixes and also allows the provisioning of static cross-connects in the midpoint of a label-switched path (LSP). The feature is primarily designed to permit connection to neighbor routers that do not support LDP or RSVP but do support MPLS forwarding.

If static labels were enabled on a CE router in a CsC environment, then it would be possible for the labels provided by the PE router to be changed at the CE router. However, as discussed in the previous section, any packets that arrive with an incorrect label are dropped due to the antilabel spoofing capabilities. In addition, Cisco IOS does not allow a label for a prefix to be modified by using static commands if an LDP peer has previously provided a label.

Example 5-3 shows an attempt to change the outgoing label for prefix 196.7.26.0/24 to use 77. Because the Paris PE router has already provided label 27 as the outgoing label, it will take precedence over the static binding.

Example 5-3 *Static Binding Command*

```
EuroBank_Paris#show mpls forwarding
Local  Outgoing    Prefix              Bytes tag  Outgoing     Next Hop
tag    tag or VC   or Tunnel Id        switched   interface
17     23          10.2.1.0/24         0          Et1/0        192.168.2.26
18     24          192.168.2.12/30     0          Et1/0        192.168.2.26
19     26          192.168.2.32/30     0          Et1/0        192.168.2.26
20     27          196.7.26.0/24       0          Et1/0        192.168.2.26

EuroBank_Paris(config)#mpls static binding ipv4 196.7.26.0 255.255.255.0 output
192.168.2.26 77
% Warning: Next hop 192.168.2.26 is an TDP/LDP peer (192.168.2.26:0)
% Label learned from peer, if any, takes precedence
% Continuing with configuration of the label
```

Neighbor Authentication

Many points of vulnerability in an MPLS VPN network can be minimized through the use of neighbor authentication. This type of authentication prevents a router from receiving fraudulent updates from a routing neighbor and can also be used to verify updates it receives from a label distribution peer.

If routing protocol authentication is not enabled between neighbors, then security of the network could be compromised by the introduction of bogus routes. An unauthorised router could inject routes to divert traffic toward a monitoring point, where the data in the IP packets could be analyzed. Routes could also be introduced for no other reason than to disrupt the network and cause DoS.

In Cisco IOS, neighbor authentication can be enabled for BGP; Intermediate System-to-Intermediate System (IS-IS); Enhanced Interior Gateway Routing Protocol (EIGRP); Open Shortest Path First (OSPF); Routing Information Protocol, version 2 (RIPv2); and the Label Distribution Protocol (LDP).

NOTE   Neighbor authentication is not supported by using the Tag Distribution Protocol (TDP). Therefore, to enable the highest level of authentication in an MPLS VPN network, LDP must be used on the P/PE-network interfaces.

All the aforementioned protocols support authentication for the various neighbor combinations that can exist in an MPLS VPN network, as shown in Table 5-1.

Table 5-1   *Neighbor Combination and Authentication*

Neighbor	Authentication Required
PE to CE	Selected PE-CE routing protocol plus LDP if CsC is enabled. If BGP+labels is being used on CsC, then authentication is required only on the BGP session (no LDP required).
PE to PE	BGP authentication for the secure exchange of VPNv4 routes.
PE to P and P to P	Authentication for the backbone routing protocol (IGP) plus LDP

When neighbor authentication is enabled, the receiving router authenticates the source of routing updates by using a shared key that the source and the receiver know. You can use two types of authentication: plain text or message digest algorithm 5 (MD5). Plain text, as the name implies, sends the authenticating key as a clear text transmission over the circuit. MD5 does not send the key; instead, it creates a message digest by using the key and the message as a hash to MD5. The resulting message digest is then exchanged among neighbors, which ensures that the key cannot be learned through unauthorized monitoring.

NOTE   Service provider "best practice" is to use MD5 authentication; therefore, this type of authentication will be used in all the examples that follow.

PE to CE Authentication

This section provides an example of how to configure MD5 authentication on PE/CE circuits for dynamic routing protocols. Obviously, if routing on the PE/CE circuit is limited to static entries, then authentication will be superfluous because the service provider has control over the routes that are injected into the VRF table.

For our examples, we will use the usual SuperCom network, as shown in Figure 5-3. The FastFoods and EuroBank CE routers have been configured for dynamic routing to the SuperCom PE routers. EuroBank will use RIPv2 for its PE/CE routing protocol, and FastFoods has selected OSPF.

Figure 5-3 *PE/CE Routing in the SuperCom Network*

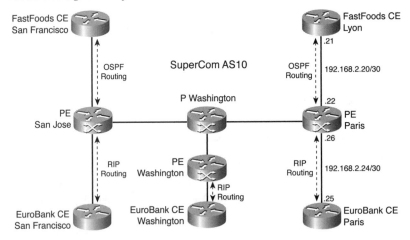

To provide a secure connection between the SuperCom network and the CE routers, MD5 authentication is enabled on the routing protocols that FastFoods and EuroBank use. The following sections describe the configurations that are necessary to enable neighbor routing authentication.

RIPv2 Authentication for EuroBank

Example 5-4 shows the PE router configuration to set up RIPv2 authentication to the EuroBank CE router.

Example 5-4 *Paris PE Router RIPv2 Authentication Configuration*

```
service password-encryption

interface Ethernet0/0
 ip vrf forwarding EuroBank
 ip address 192.168.2.26 255.255.255.252
 ip rip authentication mode md5
```

Example 5-4   *Paris PE Router RIPv2 Authentication Configuration (Continued)*

```
 ip rip authentication key-chain CE-Neighbor
 no cdp enable

router rip
 version 2
 !
 address-family ipv4 vrf EuroBank
 version 2
 redistribute bgp 100 metric 5
 network 192.168.2.0
 no auto-summary
 exit-address-family

key chain CE-Neighbor
 key 1
   key-string 7 000816120C5E19140631
```

The first item to be enabled is the **service password-encryption** command; this command ensures that the passwords are not readable in the routers' NVRAM configuration.

For the EuroBank circuit, MD5 authentication is enabled for RIPv2 by using two **ip rip authentication** interface commands. The first command configures MD5 authentication for the specified interface, whereas the second command specifies the key to be used via a key chain.

NOTE   A *key chain* is a sophisticated mechanism that RIPv2 (and EIGRP) uses to provide a key for MD5. A key chain allows a series of keys to be specified, which will be cycled through by the router. Each key within the key chain has a specific lifetime; when the lifetime expires, the next key in the chain is activated, if it is configured.

If key chains are used, both authentication neighbors need to be synchronized to the same time so that they are using the same keys at a particular time. The Network Time Protocol (NTP) is best suited for this purpose.

NOTE   For more complete information on key chains, refer to the "Managing Authentication Keys" section in the *Configuring IP Routing Protocol-Independent Features of the Cisco IOS IP Configuration Guide*, which can be found at www.cisco.com.

To simplify the configuration example, the **key chain CE-Neighbor** that is used for the EuroBank VPN does not use the lifetime feature; instead, it uses a permanent key. Example 5-5 shows the corresponding RIPv2 configuration for the EuroBank Paris CE router.

Example 5-5 *EuroBank Paris CE Router RIPv2 Authentication Configuration*

```
service password-encryption
 !
key chain PE-Neighbor
 key 1
   key-string 7 020A014F03031D33455E
 !
interface Ethernet1/0
 ip address 192.168.2.25 255.255.255.252
 ip rip authentication mode md5
 ip rip authentication key-chain PE-Neighbor
router rip
 version 2
 redistribute connected
 redistribute static
 network 192.168.2.0
```

OSPF Authentication for FastFoods

Example 5-6 shows the PE router configuration to set up OSPF authentication to the FastFoods CE router.

Example 5-6 *Paris PE Router OSPF Authentication Configuration*

```
interface Serial5/0
 ip vrf forwarding FastFoods
 ip address 192.168.2.22 255.255.255.252
 ip ospf message-digest-key 1 md5 7 00051F09104F0A140034584B1A
 no cdp enable

router ospf 200 vrf FastFoods
 log-adjacency-changes
 area 2 authentication message-digest
 redistribute connected subnets
 redistribute bgp 100 metric-type 1 subnets
 network 192.168.2.0 0.0.0.255 area 2
```

For the FastFoods circuit, MD5 is activated for an area using the **area** command under the OSPF process configuration. The value of the key and the message digest algorithm to be used are specified with the **ip ospf message-digest-key** interface command. Unlike the

RIPv2 protocol, OSPF does not support key chains. Example 5-7 shows the corresponding OSPF configuration for the FastFoods CE router.

Example 5-7   *FastFoods Lyon CE Router RIPv2 Authentication Configuration*

```
interface 4/0
 ip address 192.168.2.21 255.255.255.252
 ip ospf message-digest-key 1 md5 7 130912061818052620
 no fair-queue
!
router ospf 200
 router-id 192.168.2.21
 log-adjacency-changes
 area 2 authentication message-digest
 redistribute connected subnets
 redistribute static subnets
 network 192.168.2.0 0.0.0.255 area 2
```

NOTE   OSPF supports authentication on an interfaces basis; therefore, not all interfaces in an area configured with message-digest authentication require a key to be configured.

PE to PE Authentication

MD5 authentication can be enabled on the Multiprotocol BGP sessions between PE routers, as shown in Figure 5-4.

Figure 5-4   *BGP VPNv4 Sessions in the SuperCom Network*

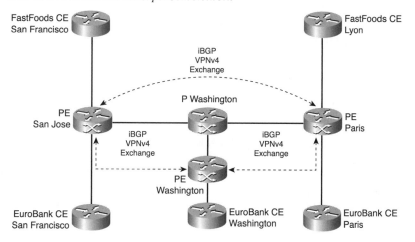

Example 5-8 shows the necessary configuration to activate BGP authentication for peers of the Paris PE router. Activation of MD5 authentication is performed in the global portion of the BGP process configuration. This means that both IPv4 and VPNv4 address families, if they are active, will have their routing updates authenticated between peers.

The configuration to activate BGP authentication is simple. It requires only the **neighbor password** command, which implicitly uses the MD5 algorithm to authenticate TCP sessions for a BGP neighbor. This configuration should be replicated on all other BGP PE router peers.

Example 5-8 *Paris PE Router BGP Authentication Configuration*

```
router bgp 10
 no synchronization
 no bgp default ipv4-unicast
 bgp log-neighbor-changes
 neighbor 194.22.15.2 remote-as 10
 neighbor 194.22.15.2 password 7 071A354D4202100B031D0609
 neighbor 194.22.15.2 update-source Loopback0
 neighbor 194.22.15.3 remote-as 10
 neighbor 194.22.15.2 password 7 071A354D4202100B031D0609
 neighbor 194.22.15.3 update-source Loopback0
 no auto-summary
```

NOTE   With many PE routers, route reflectors are most likely used for VPNv4 route exchange. In this case, the configuration for MD5 neighbor authentication is the same as shown in the previous example.

P-Network Authentication

Authentication in the P-network consists of ensuring that all IGP and LDP neighbors are configured with an MD5 authentication key.

IGP Authentication

The IGP used in all examples throughout this book for the SuperCom network is OSPF; therefore, the configuration that is applied is similar to that used for OSPF on the FastFoods PE/CE circuit. Example 5-9 shows the configuration for the Washington P router that interconnects all the other PE routers at San Jose, Paris, and Washington in the SuperCom network. The OSPF authentication configuration is similar for all other PE and P routers in the network.

Example 5-9   *Washington P Router OSPF Authentication Configuration*

```
service password-encryption

mpls label protocol ldp

router ospf 1
 router-id 194.22.15.4
 log-adjacency-changes
 area 0 authentication message-digest
 network 194.22.15.0 0.0.0.255 area 0

interface Serial4/0
 Description Link to San Jose PE-router
 ip address 194.22.15.18 255.255.255.252
 ip ospf message-digest-key 1 md5 7 12180918061F0D16253E302D20
 tag-switching ip
!
interface Serial5/0
 Description Link to Paris PE-router
 ip address 194.22.15.21 255.255.255.252
 ip ospf message-digest-key 1 md5 7 070E2D435A1D181718071F0917
  tag-switching ip
!
interface Serial6/0
 Description Link to Washington PE-router
 ip address 194.22.15.25 255.255.255.252
 ip ospf message-digest-key 1 md5 7 0607032E585A080B0A02060E1F
 tag-switching ip
```

LDP Authentication

In addition to the IGP authentication, all LDP sessions should be enabled for MD5 authentication. This includes CsC environments in which the PE router is providing the upstream CE router with labels for IGP routes in the VPN.

MD5 authentication is only supported with LDP. In environments that are using TDP globally, LDP can be enabled on a per-circuit basis if authentication is required. Once again, the configuration is straightforward, as Example 5-10 for the Washington P router shows.

Example 5-10   *Washington P Router LDP Authentication Configuration*

```
mpls ldp neighbor 194.22.15.2 password 7 0005110A014F040A0E234942
mpls ldp neighbor 194.22.15.1 password 7 11081B091206040005282E28
mpls ldp neighbor 194.22.15.3 password 7 15130900013E24282931302E
```

In the case of LDP sessions being used for CsC, the **vrf** keyword is added to the **mpls ldp neighbor** command on the PE router so that the LDP peering address of the CE router can be specified. Examples 5-11 and 5-12 show the necessary commands at the PE router and CE router to enable authentication when the EuroBank CE router is using the CsC feature.

Example 5-11 *PE Router LDP Authentication Configuration for CsC*

```
mpls ldp neighbor vrf EuroBank 192.168.2.25 password 7 104F0B1500031D070D062F27
```

Example 5-12 *EuroBank CE Router LDP Authentication Configuration for CsC*

```
mpls ldp neighbor 192.168.2.26 password 7 104F0B1500031D070D062F27
```

CE-to-CE Authentication

An area that is currently being addressed in the IETF is that of CE-to-CE authentication. When a CE router is connected to a PE router, mechanisms are available to ensure that the direct connection to the network is validated. These include PPP authentication and neighbor authentication using MD5. However, no mechanism is presently available to verify that the CE router and the customer network are indeed connected to the correct VPN in the MPLS network.

The basic premise is that the customer can expect to be connected to the correct VPN by the service provider, and that the customer's traffic will not be transported outside the VPN. Furthermore, it is assumed that unauthorized traffic will not be allowed into the customer's VPN. However, a security breach of the VPN is quite possible if there is an error in the VPN configuration. Because the service provider is responsible for the infrastructure providing the MPLS-VPN—which includes route distinguishers, route targets, VRF-to-interface allocations, and VPN route distribution—it is quite possible that an error in any of these areas could allow unauthorized parties access to the VPN, while the legitimate VPN customer is unaware of the security breach.

To avoid this problem, a process or mechanism is needed to detect accidental misconfigurations in the service provider network. Because the various solutions are still being proposed and debated, a CE-to-CE authentication feature has yet to be implemented for MPLS-VPN.

However, to provide a better understanding of the concept and the problem it is trying to solve, the solution proposed in draft-ietf-ppvpn-l3vpn-auth, which is available from http://www.ietf.org/internet-drafts, will be discussed. This draft proposes the use of a token that customer networks must hold to permit access to a VPN. The customer can hold more than one token to allow participation in overlapping VPNs or extranets.

Figure 5-5 shows each step in the operation of CE-to-CE authentication (also referred to as CE-to-CE member verification) using the token-based approach.

The CE-to-CE authentication process illustrated in Figure 5-5 can be divided into three components:

- Customer-to-PE signaling
- PE-to-PE signaling
- PE-to-Customer signaling

Figure 5-5   *CE-to-CE Authentication Using Tokens*

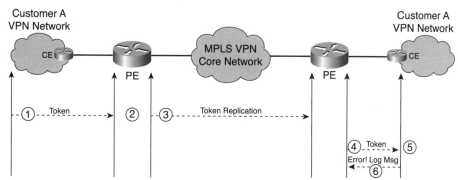

The steps required for each of these components are described as follows:

Step 1   Each customer VPN site originates and forwards one or more tokens toward the PE router to which it is connected. These tokens indicate membership of a particular VPN. Under normal circumstances, the tokens originate from a customer-managed device, which in most cases is the customer-owned CE router. When the CE-router is managed by the Service Provider, it is unlikely that the customer will allow the service provider to manage the tokens because it defeats the original intent of the authentication—that is, to avoid configuration mishaps by the service provider.

If a managed CE router service is being provided, then tokens can be originated from a customer-controlled device or router within the VPN site that is not the CE router. Tokens can be propagated to the PE router from the customer through BGP or a new UDP-based token propagation protocol.

If the routing protocol that is used on the PE/CE circuit is BGP, then the tokens can be transferred via the existing BGP session via a new extended community attribute.

If BGP routing is not enabled on the PE/CE circuit, then the UDP-based protocol will provide the token-forwarding function. Note that the BGP session or the VPN Token propagation protocol can originate from a router or device in the customer site behind the CE router.

If the customer site requires CE-to-CE based authentication, then the PE router will not advertise routes (to other PE routers) that originate from the customer site until a token has been received.

Step 2   When a token is received, the PE router advertises the destination routes originated by the CE router to all other PE routers by using the standard Multiprotocol BGP mechanism. In addition to the VPNv4 routes that are advertised, each Multiprotocol BGP update contains the associated token carried as a new extended community attribute called the *CE-to-CE Authentication Token*. (This is the same extended community attribute referred to in Step 1) Therefore, each route in the forwarding table is associated with a token. If Multiprotocol BGP is not being used to distribute routes between PE routers, then the VPN Token Propagation Protocol could have provided this function.

Step 3   When the remote PE router receives routes with a new token, either through Multiprotocol BGP or the VPN Token propagation protocol, it must relay the token to the attached CE router. However, the PE router must not pass a token to a CE router, if a token has not been previously received from that site. The token can be forwarded from the PE router to the customer network by using either BGP or the VPN Token propagation protocol.

Step 4   When the CE router receives the token, it authenticates against known tokens for particular VPNs it has configured.

Step 5   If the authentication fails, the CE issues an alarm requiring operator intervention. Optionally, it might withdraw from the VPN completely until the fault is rectified.

The advantage of the token-based approach to CE-to-CE authentication is that it provides the flexibility of supporting multiple overlapping VPNs for a customer. On the down side, this approach is incumbent upon the customer to perform additional configurations in his network, as well as maintain additional protocols—that is the VPN Token propagation protocol or BGP on the PE/CE circuit.

One of the advantages for a separate VPN token distribution protocol is that although it is easy to extend the BGP protocol to support the propagation of tokens, it is not necessarily easy to do so with other protocols used on the PE/CE circuit such as RIP, OSPF, ISIS, EIGRP, or static routing. A separate VPN token distribution protocol will allow a customer site to maintain its existing PE/CE routing protocol (assuming that BGP is not being used) in addition to enabling the CE-to-CE authentication feature.

Another draft that is currently in circulation is draft-behringer-mpls-vpn-auth, which is available from http://www.ietf.org/internet-drafts. This proposal needs no new protocols, no software upgrades at the CE routers, and no additional configuration in the customer network. It bases its solution on the premise that MD5 neighbor authentication (as discussed previously) should be run on PE/CE circuits. BGP UPDATE messages between PE routers will include a new BGP attribute, referred to as the "UPDATE authenticator."

The "UPDATE authenticator" attribute carries two entities: a generator value and a keyed HMAC MD5 signature of the generator value. The signature is obtained by running the

MD5 key used by the particular VPN whose routes are carried within the BGP update against the generator value.

On receipt of a BGP update that contains the UPDATE authenticator attribute, a receiving PE router can use its local copy of the VPNs MD5 key to generate a keyed HMAC MD5 signature of the generator value that is contained within the attribute. If the result is different from the value that is transmitted in the UPDATE authenticator attribute, the UPDATE is discarded and a warning is logged.

There are some constraints imposed by this proposal:

- Routing with MD5 authentication [RFC 2082, RFC 2154, RFC 2385] must be configured for all PE-CE links. Therefore, static routing is not possible for CE-CE authentication unless the VPN customer is willing to accept that the service provider will correctly configure its static routing information.

- The same key must be used for all CE routers in the same VPN. This causes some operational issues with extranets, where VPNs essentially overlap, although extranets can be supported either centrally or distributed by maintaining all VPN keys within a list at the PE routers.

- If the service provider manages the CE routers on behalf of the customer, then downstream C routers must use the same MD5 key as other sites within the same VPN. This is because the service provider might misconfigure either the PE or CE router; therefore, the VPN client must be able to authenticate on equipment that it manages.

Control of Routes That Are Injected into a VRF

An area that can cause DoS in an MPLS VPN network is an excessive number of routes being injected from the CE router to the VRF in the PE router, resulting in memory exhaustion and possible failure of the PE router. A VRF on a PE router can be populated with customer routes in several ways:

- Through direct configuration into the VRF of static routes that the service provider enters

- Through the use of a dynamic routing protocol between the CE router and the PE router

- Through Multiprotocol BGP for exchange of VPNv4 routes between PE routers (including intranet, extranet, and Internet VPNs)

The use of static routing provides the greatest security because the service provider controls the destinations and number of prefixes injected into the VRF. In contrast, a PE/CE routing protocol and Multiprotocol BGP are dynamic in nature; therefore, any number of routes could be injected or removed at any time. This poses a problem because the PE router could be flooded with updates from a local CE router or via Multiprotocol BGP from a remote CE router. Therefore, the PE router could be open to a DoS attack (an excessive number of

VRF routes might result in memory overflow, causing CEF to be disabled and MPLS VPN functionality to fail), either through malicious intent, a malfunctioning CE router, or a configuration error somewhere in the network that results in an excessive number of routes being injected into the VRF.

To address this problem, the number of routes that a VRF accepts can be limited by the **maximum routes** command under the VRF definition configuration, as shown in Example 5-13. The first parameter on the command is the limit of routes permitted within the VRF; any routes that exceed this number will be dropped, unless the **warning-only** keyword is used. The second parameter defines a percentage threshold, which, if exceeded, generates a warning message.

Example 5-13 *maximum routes Command*

```
ip vrf EuroBank
 rd 10:27
 route-target export 10:27
 route-target import 10:27
 maximum routes <maximum number of routes> <warning threshold % | warning-only>
```

To demonstrate the behavior of the **maximum routes** command, the PE/CE routing protocols used in the SuperCom network—which include RIPv2, eBGP, and OSPF—will be discussed in the following sections. The **maximum routes** command will be configured for each of these protocols, and then an excessive number of routes will be injected. As will be discussed, the behavior of the **maximum routes** command varies depending on which routing protocol is used.

Using RIPv2 as the PE/CE Routing Protocol

As an example, we will use the EuroBank VRF on the Paris PE router. As described previously, EuroBank uses RIPv2 to inject routes into its VRFs. Example 5-14 shows the EuroBank VRF in the steady state. Six routes are active in the EuroBank VRF. The first route is injected by the EuroBank CE router in Paris using RIPv2, the next four are injected by Multiprotocol BGP from remote PE routers indicated by the "B" at the beginning of each entry, and the last entry is the connected route for the PE/CE circuit.

Example 5-14 *Paris PE Router EuroBank VRF Routes*

```
Paris_PE#show ip route vrf EuroBank
[snip]
R    196.7.25.0/24 [120/1] via 192.168.2.25, 00:00:21, Ethernet0/0
B    196.7.26.0/24 [200/0] via 194.22.15.3, 00:18:21
     10.0.0.0/24 is subnetted, 1 subnets
B       10.2.1.0 [200/0] via 194.22.15.2, 00:18:21
     192.168.2.0/30 is subnetted, 3 subnets
B       192.168.2.32 [200/0] via 194.22.15.3, 00:18:21
B       192.168.2.12 [200/0] via 194.22.15.2, 00:18:21
C       192.168.2.24 is directly connected, Ethernet0/0
```

Inspecting the BGP VPNv4 table for the EuroBank VRF in Example 5-15, you can see that the routes correspond to those installed in the VRF.

Example 5-15 *Paris PE Router EuroBank VPNv4 Table*

```
Paris_PE#show ip bgp vpnv4 vrf EuroBank
[snip]
    Network              Next Hop          Metric LocPrf Weight Path
Route Distinguisher: 10:27 (default for vrf EuroBank)
  *>i10.2.1.0/24        194.22.15.2            0    100      0 ?
  *>i192.168.2.12/30    194.22.15.2            0    100      0 ?
  *> 192.168.2.24/30    0.0.0.0                0         32768 ?
  *>i192.168.2.32/30    194.22.15.3            0    100      0 ?
  *> 196.7.25.0         192.168.2.25           1         32768 ?
  *>i196.7.26.0         194.22.15.3            0    100      0 ?
```

To demonstrate the **maximum routes** command on the EuroBank VRF, we will apply a limit of **10** on the Paris PE router, as shown in Example 5-16. The **100** value is the percentage threshold at which to generate a log message. (Although 100% is used for purposes of this example, a smaller value would normally be configured to generate a syslog message before the limit was reached.) Any routes that are injected into the EuroBank VRF above the limit will be dropped. This behavior can be changed to logging a message only (and not dropping the route) by replacing the threshold value with the **warning-only** keyword.

Example 5-16 *Maximum Route Limit*

```
ip vrf EuroBank
 rd 10:27
 route-target export 10:27
 route-target import 10:27
 maximum routes 10 100
```

To check that the **maximum routes** command is working, the EuroBank Paris CE router has been configured to originate 10 additional prefixes from 192.168.20.0/24 through 192.168.29.0/24. Example 5-17 shows the warning message that is generated when the maximum route limit is exceeded.

Example 5-17 *Route Limit Warning*

```
%IPRT-3-ROUTELIMITEXCEEDED: IP routing table limit exceeded - EuroBank,
 192.168.24.0/24
```

Examining the EuroBank VRF and the associated entries in the BGP VPNv4 table as shown in Example 5-18, you see that there are indeed only 10 routes injected into the VRF and the VPNv4 table. Only four of the new routes were accepted: 192.168.20.0/24 through 192.168.23.0/24.

NOTE   The RIPv2 database on the Paris PE router only contains the routes that have been accepted in the VRF. Any routes that were dropped do not appear in the RIP database. This is contrary to the behavior of eBGP and OSPF, as will be discussed later in this section. With eBGP and OSPF, although a route might be dropped from a VRF, it still appears in the Multiprotocol BGP VPNv4 table or OSPF link-state database. This is an important point to note because an excessive number of routes can affect memory consumption with eBGP and OSPF.

Example 5-18 *Paris PE Router VRF and VPNv4 Table After Routes from EuroBank CE Router*

```
Paris_PE#show ip route vrf EuroBank
[snip]
R      196.7.25.0/24 [120/1] via 192.168.2.25, 00:00:13, Ethernet0/0
B      196.7.26.0/24 [200/0] via 194.22.15.3, 00:08:20
R      192.168.21.0/24 [120/1] via 192.168.2.25, 00:00:13, Ethernet0/0
R      192.168.20.0/24 [120/1] via 192.168.2.25, 00:00:13, Ethernet0/0
       10.0.0.0/24 is subnetted, 1 subnets
B         10.2.1.0 [200/0] via 194.22.15.2, 00:08:51
R      192.168.23.0/24 [120/1] via 192.168.2.25, 00:00:13, Ethernet0/0
R      192.168.22.0/24 [120/1] via 192.168.2.25, 00:00:13, Ethernet0/0
       192.168.2.0/30 is subnetted, 3 subnets
B         192.168.2.32 [200/0] via 194.22.15.3, 00:08:20
B         192.168.2.12 [200/0] via 194.22.15.2, 00:08:51
C         192.168.2.24 is directly connected, Ethernet0/0
Paris_PE#show ip bgp vpnv4 vrf EuroBank
[snip]
   Network          Next Hop          Metric LocPrf Weight Path
Route Distinguisher: 10:27 (default for vrf EuroBank)
*>i10.2.1.0/24      194.22.15.2            0    100      0 ?
*>i192.168.2.12/30  194.22.15.2            0    100      0 ?
*> 192.168.2.24/30  0.0.0.0                0          32768 ?
*>i192.168.2.32/30  194.22.15.3            0    100      0 ?
*> 192.168.20.0     192.168.2.25           1          32768 ?
*> 192.168.21.0     192.168.2.25           1          32768 ?
*> 192.168.22.0     192.168.2.25           1          32768 ?
*> 192.168.23.0     192.168.2.25           1          32768 ?
*> 196.7.25.0       192.168.2.25           1          32768 ?
*>i196.7.26.0       194.22.15.3            0    100      0 ?
```

The output in Example 5-19 confirms that the RIPv2 database contains the same routes as held in the VRF.

Example 5-19 *EuroBank VRF RIPv2 Database*

```
Paris_PE#show ip rip database vrf EuroBank
10.0.0.0/8      auto-summary
10.2.1.0/24     redistributed
    [5] via 194.22.15.2,
```

Example 5-19 *EuroBank VRF RIPv2 Database (Continued)*

```
192.168.2.0/24      auto-summary
192.168.2.12/30     redistributed
    [5] via 194.22.15.2,
192.168.2.24/30     directly connected, Ethernet0/0
192.168.2.32/30     redistributed
    [5] via 194.22.15.3,
192.168.20.0/24     auto-summary
192.168.20.0/24
    [1] via 192.168.2.25, 00:00:01, Ethernet0/0
192.168.21.0/24     auto-summary
192.168.21.0/24
    [1] via 192.168.2.25, 00:00:01, Ethernet0/0
192.168.22.0/24     auto-summary
192.168.22.0/24
    [1] via 192.168.2.25, 00:00:01, Ethernet0/0
192.168.23.0/24     auto-summary
192.168.23.0/24
    [1] via 192.168.2.25, 00:00:01, Ethernet0/0
196.7.25.0/24       auto-summary
196.7.25.0/24
    [1] via 192.168.2.25, 00:00:02, Ethernet0/0
196.7.26.0/24       auto-summary
196.7.26.0/24       redistributed
    [5] via 194.22.15.3,
```

Using Multiprotocol BGP to Exchange VPNv4 Routes

The output from the RIPv2 scenario shows that the route limit command is working as expected; however, we only configured a limit on the EuroBank VRF in Paris. If additional routes were injected by other EuroBank CE routers (or static routes added by the service provider), they would be received via Multiprotocol BGP at the Paris PE router.

To illustrate the effect of not applying the route limit on all PE routers that have VRFs for EuroBank, we have configured the San Jose CE router to originate another 10 routes: 192.168.30.0/24 through 192.168.39.0/24. An interesting thing happens. Although these additional routes from EuroBank San Jose are not installed in the Paris EuroBank VRF, they are retained in the BGP VPNv4 table for the EuroBank VRF. The output in Example 5-20 shows the current state of the BGP VPNv4 table at the Paris PE router. The additional routes were received from the San Jose PE router (next-hop of 194.22.15.2), but they all have an "r" flag associated with them, which indicates a routing information base (RIB) failure. Although these routes were received via Multiprotocol BGP and stored into the BGP table on the Paris PE router, they could not be installed into the VRF table due to the limit imposed by the **maximum routes** command.

Example 5-20 *Paris PE Router EuroBank VPNv4 Table with Routes from San Jose*

```
Paris_PE#show ip bgp vpnv4 vrf EuroBank
BGP table version is 153, local router ID is 194.22.15.1
Status codes: s suppressed, d damped, h history, * valid, > best, i - internal,
              r RIB-failure
Origin codes: i - IGP, e - EGP, ? - incomplete

   Network          Next Hop         Metric LocPrf Weight Path
Route Distinguisher: 10:27 (default for vrf EuroBank)
*>i10.2.1.0/24      194.22.15.2           0    100      0 ?
*>i192.168.2.12/30  194.22.15.2           0    100      0 ?
*> 192.168.2.24/30  0.0.0.0               0         32768 ?
*>i192.168.2.32/30  194.22.15.3           0    100      0 ?
*> 192.168.20.0     192.168.2.25          1         32768 ?
*> 192.168.21.0     192.168.2.25          1         32768 ?
*> 192.168.22.0     192.168.2.25          1         32768 ?
*> 192.168.23.0     192.168.2.25          1         32768 ?
r>i192.168.30.0     194.22.15.2           0    100      0 ?
r>i192.168.31.0     194.22.15.2           0    100      0 ?
r>i192.168.32.0     194.22.15.2           0    100      0 ?
r>i192.168.33.0     194.22.15.2           0    100      0 ?
r>i192.168.34.0     194.22.15.2           0    100      0 ?
r>i192.168.35.0     194.22.15.2           0    100      0 ?
r>i192.168.36.0     194.22.15.2           0    100      0 ?
r>i192.168.37.0     194.22.15.2           0    100      0 ?
r>i192.168.38.0     194.22.15.2           0    100      0 ?
r>i192.168.39.0     194.22.15.2           0    100      0 ?
*> 196.7.25.0       192.168.2.25          1         32768 ?
*>i196.7.26.0       194.22.15.3           0    100      0 ?
```

The end result is that even though the EuroBank CE router is prevented from accidentally or maliciously flooding the Paris PE router with routes, a DoS could still occur on the PE router by exhausting the memory in the Multiprotocol BGP VPNv4 table with routes that are accepted from other PE routers.

To avoid this situation, apply the **maximum routes** command to all VRFs. Give some consideration to the value of the limit imposed; if the value is too low, valid routes will be rejected, causing a DoS for some customer routes. Also note that the **maximum routes** value must cater for all types of routes that are injected into the VRF, which includes statics, connected, and routes learned dynamically.

Applying a consistent value for the **maximum routes** to all VRFs prevents Multiprotocol BGP from distributing VPNv4 routes that are accepted in one part of the network but not another.

NOTE	The **maximum routes** command is not selective on which routes it drops; it essentially drops them on a last-in, first-dropped basis. This is not really a problem because the main function of this command is to avoid memory overflow in the PE router due to routing instability in the customer network. It is the service provider's responsibility to monitor system logs and rectify the problem immediately if one is detected.

Using eBGP as the PE/CE Routing Protocol

The same RIB-failure problem can occur if eBGP is used as the PE/CE routing protocol between the Paris PE router and the Paris EuroBank CE router. In this case, the EuroBank VRF will reject the locally originating routes, but the entries received from the eBGP session will be retained in the BGP VPNv4 table for the VRF. This is shown in the output in Example 5-21. As you can see in the example, when the BGP session is established, a warning message is logged indicating the limit has been exceeded. However, the additional six routes that were rejected from the VRF exist in the VPNv4 table with the "r" status code.

Example 5-21 *Paris PE Router EuroBank VRF Routes Using eBGP*

```
%BGP-5-ADJCHANGE: neighbor 192.168.2.25 vpn vrf EuroBank Up
%IPRT-3-ROUTELIMITEXCEEDED: IP routing table limit exceeded - EuroBank,
  192.168.24.0/24
Paris_PE#show ip route vrf EuroBank
[snip]
B    196.7.25.0/24 [20/0] via 192.168.2.25, 00:38:21
B    196.7.26.0/24 [200/0] via 194.22.15.3, 00:38:21
B    192.168.21.0/24 [20/0] via 192.168.2.25, 00:21:53
B    192.168.20.0/24 [20/0] via 192.168.2.25, 00:22:24
     10.0.0.0/24 is subnetted, 1 subnets
B       10.2.1.0 [200/0] via 194.22.15.2, 00:38:21
B    192.168.23.0/24 [20/0] via 192.168.2.25, 00:21:53
B    192.168.22.0/24 [20/0] via 192.168.2.25, 00:21:53
     192.168.2.0/30 is subnetted, 3 subnets
B       192.168.2.32 [200/0] via 194.22.15.3, 00:38:21
B       192.168.2.12 [200/0] via 194.22.15.2, 00:38:21
C       192.168.2.24 is directly connected, Ethernet0/0
Paris_PE#show ip bgp vpnv4 vrf EuroBank
[snip]
   Network          Next Hop         Metric LocPrf Weight Path
Route Distinguisher: 10:27 (default for vrf EuroBank)
*>i10.2.1.0/24      194.22.15.2           0    100      0 ?
*>i192.168.2.12/30  194.22.15.2           0    100      0 ?
*  192.168.2.24/30  192.168.2.25          0             0 20 ?
*>                  0.0.0.0               0         32768 ?
*>i192.168.2.32/30  194.22.15.3           0    100      0 ?
*> 192.168.20.0     192.168.2.25          0             0 20 ?
*> 192.168.21.0     192.168.2.25          0             0 20 ?
*> 192.168.22.0     192.168.2.25          0             0 20 ?
*> 192.168.23.0     192.168.2.25          0             0 20 ?
```

continues

Example 5-21 *Paris PE Router EuroBank VRF Routes Using eBGP (Continued)*

```
r> 192.168.24.0      192.168.2.25              0            0 20 ?
r> 192.168.25.0      192.168.2.25              0            0 20 ?
r> 192.168.26.0      192.168.2.25              0            0 20 ?
r> 192.168.27.0      192.168.2.25              0            0 20 ?
r> 192.168.28.0      192.168.2.25              0            0 20 ?
r> 192.168.29.0      192.168.2.25              0            0 20 ?
*> 196.7.25.0        192.168.2.25              0            0 20 ?
```

NOTE It is worth noting that when a route is marked as "r," it will *not be* advertised in BGP. This is to prevent customer traffic from being black-holed due to inconsistent routing at the PE routers.

To contain the number of routes that eBGP accepts, the BGP **neighbor maximum-prefix** command should be configured on the PE router for the CE router neighbor, as shown in Example 5-22. This prevents the PE router from accepting excessive routes through the PE/CE BGP session. Note that MD5 authentication is also enabled for the PE/CE BGP session.

Example 5-22 *Configuring Maximum Prefixes for PE/CE eBGP*

```
router bgp 10
 address-family ipv4 vrf EuroBank
  redistribute connected
  redistribute static
  neighbor 192.168.2.25 remote-as 20
  neighbor 192.168.2.25 password 7 1211041B17060D1633
  neighbor 192.168.2.25 activate
  neighbor 192.168.2.25 maximum-prefix 10
 bgp dampening
  no auto-summary
  no synchronization
  exit-address-family
```

By default, exceeding the maximum prefix value causes the BGP session to be dropped between the PE router and CE router and a message to be sent to the system log, as shown in Example 5-23.

NOTE The BGP dampening command is also included in the configuration in Example 5-23. This command controls a flapping route or interface when a CE router is sending too many prefixes and causing network instability.

Example 5-23 *BGP Session Drop Due to Maximum Prefix Exceeded*

```
%BGP-5-ADJCHANGE: neighbor 192.168.2.25 vpn vrf EuroBank Up
%BGP-4-MAXPFX: No. of prefix received from 192.168.2.25 (afi 2) reaches 8,
 max 10
%BGP-3-MAXPFXEXCEED: No. of prefix received from 192.168.2.25 (afi 2): 11
 exceed limit 10
%BGP-5-ADJCHANGE: neighbor 192.168.2.25 vpn vrf EuroBank Down BGP Notification
 sent
%BGP-3-NOTIFICATION: sent to neighbor 192.168.2.25 3/1 (update malformed) 0
 bytes
%IPRT-3-ROUTELIMITEXCEEDED: IP routing table limit exceeded - EuroBank,
 192.168.26.0/24
Paris_PE#show ip bgp vpnv4 vrf EuroBank neighbor
BGP neighbor is 192.168.2.25,  vrf EuroBank,  remote AS 20, external link
  BGP version 4, remote router ID 0.0.0.0
  BGP state = Idle
  Last read 00:05:34, hold time is 180, keepalive interval is 60 seconds
  Received 69 messages, 0 notifications, 0 in queue
  Sent 69 messages, 1 notifications, 0 in queue
  Default minimum time between advertisement runs is 30 seconds

 For address family: VPNv4 Unicast
  Translates address family IPv4 Unicast for VRF EuroBank
  BGP table version 260, neighbor version 0
  Index 3, Offset 0, Mask 0x8
  Route refresh request: received 0, sent 0, maximum limit 10
  Threshold for warning message 75%

  Connections established 2; dropped 2
  Last reset 00:05:35, due to BGP Notification sent, update malformed
  Peer had exceeded the max. no. of prefixes configured.
  Reduce the no. of prefix and clear ip bgp 192.168.2.25 to restore peering
  No active TCP connection
```

As soon as the BGP prefix limit has been exceeded, the offending BGP neighbor is shut down and the BGP session must be restarted manually. (A new automatic restart feature is available from Cisco IOS 12.0(22)S onward.) It is then up to the service provider to rectify the problem and reset the BGP peering session. If it is not desirable for the peering session to be shut down, then the **warning-only** keyword can be appended to the **maximum-prefix** command. In this case, only a warning message is logged, but the prefixes are accepted and stored in the VPNv4 table.

NOTE   As of IOS release 12.0(22)S, a **restart** keyword has been added to the **maximum-prefix** command. This keyword allows the operator to specify an interval in minutes that the peering session should stay down before being automatically activated. However, this does not mitigate the operator from correcting the underlying problem.

Using OSPF as the PE/CE Routing Protocol

In Example 5-24, the PE/CE circuit that is between the Paris PE router and the FastFoods Lyon CE router has been configured for OSPF. As in the EuroBank case, the FastFoods VRF has been configured with a maximum route limit of 10. The steady state for the FastFoods VRF shows that 4 routes are installed.

Example 5-24 *Paris PE Router FastFoods VRF Routes*

```
Paris_PE#show ip route vrf FastFoods
[snip]
      10.0.0.0/24 is subnetted, 1 subnets
O E2    10.2.1.0 [110/20] via 192.168.2.21, 02:01:31, Serial5/0
B     195.12.2.0/24 [200/0] via 194.22.15.2, 00:21:38
      192.168.2.0/30 is subnetted, 2 subnets
B        192.168.2.16 [200/0] via 194.22.15.2, 00:21:38
C        192.168.2.20 is directly connected, Serial5/0
```

The FastFoods CE router has subsequently been configured to originate 10 routes: 192.168.40.0/24 through 192.168.49/24. As expected, a warning message is sent to the Paris PE router console to indicate that the maximum number of routes for the FastFoods VRF has been exceeded. The routes that exceed the limit are dropped from the VRF. As Example 5-25 shows, only 6 of the 10 routes have been accepted.

Example 5-25 *Paris PE Router FastFoods VRF Routes After Routes from FastFoods CE Router*

```
%IPRT-3-ROUTELIMITEXCEEDED: IP routing table limit exceeded - FastFoods,
  192.168.46.0/24
Paris_PE#show ip route vrf FastFoods
[snip]
O E2 192.168.44.0/24 [110/20] via 192.168.2.21, 00:01:17, Serial5/0
O E2 192.168.45.0/24 [110/20] via 192.168.2.21, 00:01:16, Serial5/0
O E2 192.168.42.0/24 [110/20] via 192.168.2.21, 00:01:19, Serial5/0
O E2 192.168.43.0/24 [110/20] via 192.168.2.21, 00:01:18, Serial5/0
O E2 192.168.40.0/24 [110/20] via 192.168.2.21, 00:01:21, Serial5/0
O E2 192.168.41.0/24 [110/20] via 192.168.2.21, 00:01:20, Serial5/0
      10.0.0.0/24 is subnetted, 1 subnets
O E2    10.2.1.0 [110/20] via 192.168.2.21, 00:04:56, Serial5/0
B     195.12.2.0/24 [200/0] via 194.22.15.2, 00:04:56
      192.168.2.0/30 is subnetted, 2 subnets
B        192.168.2.16 [200/0] via 194.22.15.2, 00:04:56
C        192.168.2.20 is directly connected, Serial5/0
```

However, all the routes received, including those dropped from the VRF, have been kept in the OSPF link-state database. The link-state database for the FastFoods VPN is shown in Example 5-26.

Example 5-26 *Paris PE Router FastFoods OSPF Link-State Database*

```
Paris_PE#show ip ospf 200 database

              OSPF Router with ID (192.168.2.22) (Process ID 200)

              Router Link States (Area 2)

Link ID          ADV Router       Age         Seq#         Checksum Link count
192.168.2.21     192.168.2.21     1550        0x80000005 0xD12      2
192.168.2.22     192.168.2.22     1614        0x80000005 0x418      2

              Type-5 AS External Link States

Link ID          ADV Router       Age         Seq#         Checksum Tag
10.2.1.0         192.168.2.21     1550        0x80000004 0xA36C     0
192.168.2.16     192.168.2.22     1631        0x80000001 0xD72D     3489661028
192.168.40.0     192.168.2.21     27          0x80000001 0xE3AA     0
192.168.41.0     192.168.2.21     26          0x80000001 0xD8B4     0
192.168.42.0     192.168.2.21     25          0x80000001 0xCDBE     0
192.168.43.0     192.168.2.21     24          0x80000001 0xC2C8     0
192.168.44.0     192.168.2.21     23          0x80000001 0xB7D2     0
192.168.45.0     192.168.2.21     22          0x80000001 0xACDC     0
192.168.46.0     192.168.2.21     21          0x80000001 0xA1E6     0
192.168.47.0     192.168.2.21     20          0x80000001 0x96F0     0
192.168.48.0     192.168.2.21     19          0x80000001 0x8BFA     0
192.168.49.0     192.168.2.21     16          0x80000001 0x8005     0
195.12.2.0       192.168.2.22     1633        0x80000001 0xBAF0     3489661028
```

At present, there is no mechanism in Cisco IOS to control or limit the behavior of OSPF keeping all routes in its link-state database, regardless of the limit value on the **maximum routes** command. Assigning an inbound distribute-list to allow known customer subnets or prefixes is not effective. Although the list prevents routes from being installed into the VRF, these routes are still kept in the link-state database. Future IOS releases will address this issue by restricting the number of non-self-generated link-state advertisements (LSAs) that are allowed within a given OSPF processes link-state database.

NOTE

Even though OSPF routes cannot be restricted from entry into the local link-state database, they can be prevented from being populated into Multiprotocol BGP and to other PE routers and VPN sites. To get the OSPF routes into BGP, they must be redistributed at the originating PE router. Because redistribution is performed from the routing table, the routes are not populated into BGP.

In conclusion, if a dynamic routing protocol is necessary on the PE/CE circuit, the most effective way to limit routes and prevent a PE router from being flooded by IP prefixes that are announced from the customer network is to use a combination of maximum route limits on VRFs and eBGP with maximum prefixes configured.

PE to CE Circuits

As discussed earlier in this chapter, the MPLS core infrastructure is neither reachable nor visible from within a customer VPN; therefore, it is protected from potential customer DoS attacks. An exception to this rule is the peering interface of the PE router for the PE/CE circuit. Because the customer VRF is defined on this interface, it is reachable by the customer network. Therefore, the PE router might be subject to intrusion of DoS attempts from the customer network.

To mitigate unauthorized access to the service provider network, access-list filters should be placed on the PE router ingress interface to limit access, for example, to the peering addresses (PE/CE endpoints) used by the PE/CE routing protocol. Also, distribution filters can be applied on the routing process such that none of the subnets used for PE/CE circuits are made available to the customer network. If SuperCom is providing a managed router service, then these filters can be configured at the CE router instead of the PE router.

To better understand the filtering that is possible, we will examine the PE/CE circuit between the SuperCom Paris PE router and the FastFoods Lyon CE router. The IP addresses used on the Paris/Lyon PE/CE circuit are 192.168.2.22 at the PE router and 192.168.2.21 at the CE router. As has been previously discussed, this circuit uses OSPF to exchange routes and at present, no access-list or distribution filters have been applied. This means that the customer network has full visibility of all the subnets that SuperCom uses to provide PE/CE circuits for FastFoods. If we examine the FastFoods Lyon routing table in Example 5-27, we can see that all the circuit subnets starting with 192.168.2.0/30 are visible. This could potentially lead to an unscrupulous individual compromising the PE routers via Telnet attempts or access to any number of TCP/UDP ports.

Example 5-27 *FastFoods Lyon Routing Table*

```
FastFoods_Lyon#show ip route
[snip]
     10.0.0.0/24 is subnetted, 1 subnets
C       10.2.1.0 is directly connected, Ethernet0/0
O E1 195.12.2.0/24 [110/65] via 192.168.2.22, 3d18h, Serial4/0
     192.168.2.0/30 is subnetted, 2 subnets
O E1    192.168.2.16 [110/65] via 192.168.2.22, 3d18h, Serial4/0
C       192.168.2.20 is directly connected, Serial4/0
```

The only communication that is directly required between the Paris PE router and the FastFoods CE router is for OSPF routing exchanges and possibly ICMP for reachability testing. Therefore, you can create the filter for the PE router as shown in Example 5-28 based on this requirement.

Example 5-28 *FastFoods CE Router Filter*

```
ip access-list extended FastFoods-CE-Filter
 permit icmp host 192.168.2.21 host 192.168.2.22
 permit ospf host 192.168.2.21 224.0.0.0 0.0.0.255
 deny   ip any 192.168.2.0 0.0.0.255
 permit ip any any
```

The first line of the access list permits ICMP packets (pings and so on) to be sent from the FastFoods CE router only to the directly connected PE router interface, on which the FastFoods VRF is defined. Allowing pings is useful for diagnostics and management. The second line permits OSPF to exchange routes by allowing communication between the CE router and multicast destinations that OSPF uses (that is, 224.0.0.2, 224.0.0.5, and 224.0.0.6) on a serial point-to-point and broadcast circuit.

NOTE   The filter used within the previous example might need to be modified depending on which other types of media are used. Some OSPF configurations use unicast packets rather than multicast for neighbor discovery.

The third line denies access to PE/CE circuit subnets for any protocol from any source in the FastFoods Lyon network. This prevents access by using applications such as Telnet. The last line permits all other access, essentially between FastFoods sites. A permit filter must be included for a remote management workstation if the CE router interfaces are being polled for reachability.

NOTE   The OSPF router-id must be set to the interface addresses on both the PE router and the CE router; otherwise, the access-list prevents OSPF from operating.

Example 5-29 shows how the access-list is applied to the PE router serial interface for FastFoods inbound traffic.

Example 5-29 *Appling In-Bound Filter on PE/CE Circuit*

```
interface Serial5/0
 ip vrf forwarding FastFoods
 ip address 192.168.2.22 255.255.255.252
 ip access-group FastFoods-CE-Filter in
 ip ospf message-digest-key 1 md5 7 020A014F18120E2D47
 no cdp enable
```

The next thing that you should do is prevent distribution of SuperCom PE/CE circuit addresses (used by other FastFoods PE/CE circuits) to the CE router by applying an outbound distribute list to the FastFoods OSPF process on the PE router. Although the inbound access-group filter described previously prevents unauthorized access to PE/CE-circuits, it is still good practice to minimize network visibility to only what the C-network is required to see.

The configuration shown in Example 5-30 allows OSPF to distribute all routes to the CE router except for those that begin with the prefix 192.168.2.0/24, which is the PE/CE circuit address range used in the SuperCom network. The PE router should not accept routes from the FastFoods CE router for address ranges that are used in the SuperCom core network. This includes PE/CE circuits and the registered addresses used for core links and loopback addresses. This prevents the CE router from injecting false PE/CE addresses that might cause routing issues to other FastFoods sites or spoofing SuperCom infrastructure addresses.

Example 5-30 *Filtering PE/CE Circuit Routes*

```
ip access-list standard PE-CE-Circuits
 deny   192.168.2.0 0.0.0.255
 permit any

ip access-list standard SuperCom-Address-Range
 deny   192.168.2.0 0.0.0.255
 deny   194.22.0.0 0.0.255.255

router ospf 200 vrf FastFoods
 router-id 192.168.2.22
 log-adjacency-changes
 area 2 authentication message-digest
 redistribute connected subnets
 redistribute bgp 100 metric-type 1 subnets
 network 192.168.2.0 0.0.0.255 area 2
 distribute-list PE-CE-Circuits OUT
 distribute-list SuperCom-Address-Range IN

no mpls ip propagate-ttl forwarded
```

NOTE   The example also shows that the SuperCom core network is hidden from the FastFoods site by use of the **no mpls ip propagate-ttl** command.

After applying the access filter and distribute list, you can examine the Lyon CE router, as shown in Example 5-31. Only the directly connected circuit subnet is visible on the CE router; therefore, no other PE router is reachable.

NOTE   A similar **distribute-list out** can be configured on the CE router OSPF process to prevent the PE/CE circuit subnet from being seen by any FastFoods routers that might be behind FastFoods Lyon CE router.

Example 5-31 *Checking Access from the Lyon CE Router*

```
FastFoods_Lyon#show ip route
[snip]


     10.0.0.0/24 is subnetted, 1 subnets
C       10.2.1.0 is directly connected, Ethernet0/0
O E1 195.12.2.0/24 [110/65] via 192.168.2.22, 01:11:31, Serial4/0
     192.168.2.0/30 is subnetted, 1 subnets
C        192.168.2.20 is directly connected, Serial4/0
FastFoods_Lyon#ping 192.168.2.22

Type escape sequence to abort.
Sending 5, 100-byte ICMP Echos to 192.168.2.22, timeout is 2 seconds:
!!!!!
Success rate is 100 percent (5/5), round-trip min/avg/max = 20/24/32 ms
FastFoods_Lyon#telnet 192.168.2.22
Trying 192.168.2.22 ...
% Destination unreachable; gateway or host down

FastFoods_Lyon#traceroute 195.12.2.1

Type escape sequence to abort.
Tracing the route to 195.12.2.1

  1 192.168.2.22 20 msec 20 msec 20 msec
  2 192.168.2.17 20 msec 20 msec *
```

A ping can still be issued to the directly connected PE router, but applications such as Telnet will not be permitted. The **traceroute** (to the FastFoods San Jose LAN) in Example 5-31 shows the PE/CE addresses in the FastFoods VPN, but no other core addresses are visible.

Examining the FastFoods inbound access list on the Paris PE router in Example 5-32 shows how many packets have been permitted or denied for originating from the FastFoods Lyon network.

Example 5-32 *FastFoods CE Router Filter on the Paris PE Router*

```
Paris_PE#show access-list FastFoods-CE-Filter
Extended IP access list FastFoods-CE-Filter
    permit icmp host 192.168.2.21 host 192.168.2.22 (20 matches)
    permit ospf host 192.168.2.21 224.0.0.0 0.0.0.255 (517 matches)
    deny ip any 192.168.2.0 0.0.0.255 (8 matches)
    permit ip any any (77 matches)
```

The inbound filters and outbound distribute lists described in the previous section are equally applicable when using other PE/CE routing protocols such as eBGP, RIPv2, and EIGRP. If static routing were used, then only an inbound filter would be required on the PE router.

If a point-to-point (non multiaccess) connection is being used for the PE/CE circuit and dynamic routing is not required, then a combination of unnumbered and static routes (pointing to the interface) can be configured to provide strict control of routes into the C-network and to minimize the access and visibility that the CE router has of the P-network. The disadvantage of unnumbered addresses is that the interfaces are unavailable for remote testing and management. Therefore, unnumbered interfaces are not suitable for service providers who depend on reachability status by polling the CE router interface. Another disadvantage is that the routing table must be manually maintained, which might not be desirable for a large network.

Although unnumbered interfaces hide the address of the PE router circuit, it does not prevent **traceroute** from being used to obtain the value of the address being used. Therefore, it is still necessary to apply inbound filters to prevent access to the PE router interface address, as was discussed in Example 5-28.

A common and simple method for denying Telnet access to a PE router from a CE router is to place an access list on the Virtual Terminal Interfaces (VTY).

Example 5-33 shows a typical configuration of a service provider router. An access list is configured to only accept Telnet connections from IP source addresses that are part of the SuperCom core network address space (194.22.15.0/24). This access list is then applied to the range of virtual terminals that are used for remote login. If the inbound access lists discussed previously *did not* exclude Telnet access, and a PE router relied on this access list to prevent Telnet access from the CE routers, then a potential security breach could exist.

Example 5-33 *Preventing Telnet Access*

```
line vty 0 4
 access-class SuperCom_Network-TELNET in
 password 7 051B091B2E4A49061501
 login

ip access-list standard SuperCom_Network-TELNET
 permit 194.22.15.0 0.0.0.255 log
 deny   any log
 !
```

Extranet Access

One of the great advantages of the MPLS VPN architecture is that VPNs can be merged easily between different customers' intranets to create specific extranet VPNs. You can create an extranet by importing and exporting routes between different customer VRFs.

If IP address overlap between customers is not an issue (that is, the IP address space is unique between customers), then you can import routes directly between the VRF tables.

After an extranet is created between different VPNs, the customer intranets are subject to access by hosts outside their own VPNs (from the extranet). Although the intention to allow an extranet might have bona fide business reasons (for example, to allow ordering between supplier and manufacturer), it is perhaps slightly misguided to assume a level of trust between intranets. It is important that a logical separation is maintained between intranets that are participating in an extranet. This is achieved through the traditional method of using a firewall between the intranets.

Prior to MPLS-VPNs, provisioning a circuit between two companies created an extranet. It was then the responsibility of each company to secure its end of the circuit by using a privately maintained and managed firewall. This is illustrated in Figure 5-6. Assume that FastFoods and EuroBank had an extranet prior to the days of subscribing to the excellent SuperCom MPLS-VPN service. Both FastFoods and EuroBank configured their own firewalls to adhere to the security policies of their respective organizations.

Figure 5-6   *Traditional Extranet Firewalling*

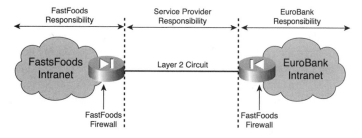

In the case of an extranet created in an MPLS-VPN environment, the firewall function can be under the control of the service provider, which is located at a common service or peering point, as shown in Figure 5-7.

In this scenario, SuperCom provides the extranet between FastFoods and EuroBank at a central point (PE router) in the network. This common service PE router has a separate VRF defined for FastFoods and EuroBank. Each of the VRFs then connect to a separate interface on the Firewall, which not only provides the security and logical separation required, but also any necessary address translation, if EuroBank and FastFoods have overlapping address spaces. In the illustration, you can see that the $\mathbf{F}$ routes belong to FastFoods, whereas the $\mathbf{E}$ routes belong to EuroBank. If address translation is required, then a static route is injected into each of the VRFs at the common service PE router that represents the translated routes through the firewall, which can be seen as the $\mathbf{E^T}$ and $\mathbf{F^T}$ routes. The translated routes are distributed through the respective intranets using standard Multiprotocol BGP VPNv4 procedures.

Figure 5-7   *Extranet Firewall at a Common Service Point*

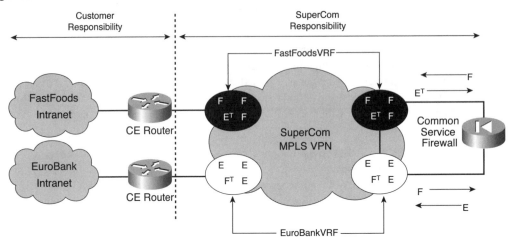

Although the example discussed places the firewall at a common service point that
SuperCom controls, there is no reason why EuroBank and FastFoods could not emulate
their original extranet connection by providing individually owned firewalls that are interconnected using the MPLS-VPN. In this case, the extranet routing occurs in the VPN that
connects the two firewalls, as illustrated in Figure 5-8. The extranet VRF that connects the two
firewalls uses the same route distinguishers and import/export route targets to exchange the
translated routes (if NAT is necessary) because they should hold identical routing entries.

Figure 5-8   *Customer-Controlled Extranet Firewall*

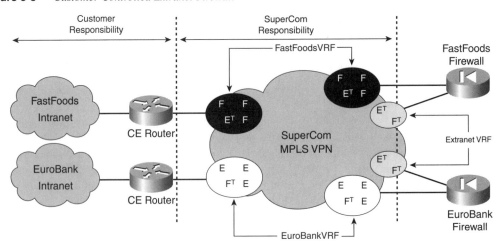

You can create an extranet directly between VRFs without using firewalls. This might occur if only a few trusted devices in each intranet need to communicate with each other, and the address space that each intranet uses is unique. Consider Figure 5-9, where FastFoods San Jose and EuroBank Paris require two specific hosts to communicate with each other. The FastFoods San Jose host is allocated the IP address **F1**, and the EuroBank Paris host is allocated the address **E1**. Because the extranet only needs to be formed between specific devices located at these particular sites, only the host addresses of **E1** and **F1** need to be imported into the VRFs at FastFoods San Jose and EuroBank Paris. This can be achieved through the use of route maps, where a unique route target can be exported with the host address. The nominated VRFs at San Jose and Paris then import this unique route target, and all other VRFs are excluded from importing the unique route target. In addition, an access list can be applied at the CE router interfaces to further restrict communication between **F1** and **E1**. If more security than an access list is required, the CE routers' routes can be upgraded with a version of Cisco IOS that provides firewalling capability.

Figure 5-9   *Simple Extranet Between Two VRFs*

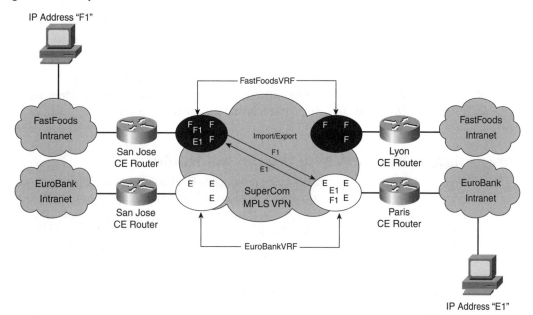

Internet Access

The provision of Internet access in an MPLS VPN network can be as straightforward as provisioning a default route within a VRF that points to one or more egress gateways. When a customer requires the full or partial BGP Internet routing table via one or more egress gateways, then the global routing table should be used.

The provision of simple Internet access using the default route to an MPLS-VPN uses the same procedures as for provisioning extranets. In fact, from an MPLS-VPN perspective, you could consider Internet access using the default route as nothing more than a giant extranet with a much larger potential for security breaches.

The provision of Internet access to most small- to medium-sized enterprise customers generally requires not much more that injecting a default route into the customer VPN pointing to the service provider Internet gateway.

If multiple Internet gateways were available from the service provider, then each could inject a default route, with the best one being imported into the VRF based on standard BGP path selection.

The disadvantage of using the default route for multiple Internet gateways is that optimal routing is not achieved. All Internet access within a VRF would follow the same path through the MPLS-VPN network, regardless of whether a better gateway were available for a particular Internet destination. You could solve this problem by injecting the Internet routes into the VRF; in that way, each Internet prefix would point to the best egress gateway. However, this is strongly discouraged due to the router resource and processing overheads required to maintain Internet routes within multiple VRFs. In this case, the global routing table should be used.

Regardless of the type of Internet access required, some form of firewall is necessary to protect the VPN customer from unauthorized access and DoS attacks. The following sections discuss the various firewall scenarios that can be deployed.

Shared Internet Access Using the Default Route

Figure 5-10 shows Internet access being provided to FastFoods and EuroBank via a shared firewall service. In this scenario, both FastFoods and EuroBank import the default route, indicated as **D** in the VRFs. Conversely, the shared Internet VRF imports the necessary routes from the FastFoods and EuroBank VPNs. The default route can be exported to all the VRFs that comprise the FastFoods and EuroBank VPNs. The result is that all sites in both these VPNs would have direct access to the Internet (no need to traverse a hub within FastFoods or EuroBank) with protection being provided by the SuperCom shared firewall. This solution assumes that the IP addressing between FastFoods and EuroBank is unique so that the same shared VRF can be used, or the use of PE-NAT is in effect at the PE routers. The firewall in this case is not required to perform NAT unless the addresses in either the FastFoods or EuroBank VPNs use private addressing. The disadvantage of this solution is that because the VPN customers share a common firewall, they are bound to the security policies that SuperCom imposes. Also, if multiple Internet gateways are available, optimal routing for a particular prefix will not be achieved because the best path was selected based on the default route to a particular gateway.

Figure 5-10 *Shared Internet Access*

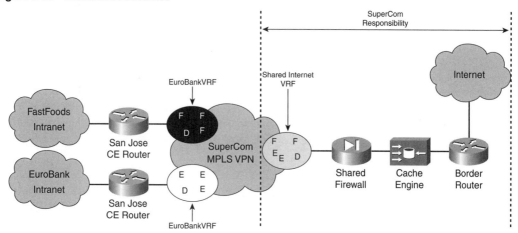

Firewall Co-Location

When address overlap is an issue or the customer requires control of his own security policies, the firewall and NAT services can be replicated as shown in Figure 5-11. A central PE router can hold a series of Internet access VRFs, some of which connect to co-located customer firewalls, and others that support a shared managed firewall service. To minimize the number of physical interfaces required on the shared PE router, VLANs can be used to direct Internet access from a VRF to the associated firewall. The advantage of providing address translation at a central point is that a small address pool is required that you can apply to all sites in the VPN. The closer that NAT is performed to the customer, the more registered addresses that are required because each CE or aggregation point needs an address pool.

Figure 5-11 *Shared Internet Access and Firewall Co-Location*

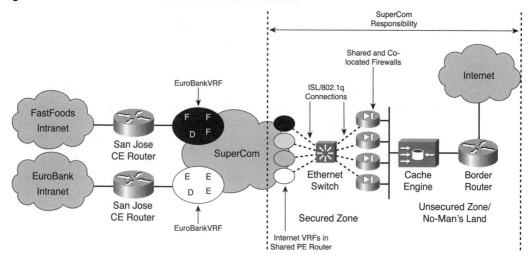

Hub and Spoke Internet Access Using the Global Routing Table

The previous scenario showed a customer firewall co-located in the SuperCom POP. To a highly security-conscious customer, this scenario will not be desirable at all.

If a customer requires total control of access to the Internet for all its sites—including physically locating the firewall on its own premises—then a hub and spoke topology should be deployed with Internet access provided by the global routing table of the MPLS-VPN service provider. Consider the scenario that is depicted in Figure 5-12. EuroBank is providing Internet access to all its sites via a hub at its San Jose headquarters. A default route is exported from the San Jose hub to all its spoke sites as indicated by the **D**.

NOTE	The EuroBank hub-and-spoke topology is only required for Internet access using the default route. All EuroBank intranet traffic is transported directly between VRFs using a fully meshed topology.

At EuroBank San Jose, a firewall is connected to a global interface in the SuperCom network; that is, no VRF is defined on the PE router to which the firewall connects. Any traffic destined to the Internet from a EuroBank site would be picked up by the default route and directed to the San Jose hub site. From San Jose, the firewall translates the traffic (if necessary) and sends it into the global routing table of SuperCom. The Internet traffic then traverses the SuperCom network and egresses the appropriate SuperCom Internet border router. One benefit of this solution is that the customer has total control over all aspects of Internet access. Because the Internet traffic is carried in the SuperCom global routing table, the best path can be selected for a particular Internet prefix if there was more than one Internet egress point in the network. The Internet BGP routing table only needs to be held in the PE routers that connect the Internet border routers and customers that require global connectivity. The core routes do not require the Internet routing table because they forward on labels, not IP prefixes. (In this case, it is the label of the destination edge PE router.) A disadvantage is that all Internet traffic for EuroBank must traverse the SuperCom network twice, first to get to the EuroBank hub and then back out into the SuperCom global routing table. If NAT is required, then a dedicated registered pool must be allocated to EuroBank. (However, this is less of an issue due to the availability of PAT). Two connections are required from the San Jose EuroBank site, although they could be logical circuits provisioned over a single physical link. With some smart configuration, it might even be possible to combine the firewall and CE router function at San Jose into a single unit, but two circuits would still be required.

Figure 5-12   *Hub-and-Spoke Internet Access*

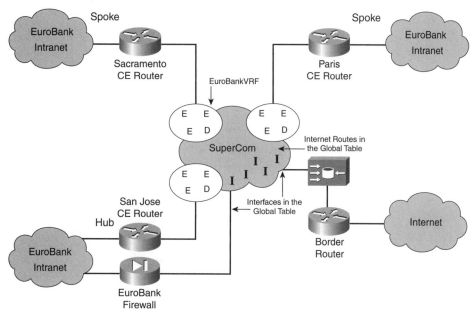

Firewall at the CE Router

Another option is to configure all CE routers in a VPN with firewall functionality available in Cisco IOS, as shown in Figure 5-13. In this scenario, all traffic exiting any EuroBank sites is subject to firewall restrictions, which could include intranet access as well as Internet access. No firewalls are required at the Internet egress point, but more configuration and management are necessary at each of the CE routers. This includes providing a NAT pool for every site, although using Port Address Translation (PAT) minimizes the number of registered addresses required.

The example shows the default route being used for Internet access; however, if there were multiple egress gateways and optimal routing were desirable, then you could use the global routing table. In this case, two circuits will be required from the CE router to connect to the PE router VRF interface and the global routing table. Access to the global routing table could also be achieved through the use of a static route within the VRF using the **global** keyword and a corresponding static route in the global routing table pointing back to the CE router (for the registered address pool the CE router firewall holds).

Figure 5-13 *Firewalls at All CE Routers*

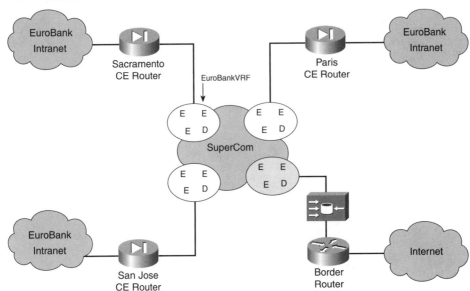

IPSec over MPLS

Generally, the MPLS-VPN service provider must be trusted to some extent to fully secure the network. However, there might be an occasion where a customer requires total control over traffic that passes through the core. You cannot control the service provider portion of the network after traffic has left the CE router. For customers who have a requirement for a high level of security, consider the use of IPSec tunnels over the MPLS core.

View IPSec as an overlay network to the MPLS-VPN network. The MPLS infrastructure is not aware of the IPSec layer, nor is the IPSec layer aware of the MPLS-VPN network. IPSec merely requires IP connectivity between two endpoints in the customer network. An IPSec tunnel could be provisioned between two CE routers, assuming the customer owns them. If the service provider is providing a managed CE router service, then the IPSec tunnels can be established further back in the customer network, avoiding the customer depending on the service provider to configure the IPSec tunnels.

IPSec is advantageous. It allows secure communication in a customer network, including encrypting the data, authenticating customer endpoints, guaranteeing integrity of the data, and providing replay detection. The disadvantage is that IPSec turns the MPLS-VPN into a series of point-to-point tunnels, which are not scalable in a large network that might require full meshing.

Summary

This chapter covered some aspects of how to make an MPLS-VPN more secure from unauthorized access and attack. No network is impervious to attack, but by following simple configuration rules, you can minimize security breaches. In summary:

- MPLS-VPNs provide a high level of security, including address separation, no visibility of the core network, and resistance to label spoofing.

- Use registered addresses for the core infrastructure and PE/CE circuits. This avoids an overlap problem on PE/CE circuits and allows the service provider to filter core addressing for CE routers that are using dynamic routing protocols.

- Always apply filters inbound on the PE routers to limit access to the PE circuit address for routing protocols and pings only. If the service provider manages the CE router, then the filter can be applied on the outbound interface to the PE router.

- If dynamic routing protocols are being used on the PE/CE circuits, filter out the address range that is used for PE/CE circuits.

- Always use MD5 neighbor authentication routing adjacencies and LDP neighbors.

- Be aware that limiting routes into a VRF does not necessarily stop those routes from being held in other memory structures. If VRF route limiting is required, try to use eBGP or static routes for PE/CE circuits.

- MPLS-VPNs provide a comparable level of security to Frame Relay and the ATM network. However, like these Layer 2 technologies, data encryption is not provided. To further increase security, you can deploy IPSec as an overlay to the MPLS-VPN network.

CHAPTER 6

Large-Scale Routing and Multiple Service Provider Connectivity

As interest in the service benefits provided by a Multiprotocol Label Switching (MPLS) virtual private network (VPN) backbone have grown, so have the size and type of end-customers who are seeking their use. This has an impact on the basic connectivity model that the architecture provides because it might not satisfy all the requirements of each client. In many cases, scaling the amount of routing information exchanged with the service provider might be a challenge, or the geographic location of each of the customer's sites might expand beyond the reach of a single service provider. Therefore, different service models are required to address each of these scenarios and provide appropriate mechanisms to facilitate connectivity between VPN sites.

Chapter 14 of *MPLS and VPN Architectures*, Volume 1 (ISBN: 1-58705-081-1) introduced the concepts of the Carrier's Carrier and Interprovider solutions. As with several other emerging technologies at the time, various aspects of these architectures have matured since the initial publication, and more deployment experience has been gained. Therefore, this chapter will review each of these technology areas and provide a more in-depth discussion on each topic so that you can successfully implement each of these solutions.

While working through example configurations in this chapter, we will refer to the sample service provider topology, as shown in Figure 6-1. All relevant IP address ranges for the service provider backbones are shown in Table 6-1.

Figure 6-1   *SuperCom and EuroCom Network Backbone Topology*

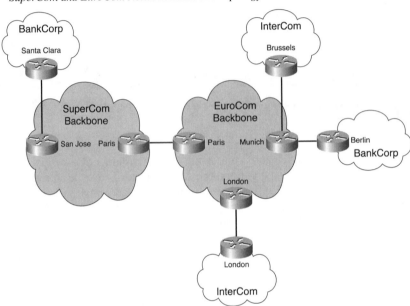

Table 6-1   *IP Address Assignment for SuperCom Backbone*

Company	Site	Subnet
EuroCom	Paris (loopback0)	196.49.1.1/32
	London (loopback0)	196.49.1.2/32
	Munich (loopback0)	196.49.1.3/32
	Management LAN	196.49.2.0/24
	PE-CE Interface Addresses	194.69.27.0/24
SuperCom	San Jose (Loopback0)	194.22.15.1/32
	Paris (Loopback 0)	194.22.15.3/32
	Management LAN	194.22.16.0/24
	PE-CE Interface Addresses	192.168.2.0/24

Large Scale Routing: Carrier's Carrier Solution Overview

When the MPLS VPN architecture was first introduced, it was envisaged that it would be used primarily to provide Layer-3 services to Enterprise customers who had a limited subset of IP routes. However, due to the popularity and large deployment base of this type of solution, many large Enterprises, smaller MPLS VPN service providers, and Internet service providers (ISPs) have seen advantages in the MPLS architecture and requested connectivity from an MPLS VPN backbone provider.

The primary advantage that these end-customers see is that they can avoid building their own Layer-2 infrastructures and use an MPLS VPN provider instead to interconnect their sites. Apart from reducing infrastructure costs, each site can be fully meshed with its peer sites, thereby providing the most optimal routing. To provide maximum availability, the end-customer can also be dual-homed to different PE routers of the carrier's MPLS VPN backbone.

The implication of allowing these types of customer access to an MPLS VPN backbone is that the backbone might have to carry large amounts of routing information for each individual customer. An ISP, for example, almost certainly needs to exchange a partial—if not the entire—Internet routing table between its sites. This is because the customers might need access to the full spectrum of Internet routes, such as when they are dual-homed to different ISPs. In the case of a large Enterprise or another MPLS VPN service provider, a substantial number of prefixes might need to be reachable from within each site.

Providing access to these customers creates a potential scaling issue because each PE router must maintain all the local routing information within a VRF. This routing information then needs to be distributed to all relevant PE routers so that remote CE routers can obtain appropriate routing information. Although there are no restrictions within the base MPLS VPN architecture to prevent the exchange of large amounts of routes between PE routers and CE routers, it is important to understand the ramifications of such connectivity. Because of these potential scaling issues, a new solution is needed, which is provided through the Carrier's Carrier architecture.

NOTE   The name *Carrier's Carrier* might imply that the architecture is only relevant to large service providers, but the architecture is not specific to a single type of organization. For example, mid-range service providers or large Enterprises might deploy this solution for scalability reasons, such as their PE routers becoming over-provisioned with routing information.

Carrier's Carrier Route Types

To understand how the Carrier's Carrier solution assists with scaling and carrier backbone isolation, it is necessary to first draw a line between which routes are used for internal connectivity of a particular VPN and which routes belong to external customers of that VPN. To better comprehend this, refer to the InterCom VPN that is shown in Figure 6-2.

Figure 6-2 *Carrier's Carrier: InterCom VPN Connectivity*

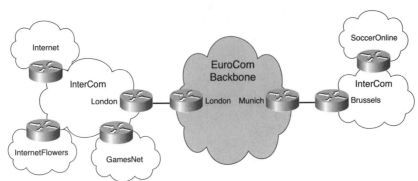

Figure 6-2 shows that InterCom is attached to the EuroCom backbone in two places: London and Brussels. InterCom has connectivity to the Internet within the London site and has two of its own Internet clients: InterFlowers and GamesNet. In the Brussels site, InterCom has a further Internet client: SoccerOnline.

Within the London and Brussels sites, InterCom has various links between each of its routers in addition to loopback interfaces on each router. The loopback interfaces are used for network management, BGP peering, and so on. InterCom also provides various internal services to its customers, such as web hosting, DHCP, and so on. All the routes associated with these aspects of the InterCom network are classified as *internal* routes.

The London InterCom site has access to the Internet via a local peering connection. The InterCom site learns the entire Internet routing table from this peering session. Both the London and Brussels sites have Internet clients attached, and Internet routes are exchanged with these customers. All the routes learned from the Internet and from external customers of the InterCom network are classified as *external* routes.

In addition to the internal and external route types, there are several other terms that are used to help define the Carrier's Carrier architecture. An illustration of each of these components is provided in Figure 6-3, and they are also listed here:

- **CSC**—This is an abbreviation used in the text to mean Carrier's Carrier.
- **CSC PE router**—This is the same as a normal PE router except that it provides MPLS-to-MPLS label forwarding rather than IP-to-MPLS label imposition.
- **CSC CE router**—This is the same as a normal CE router except that it runs a label distribution protocol with the PE router.
- **Carrier network**—This is an MPLS VPN service provider that provides CSC functionality.
- **Carrier's Carrier network**—This is the network of the VPN customer that is attached to the Carrier network.

Figure 6-3   *Carrier's Carrier Terminology*

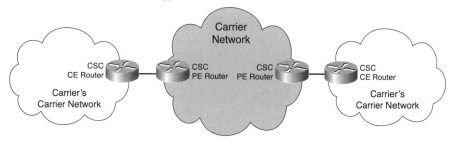

Table 6-2 provides all the relevant IP address assignments for EuroCom, InterCom, and each of InterCom's Internet customers, which you saw in Figure 6-2.

Table 6-2   *IP Address Assignment for EuroCom, InterCom, and End-Customers*

Company	Site	Subnet
EuroCom (autonomous system# 20)	PE-CE interface addresses	194.69.27.0/24
InterCom (autonomous system# 100)	London	145.27.62.0/24
	London CE router (loopback0)	145.27.62.1/32
	GamesNet peering router	145.27.62.2/32
	Brussels	145.27.63.0/24
	Brussels CE router (loopback0)	145.27.63.1/32
	SoccerOnline peering router	145.27.63.2/32
InterFlowers	London	201.16.4.0/24
GamesNet	London	222.27.5.0/24
SoccerOnline	Brussels	216.49.24.0/24

Carrier Backbone Connectivity

The previous section clearly shows that InterCom is providing ISP type services within its VPN to its customers; therefore, it has the potential to carry a substantial amount of routing information between its sites. In our example, InterCom receives the entire Internet routing table from its upstream ISP within the London site. It also receives routing information from each of its Internet end-customers. All of this routing information needs to be distributed between the InterCom London and Brussels CE routers by the EuroCom backbone; this includes end-customer routes and full Internet routing.

Due to the large amount of routing information and the desire for InterCom to keep a tight control on its intersite routing information, InterCom and EuroCom decided to utilize the Carrier's Carrier architecture. Deployment of this solution provides the routing policy control desired by InterCom. This is because InterCom is able to advertise external routes between its sites by using BGP-4 and distribute all internal routes to the neighboring EuroCom PE router by using static or dynamic routing.

As with normal MPLS VPN deployments, routes are exchanged between CSC PE routers and CSC CE routers and placed into the VRF that corresponds to that particular VPN client. Because all external routes are exchanged directly between the InterCom sites by using BGP-4, only routes that belong to the InterCom internal network are advertised from the CSC CE router to the CSC PE router. This substantially reduces the amount of routing information that the EuroCom MPLS VPN backbone network must carry. Figure 6-4 illustrates this concept and how InterCom exchanges routes with EuroCom.

Figure 6-4   *Internal and External Route Exchange*

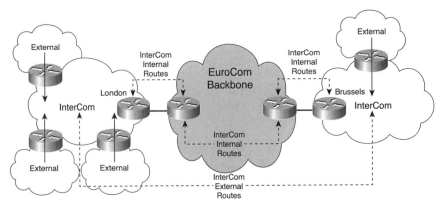

Because only internal InterCom routes are exchanged between the CSC CE routers and PE routers, all external routing information that InterCom carries is lost from the EuroCom CSC PE routers. This means that the EuroCom CSC PE routers have limited visibility into the InterCom routing domain; therefore, they need a forwarding paradigm other than IP hop-by-hop routing. This is required because packets that have an IP destination address external to the InterCom network are not routable at the CSC PE routers because the destination IP prefix will not have been distributed to EuroCom.

We have seen in *MPLS and VPN Architectures,* Volume 1, that MPLS forwarding to BGP destinations is based on label forwarding toward the next-hop of the route. Because InterCom distributes all external routes by using BGP-4, you should be able to use this mechanism also. However, this requires an end-to-end MPLS label-switched path (LSP) between the ingress and egress BGP-4 peers. Therefore, InterCom must be able to provide this LSP, both within its own sites (optional) and across the EuroCom backbone network.

To provide an LSP across the EuroCom network, the layer distribution protocol needs to be extended into the attached InterCom sites. You will see later in this chapter how to achieve this and how the LSPs are built through the CSC PE routers and between Carrier's Carrier sites.

Exchange of Internal Routes Between VPN Sites

There is nothing particularly special about the MPLS VPN backbone with respect to the Carrier's Carrier architecture. In other words, all internal routes are placed into the VRF, which corresponds to the end-customer, and are distributed among CSC PE routers using Multiprotocol BGP. The fundamental difference between this architecture and the base MPLS VPN service is that not all VPN routes are sent to the CSC PE routers; instead, they are distributed directly between sites using BGP-4. This results in CSC PE routers having partial visibility of customer's routing. Thus, they must rely on a packet forwarding capability that is different from the default hop-by-hop IP routing to carry customer IP datagrams between sites.

Example 6-1 provides the initial configuration of the EuroCom London CSC PE router that will support the exchange of InterCom internal routes from the London site between the London and Munich CSC PE routers.

Example 6-1   *CSC PE Router Configuration for Internal Route Exchange*

```
hostname EuroCom_LondonPE
!
ip vrf InterCom
 rd 20:1234
 route-target export 20:99
 route-target import 20:99
!
interface Ethernet10/1/1
 description ** interface to InterCom London
 ip vrf forwarding InterCom
 ip address 194.69.27.6 255.255.255.252
!
router bgp 20
 no bgp default ipv4-unicast
 bgp log-neighbor-changes
 neighbor 196.49.1.3 remote-as 20
 neighbor 196.49.1.3 update-source Loopback0
 !
 address-family ipv4 vrf InterCom
 no auto-summary
 no synchronization
 exit-address-family
 !
 address-family vpnv4
 neighbor 196.49.1.3 activate
 neighbor 196.49.1.3 send-community extended
 exit-address-family
```

Routing Information Exchange Between CSC PE Routers and CE Routers

In theory, any IGP that is supported for base MPLS VPN PE router/CE router route exchange can be used with the Carrier's Carrier architecture. The CSC CE router will use this routing protocol to advertise internal routes from the attached VPN site. These internal routes will then be placed into the corresponding VRF for subsequent distribution across the MPLS VPN backbone using Multiprotocol BGP. The use of Border Gateway Protocol (BGP-4) across the PE/CE links within the Carrier's Carrier architecture is a special case that requires some extensions to the protocol to support the requirement of label distribution described earlier in this chapter. This case will be covered in detail later in this chapter.

Static Routing Between CSC PE/CE Routers

The first option that you might consider for PE/CE router connectivity is static routing; indeed, static routing is widely deployed today for normal MPLS VPN customers. Static routing is a good option if the number of routes within the attached site is small and does not change on a regular basis. This might not be the case where the Carrier's Carrier architecture is deployed because the end-customer is typically an ISP or large enterprise, which might have a substantial number of internal routes to exchange. If a large number of routes must be exchanged, then the configuration of the CSC PE router might become complex due to the number of static routes. If the routing information changes regularly, then management of the static routes might become prohibitive. Because of these reasons, the use of static routing within a Carrier's Carrier environment is discouraged.

From the CSC CE router's perspective, a static default route that points toward the CSC PE router might be desirable because this removes the requirement of maintaining a number of static routes at the CSC CE router. However, the design concept of forwarding IP packets toward external VPN destinations by using the MPLS label of the BGP next-hop prevents this. This is because an end-to-end LSP is required across the VPN and MPLS VPN backbone, and any summarization (including, of course, the default route) breaks the end-to-end LSP, as explained in Chapter 13 of *MPLS and VPN Architectures,* Volume 1. You will see later in this chapter that the use of a static default route at the CSC CE router is impossible within the Carrier's Carrier environment.

To enable the successful transport of packets toward InterCom external destinations, the only routes that you need to exchange between the InterCom sites are the BGP-4 next-hop addresses of these routes. These next-hop addresses would typically be the PE routers through which the external destinations are reachable. This means that in our example, the number of static routes at the EuroCom CSC PE routers is minimal because the InterCom VPN has only two sites.

NOTE   As stated earlier in this chapter, InterCom also has some local services within its sites, and the routes for these services need to be exchanged with the EuroCom MPLS VPN backbone. However, to simplify the configuration examples within this chapter, these routes will not be considered further.

The relevant configurations for the InterCom London site, to support the use of static routing, are shown in Example 6-2. For the sake of simplicity, only the BGP-4 next-hop addresses of the InterCom GamesNet and SoccerOnline peering routers are shown, although to complete the configuration, the next-hop addresses of the InterFlowers and Internet peering routers would need to be added.

Example 6-2   *Static Route Configuration for InterCom VPN*

```
hostname EuroCom_LondonPE
!
router bgp 20
 !
 address-family ipv4 vrf InterCom
 redistribute static
 no auto-summary
 no synchronization
 exit-address-family
 !
 ! Route to GamesNet BGP next hop
 ip route vrf InterCom 145.27.62.2 255.255.255.255 194.69.27.5
----------------------------------------------------------------
hostname InterCom_LondonCE
!
! Route to SoccerOnline BGP next hop
ip route 145.27.63.2 255.255.255.255 194.69.27.6
```

This configuration shows that the EuroCom London CSC PE router has a static route pointing to the 145.27.62.2/32 prefix, which is the address used for the loopback0 interface on the InterCom GamesNet peering router within the London site. The InterCom London CSC CE router has a static route pointing to the 145.27.63.2/32 prefix, which is the address used for the loopback0 interface on the SoccerOnline peering router within the Brussels site. These addresses will be used as the BGP next-hop when exchanging GamesNet and SoccerOnline routes directly between the InterCom London and Brussels sites.

NOTE   You might question why the 145.27.62.2/32 and 145.27.63.2/32 prefixes are used as the BGP-4 next-hops of all GamesNet and SoccerOnline routes advertised between the InterCom London and Brussels sites. In normal BGP-4 operation, the next-hop of external routes is not changed when advertising across an internal session. However, InterCom is using the **next-hop-self** feature on its edge routers (that peer with GamesNet and SoccerOnline) to change the next-hop to one of its own addresses. This eliminates the need to carry any external customer interface addresses within the InterCom network.

Dynamic Routing Between CSC PE/CE Routers

In most cases where the Carrier's Carrier architecture is deployed, static routing is not desirable for CSC PE router to CE router connectivity. This might be because of the number of routes within the site, or perhaps these routes change on a regular basis. Also, the site might have multiple connections into the MPLS VPN backbone, which would dictate a more dynamic method of route exchange. Whatever the case, any of the currently supported IGP protocols can be used in a Carrier's Carrier environment.

The configuration of the dynamic routing protocol is the same as in the base MPLS VPN environment. You can find detailed information on the configurations for RIP version 2 (RIPv2) and Open Shortest Path First (OSPF) in Chapter 9, "MPLS/VPN Architecture Operation" of *MPLS and VPN Architectures,* Volume 1. You can find this information for IS-IS, EIGRP, and advanced OSPF in this book's Chapter 3, "PE-CE Routing Protocol Enhancements and Advanced Features." Sample configurations for the EuroCom London CSC PE router (for each routing protocol) are provided for completeness in Example 6-3.

Example 6-3   *Dynamic Routing Protocol Configurations for InterCom*

```
OSPF Configuration:

router ospf 101 vrf InterCom
 network 194.69.27.4 0.0.0.3 area 1
 redistribute bgp 20 subnets metric 20
 !
router bgp 20
 !
 address-family ipv4 vrf InterCom
 redistribute ospf 101 match internal external 1 external 2

RIP V2 Configuration:

router rip
 version 2
 !
 address-family ipv4 vrf InterCom
  version 2
  redistribute bgp 20 metric transparent
  network 194.69.27.0

router bgp 20
 !
 address-family ipv4 vrf InterCom
 redistribute rip

EIGRP Configuration:

router eigrp 1
 !
 address-family ipv4 vrf InterCom
 redistribute bgp 20
 network 194.69.27.4 0.0.0.3
```

Example 6-3 *Dynamic Routing Protocol Configurations for InterCom (Continued)*

```
 no auto-summary
 autonomous-system 21

router bgp 20
 !
 address-family ipv4 vrf InterCom
 redistribute eigrp 21
```

IS-IS Configuration:

```
router isis InterCom vrf InterCom
 net 47.1234.0000.0000.0020.00
 redistribute bgp 10 metric transparent level-1-2
 metric-style wide
 !
router bgp 20
 !
 address-family ipv4 vrf InterCom
 redistribute isis InterCom vrf InterCom level-1-2
```

Exchange of External Routes Between VPN Sites

You learned earlier in this chapter that customer external routes within the Carrier's Carrier architecture are not exchanged directly with the MPLS VPN backbone. This implies that direct BGP-4 sessions between C routers are required to distribute these external routes. In most cases, the BGP-4 session between sites will be established within the same autonomous system; therefore, internal BGP-4 will be used. Figure 6-5 shows that the InterCom GamesNet and SoccerOnline routers are connected by using an internal BGP-4 session for the exchange of GamesNet and SoccerOnline routes.

Figure 6-5 *Internal BGP Peering Between InterCom C Routers*

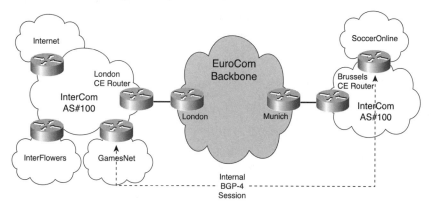

NOTE   There is no restriction within the Carrier's Carrier architecture to prevent the use of external BGP sessions between customer sites.

For clarity and to simplify our example configuration, Figure 6-5 only shows a BGP session between the GamesNet and SoccerOnline edge routers and not between all InterCom routers. However, if internal BGP-4 is used between customer sites, then standard internal BGP-4 rules apply. This means that a full mesh of sessions is required between all sites; otherwise, to reduce the number of sessions, route reflectors or BGP confederations must be deployed.

NOTE   The full mesh requirement includes the CSC CE routers at this point because a label distribution protocol has not yet been deployed within the InterCom sites or across the PE/CE links. This means that *all* the external routes known within the InterCom autonomous system will be carried on the CSC CE routers, although these routes will not be exchanged with the CSC PE routers. You have already seen in this chapter that packets are dropped by the CSC PE routers if the IP destination addresses are unavailable, and this is also the case for the CSC CE routers. You will see later in this chapter that the requirement for BGP on the CSC CE routers will be removed when a label distribution protocol is deployed on the PE/CE links and within the Intercom sites.

In a real deployment, it is likely that InterCom would use route reflectors. All internal BGP-4 sessions would peer with these route reflectors rather than direct peering between edge routers. Example 6-4 shows the BGP-4 configuration on the InterCom edge routers that will allow the exchange of routes between the GamesNet and SoccerOnline routers.

Example 6-4   *BGP-4 Configuration for InterCom Edge Routers*

```
hostname InterCom-GamesNet
!
router bgp 100
 no synchronization
 neighbor 145.27.63.2 remote-as 100
 neighbor 145.27.63.2 update-source Loopback0
------------------------------------------------------------------
hostname InterCom-SoccerOnline
!
router bgp 100
 no synchronization
 neighbor 145.27.62.2 remote-as 100
 neighbor 145.27.62.2 update-source Loopback0
```

This configuration shows that the InterCom-GamesNet router (IP address 145.27.62.2) has an internal BGP-4 session with the InterCom-SoccerOnline router (IP address 145.27.63.2). (It is an internal BGP-4 session because the remote autonomous system numbers are the same.) You can see in Example 6-5 that the InterCom-GamesNet router has learned the SoccerOnline subnet 216.49.24.0/24 from the InterCom-SoccerOnline router with a next-hop of 145.27.63.2, which is the SoccerOnline peering router. The InterCom-SoccerOnline router has learned the GamesNet subnet 222.27.5.0/24 from the InterCom-GamesNet router with a next-hop of 145.27.62.2, which is the GamesNet peering router.

Example 6-5   *Carrier's Carrier External BGP-4 Exchange*

```
InterCom-GamesNet# show ip route
Codes: C - connected, S - static, I - IGRP, R - RIP, M - mobile, B - BGP
       D - EIGRP, EX - EIGRP external, O - OSPF, IA - OSPF inter area
       N1 - OSPF NSSA external type 1, N2 - OSPF NSSA external type 2
       E1 - OSPF external type 1, E2 - OSPF external type 2, E - EGP
       i - IS-IS, L1 - IS-IS level-1, L2 - IS-IS level-2, ia - IS-IS inter area
       * - candidate default, U - per-user static route, o - ODR
       P - periodic downloaded static route

Gateway of last resort is not set

i L2    145.27.63.2/32 [115/10] via 145.27.62.6, Ethernet3/1
B     216.49.24.0/24 [200/0] via 145.27.63.2, 3d00h

InterCom-SoccerOnline# show ip route
Codes: C - connected, S - static, I - IGRP, R - RIP, M - mobile, B - BGP
       D - EIGRP, EX - EIGRP external, O - OSPF, IA - OSPF inter area
       N1 - OSPF NSSA external type 1, N2 - OSPF NSSA external type 2
       E1 - OSPF external type 1, E2 - OSPF external type 2, E - EGP
       i - IS-IS, L1 - IS-IS level-1, L2 - IS-IS level-2, ia - IS-IS inter area
       * - candidate default, U - per-user static route, o - ODR
       P - periodic downloaded static route

Gateway of last resort is 194.69.27.10 to network 0.0.0.0

i L2    145.27.62.2/32 [115/10] via 145.27.63.10, Ethernet4/0
B     222.27.5.0/24 [200/0] via 145.27.62.2, 3d00h
```

The next-hops for the GamesNet and SoccerOnline subnets have been learned via the InterCom IGP, which in this case is Intermediate System-to-Intermediate System (IS-IS). These routes were injected into the InterCom IGP at the CSC CE routers, through redistribution of static routes into the IS-IS process, as shown in Example 6-6. If a dynamic routing protocol is used across the PE/CE links, then this redistribution step is not required because the next-hop addresses will be learned from the local CSC PE router.

Example 6-6   *Redistribution of BGP Next-Hops into Site IGP*

```
router isis InterCom
 redistribute static ip
```

Label Distribution Protocols on PE-CE Links

The previous sections have shown how routes are exchanged directly between VPN sites and also with the MPLS VPN backbone. Having distributed all of the routing information, you might think that connectivity is achieved between the customer sites, but you have already seen that this is not the case. Example 6-7 shows that ping tests result in no reachability between the VPN endpoints (in this case the InterCom-GamesNet router and a host on the SoccerOnline 216.29.24.0/24 subnet).

Example 6-7 *Connectivity Failure Between C Routers*

```
InterCom-GamesNet# ping 216.29.24.1

Type escape sequence to abort.
Sending 5, 100-byte ICMP Echos to 216.29.24.1, timeout is 2
             seconds:
.....
Success rate is 0 percent (0/5)
```

Let's remind ourselves what the problem is and inspect the InterCom routing table at the London CSC PE router. Having distributed everything within the control plane, data forwarding should be available, but the routing table shows that the destination subnet 216.29.24.0/24 does not exist within the InterCom VRF, as shown in Example 6-8.

Example 6-8 *Missing Routing Information at CSC PE Router*

```
EuroCom_LondonPE# show ip route vrf InterCom
Codes: C - connected, S - static, I - IGRP, R - RIP, M - mobile, B - BGP
       D - EIGRP, EX - EIGRP external, O - OSPF, IA - OSPF inter area
       N1 - OSPF NSSA external type 1, N2 - OSPF NSSA external type 2
       E1 - OSPF external type 1, E2 - OSPF external type 2, E - EGP
       i - IS-IS, L1 - IS-IS level-1, L2 - IS-IS level-2
       IT - IS-IS inter area or inter level
       * - candidate default, U - per-user static route, o - ODR
       P - periodic downloaded static route

Gateway of last resort is not set

     194.69.27.0/30 is subnetted, 1 subnets
C       194.69.27.4 is directly connected, Ethernet10/1/1
     145.27.0.0/32 is subnetted, 3 subnets
B       145.27.63.1 [200/0] via 196.49.1.3, 3d03h
S       145.27.62.2 [1/0] via 194.69.27.5
B       145.27.63.2 [200/0] via 196.49.1.3, 3d03h
```

Remember that the fundamental principle of the Carrier's Carrier architecture is to offload the MPLS VPN backbone from having to carry end-customer external routes. In our ping test example, the destination address of the ping is indeed a prefix that belongs to one of InterCom's external customers. This route was never distributed to the CSC PE router; therefore, the CSC PE router has no means of forwarding an incoming packet that contains a destination address that is external to the InterCom VPN. This means that the CSC PE router has no choice but to drop the packet and inform the CSC CE router that the destination host is unreachable.

To overcome this fundamental routing problem, the CSC PE routers must be able to forward packets from the CSC CE router based on something other than the destination IP address. One of the basic concepts of MPLS is that it separates routing from forwarding. MPLS forwards a packet based on the value of the label only; the IP address is not examined by label switch routers in the packet-forwarding path (except in the case of load balancing). If a label were pushed onto a packet *before* it got to the CSC PE router, then the CSC PE router would be able to forward all packets from the CSC CE router based on the label, regardless of whether the destination of the packet were an internal or external address. To enable this functionality, label distribution must be extended from the service provider backbone down to the CSC CE routers.

Figure 6-6 shows that LDP is extended from the EuroCom MPLS VPN backbone down to the InterCom London and Brussels CSC CE routers.

NOTE   LDP and BGP are the only label distribution protocols that are supported in a Carrier's Carrier environment; therefore, you cannot use the Tag Distribution Protocol (TDP) on the PE/CE links, although you can continue to use it within the rest of the network if you so desire.

Figure 6-6   *LDP Extension from CSC PE Router to CE Router*

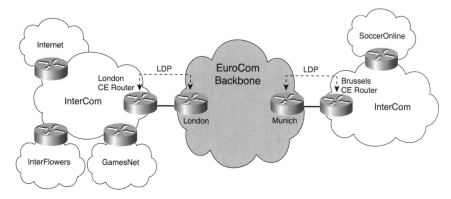

To enable LDP across the CSC PE router to CE router links, you must configure the **mpls ip** interface command on the interface. The selection of LDP as the label distribution protocol is automatic and does not need to be configured by using the **mpls label protocol**

ldp command. Example 6-9 shows the configuration of the EuroCom London CSC PE router, as well as the automatic selection of LDP.

Example 6-9 *Enabling LDP on the PE Router/CE Router Interface*

```
hostname EuroCom_LondonPE
!
interface Ethernet10/1/0
 description ** interface to InterCom London
 ip vrf forwarding InterCom
 ip address 194.69.27.6 255.255.255.252
 tag-switching ip

00:04:44: Set CSC label distribution protocol to LDP for VRF InterCom
```

After you have configured the CSC PE router and CE router for LDP label distribution, you can confirm successful establishment of the LDP session by using the **show mpls ldp discovery <vrf>** and **show mpls ldp neighbor <vrf>** commands, as illustrated in Example 6-10.

NOTE Each of the LDP commands has been extended to support the Carrier's Carrier architecture so that information for each LDP-in-a-VRF context can be displayed.

Example 6-10 *Use of show mpls ldp discovery/neighbor Commands*

```
EuroCom_LondonPE# show mpls ldp discovery vrf InterCom
 Local LDP Identifier:
    194.69.27.6:0
    Discovery Sources:
    Interfaces:
        Ethernet10/1/1 (ldp): xmit/recv
          LDP Id: 145.27.62.1:0

EuroCom_LondonPE# show mpls ldp neighbor vrf InterCom
    Peer LDP Ident: 145.27.62.1:0; Local LDP Ident 194.69.27.6:0
        TCP connection: 145.27.62.1.646 - 194.69.27.6.11002
        State: Oper; Msgs sent/rcvd: 14/19; Downstream
        Up time: 00:08:18
        LDP discovery sources:
          Ethernet10/1/1, Src IP addr: 194.69.27.5
        Addresses bound to peer LDP Ident:
          145.27.62.6    145.27.62.1    194.69.27.5
```

This example shows that an LDP session between the EuroCom London CSC PE router and the InterCom London CSC CE router has been successfully established. In this particular example, the EuroCom CSC PE router has an LDP identifier of 194.69.27.6:0, and the InterCom CSC CE router has an LDP identifier of 145.27.62.1:0. The LDP identifier is selected as the highest loopback interface address within the VRF; if no loopback interface exists, then the highest IP address available within the VRF is used.

The InterCom VRF on the EuroCom London CSC PE router contains no loopback interface. This means that the highest available IP address is the address assigned to the interface that connects to the InterCom CSC CE router. However, the InterCom CSC CE router does have a loopback address, 145.27.62.1/32; therefore, this address is used as the LDP identifier rather than the address of the link to the EuroCom CSC PE router. This is an important observation to understand, especially if static routing is used across the PE/CE link. The IP address that is used for the LDP identifier must be reachable from the LDP neighbor because the LDP sessions are established between LDP identifiers.

In our example, a static route has been provisioned at the EuroCom London CSC PE router that points toward the InterCom CSC CE router loopback address, 145.27.62.1/32. If the static route is removed from the EuroCom CSC PE router, then you can no longer establish an LDP session with the InterCom CSC CE router (see Example 6-11).

Example 6-11 *LDP Identifier Usage with Static Routing*

```
EuroCom_London-PE# show mpls ldp discovery vrf InterCom
  Local LDP Identifier:
    194.69.27.6:0
    Discovery Sources:
    Interfaces:
        Ethernet10/1/1 (ldp): xmit/recv
            LDP Id: 145.27.62.1:0; no route
```

This example clearly shows that *no route* exists at the EuroCom CSC PE router for the remote LDP identifier (145.27.62.1:0); therefore, a problem exists. A session cannot be established because this address is used as the transport address for the TCP connection.

LDP Discovery: Transport Address Usage

You can clearly avoid the problem in the previous example by configuring a static route within the VRF on the CSC PE router. However, this problem occurs because the transport address used to establish the TCP session between the CSC PE router and CE router is the same as the LDP identifier address. You can change this default behavior by using the **mpls ldp discovery transport-address** command on the link that attaches the CSC PE router to the CE router, as shown in Example 6-12.

Example 6-12 *mpls ldp discovery transport-address*

```
EuroCom_LondonPE(config)# interface e10/1/1
EuroCom_LondonPE(config-if)# mpls ldp discovery transport-address interface

InterCom_LondonCE# interface e5/1
InterCom_LondonCE(config-if)# mpls ldp discovery transport-address interface
```

Having specified that the transport address should be the same as the local interface address, Example 6-13 shows that the LDP session is successfully established.

Example 6-13 *Successful LDP Discovery with transport-address*

```
EuroCom_LondonPE# show mpls ldp discovery vrf InterCom
 Local LDP Identifier:
    194.69.27.6:0
    Discovery Sources:
    Interfaces:
        Ethernet10/1/1 (ldp): xmit/recv
            LDP Id: 145.27.62.1:0; IP addr: 194.69.27.5

EuroCom_LondonPE# show mpls ldp neighbor vrf InterCom
    Peer LDP Ident: 145.27.62.1:0; Local LDP Ident 194.69.27.6:0
        TCP connection: 194.69.27.5.646 - 194.69.27.6.11296
        State: Oper; Msgs sent/rcvd: 9/15; Downstream
        Up time: 00:03:41
        LDP discovery sources:
          Ethernet10/1/1, Src IP addr: 194.69.27.5
        Addresses bound to peer LDP Ident:
          145.27.62.6    145.27.62.1    194.69.27.5
```

As Example 6-13 shows, the LDP identifier is not affected by the **mpls ldp discovery transport-address** command. However, the TCP connection between the CSC CE router and PE router is now between **194.69.27.5.646 – 194.69.27.6.11296**, which are the local interface addresses. (646 is the TCP port used for LDP.)

NOTE   A further option to resolve the LDP session establishment problem is to configure the LDP router-id manually at the CSC CE router by using the **mpls ldp router-id** command. This forces the LDP identifier to be the IP address of the specified interface. However, the problem with this solution is that the link to the CSC PE router might flap, causing the router-id to change and creating potential instability. Therefore, it is recommended that you set the router-id to a loopback interface on the CSC CE router and specify the transport address to be used via the **mpls ldp discovery transport-address** command. You should also use this command at the CSC PE router if more than one interface is associated with the CSC VRF.

Label Distribution Between CSC PE Router and CE Router

After LDP has been enabled on the CSC PE router to CE router links, labels for internal routes are exchanged between the CSC PE router and the CE router. Example 6-14 shows the label exchange between the EuroCom London CSC PE router and the InterCom London CSC CE router.

Example 6-14 *Label Exchange Confirmation Between PE/CE Routers*

```
EuroCom_LondonPE# show mpls forwarding vrf InterCom
Local  Outgoing     Prefix           Bytes tag  Outgoing   Next Hop
tag    tag or VC    or Tunnel Id     switched   interface
19     Pop tag      145.27.62.1/32[V] 9934        Et10/1/1   194.69.27.5
20     17           145.27.62.2/32[V] 12084       Et10/1/1   194.69.27.5
21     27           145.27.63.2/32[V] 8404        AT9/0/0    10.2.1.10
22     27           145.27.63.1/32[V] 7930        AT9/0/0    10.2.1.10


InterCom_LondonCE# show mpls forwarding
Local  Outgoing     Prefix           Bytes tag  Outgoing   Next Hop
tag    tag or VC    or Tunnel Id     switched   interface
16     22           145.27.63.1/32   0           Et5/1      194.69.27.6
17     Untagged     145.27.62.2/32   11714       Et5/0      145.27.62.5
18     21           145.27.63.2/32   0           Et5/1      194.69.27.6
```

The output for the EuroCom London CSC PE router shows that subnets 145.27.62.1/32 and 145.27.62.2 (the loopbacks of the InterCom London CSC CE router and the InterCom GamesNet router) are reachable via 194.69.27.5 (the InterCom London CSC CE router). Subnets 145.27.63.1/32 and 145.27.63.2/32 (the InterCom Brussels CSC CE router and the InterCom SoccerOnline router) are reachable via 10.2.1.20 (a P router within the EuroCom MPLS VPN backbone).

The output for the InterCom London CSC CE router shows that subnets 145.27.63.1/32 and 145.27.63.2/32 are reachable via 194.69.27.6 (the EuroCom London CSC PE router). The 145.27.62.2/32 subnet (the InterCom GamesNet router) is reachable via 145.27.62.5 (the directly connected interface address on the InterCom GamesNet router). The link between the London CSC CE router and the GamesNet router does not have label switching enabled; therefore, packets that are destined to 145.27.62.2 are *untagged*.

Using this label forwarding information, connectivity within the InterCom VPN is established, as shown in Example 6-15. The full data-path from the InterCom-GamesNet router to the InterCom-SoccerOnline router is provided within the example and in Figure 6-7.

Example 6-15 *Successful Connectivity Within the InterCom VPN*

```
InterCom-GamesNet# ping 216.49.24.1

Type escape sequence to abort.
Sending 5, 100-byte ICMP Echos to 216.49.24.1, timeout is 2
            seconds:
!!!!!
Success rate is 100 percent (5/5), round-trip min/avg/max = 1/3/4 ms

InterCom-Gamesnet# show ip cef 216.49.24.0
216.49.24.0/24, version 81, cached adjacency 145.27.62.6
0 packets, 0 bytes
  via 145.27.63.2, 0 dependencies, recursive
    next hop 145.27.62.6, Ethernet3/1 via 145.27.63.2/32
    valid cached adjacency
```

continues

Example 6-15   *Successful Connectivity Within the InterCom VPN (Continued)*

```
InterCom-GamesNet# show ip cef 145.27.63.2
145.27.63.2/32, version 80, cached adjacency 145.27.62.6
0 packets, 0 bytes
  via 145.27.62.6, Ethernet3/1, 1 dependency
    next hop 145.27.62.6, Ethernet3/1
    valid cached adjacency

InterCom_LondonCE# show ip cef 216.49.24.0
216.49.24.0/24, version 44, cached adjacency 194.69.27.6
0 packets, 0 bytes
  tag information from 145.27.63.2/32, shared, unshareable
    local tag: 18
    fast tag rewrite with Et5/1, 194.69.27.6, tags imposed {21}
  via 145.27.63.2, 0 dependencies, recursive
    next hop 194.69.27.6, Ethernet5/1 via 145.27.63.2/32
    valid cached adjacency
    tag rewrite with Et5/1, 194.69.27.6, tags imposed {21}
NOTE## the label value of <21> corresponds to the BGP next-hop of
the 216.49.24.0/24 subnet

EuroCom_LondonPE# show mpls forwarding label 21
Local  Outgoing     Prefix          Bytes tag  Outgoing    Next Hop
tag    tag or VC    or Tunnel Id    switched   interface
21     27           145.27.63.2/32[V] 11106     AT9/0/0     10.2.1.10

EuroCom_LondonPE# show ip cef vrf InterCom 145.27.63.2
145.27.63.2/32, version 16, cached adjacency 10.2.1.10
0 packets, 0 bytes
  tag information set
    local tag: 21
    fast tag rewrite with AT9/0/0, 10.2.1.10, tags imposed {27 20}
  via 196.49.1.3, 0 dependencies, recursive
    next hop 10.2.1.10, ATM9/0/0 via 196.49.1.3/32
    valid cached adjacency
    tag rewrite with AT9/0/0, 10.2.1.10, tags imposed {27 20}

EuroCom_P# show mpls forwarding
Local  Outgoing     Prefix          Bytes tag  Outgoing    Next Hop
tag    tag or VC    or Tunnel Id    switched   interface
27     Pop tag      196.49.1.3/32   134180     AT0/0       10.2.1.21

EuroCom_MunichPE# show mpls forwarding label 20
Local  Outgoing     Prefix          Bytes tag  Outgoing    Next Hop
tag    tag or VC    or Tunnel Id    switched   interface
20     18           145.27.63.2/32[V] 0         Se10/0/1    point2point

InterCom_BrusselsCE# show mpls forwarding label 18
Local  Outgoing     Prefix          Bytes tag  Outgoing    Next Hop
tag    tag or VC    or Tunnel Id    switched   interface
18     Untagged     145.27.63.2/32  200        Et3/0       145.27.63.9
```

Figure 6-7   *LSP for InterCom VPN*

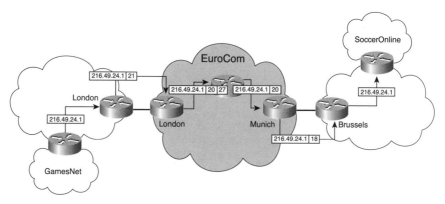

NOTE	A successful ping of the SoccerOnline subnet from the InterCom London site relies on the fact that the InterCom London CSC CE router knows of the SoccerOnline subnet. This is because the London CSC CE router receives an IP packet that has a destination address of 216.49.24.1 and must perform a lookup in the forwarding information base (FIB) for this destination. To remove this requirement, you must extend label distribution into the attached site so that an LSP is available from the ingress edge router to the egress edge router. This means that in our example, you need to extend LDP to the GamesNet and SoccerOnline edge routers so that the InterCom CSC CE routers perform label switching only. As explained earlier in this chapter, extending LDP into each Carrier's Carrier site removes the requirement for BGP-4 peering at the CSC CE routers and reduces the complexity of the BGP topology.

Use of Static Default Routes at CSC CE Routers

The use of static default routes (that point toward the CSC PE router for external next-hop reachability) at the CSC CE router are not possible within the Carrier's Carrier architecture. To help illustrate this restriction, let's assume that the InterCom CSC CE routers have been configured with static default routes instead of the specific static routes that we described earlier. Example 6-16 shows that because of the static default route configuration, no connectivity is available from the InterCom London CSC CE router to the SoccerOnline subnet 216.49.24.0/24.

Example 6-16   *Connectivity Between InterCom CSC CE Routers*

```
InterCom_LondonCE# ping 216.49.24.1

Type escape sequence to abort.
Sending 5, 100-byte ICMP Echos to 216.49.24.1, timeout is 2
                seconds:
.....
Success rate is 0 percent (0/5)
```

This loss of connectivity occurred because the CSC PE router must rely on label switching to forward traffic within the VPN for external routes. Because no label is available for the default route, forwarding fails. Even if a label were available at the CSC PE router, forwarding might still fail because packets might be sent to one exit point rather than to the correct egress CSC PE router.

Example 6-17 *Default Restriction in Carrier's Carrier Environment*

```
InterCom_LondonCE# show ip route 216.49.24.0
Routing entry for 216.49.24.0/24
  Known via "bgp 10", distance 200, metric 0, type internal
  Last update from 145.27.63.2 00:32:17 ago
  Routing Descriptor Blocks:
  * 145.27.63.2, from 145.27.63.1, 00:32:17 ago
      Route metric is 0, traffic share count is 1
      AS Hops 0

InterCom_LondonCE# show ip route 145.27.63.2
% Subnet not in table

InterCom_LondonCE# show ip route 0.0.0.0
Routing entry for 0.0.0.0/0, supernet
  Known via "static", distance 1, metric 0, candidate default path
  Routing Descriptor Blocks:
  * 194.69.27.6
      Route metric is 0, traffic share count is 1

InterCom_LondonCE# show ip cef 216.49.24.1
216.49.24.0/24, version 1735, cached adjacency 194.69.27.6
0 packets, 0 bytes
  tag information from 0.0.0.0/0, shared, unshareable
    local tag: implicit-null
  via 145.27.63.2, 0 dependencies, recursive
    next hop 194.69.27.6, Ethernet5/1 via 0.0.0.0/0
    valid cached adjacency
```

As illustrated in Example 6-17, the 216.49.24.0/24 subnet is reachable via a next-hop of 145.27.63.2 (the InterCom SoccerOnline peering router). This next-hop does not exist within the routing table, so you must use the default route. This default points to a next-hop of 194.69.27.6, which is the EuroCom London CSC PE router. The CEF entry for the 216.49.24.0/24 subnet shows that no label stack is prepended to the outgoing packets when they are sent toward the CSC PE router; therefore, forwarding fails because the CSC PE router has no forwarding entry for the 216.49.24.0/24 subnet. To overcome this issue, the CSC CE router must have static routes pointing toward the BGP next-hop for external routes. A default that points from the CSC CE router to the CSC PE router is impossible within the Carrier's Carrier environment.

BGP-4 Between PE/CE Routers

Previous examples of the Carrier's Carrier architecture used LDP on the CSC PE router to CE router links to distribute labels for the IGP routes. However, in many cases, such as an ISP environment, BGP-4 is the preferred protocol for routing exchange (more so because the PE-CE protocol is usually dictated by the service providers, and many of them prefer BGP-4). Therefore, support for this protocol has been added to Cisco IOS. This support is referred to as *IPv4 + Labels*, or RFC 3107 support. It provides the ability to assign labels to BGP routes, which is not available in standard MPLS software, and removes the requirement of running LDP on the PE-CE links.

Figure 6-8 shows that InterCom has chosen to use BGP-4 on its link to the EuroCom backbone. LDP has also been enabled within each of its sites so that it does not have to hold all its external routes on its CSC CE routers.

Figure 6-8   *BGP-4 on PE Router/CE Router Links for Carrier's Carrier*

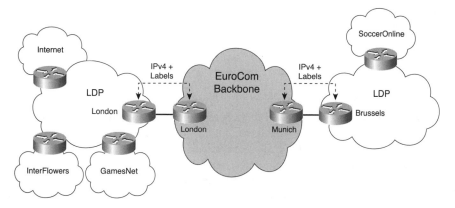

To enable the exchange of labels with BGP-4 routes, a new extension, **send-labels**, has been added to the BGP **neighbor** command, as you can see in Example 6-18.

Example 6-18   *send-labels Extension to neighbor Command*

```
hostname EuroCom_LondonPE
!
router bgp 20
 no bgp default ipv4-unicast
 bgp log-neighbor-changes
 neighbor 196.49.1.3 remote-as 20
 neighbor 196.49.1.3 update-source Loopback0
 no auto-summary
 !
 address-family vpnv4
 neighbor 196.49.1.3 activate
 neighbor 196.49.1.3 send-community extended
 exit-address-family
 !
```

continues

Example 6-18   *send-labels Extension to neighbor Command (Continued)*

```
  address-family ipv4 vrf InterCom
  neighbor 194.69.27.5 remote-as 100
  neighbor 194.69.27.5 activate
  neighbor 194.69.27.5 as-override
  neighbor 194.69.27.5 send-label
 no auto-summary
 no synchronization
 exit-address-family
- - - - - - - - - - - - - - - - - - - - - - - - - - - - - - - - - - - - - - - - - -
hostname InterCom_LondonCE
!
router bgp 100
 neighbor 194.69.27.6 remote-as 20
 !
 address-family ipv4
 neighbor 194.69.27.6 activate
 neighbor 194.69.27.6 send-label
 no auto-summary
 no synchronization
 exit-address-family
```

NOTE   Example 6-18 also shows the use of the **as-override** command. This command (extensively covered in Chapter 11 of *MPLS and VPN Architectures*, Volume 1) is necessary within the InterCom VPN because each of its sites uses the same autonomous system number. In normal operation, a BGP-4 speaker ignores any update that contains its own autonomous system number. However, when **as-override** is configured, the CSC PE router replaces the InterCom autonomous system number with the autonomous system number of the MPLS VPN backbone, thus allowing successful reachability between end-customer sites.

The **neighbor <IP-address> send-label** command is configured within the ipv4 address-family. You can check successful establishment of this BGP-4 capability for each neighbor, as illustrated in Example 6-19.

Example 6-19   *Confirmation of send-label Capability*

```
EuroCom_LondonPE# show ip bgp neighbor
BGP neighbor is 194.69.27.5, vrf InterCom, remote AS 100, external link
  BGP version 4, remote router ID 145.27.62.1
  BGP state = Established, up for 00:58:53
  Last read 00:00:53, hold time is 180, keepalive interval is 60 seconds
  Neighbor capabilities:
    Route refresh: advertised and received(new)
    Address family IPv4 Unicast: advertised and received
    IPv4 MPLS Label capability: advertised and received

...rest clipped
```

After a BGP-4 session has been successfully established between the CSC PE router and the CE router, exchange of routes using IPv4 + Labels can occur, and InterCom can exchange its internal routes with the EuroCom backbone. Example 6-20 provides an illustration of how the InterCom London CSC CE router receives a label for the SoccerOnline edge router address 145.27.63.2/32 from the EuroCom London CSC PE router.

Example 6-20 *IPv4 + Labels Receipt by CE Router*

```
InterCom_LondonCE# show ip bgp label
Network          Next Hop          In Label/Out Label
145.27.63.2/32   194.69.27.6       18/20
```

This example shows that a label value of <20> has been received from the EuroCom London CSC PE router for the SoccerOnline edge router address 145.27.63.2/32. The InterCom CSC CE router uses this label for all traffic that it sends toward 145.27.63.2, including all external BGP-4 routes that are reachable via this next-hop address.

Filtering Routes on CSC CE Router to PE Router Links

The injection of internal routes into the BGP process that runs across the CSC CE router to PE router link is achieved through redistribution. The CSC CE router injects internal routes into IPv4 + Labels by redistributing from the local routing process, as shown in Example 6-21.

Example 6-21 *Redistribution from IGP into IPv4 + Labels*

```
hostname InterCom_LondonCE
!
router bgp 100
  neighbor 194.69.27.6 remote-as 20
  !
  address-family ipv4
  redistribute isis InterCom level-2
```

By default, all internal routes within the local IGP process are redistributed. To prevent this and only redistribute selected routes such as the BGP-4 next-hop addresses, you must apply filtering, either during the redistribution or when the routes are sent to the CSC PE router across the BGP-4 session. Example 6-22 provides an example of how the InterCom London CSC CE router filters everything except the loopback address of the GamesNet edge router, 145.27.62.2/32.

Example 6-22 *Filtering of IPv4 + Labels Updates*

```
hostname InterCom_LondonCE
!
router bgp 100
  neighbor 194.69.27.6 remote-as 20
  !
  address-family ipv4
  redistribute isis InterCom level-1-2
  neighbor 194.69.27.6 activate
```

continues

Example 6-22 *Filtering of IPv4 + Labels Updates (Continued)*

```
 neighbor 194.69.27.6 route-map INTERNAL out
 neighbor 194.69.27.6 send-label
 no auto-summary
 no synchronization
 exit-address-family
!
access-list 1 permit 145.27.62.2
route-map INTERNAL permit 10
 match ip address 1
 set mpls-label
```

This example shows that routes are filtered when they are advertised toward the BGP-4 neighbor (to illustrate the need for the **set mpls-label** command). However, if this filtering were to be performed during redistribution, then the undesirable routes would never make it into the BGP table and filtering at the BGP-4 level would not be required. Therefore, the recommended filtering mechanism in this environment is to use route maps and filter during redistribution.

NOTE

You can use a *route map* that you apply to a BGP neighbor to control MPLS label propagation in BGP-4 updates. When you are setting a route map, as shown in Example 6-22, you must configure the **set mpls-label** command to allow label allocation for BGP-4 routes. By default, when you set a route map, all prefixes are sent unlabelled. Therefore, this command is required if you want MPLS labels attached to BGP-4 routes.

Having distributed all of the necessary label information, Example 6-23 shows the complete LSP between the GamesNet edge router and the SoccerOnline edge router, to reach the 216.49.24.0/24 subnet. Figure 6-9 provides an illustration of this LSP.

Example 6-23 *IPv4 + Labels LSP Between GamesNet and SoccerOnline*

```
InterCom-GamesNet# ping 216.49.24.1

Type escape sequence to abort.
Sending 5, 100-byte ICMP Echos to 216.49.24.1, timeout is 2
             seconds:
!!!!!

InterCom-GamesNet# show ip cef 216.49.24.0
216.49.24.0/24, version 56, cached adjacency 145.27.62.6
0 packets, 0 bytes
  tag information from 145.27.63.2/32, shared
    local tag: 17
    fast tag rewrite with Et3/1, 145.27.62.6, tags imposed {18}
  via 145.27.63.2, 0 dependencies, recursive
    next hop 145.27.62.6, Ethernet3/1 via 145.27.63.2/32
```

Example 6-23 *IPv4 + Labels LSP Between GamesNet and SoccerOnline (Continued)*

```
        valid cached adjacency
        tag rewrite with Et3/1, 145.27.62.6, tags imposed {18}

InterCom_LondonCE# show mpls forwarding label 18
Local  Outgoing    Prefix          Bytes tag  Outgoing   Next Hop
tag    tag or VC   or Tunnel Id    switched   interface
18     20          145.27.63.2/32  12594      Et5/1      194.69.27.6

EuroCom_LondonPE# show mpls forwarding label 20
Local  Outgoing    Prefix             Bytes tag  Outgoing   Next Hop
tag    tag or VC   or Tunnel Id       switched   interface
20     27          145.27.63.2/32[V]  13089      AT9/0/0    10.2.1.10

EuroCom_LondonPE# show ip cef vrf InterCom 145.27.63.2
145.27.63.2/32, version 10, cached adjacency 10.2.1.10
0 packets, 0 bytes
  tag information set
    local tag: 20
    fast tag rewrite with AT9/0/0, 10.2.1.10, tags imposed {27 19}
  via 196.49.1.3, 0 dependencies, recursive
    next hop 10.2.1.10, ATM9/0/0 via 196.49.1.3/32
    valid cached adjacency
    tag rewrite with AT9/0/0, 10.2.1.10, tags imposed {27 19}

EuroCom_MunichPE# show mpls forwarding label 19
Local  Outgoing    Prefix             Bytes tag  Outgoing   Next Hop
tag    tag or VC   or Tunnel Id       switched   interface
19     16          145.27.63.2/32[V]  10282      Se10/0/1   point2point

InterCom_LondonCE# show mpls forwarding label 16
Local  Outgoing    Prefix          Bytes tag  Outgoing   Next Hop
tag    tag or VC   or Tunnel Id    switched   interface
16     Pop tag     145.27.62.2/32  0          Et5/0      145.27.62.5
```

Figure 6-9 *IPv4 + Labels LSP Between GamesNet and SoccerOnline*

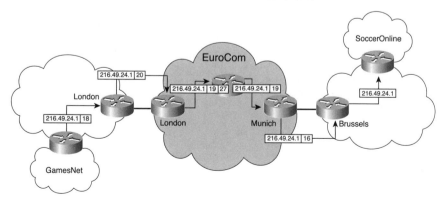

Hierarchical VPNs: Carrier's Carrier MPLS VPNs

In some cases, the customer of the Carrier MPLS VPN backbone network might also want to provide MPLS VPN services to its own customers. This type of connectivity is referred to as *hierarchical VPNs*, with multiple levels of VPNv4 label allocation.

Figure 6-10 shows that InterCom is now providing MPLS VPN services to GamesNet and SoccerOnline, and they have connectivity within their own extranet.

Figure 6-10   *MPLS VPN Extranet Between GamesNet and SoccerOnline*

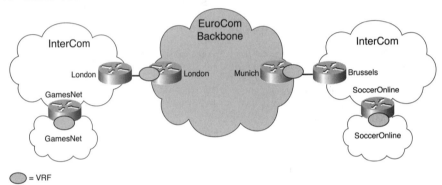

As you can see in Figure 6-10, the InterCom GamesNet and SoccerOnline edge routers now provide MPLS VPN PE router functionality to GamesNet and SoccerOnline. You can see the configuration of the InterCom GamesNet PE router in Example 6-24. For the sake of simplicity, only a single IP prefix that is assigned to a loopback interface belonging to the GamesNet VPN is shown in the printouts and configuration examples that follow.

Example 6-24   *Configuration of GamesNet and SoccerOnline PE Routers*

```
hostname InterCom_GamesNet
!
ip vrf GamesNet
 rd 99:1234
 route-target export 100:99
 route-target import 100:99
!
interface loopback0
 description ** loopback for GamesNet
 ip vrf forwarding GamesNet
 ip address 222.27.5.1 255.255.255.255
!
router bgp 100
 no bgp default ipv4-unicast
 bgp log-neighbor-changes
 neighbor 145.27.63.2 remote-as 100
 neighbor 145.27.63.2 update-source Loopback0
 no auto-summary
 !
```

Example 6-24   *Configuration of GamesNet and SoccerOnline PE Routers (Continued)*

```
address-family vpnv4
neighbor 145.27.63.2 activate
neighbor 145.27.63.2 send-community extended
exit-address-family
!
address-family ipv4 vrf GamesNet
redistribute connected
no auto-summary
no synchronization
exit-address-family
```

The main change from the previous Carrier's Carriers configuration examples is that the BGP session between the GamesNet and SoccerOnline edge routers is now Multiprotocol BGP rather than IPv4 BGP. This change does not affect the InterCom or EuroCom backbone at all because the BGP session is transported as application data across the network. The forwarding among InterCom sites, PE-CE links, and the EuroCom backbone is also unchanged; MPLS is still used to transport the VPN traffic. The only difference between this architecture and the simpler Carrier's Carrier architecture is that the VPN traffic is transported across the network with an extra MPLS label (InterCom's VPN label) attached.

Using the configuration from Example 6-24, you can see in Example 6-25 the LSP used to provide connectivity within the GamesNet/SoccerOnline extranet. Figure 6-11 shows an illustration of this LSP.

Example 6-25   *Hierarchical VPN LSP Example*

```
InterCom_GamesNet# show ip cef vrf GamesNet 216.49.24.1
216.49.24.1/32, version 5, cached adjacency 145.27.62.6
0 packets, 0 bytes
  tag information set
    local tag: VPN route head
    fast tag rewrite with Et3/1, 145.27.62.6, tags imposed {19 18}
  via 145.27.63.2, 0 dependencies, recursive
    next hop 145.27.62.6, Ethernet3/1 via 145.27.63.2/32
    valid cached adjacency
    tag rewrite with Et3/1, 145.27.62.6, tags imposed {19 18}

InterCom_LondonCE# show mpls forwarding label 19
Local  Outgoing    Prefix         Bytes tag  Outgoing    Next Hop
tag    tag or VC   or Tunnel Id   switched   interface
19     20          145.27.63.2/32    13902    Et5/1       194.69.27.6

EuroCom_LondonPE# show mpls forwarding label 20
Local  Outgoing    Prefix         Bytes tag  Outgoing    Next Hop
tag    tag or VC   or Tunnel Id   switched   interface
20     27          145.27.63.2/32[V] 16196   AT9/0/0     10.2.1.10

EuroCom_LondonPE# show ip cef vrf InterCom 145.27.63.2
145.27.63.2/32, version 12, cached adjacency 10.2.1.10
0 packets, 0 bytes
```

continues

Example 6-25 *Hierarchical VPN LSP Example (Continued)*

```
   tag information set
     local tag: 20
     fast tag rewrite with AT9/0/0, 10.2.1.10, tags imposed {27 21}
   via 196.49.1.3, 0 dependencies, recursive
     next hop 10.2.1.10, ATM9/0/0 via 196.49.1.3/32
     valid cached adjacency
     tag rewrite with AT9/0/0, 10.2.1.10, tags imposed {27 21}

EuroCom_MunichPE# show mpls forwarding label 21
Local  Outgoing     Prefix           Bytes tag  Outgoing     Next Hop
tag    tag or VC    or Tunnel Id     switched   interface
21     16           145.27.63.2/32[V] 13697      Se10/0/1     point2point

InterCom_BrusselsCE# show mpls forwarding label 16
Local  Outgoing     Prefix           Bytes tag  Outgoing     Next Hop
tag    tag or VC    or Tunnel Id     switched   interface
16     Pop tag      145.27.63.2/32   14968      Et3/0        145.27.63.9

InterCom_SoccerOnline# show mpls forwarding label 18
Local  Outgoing     Prefix           Bytes tag  Outgoing     Next Hop
tag    tag or VC    or Tunnel Id     switched   interface
18     Aggregate    216.49.24.1/32[V] 1040
```

Figure 6-11 *LSP*

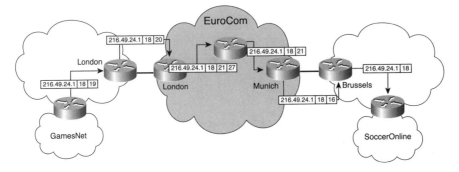

VPN Connectivity Between Different Service Providers

As the popularity of the MPLS VPN solution has grown, so has the size and reach of the end-customers of the service. The greater the number of sites within a particular Enterprise, the greater the likelihood that certain geographic locations will attach to different service providers. This requires a different connectivity model than the base MPLS VPN architecture provides.

In this situation, transit traffic between customer sites must pass through more than one autonomous system and more than one MPLS VPN backbone. Consider Figure 6-12, which shows how the sites within the BankCorp VPN attach to their local carriers.

Figure 6-12 *BankCorp Interprovider Topology*

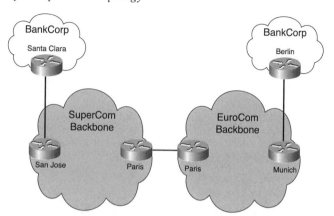

Figure 6-12 illustrates that BankCorp has two sites: Santa Clara, which attaches to the SuperCom MPLS VPN backbone via the San Jose PE router; and Berlin, which attaches to the EuroCom MPLS VPN backbone via the Munich PE router. The relevant IP address assignments for BankCorp are shown in Table 6-3.

Clearly, BankCorp would like to have connectivity between these sites, but that requires the exchange of VPN-specific routes between the SuperCom and EuroCom networks. This type of connectivity is collectively referred to as *InterAS* or *Interprovider VPN*.

Table 6-3   *IP Address Assignment for BankCorp VPN*

Company	Site	Subnet
BankCorp	Santa Clara	198.121.63.0/24
	Berlin	198.121.62.0/24

Interprovider Connectivity Requirements

To support the exchange of VPN routing information between service providers, a new mechanism is required so that prefix and label details can be advertised across the interprovider links. As Figure 6-13 shows, normal MPLS VPN procedures are run within each autonomous system, and any PE routers that have relevant customer sites attached can import the routing information through use of the route-target extended community attribute. However, the base architecture does not provide the ability to advertise this information to other service providers, which means that extensions to the protocols are required.

Figure 6-13   *InterAS Connectivity Model*

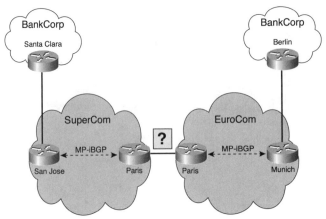

As illustrated in Figure 6-13, the SuperCom and EuroCom autonomous system boundary routers (ASBRs) have no means with which to exchange the routes for the BankCorp VPN. As you will see in the sections that follow, there are actually several ways to support the exchange of VPN routing information among service providers:

- Back-to-back VRF solution
- External Multiprotocol BGP
- Multihop MP-eBGP for VPNv4 prefix exchange
- Multihop MP-eBGP between route reflectors

The option selected for deployment depends on a number of factors, such as the number of InterAS VPN clients, the amount of VPN routing information to exchange, filtering policies, and so on.

Back-to-Back VRF Solution

The simplest solution to implement is *back-to-back* VRFs. This method essentially turns each of the ASBR routers into PE routers that treat the adjacent service provider ASBR as a CE router. This means that in our example, the SuperCom Paris ASBR sees the EuroCom Paris ASBR as a CE router, and vice versa. This is illustrated in Figure 6-14, with the relevant configuration of each ASBR provided in Example 6-26.

Figure 6-14 *Back-to-Back VRF Deployment*

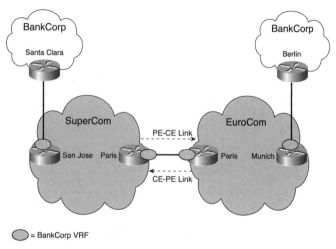

= BankCorp VRF

Example 6-26 *Back-to-Back VRF ASBR Configuration*

```
hostname SuperComParis-ASBR
!
ip vrf BankCorp
 rd 10:4972
 route-target export 20:123
 route-target import 20:123
!
interface POS10/0/0
 description ** interface to EuroCom Paris-ASBR
 ip vrf forwarding BankCorp
 ip address 192.168.2.37 255.255.255.252


------------------------------------------------------------------------
hostname EuroComParis-ASBR
!
ip vrf BankCorp
 rd 99:5432
 route-target export 20:123
 route-target import 20:123
!
interface POS8/1/0
 description ** interface to SuperCom Paris-ASBR
 ip vrf forwarding BankCorp
 ip address 192.168.2.38 255.255.255.252
```

This configuration results in each of the ASBR routers learning routes for BankCorp sites within their own autonomous system. The EuroCom Paris ASBR learns routes 194.69.27.16/30 (the PE-CE link on the Munich PE router) and 198.121.62.0/24 (the

BankCorp Berlin site reachable via Munich). The SuperCom Paris ASBR learns routes 192.168.2.32/30 (the PE-CE link on the San Jose PE router) and 198.121.63.0/24 (the BankCorp Santa Clara site reachable via San Jose).

NOTE	Example 6-27 shows the connectivity requirements of only one VPN client. However, a real deployment would clearly have multiple VPN clients, each of which would require their own back-to-back VRF connection between the ASBRs. The only way to scale such connectivity is to implement a logical interface per-VPN across the physical link. Frame Relay subinterfaces are an example of this, in which a single data-link connection identifier (DLCI) is used per-client. Such connectivity is discussed in detail in Chapter 4, "Virtual Router Connectivity."

Example 6-27 *BankCorp Routes Within ASBR Prior to InterAS Distribution*

```
EuroComParis-ASBR# show ip route vrf BankCorp
Codes: C - connected, S - static, I - IGRP, R - RIP, M - mobile, B - BGP
       D - EIGRP, EX - EIGRP external, O - OSPF, IA - OSPF inter area
       N1 - OSPF NSSA external type 1, N2 - OSPF NSSA external type 2
       E1 - OSPF external type 1, E2 - OSPF external type 2, E - EGP
       i - IS-IS, L1 - IS-IS level-1, L2 - IS-IS level-2, ia - IS-IS inter area
       * - candidate default, U - per-user static route, o - ODR

Gateway of last resort is not set

     194.69.27.0/30 is subnetted, 1 subnets
B       194.69.27.16 [200/0] via 196.49.1.3, 21:39:37
B    198.121.62.0/24 [200/1] via 196.49.1.3, 21:39:37
     192.168.2.0/30 is subnetted, 1 subnets
C       192.168.2.36 is directly connected, POS8/1/0

SuperComParis-ASBR# show ip route vrf BankCorp
Codes: C - connected, S - static, I - IGRP, R - RIP, M - mobile, B - BGP
       D - EIGRP, EX - EIGRP external, O - OSPF, IA - OSPF inter area
       N1 - OSPF NSSA external type 1, N2 - OSPF NSSA external type 2
       E1 - OSPF external type 1, E2 - OSPF external type 2, E - EGP
       i - IS-IS, L1 - IS-IS level-1, L2 - IS-IS level-2, ia - IS-IS inter area
       * - candidate default, U - per-user static route, o - ODR

Gateway of last resort is not set

B    198.121.63.0/24 [200/1] via 194.22.15.1, 21:57:36
     192.168.2.0/30 is subnetted, 2 subnets
B       192.168.2.32 [200/0] via 194.22.15.1, 21:57:37
C       192.168.2.36 is directly connected, POS10/0/0
```

Distribution of Routes Across ASBR-ASBR Link

Having imported all the local routes into the ASBR VRFs, the next step is to distribute the routes to the adjacent service provider by using a dynamic routing protocol per-VRF. After this step is complete, any packets received across the ASBR-ASBR link and destined for one of the subnets within the VRF will be label switched by using the normal MPLS VPN forwarding mechanisms.

You can use any of the currently supported PE-CE routing protocols across the ASBR-ASBR link. Although IGP protocols can theoretically be used because the link is an inter-autonomous system connection, in most cases, the service provider prefers to use BGP-4 for the exchange of routing information. Using an IGP protocol requires redistribution at the border routers, and static routing involves coordination of the ASBR configuration (which is simply not feasible). In contrast, no extra configuration is needed when you are running BGP between the ASBRs. In addition, BGP-4 provides better policy and security mechanisms; therefore, it is the protocol of choice in this environment.

Both EuroCom and SuperCom have chosen to use BGP-4 on the ASBR-ASBR link. The configuration of both ASBRs is shown in Example 6-28.

Example 6-28 *BGP-4 Configuration of ASBR Routers*

```
hostname SuperComParis-ASBR
!
router bgp 10
 no bgp default ipv4-unicast
 bgp log-neighbor-changes
 neighbor 194.22.15.1 remote-as 10
 neighbor 194.22.15.1 update-source Loopback0
 no auto-summary
 !
 address-family vpnv4
 neighbor 194.22.15.1 activate
 neighbor 194.22.15.1 send-community extended
 exit-address-family
 !
 address-family ipv4 vrf BankCorp
 neighbor 192.168.2.38 remote-as 20
 neighbor 192.168.2.38 activate
 no auto-summary
 no synchronization
 exit-address-family
-----------------------------------------------------------------
hostname EuroComParis-ASBR
!
router bgp 20
 no bgp default ipv4-unicast
 bgp log-neighbor-changes
 neighbor 196.49.1.3 remote-as 20
 neighbor 196.49.1.3 update-source Loopback0
 no auto-summary
 !
```

continues

Example 6-28 *BGP-4 Configuration of ASBR Routers (Continued)*

```
address-family vpnv4
neighbor 196.49.1.3 activate
neighbor 196.49.1.3 send-community extended
exit-address-family
!
address-family ipv4 vrf BankCorp
neighbor 192.168.2.37 remote-as 10
neighbor 192.168.2.37 activate
no auto-summary
no synchronization
exit-address-family
```

Now that a BGP-4 session is available within the BankCorp VRF, Example 6-29 shows that all the BankCorp routes are available at each ASBR.

Example 6-29 *BankCorp Routes at ASBRs After BGP-4 Distribution*

```
SuperComParis-ASBR# show ip route vrf BankCorp
Codes: C - connected, S - static, I - IGRP, R - RIP, M - mobile, B - BGP
       D - EIGRP, EX - EIGRP external, O - OSPF, IA - OSPF inter area
       N1 - OSPF NSSA external type 1, N2 - OSPF NSSA external type 2
       E1 - OSPF external type 1, E2 - OSPF external type 2, E - EGP
       i - IS-IS, L1 - IS-IS level-1, L2 - IS-IS level-2, ia - IS-IS inter area
       * - candidate default, U - per-user static route, o - ODR

Gateway of last resort is not set

     194.69.27.0/30 is subnetted, 1 subnets
B       194.69.27.16 [20/0] via 192.168.2.38, 00:02:20
B    198.121.63.0/24 [200/1] via 194.22.15.1, 22:23:35
B    198.121.62.0/24 [20/0] via 192.168.2.38, 00:02:20
     192.168.2.0/30 is subnetted, 2 subnets
B       192.168.2.32 [200/0] via 194.22.15.1, 22:23:35
C       192.168.2.36 is directly connected, POS10/0/0

EuroComParis-ASBR# show ip route vrf BankCorp
Codes: C - connected, S - static, I - IGRP, R - RIP, M - mobile, B - BGP
       D - EIGRP, EX - EIGRP external, O - OSPF, IA - OSPF inter area
       N1 - OSPF NSSA external type 1, N2 - OSPF NSSA external type 2
       E1 - OSPF external type 1, E2 - OSPF external type 2, E - EGP
       i - IS-IS, L1 - IS-IS level-1, L2 - IS-IS level-2, ia - IS-IS inter area
       * - candidate default, U - per-user static route, o - ODR

Gateway of last resort is not set

     194.69.27.0/30 is subnetted, 1 subnets
B       194.69.27.16 [200/0] via 196.49.1.3, 22:06:30
B    198.121.63.0/24 [20/0] via 192.168.2.37, 00:02:13
B    198.121.62.0/24 [200/1] via 196.49.1.3, 22:06:30
     192.168.2.0/30 is subnetted, 2 subnets
B       192.168.2.32 [20/0] via 192.168.2.37, 00:02:13
C       192.168.2.36 is directly connected, POS8/1/0
```

These routes will now be advertised within the SuperCom and EuroCom MPLS VPN backbones and will be imported by any PE routers that have BankCorp sites attached. If you look at the SuperCom San Jose PE router in Example 6-30, you can see that the BankCorp 198.121.62.0/24 subnet (which is the Berlin site) is available.

Example 6-30 *Successful Distribution of BankCorp Routes via InterAS*

```
SanJose-PE# show ip route vrf BankCorp
Codes: C - connected, S - static, I - IGRP, R - RIP, M - mobile, B - BGP
       D - EIGRP, EX - EIGRP external, O - OSPF, IA - OSPF inter area
       N1 - OSPF NSSA external type 1, N2 - OSPF NSSA external type 2
       E1 - OSPF external type 1, E2 - OSPF external type 2, E - EGP
       i - IS-IS, L1 - IS-IS level-1, L2 - IS-IS level-2, ia - IS-IS inter area
       * - candidate default, U - per-user static route, o - ODR

Gateway of last resort is not set

     194.69.27.0/30 is subnetted, 1 subnets
B       194.69.27.16 [200/0] via 194.22.15.3, 00:05:46
R    198.121.63.0/24 [120/1] via 192.168.2.33, 00:00:22, Ethernet6/1
B    198.121.62.0/24 [200/0] via 194.22.15.3, 00:06:02
     192.168.2.0/30 is subnetted, 1 subnets
C       192.168.2.32 is directly connected, Ethernet6/1
```

All packets directed toward the 198.121.62.0/24 subnet should be label-switched across the SuperCom and EuroCom backbones. However, the back-to-back VRF solution does not require label switching across the ASBR-ASBR links. Packets will be label-switched across each MPLS VPN backbone and then be sent as IP packets between service providers. This concept is illustrated in Figure 6-15, and a traceroute is provided in Figure 6-16. Printouts for the MPLS LSP from the BankCorp Santa Clara CE router to the 198.121.62.0/24 subnet are provided in Example 6-31. Figure 6-17 provides an illustration of the complete end-to-end LSP for the BankCorp VPN.

Figure 6-15 *Back-to-Back VRF Label Switching and IP Paths*

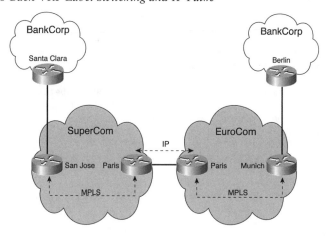

Figure 6-16 *Traceroute Between BankCorp Santa Clara and Berlin Sites*

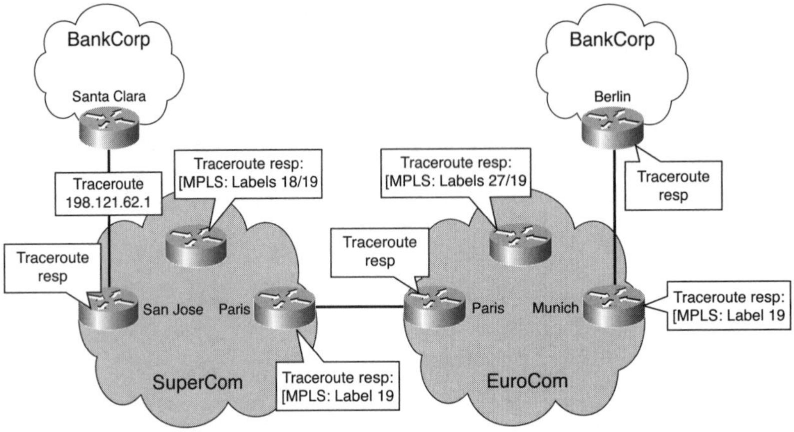

Example 6-31 *LSP Between BankCorp Sites*

```
SantaClara-CE# ping 198.121.62.1

Type escape sequence to abort.
Sending 5, 100-byte ICMP Echos to 198.121.62.1, timeout is 2 seconds:
!!!!!
Success rate is 100 percent (5/5), round-trip min/avg/max = 4/6/8 ms

SantaClara-CE# traceroute 198.121.62.1

Type escape sequence to abort.
Tracing the route to 198.121.62.1

  1 192.168.2.34 0 msec 0 msec 0 msec
! response from SuperCom SanJose PE-router
  2 194.22.15.9 [MPLS: Labels 18/19 Exp 0] 4 msec 4 msec 4 msec
! response from P-router within the SuperCom network
  3 192.168.2.37 [MPLS: Label 19 Exp 0] 4 msec 4 msec 4 msec
! response from SuperCom Paris ASBR
  4 192.168.2.38 4 msec 0 msec 4 msec
! response from EuroCom Paris ASBR (Note: no MPLS labels)
  5 10.2.1.22 [MPLS: Labels 27/19 Exp 0] 8 msec 4 msec 8 msec
! response from P-router within the EuroCom network
  6 194.69.27.18 [MPLS: Label 19 Exp 0] 8 msec 4 msec 8 msec
! response from EuroCom Munich PE-router
  7 194.69.27.17 4 msec 4 msec *
! response from BankCorp Berlin CE-router

SanJose-PE# show ip cef vrf BankCorp 198.121.62.0
198.121.62.0/24, version 16, cached adjacency to Serial4/0
```

Example 6-31 *LSP Between BankCorp Sites (Continued)*

```
0 packets, 0 bytes
  tag information set
    local tag: VPN route head
    fast tag rewrite with Se4/0, point2point, tags imposed {18 19}
  via 194.22.15.3, 0 dependencies, recursive
    next hop 194.22.15.9, Serial4/0 via 194.22.15.3/32
    valid cached adjacency
    tag rewrite with Se4/0, point2point, tags imposed {18 19}

SuperComParis-ASBR# show mpls forwarding label 19
Local  Outgoing    Prefix                Bytes tag  Outgoing   Next Hop
tag    tag or VC   or Tunnel Id          switched   interface
19     Untagged    198.121.62.0/24[V]   \
                                         1040       PO10/0/0   point2point

EuroComParis-ASBR# show ip cef vrf BankCorp 198.121.62.0
198.121.62.0/24, version 9, cached adjacency 10.2.1.22
0 packets, 0 bytes
  tag information set
    local tag: VPN route head
    fast tag rewrite with AT4/1/0, 10.2.1.22, tags imposed {27 19}
  via 196.49.1.3, 0 dependencies, recursive
    next hop 10.2.1.22, ATM4/1/0 via 196.49.1.3/32
    valid cached adjacency
    tag rewrite with AT4/1/0, 10.2.1.22, tags imposed {27 19}

Munich_PE# show mpls forwarding label 19
Local  Outgoing    Prefix                Bytes tag  Outgoing   Next Hop
tag    tag or VC   or Tunnel Id          switched   interface
19     Untagged    198.121.62.0/24[V]   \
                                         1140       Et4/0      194.69.27.17
```

Figure 6-17 *LSP Between BankCorp Sites*

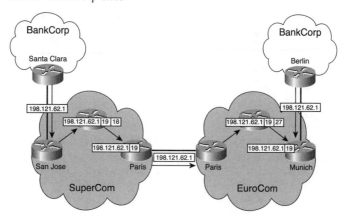

External Multiprotocol BGP

Although the back-to-back VRF solution provides an easy implementation option, it clearly has some severe scaling issues in large-scale deployments because it requires a VRF and logical interface per-InterAS VPN. This is certainly not appropriate when a large number of VPNs must be reachable between service providers; therefore, a different label/prefix distribution method is needed. This requirement is met by extending Multiprotocol BGP to support VPNv4 external neighbors as well as VPNv4 internal neighbors.

External Multiprotocol BGP provides the functionality to advertise VPNv4 prefix/label information across the service provider boundaries. The advertising ASBR replaces the label stack of the VPN prefix with a locally allocated label prior to advertising the VPN route. This is necessary because the BGP session between the two service providers is external BGP, so the ASBR becomes the next-hop of the route and terminates the LSP for that route. To preserve the LSP, the ASBR must allocate a local label that corresponds to the label stack of the route within the local MPLS VPN network. This newly allocated label is set on packets sent toward the prefix from the adjacent service provider. This InterAS model is illustrated in Figure 6-18.

Figure 6-18 *MP-eBGP Connectivity Model*

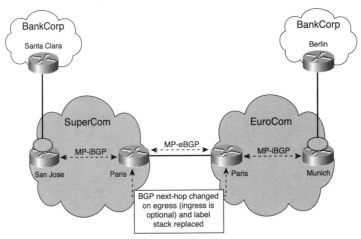

NOTE   There is no requirement to run an IGP or any other label distribution protocol other than BGP on the InterAS link when you are deploying External Multiprotocol BGP.

You can view the configuration of the SuperCom Paris ASBR and EuroCom Paris ASBR in Example 6-32. As you can see, the ASBR does not require VRF configuration, and the interface that connects the two routers is within the global routing table.

Example 6-32 *External MP-BGP Configuration of ASBRs*

```
hostname SuperComParis-ASBR
!
interface POS10/0/0
 description ** interface to EuroCom Paris-ASBR
 ip address 192.168.2.37 255.255.255.252
!
router bgp 10
 no bgp default ipv4-unicast
 bgp log-neighbor-changes
 neighbor 192.168.2.38 remote-as 20
 neighbor 194.22.15.1 remote-as 10
 neighbor 194.22.15.1 update-source Loopback0
 no auto-summary
 !
 address-family vpnv4
 neighbor 192.168.2.38 activate
 neighbor 192.168.2.38 send-community extended
 neighbor 194.22.15.1 activate
 neighbor 194.22.15.1 send-community extended
 exit-address-family

hostname EuroComParis-ASBR
!
interface POS8/1/0
 description ** interface to SuperCom Washington ASBR
 ip address 192.168.2.38 255.255.255.252
!
router bgp 20
 no bgp default ipv4-unicast
 bgp log-neighbor-changes
 neighbor 192.168.2.37 remote-as 10
 neighbor 196.49.1.3 remote-as 20
 neighbor 196.49.1.3 update-source Loopback0
 no auto-summary
 !
 address-family vpnv4
 neighbor 192.168.2.37 activate
 neighbor 192.168.2.37 send-community extended
 neighbor 196.49.1.3 activate
 neighbor 196.49.1.3 send-community extended
 exit-address-family
```

External MP-BGP VPNv4 Route Exchange

Having successfully enabled an external BGP session between the SuperCom and EuroCom ASBRs, you might think that VPNv4 routes will be exchanged automatically across the session. However, if you look at the routes available within the SuperCom backbone in Example 6-33, you will see that VPNv4 routes do not exist within the BGP table, including the BankCorp routes that are within the local autonomous system.

Example 6-33 *MP-eBGP Session Establishment with VPNv4 Prefix Exchange*

```
SuperComParis-ASBR# show ip bgp neighbor
BGP neighbor is 192.168.2.38, remote AS 20, external link
  BGP version 4, remote router ID 196.49.1.1
  BGP state = Established, up for 00:08:18
  Last read 00:00:18, hold time is 180, keepalive interval is 60 seconds
  Neighbor capabilities:
    Route refresh: advertised and received(new)
    Address family VPNv4 Unicast: advertised and received

SuperComParis-ASBR# show ip bgp vpnv4 all summary
BGP router identifier 194.22.15.3, local AS number 10
BGP table version is 28, main routing table version 28

Neighbor      V  AS MsgRcvd MsgSent  TblVer InQ OutQ Up/Down State/PfxRc
192.168.2.38  4  20     13      13      28   0    0 00:09:38       0
194.22.15.1   4  10    1470    1481     28   0    0 1d00h          0
```

The absence of VPNv4 prefix information on the ASBRs is caused by the automatic route-filtering mechanism that was described in Chapter 9, "MPLS/VPN Architecture Operation," of *MPLS and VPN Architectures*, Volume 1. With this feature enabled, the router only accepts VPNv4 routes if they contain a route target that matches one of the import statements within the local VRFs. In this case, no VRFs exist on the ASBRs; therefore, *all* VPNv4 prefix information is dropped. To resolve this issue, you must configure the **no bgp default route-target filter** command within the BGP process (see Example 6-34).

Example 6-34 *Use of no bgp default route-target filter Command*

```
hostname SuperComParis-ASBR
!
router bgp 10
 no bgp default ipv4-unicast
 no bgp default route-target filter

SuperComParis-ASBR# show ip bgp vpnv4 all summary
BGP router identifier 194.22.15.3, local AS number 10
BGP table version is 5, main routing table version 5
4 network entries and 4 paths using 724 bytes of memory
3 BGP path attribute entries using 168 bytes of memory
1 BGP AS-PATH entries using 24 bytes of memory
1 BGP extended community entries using 24 bytes of memory
0 BGP route-map cache entries using 0 bytes of memory
0 BGP filter-list cache entries using 0 bytes of memory
BGP activity 13/13 prefixes, 16/12 paths, scan interval 15 secs

Neighbor      V AS MsgRcvd MsgSent TblVer InQ OutQ Up/Down State/PfxRcd
192.168.2.38  4 20     31      31     5    0    0 00:02:41       2
194.22.15.1   4 10    1488    1499    5    0    0 00:02:52       2
```

NOTE   A route refresh is not sent when the **no bgp default route-target filter** command is entered on the ASBR; therefore, the BGP session must be cleared, or a soft clearing of the BGP session must be performed, so that the previously rejected routes can be relearned.

Having disabled the automatic route filtering feature, VPNv4 prefix information sent by other PE routers in the same MPLS VPN backbone is no longer rejected by the ASBRs. The previous example shows that the SuperCom Paris ASBR has learned routes from two different peers: 192.168.2.38, which is the EuroCom Paris ASBR, and 194.22.15.1, which is the SuperCom San Jose PE router. By examining how the SuperCom Paris ASBR sees the BankCorp 198.121.62.0/24 subnet, which is reachable via the EuroCom Munich PE router, you can see in Example 6-35 that the next-hop for this route is, in fact, the EuroCom Paris ASBR.

Example 6-35 *Change of BGP Next-Hop on InterAS Link*

```
SuperComParis-ASBR# show ip bgp vpnv4 all 198.121.62.0
BGP routing table entry for 99:5432:198.121.62.0/24, version 5
Paths: (1 available, best #1, no table)
  Advertised to non peer-group peers:
  194.22.15.1
  20
    192.168.2.38 from 192.168.2.38 (196.49.1.1)
      Origin incomplete, localpref 100, valid, external, best
      Extended Community: RT:20:123
```

As previously stated, the advertising ASBR allocates a new MPLS label to represent a particular VPNv4 prefix. This label is used to label-switch traffic across the ASBR-ASBR link. Furthermore, the advertising ASBR in one MPLS VPN backbone becomes the BGP next-hop in the adjacent MPLS VPN backbone, so that all the PE routers in the adjacent MPLS VPN backbone use the label that the advertising ASBR assigns as the second label in the MPLS label stack. Example 6-36 shows the label allocation for the BankCorp VPN client, as well as the corresponding label forwarding information base (LFIB) entries, on the EuroCom and SuperCom Paris ASBRs.

Example 6-36 *ASBR Label Allocation for VPNv4 Prefixes*

```
EuroComParis-ASBR# show ip bgp vpnv4 all tags
   Network          Next Hop        In tag/Out tag
Route Distinguisher: 10:4972
   192.168.2.32/30  192.168.2.37     notag/21
   198.121.63.0     192.168.2.37     notag/25
Route Distinguisher: 99:5432
   194.69.27.16/30  196.49.1.3       24/22
   198.121.62.0     196.49.1.3       25/19
```

continues

Example 6-36 *ASBR Label Allocation for VPNv4 Prefixes (Continued)*

```
EuroComParis-ASBR# show mpls forwarding
Local  Outgoing    Prefix          Bytes tag  Outgoing    Next Hop
tag    tag or VC   or Tunnel Id    switched   interface
16     Pop tag     192.168.2.37/32  0         PO8/1/0     point2point
17     Pop tag     196.49.1.2/32    0         AT4/1/0     10.2.1.22
18     Pop tag     192.168.2.32/30  0         AT4/1/0     10.2.1.22
19     12305       196.49.1.3/32    0         AT4/1/0     10.2.1.22
24     12305       99:5432:194.69.27.16/30  \
                                    0         AT4/1/0     10.2.1.22
25     12305       99:5432:198.121.62.0/24  \
                                    0         AT4/1/0     10.2.1.22


SuperComParis-ASBR# show ip bgp vpnv4 all tags
    Network          Next Hop        In tag/Out tag
Route Distinguisher: 10:4972
    192.168.2.32/30  194.22.15.1     21/18
    198.121.63.0     194.22.15.1     25/24
Route Distinguisher: 99:5432
    194.69.27.16/30  192.168.2.38    notag/24
    198.121.62.0     192.168.2.38    notag/25


SuperComParis-ASBR# show mpls forwarding
Local  Outgoing    Prefix          Bytes tag  Outgoing    Next Hop
tag    tag or VC   or Tunnel Id    switched   interface
17     Pop tag     194.22.15.8/30   0         Et10/1/1    194.22.15.6
18     Pop tag     194.22.16.0/24   0         Et10/1/1    194.22.15.6
19     16          194.22.15.1/32   0         Et10/1/1    194.22.15.6
22     Pop tag     192.168.2.38/32  0         PO10/0/0    point2point
21     16          10:4972:192.168.2.32/30  \
                                    0         Et10/1/1    194.22.15.6
25     16          10:4972:198.121.63.0/24  \
                                    0         Et10/1/1    194.22.15.6
```

NOTE   Example 6-36 shows that all InterAS routes are shown in VPNv4 format within the LFIB. This is so that each prefix can remain unique between the two backbones. The example also shows that only local autonomous system prefixes are shown within the LFIB. (No entries are available for routes that are learned from the adjacent provider.) You will see later in this section that this behavior is driven by the **next-hop-self** configuration at the ASBR routers.

If you examine the BankCorp 198.121.62.0/24 subnet entries on both of the ASBRs, you can see that the EuroCom Paris ASBR has allocated a label value of <25> to that VPN prefix, and this label is used as the <out> label on the SuperCom Paris ASBR for packets sent toward the subnet. The EuroCom Paris ASBR also has an outgoing label with a value of <19>. This label is the VPN label that it received from its internal session with the originating PE router. You can confirm this by looking on the Munich PE router, as shown in Example 6-37.

NOTE	The notag entries in the previous output indicate that no local label has been allocated for the prefix. If you examine the 198.121.62.0/24 subnet on the SuperCom Paris ASBR, you can see that the \<In tag\> value is \<notag\>. This means that no LFIB entry is created for the prefix on the ASBR, and this is confirmed by examining the MPLS forwarding entries for the SuperCom ASBR in Example 6-36. However, the EuroCom Paris ASBR has allocated a local label, and a corresponding LFIB entry is created. Examination of the MPLS forwarding entries for the EuroCom Paris ASBR shows that an entry is available for the 198.121.62.0/24 subnet.

Example 6-37 *Label Allocation at Originating PE Router*

```
Munich_PE# show ip bgp vpnv4 all tags
    Network           Next Hop       In tag/Out tag
Route Distinguisher: 10:4972
    192.168.2.32/30  192.168.2.37    notag/19
    198.121.63.0     192.168.2.37    notag/20
Route Distinguisher: 99:5432 (BankCorp)
    194.69.27.16/30  0.0.0.0         17/aggregate(BankCorp)
    198.121.62.0     194.69.27.17    19/notag
```

Having distributed all the label information across the SuperCom and EuroCom backbone networks, connectivity should be available within the BankCorp VPN. However, as Example 6-38 shows, for some reason, connectivity to the 198.121.62.0/24 subnet is not available at the BankCorp Santa Clara CE router.

Example 6-38 *Loss of Connectivity to BankCorp Berlin in Santa Clara*

```
SantaClara-CE# show ip route 198.121.62.0 255.255.255.0
% Network not in table
```

Examination of the San Jose PE router in Example 6-39 highlights the cause of the problem. It is a classic BGP-4 next-hop problem associated with the combination of internal and external BGP. The BGP-4 next-hop of the 198.121.62.0/24 subnet is set to 192.168.2.38, which is the EuroCom Paris ASBR. This prefix is not accessible within the SuperCom backbone; therefore, the BGP route is not imported into the BankCorp VRF.

Example 6-39 *BGP Next-Hop Inaccessible to SuperCom Backbone*

```
SanJose-PE# show ip bgp vpnv4 all 198.121.62.0
BGP routing table entry for 99:5432:198.121.62.0/24, version 0
Paths: (1 available, no best path)
  Not advertised to any peer
  20
    192.168.2.38 (inaccessible) from 194.22.15.3 (194.22.15.3)
      Origin incomplete, localpref 100, valid, internal
      Extended Community: RT:20:123
```

To rectify this problem, SuperCom can do one of two things. It can either make the ASBR link available within its IGP, or it can change the BGP-4 next-hop of any routes it receives from EuroCom, prior to advertisement within the local autonomous system.

To inject the ASBR link into the SuperCom IGP, you could configure redistribution of connected subnets at the ASBR, or you could include connected subnets into the IGP running on the ASBR and turn them into *passive interfaces*. However, whenever external Multiprotocol BGP is configured for a VPNv4 adjacency, a /32 host route for the adjacent ASBR is automatically created so that an LSP can be built from an ingress PE router to the ASBR. Therefore, injection of the ASBR address into the IGP is straightforward; you only need to redistribute connected host routes into the IGP routing process.

SuperCom has elected to change the next-hop of the routes rather than inject the adjacent ASBR's IP address into the IGP. As Example 6-40 shows, connectivity within the BankCorp VPN is now available.

Example 6-40 *Change of BGP Next-Hop at SuperCom Paris ASBR*

```
hostname SuperComParis-ASBR
!
router bgp 10
 no bgp default ipv4-unicast
 no bgp default route-target filter
 bgp log-neighbor-changes
 neighbor 192.168.2.38 remote-as 20
 neighbor 194.22.15.1 remote-as 10
 neighbor 194.22.15.1 update-source Loopback0
 no auto-summary
 !
 address-family vpnv4
 neighbor 192.168.2.38 activate
 neighbor 192.168.2.38 send-community extended
 neighbor 194.22.15.1 activate
 neighbor 194.22.15.1 next-hop-self
 neighbor 194.22.15.1 send-community extended
 exit-address-family

SanJose-PE# show ip bgp vpnv4 all 198.121.62.0
BGP routing table entry for 10:4972:198.121.62.0/24, version 32
Paths: (1 available, best #1, table BankCorp)
  Not advertised to any peer
  20, imported path from 99:5432:198.121.62.0/24
    194.22.15.3 (metric 20) from 194.22.15.3 (194.22.15.3)
      Origin incomplete, localpref 100, valid, internal, best
      Extended Community: RT:20:123

SantaClara-CE# show ip route 198.121.62.0 255.255.255.0
Routing entry for 198.121.62.0/24
  Known via "rip", distance 120, metric 1
  Tag 20
  Redistributing via rip
  Advertised by rip (self originated)
  Last update from 192.168.2.34 on Ethernet3/1, 00:00:22 ago
```

Example 6-40 *Change of BGP Next-Hop at SuperCom Paris ASBR (Continued)*

```
     Routing Descriptor Blocks:
     * 192.168.2.34, from 192.168.2.34, 00:00:22 ago, via Ethernet3/1
         Route metric is 1, traffic share count is 1

SantaClara-CE# ping 198.121.62.1

Type escape sequence to abort.
Sending 5, 100-byte ICMP Echos to 198.121.62.1, timeout is 2 seconds:
!!!!!
Success rate is 100 percent (5/5), round-trip min/avg/max = 4/6/8 ms
```

Changing of the next-hop address at the advertising ASBR has some implications.
Whenever the BGP next-hop of a VPNv4 prefix is changed, a new label has to be assigned
by the BGP router that changed the next-hop attribute. Therefore, when the BGP next-hop
of an eBGP VPNv4 prefix is changed by the receiving ASBR, it has to allocate another
MPLS label for the VPNv4 prefix prior to advertisement of the route into the local MPLS
VPN backbone. As a result, if the **next-hop-self** command is used on both the sending
ASBR and the receiving ASBR, they each have to allocate an MPLS label for every VPN
route exchange between the MPLS VPN backbones.

If you examine in Example 6-41 the Multiprotocol BGP and LFIB entries for the
198.121.62.0/24 subnet on the SuperCom Paris ASBR again, you can see that a local label
has been allocated and a subsequent LFIB entry has been created.

Example 6-41 *End-to-End LSP Within BankCorp VPN*

```
SuperComParis-ASBR# show ip bgp vpnv4 all tags
   Network          Next Hop       In tag/Out tag
Route Distinguisher: 10:4972
   192.168.2.32/30  194.22.15.1      21/18
   198.121.63.0     194.22.15.1      25/24
Route Distinguisher: 99:5432
   194.69.27.16/30  192.168.2.38     26/24
   198.121.62.0     192.168.2.38     27/25

SuperComParis-ASBR# show mpls forwarding
Local  Outgoing    Prefix          Bytes tag  Outgoing    Next Hop
tag    tag or VC   or Tunnel Id    switched   interface
17     Pop tag     194.22.15.8/30    0         Et10/1/1    194.22.15.6
18     Pop tag     194.22.16.0/24    0         Et10/1/1    194.22.15.6
19     16          194.22.15.1/32    0         Et10/1/1    194.22.15.6
21     16          10:4972:192.168.2.32/30  \
                                     0         Et10/1/1    194.22.15.6
22     Pop tag     192.168.2.38/32   0         PO10/0/0    point2point
25     16          10:4972:198.121.63.0/24  \
                                     0         Et10/1/1    194.22.15.6
26     24          99:5432:194.69.27.16/30  \
                                     0         PO10/0/0    point2point
27     25          99:5432:198.121.62.0/24  \
                                     0         PO10/0/0    point2point
```

Example 6-42 shows the LSP for the 198.121.62.0/24 subnet, from the viewpoint of the SuperCom San Jose PE router. Figure 6-19 provides an illustration of this LSP.

Example 6-42 *End-to-End LSP Within BankCorp VPN*

```
SanJose-PE# show ip cef vrf BankCorp 198.121.62.0
198.121.62.0/24, version 19, cached adjacency to Serial4/0
0 packets, 0 bytes
  tag information set
    local tag: VPN route head
    fast tag rewrite with Se4/0, point2point, tags imposed {18 23}
  via 194.22.15.3, 0 dependencies, recursive
    next hop 194.22.15.9, Serial4/0 via 194.22.15.3/32
    valid cached adjacency
    tag rewrite with Se4/0, point2point, tags imposed {17 27}


SuperComParis-ASBR# show mpls forwarding label 27
Local  Outgoing    Prefix          Bytes tag  Outgoing    Next Hop
tag    tag or VC   or Tunnel Id    switched   interface
27     25          99:5432:198.121.62.0/24    \
                                   1080       PO10/0/0    point2point


EuroComParis-ASBR# show mpls forwarding label 25
Local  Outgoing    Prefix          Bytes tag  Outgoing    Next Hop
tag    tag or VC   or Tunnel Id    switched   interface
25     27          99:5432:198.121.62.0/24    \
                                   1200       AT4/1/0     10.2.1.22


EuroComParis-ASBR# show mpls forwarding label 25 detail
Local  Outgoing    Prefix          Bytes tag  Outgoing    Next Hop
tag    tag or VC   or Tunnel Id    switched   interface
25     27          99:5432:198.121.62.0/24    \
                                   1200       AT4/1/0     10.2.1.22
           MAC/Encaps=12/20, MTU=4466, Tag Stack{27 19}
           00040000AAAA030000008847 0001B00000013000
           No output feature configured


Munich_PE# show mpls forwarding label 19
Local  Outgoing    Prefix          Bytes tag  Outgoing    Next Hop
tag    tag or VC   or Tunnel Id    switched   interface
19     Untagged    198.121.62.0/24[V]   \
                                   2280       Et4/0       194.69.27.17
```

Figure 6-19 *LSP for BankCorp InterAS Connectivity*

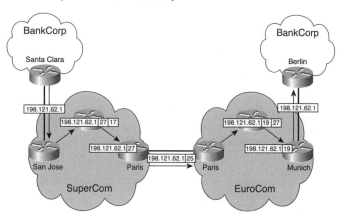

Multihop Multiprotocol eBGP for VPNv4 Prefix Exchange

With the growing success of the VPN service within each of the service provider's backbones, SuperCom and EuroCom have a requirement to increase the amount of bandwidth available between their two autonomous systems. To achieve this, an extra link is added between the Paris ASBRs. The links will be used to load balance traffic between the routers. The configuration of the new link is shown in Example 6-43.

Example 6-43 *Additional Link Between Paris ASBRs*

```
hostname SuperComParis-ASBR
!
interface POS1/0/0
 description ** first interface to EuroCom Paris-ASBR
 ip address 192.168.2.41 255.255.255.252
!
interface POS10/0/0
 description ** second interface to EuroCom Paris-ASBR
 ip address 192.168.2.37 255.255.255.252

hostname EuroComParis-ASBR
!
interface POS8/1/0
 description ** first interface to SuperCom Paris-ASBR
 ip address 192.168.2.38 255.255.255.252
!
interface POS9/0/0
 description ** second interface to SuperCom Paris-ASBR
 ip address 192.168.2.42 255.255.255.252
```

Having deployed the new link, it is necessary to make some changes to the previous BGP configuration so that both links can be used to carry traffic. Adding the new link is not enough to distribute the traffic because all the InterAS routes are seen with a BGP next-hop address that is directly connected to the ASBR. This is illustrated in Example 6-44, which shows that the SuperCom Paris ASBR sees all routes from EuroCom with a BGP next-hop of 192.168.2.38. This next-hop is reachable via the directly connected interface POSS10/0/0.

Example 6-44 *BGP Next-Hop Usage on SuperCom Paris ASBR*

```
SuperComParis-ASBR# show ip bgp vpnv4 rd 99:5432
BGP table version is 13, local router ID is 194.22.15.3
Status codes: s suppressed, d damped, h history, * valid, > best, i - internal
Origin codes: i - IGP, e - EGP, ? - incomplete

   Network          Next Hop          Metric LocPrf Weight Path
Route Distinguisher: 99:5432
*> 194.69.27.16/30  192.168.2.38                     0 20 ?
*> 198.121.62.0     192.168.2.38                     0 20 ?

SuperComParis-ASBR# show ip route 192.168.2.38
Routing entry for 192.168.2.38/32
  Known via "connected", distance 0, metric 0 (connected, via interface)
  Redistributing via isis
  Advertised by isis metric 0 metric-type internal level-2
  Routing Descriptor Blocks:
  * directly connected, via POS10/0/0
      Route metric is 0, traffic share count is 1
```

To achieve the required load balancing, you can use a Multihop Multiprotocol BGP session between the SuperCom and EuroCom ASBRs. This session should run between two loopback interfaces (for stability reasons). You can achieve load balancing by recursion of the BGP next-hop to the directly connected interfaces.

SuperCom and EuroCom do not want to run an IGP between their ASBRs, so the first part of the new configuration is to add static routes that point to each other's loopback interfaces. To make sure that the loopback interfaces are reachable via both of the links, you need two static routes, as shown in Example 6-45. Figure 6-20 shows how the two ASBRs are connected in this environment.

Example 6-45 *Static Routes Between ASBRs*

```
hostname SuperComParis-ASBR
!
ip route 196.49.1.1 255.255.255.255 192.168.2.42
ip route 196.49.1.1 255.255.255.255 192.168.2.38

hostname EuroComParis-ASBR
!
ip route 194.22.15.3 255.255.255.255 192.168.2.41
ip route 194.22.15.3 255.255.255.255 192.168.2.37
```

Figure 6-20 *Multihop MP-eBGP Between ASBRs*

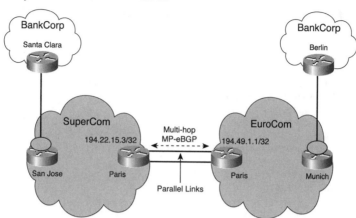

With the relevant static routes in place, you can configure the ASBRs for a Multihop Multi-protocol BGP session. You can use the loopback interface addresses as the BGP peering endpoints. The relevant configuration for both ASBRs is shown in Example 6-46.

Example 6-46 *Multihop MP-eBGP Configuration of ASBRs*

```
hostname SuperComParis-ASBR
!
router bgp 10
 neighbor 196.49.1.1 remote-as 20
 neighbor 196.49.1.1 ebgp-multihop 255
 neighbor 196.49.1.1 update-source Loopback0
 !
 address-family vpnv4
 neighbor 196.49.1.1 activate
 neighbor 196.49.1.1 send-community extended

hostname EuroComParis-ASBR
!
router bgp 20
 neighbor 194.22.15.3 remote-as 10
 neighbor 194.22.15.3 ebgp-multihop 255
 neighbor 194.22.15.3 update-source Loopback0
 !
 address-family vpnv4
 neighbor 194.22.15.3 activate
 neighbor 194.22.15.3 send-community extended
```

Now that a Multihop Multiprotocol BGP session is available between the ASBRs, we can compare the reachability information provided in Example 6-47 with the output of Example 6-44 to see that the BGP next-hop has changed. This next-hop is reachable via the two parallel links between the ASBRs.

Example 6-47 *Change of BGP Next-Hop with Multihop MP-eBGP*

```
SuperComParis-ASBR# show ip bgp vpnv4 rd 99:5432
BGP table version is 5, local router ID is 194.22.15.3
Status codes: s suppressed, d damped, h history, * valid, > best, i - internal
Origin codes: i - IGP, e - EGP, ? - incomplete

   Network          Next Hop          Metric LocPrf Weight Path
Route Distinguisher: 99:5432
*> 194.69.27.16/30   196.49.1.1                        0 20 ?
*> 198.121.62.0      196.49.1.1                        0 20 ?


SuperComParis-ASBR# show ip route 196.49.1.1
Routing entry for 196.49.1.1/32
  Known via "static", distance 1, metric 0
  Routing Descriptor Blocks:
  * 192.168.2.42
      Route metric is 0, traffic share count is 1
    192.168.2.38
      Route metric is 0, traffic share count is 1
```

Whenever you use Multihop BGP between two ASBRs, there is the possibility that further routers lie in the path between the two BGP speakers. The MPLS VPN architecture requires that a packet be label-switched to the originator of a particular VPN route, and this includes ASBRs when you are running InterAS solutions.

You can see from Example 6-48 that the SuperCom Paris ASBR learns all routes from EuroCom with a next-hop of 196.49.1.1/32, which is the EuroCom Paris ASBR. The subsequent LFIB entry shows that it has two paths to this next-hop, but the outgoing label is set to *untagged*.

Example 6-48 *SuperCom ASBR LDP Requirement*

```
SuperComParis-ASBR# show ip bgp vpnv4 rd 99:5432
BGP table version is 9, local router ID is 197.1.1.1
Status codes: s suppressed, d damped, h history, * valid, > best, i - internal
Origin codes: i - IGP, e - EGP, ? - incomplete

   Network          Next Hop          Metric LocPrf Weight Path
Route Distinguisher: 99:5432
*> 194.69.27.16/30   196.49.1.1                        0 20 ?
*> 198.121.62.0      196.49.1.1                        0 20 ?


SuperComParis-ASBR# show mpls forwarding 196.49.1.1
Local  Outgoing    Prefix          Bytes tag  Outgoing    Next Hop
tag    tag or VC   or Tunnel Id    switched   interface
16     Untagged    196.49.1.1/32   0          PO1/0/0     point2point
       Untagged    196.49.1.1/32   0          PO10/0/0    point2point
```

Example 6-49 shows that the *untagged* entry causes the SuperCom Paris ASBR to send all packets for the 198.121.62.0/24 subnet with only one label: the VPN label. The VPN label has a value *<25>*, as allocated by the EuroCom ASBR.

Example 6-49 *Label Stack Prior to LDP on ASBR Links*

```
SuperComParis-ASBR# show ip bgp vpnv4 rd 99:5432 tags
   Network          Next Hop      In tag/Out tag
Route Distinguisher: 99:5432
   194.69.27.16/30  196.49.1.1       23/24
   198.121.62.0     196.49.1.1       20/25

SuperComParis-ASBR# show mpls forwarding label 20 detail
Local  Outgoing    Prefix            Bytes tag  Outgoing    Next Hop
tag    tag or VC   or Tunnel Id      switched   interface
20     Recursive   99:5432:198.121.62.0/24   \
                                     0
       Recursive rewrite via 196.49.1.1/32, Tag Stack{25}
        00019000
       No output feature configured
```

The SuperCom router has no way of knowing how many devices are between it and the adjacent ASBR. Therefore, LDP/TDP is required on the ASBR-ASBR link so that the VPN label that the EuroCom Paris ASBR allocates is not exposed on packets before they reach it. To complete the configuration of the SuperCom and EuroCom ASBRs, you must add the **mpls ip** command to the interface configuration, as shown in Example 6-50.

Example 6-50 *LDP Configuration on ASBR Links*

```
hostname SuperComParis-ASBR
!
interface POS1/0/0
 description ** first interface to EuroCom Paris-ASBR
 ip address 192.168.2.41 255.255.255.252
 tag-switching ip
!
interface POS10/0/0
 description ** second interface to EuroCom Paris-ASBR
 ip address 192.168.2.37 255.255.255.252
 tag-switching ip

hostname EuroComParis-ASBR
!
interface POS8/1/0
 description ** first interface to SuperCom Paris-ASBR
 ip address 192.168.2.38 255.255.255.252
 tag-switching ip
!
interface POS9/0/0
 description ** second interface to SuperCom Paris-ASBR
 ip address 192.168.2.42 255.255.255.252
 tag-switching ip
```

Having enabled LDP across each of the ASBR links, you can see in Example 6-51 that the LSP has been created. In this case, the LDP label is implicit-null because there are no further devices between the two ASBRs.

Example 6-51 *Label Stack After LDP Is Enabled on ASBR Links*

```
SuperComParis-ASBR# show mpls ldp binding 196.49.1.1 255.255.255.255
   tib entry: 196.49.1.1/32, rev 37
         local binding:  tag: 16
         remote binding: tsr: 196.49.1.1:0, tag: imp-null

SuperComParis-ASBR# show mpls forwarding 196.49.1.1
Local   Outgoing     Prefix           Bytes tag  Outgoing    Next Hop
tag     tag or VC    or Tunnel Id     switched   interface
16      Pop tag      196.49.1.1/32    0          PO1/0/0     point2point
        Pop tag      196.49.1.1/32    0          PO10/0/0    point2point

SuperComParis-ASBR# show mpls forwarding label 20 detail
Local   Outgoing     Prefix           Bytes tag  Outgoing    Next Hop
tag     tag or VC    or Tunnel Id     switched   interface
20      Recursive    99:5432:198.121.62.0/24   \
                                      0
        Recursive rewrite via 196.49.1.1/32, Tag Stack{25}
          00019000
        No output feature configured
```

Multihop Multiprotocol eBGP Between Route Reflectors

The last InterAS connectivity option that we will consider is a combination of the previous two options. This option uses the External Multiprotocol BGP functionality, along with Multihop between the two service providers. The option provides some advantages over the other scenarios discussed within this chapter, including enhanced scalability, removal of LFIB duplication at the ASBRs, and the ability to remove VPN routes altogether from the ASBRs.

External Multiprotocol BGP is once again used to exchange local VPNv4 prefix/label information between the service providers. However, instead of exchanging this information between the ASBRs, this option provides the ability to exchange routes directly between *route reflectors*. Because the route reflectors of the different service providers will not be directly connected, multihop functionality is required to allow for the successful establishment of a BGP session.

The PE router next-hop for the VPNv4 routes that are exchanged between the route reflectors are advertised across the ASBR link, for subsequent distribution within the adjacent service provider. This means that the loopback addresses of the PE routers that originate the VPN routes in the other autonomous system must be known to the local autonomous system. You will see later in this section that you can deploy this distribution either through the use of an IGP or static routing, or via BGP with extensions to carry MPLS label information.

Figure 6-21 shows how you can use this connectivity model between the SuperCom and EuroCom networks.

Figure 6-21 *Multihop MP-eBGP Between Route Reflectors*

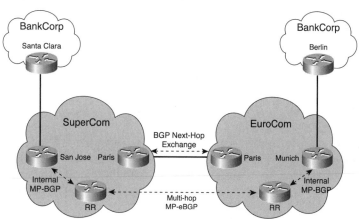

Within each of the service provider backbones, each PE router has a Multiprotocol BGP session with the local route reflector. The PE router exchanges all of its local VPNv4 routes with the route reflector. The configuration of the SuperCom and EuroCom route reflectors, to support the exchange of routes with local PE routers, is shown in Example 6-52.

NOTE   Our example configuration shows only one route reflector in each backbone. In a real deployment, you should use dual route reflectors for redundancy. Multiple route reflectors can support the edge topology.

Example 6-52 *Configuration of SuperCom and EuroCom Route Reflectors*

```
hostname SuperCom-RR
!
router bgp 10
 neighbor 194.22.15.1 remote-as 10
 neighbor 194.22.15.1 description SanJose PE-router
 neighbor 194.22.15.1 update-source Loopback0
 !
 address-family vpnv4
 neighbor 194.22.15.1 activate
 neighbor 194.22.15.1 route-reflector-client
 neighbor 194.22.15.1 send-community extended
 exit-address-family

hostname EuroCom-RR
!
router bgp 20
 neighbor 196.49.1.3 remote-as 20
```

continues

Example 6-52 *Configuration of SuperCom and EuroCom Route Reflectors (Continued)*

```
 neighbor 196.49.1.3 description Munich PE-router
 neighbor 196.49.1.3 update-source Loopback0
 !
 address-family vpnv4
 neighbor 196.49.1.3 activate
 neighbor 196.49.1.3 route-reflector-client
 neighbor 196.49.1.3 send-community extended
 exit-address-family
```

Now that you have established the local BGP sessions, all local VPNv4 prefix/label information is available at the route reflector. You must advertise this information between the two service providers via a Multihop External Multiprotocol BGP session, as shown in Figure 6-21. The additions to the previous configuration example, to support this new BGP session, are shown in Example 6-53.

Example 6-53 *Multihop MP-eBGP Session Between Route Reflectors*

```
hostname SuperCom-RR
!
router bgp 10
 neighbor 196.49.1.2 remote-as 20
 neighbor 196.49.1.2 description EuroCom-RR
 neighbor 196.49.1.2 ebgp-multihop 255
 neighbor 196.49.1.2 update-source Loopback0
 !
 address-family vpnv4
 neighbor 196.49.1.2 activate
 neighbor 196.49.1.2 send-community extended

hostname EuroCom-RR
!
router bgp 20
 neighbor 194.22.16.1 remote-as 10
 neighbor 194.22.16.1 description SuperCom-RR
 neighbor 194.22.16.1 ebgp-multihop 255
 neighbor 194.22.16.1 update-source Loopback0
 !
 address-family vpnv4
 neighbor 194.22.16.1 activate
 neighbor 194.22.16.1 send-community extended
```

So that you can successfully establish this session, each of the route reflectors must be reachable by each service provider; therefore you must leak the routes between routing domains. You can achieve this in a number of ways, but in our example, static routes have been configured at each ASBR. These static routes point to the route reflector address within the adjacent service provider. The routes are redistributed into the IGP at each ASBR, the BGP session is created, and VPNv4 prefix/label information is exchanged.

Example 6-54 *Successful Exchange of VPNv4 Routes Between Route Reflectors*

```
SuperCom-RR# show ip bgp vpnv4 all summary
BGP router identifier 194.22.16.1, local AS number 10
BGP table version is 5, main routing table version 5
4 network entries and 4 paths using 724 bytes of memory
3 BGP path attribute entries using 168 bytes of memory
1 BGP AS-PATH entries using 24 bytes of memory
1 BGP extended community entries using 24 bytes of memory
0 BGP route-map cache entries using 0 bytes of memory
0 BGP filter-list cache entries using 0 bytes of memory
BGP activity 4/12 prefixes, 4/0 paths, scan interval 15 secs

Neighbor       V   AS MsgRcvd MsgSent TblVer InQ OutQ Up/Down State/PfxRcd
194.22.15.1    4   10    75      75      5    0    0 01:09:11      2
196.49.1.2     4   20     8       8      5    0    0 00:02:19      2

SuperCom-RR# show ip bgp vpnv4 all
BGP table version is 5, local router ID is 194.22.16.1
Status codes: s suppressed, d damped, h history, * valid, > best, i - internal
Origin codes: i - IGP, e - EGP, ? - incomplete

   Network          Next Hop        Metric LocPrf Weight Path
Route Distinguisher: 10:4972
*>i192.168.2.32/30  194.22.15.1          0    100      0 ?
*>i198.121.63.0     194.22.15.1          1    100      0 ?
Route Distinguisher: 99:5432
*>  194.69.27.16/30 196.49.1.2                         0 20 ?
*>  198.121.62.0    196.49.1.2                         0 20 ?
```

Although Example 6-54 shows that the SuperCom route reflector has learned all the VPNv4 routes from the EuroCom route reflector, it also highlights a problem in the forwarding path. The BGP next-hop for the routes is 196.49.1.2, which is the address of the EuroCom route reflector. Using this IP address as the next-hop will cause all inter-site traffic between the BankCorp Santa Clara and Berlin sites to be forwarded through the EuroCom route reflector, which is clearly not desirable. You will see later how the end-to-end LSP between the BankCorp sites is built using IPv4 + Labels on the ASBR-ASBR link, but for now, assume that Figure 6-22 shows the path that traffic will take between the BankCorp sites using this configuration. Example 6-55 shows a printout of the LSP.

Figure 6-22 *BankCorp LSP via EuroCom Route Reflector*

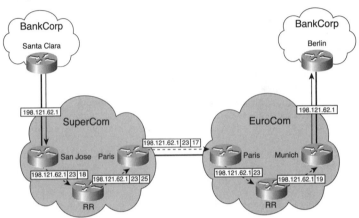

Example 6-55 *BankCorp LSP through the EuroCom Route Reflector*

```
SanJose-PE# show ip cef vrf BankCorp 198.121.62.0
198.121.62.0/24, version 35, cached adjacency to Serial4/0
0 packets, 0 bytes
  tag information set
    local tag: VPN route head
    fast tag rewrite with Se4/0, point2point, tags imposed {18 12310}
  via 196.49.1.2, 0 dependencies, recursive
    next hop 194.22.15.9, Serial4/0 via 196.49.1.2/32
    valid cached adjacency
    tag rewrite with Se4/0, point2point, tags imposed {18 23}


SuperCom-RR# show mpls forwarding label 18 detail
Local   Outgoing    Prefix         Bytes tag   Outgoing    Next Hop
tag     tag or VC   or Tunnel Id   switched    interface
18      25          196.49.1.2/32  1736        Et5/1       194.22.15.5
          MAC/Encaps=14/18, MTU=1500, Tag Stack{25}


SuperComParis-ASBR# show mpls forwarding label 25 detail
Local   Outgoing    Prefix         Bytes tag   Outgoing    Next Hop
tag     tag or VC   or Tunnel Id   switched    interface
25      17          196.49.1.2/32  3275        PO10/0/0    point2point
          MAC/Encaps=4/8, MTU=4470, Tag Stack{17}


EuroComParis-ASBR# show mpls forwarding label 17 detail
Local   Outgoing    Prefix         Bytes tag   Outgoing    Next Hop
tag     tag or VC   or Tunnel Id   switched    interface
17      Pop tag     196.49.1.2/32  8107        AT4/1/0     10.2.1.22
          MAC/Encaps=12/12, MTU=4474, Tag Stack{}


EuroCom-RR# show mpls forwarding label 23 detail
Local   Outgoing    Prefix         Bytes tag   Outgoing    Next Hop
```

Example 6-55 *BankCorp LSP through the EuroCom Route Reflector (Continued)*

```
tag     tag or VC   or Tunnel Id      switched    interface
12310   19          99:5432:198.121.62.0/24    \
                                      3286      AT1/1.1     point2point
        MAC/Encaps=12/16, MRU=4470, Tag Stack{19}


Munich_PE# show mpls forwarding label 19 detail
Local  Outgoing   Prefix             Bytes tag  Outgoing   Next Hop
tag    tag or VC  or Tunnel Id       switched   interface
19     Untagged   198.121.62.0/24[V]    \
                                     4668       Et4/0      194.69.27.17
        MAC/Encaps=0/0, MTU=1504, Tag Stack{}
```

Change of BGP Next-Hop at the Route Reflectors

So that you can overcome the forwarding issue that was highlighted in the previous section, a new feature has been introduced to prohibit the route reflector from rewriting the BGP next-hop attribute when advertising routes to external neighbors. This feature is known as *next-hop-unchanged*. You must configure the SuperCom and EuroCom route reflectors to use this feature, as shown in Example 6-56.

Example 6-56 *Next-Hop-Unchanged Feature for Route Reflectors*

```
hostname SuperCom-RR
!
router bgp 10
 neighbor 196.49.1.2 remote-as 20
 neighbor 196.49.1.2 description EuroCom-RR
 neighbor 196.49.1.2 ebgp-multihop 255
 neighbor 196.49.1.2 update-source Loopback0
 !
 address-family vpnv4
 neighbor 196.49.1.2 activate
 neighbor 196.49.1.2 next-hop-unchanged
 neighbor 196.49.1.2 send-community extended

hostname EuroCom-RR
!
router bgp 20
 neighbor 194.22.16.1 remote-as 10
 neighbor 194.22.16.1 description SuperCom-RR
 neighbor 194.22.16.1 ebgp-multihop 255
 neighbor 194.22.16.1 update-source Loopback0
 !
 address-family vpnv4
 neighbor 194.22.16.1 activate
 neighbor 194.22.16.1 next-hop-unchanged
 neighbor 194.22.16.1 send-community extended
```

Now that you have set this configuration at the route reflectors, Example 6-57 shows that the SuperCom route reflector learns all the VPNv4 routes within the EuroCom network with a next-hop of the originating PE router, which in this case is the Munich PE router. You will see later in this chapter how the LSP between the BankCorp sites has changed so that it bypasses the SuperCom and EuroCom route reflectors.

Example 6-57 *PE Router Address Used as BGP Next-Hop*

```
SuperCom-RR# show ip bgp vpnv4 all
BGP table version is 7, local router ID is 194.22.16.1
Status codes: s suppressed, d damped, h history, * valid, > best, i - internal
Origin codes: i - IGP, e - EGP, ? - incomplete

   Network          Next Hop          Metric LocPrf Weight Path
Route Distinguisher: 10:4972
*>i192.168.2.32/30  194.22.15.1           0    100      0 ?
*>i198.121.63.0     194.22.15.1           1    100      0 ?
Route Distinguisher: 99:5432
*   194.69.27.16/30 196.49.1.3                          0 20 ?
*   198.121.62.0    196.49.1.3                          0 20 ?
```

IPv4 + Labels Capability for Exchange of BGP Next-Hops

Having distributed all the necessary VPNv4 prefix information between the route reflectors, you must allow access to the PE router next-hop addresses of those routes. As previously mentioned in the Carrier's Carrier sections, you can achieve this in various ways, including the following:

- Static routing
- Dynamic IGP routing protocols
- BGP-4

The preferred option for a service provider is to use BGP-4. The problem with this approach, however, is that the LSP between PE routers is broken at the ASBR-ASBR link; therefore, you need to extend BGP to allow the addition of MPLS labels to the routes. You achieve this through the use of IPv4 + Labels that was discussed in the Carrier's Carrier sections earlier in this chapter.

Now that you have decided to use this functionality on the SuperCom/EuroCom ASBR-ASBR link, the first step of the configuration is to redistribute the local PE router addresses into BGP at the ASBRs.

NOTE   A further option for injecting the PE router loopback addresses into BGP is to run IPv4 + Labels down to the PE routers and inject the PE router loopback address either through redistribution or use of the network statement.

As with any redistribution, it is good practice to filter the specific routes via a route map so that only the desired prefixes are injected into the BGP table and propagated using IPv4 + Labels to the adjacent ASBR. These prefixes should only be the loopback addresses of PE routers that hold InterAS VPN customers. To simplify the filtering configuration of the route map, allocate these addresses from the same address block. The configuration of the SuperCom and EuroCom ASBRs to support this filtering is shown in Example 6-58.

Example 6-58 *Filtering at ASBRs During Redistribution*

```
hostname SuperComParis-ASBR
!
router bgp 10
 !
 address-family ipv4
 redistribute isis SuperCom level-2 route-map IPV4+LABELS
 !
access-list 1 permit 194.22.15.0 0.0.0.255
route-map IPV4+LABELS permit 10
 match ip address 1

hostname EuroComParis-ASBR
!
router bgp 20
 !
 address-family ipv4
 redistribute isis EuroCom level-2 route-map IPV4+LABELS
 !
access-list 1 permit 196.49.1.0 0.0.0.255
route-map IPV4+LABELS permit 10
 match ip address 1
```

NOTE   The configuration shown in Example 6-58 does not contain the **set mpls-label** command within the route map, which was required in the Carrier's Carrier example earlier in this chapter. The reason for this is that the filtering is performed during redistribution rather than at the BGP neighbor level; therefore, this command is not necessary.

Using this configuration, only the 194.22.15.1/32 (San Jose PE router) prefix is redistributed into IPv4 + Labels from the SuperCom ASBR, and only the 196.49.1.3/32 (Munich PE router) prefix is redistributed from the EuroCom ASBR.

You must also configure redistribution to allow the BGP routes that are learned from the adjacent ASBR to be injected into the local IGP. The relevant configuration for this redistribution is provided in Example 6-59.

Example 6-59 *Redistribution from IPv4 + Labels into IGP*

```
hostname SuperComParis-ASBR
!
router isis SuperCom
 redistribute bgp 10 route-map IPV4+LABELS-IN
!
access-list 2 permit 196.49.1.0 0.0.0.255
route-map IPV4+LABELS-IN permit 10
 match ip address 2
 match mpls-label

hostname EuroComParis-ASBR
!
router isis EuroCom
 redistribute bgp 20 route-map IPV4+LABELS-IN
!
access-list 2 permit 194.22.15.0 0.0.0.255
route-map IPV4+LABELS-IN permit 10
 match ip address 2
 match mpls-label
```

NOTE   Example 6-59 shows that the command **match mpls-label** is used within the route map. This ensures that only BGP routes with labels are redistributed into the IGP; these should be the only routes that are reachable across the ASBR-link for PE router/PE router connectivity.

With all the relevant filters in place, the last piece of the configuration is to activate the BGP session between the ASBRs, as shown in Example 6-60.

Example 6-60 *Activation of IPv4 + Labels Between ASBRs*

```
hostname SuperComParis-ASBR
!
router bgp 10
 !
 address-family ipv4
 redistribute isis SuperCom level-2 route-map IPV4+LABELS
 neighbor 192.168.2.38 activate
 neighbor 192.168.2.38 send-label

hostname EuroComParis-ASBR
!
router bgp 20
 !
```

Example 6-60 *Activation of IPv4 + Labels Between ASBRs (Continued)*

```
address-family ipv4
redistribute isis EuroCom level-2 route-map IPV4+LABELS
neighbor 192.168.2.37 activate
neighbor 192.168.2.37 send-label
```

Now that the VPNv4 and BGP next-hop route exchange has been successfully configured, Example 6-61 provides the end-to-end LSP path from the San Jose PE router for the BankCorp Berlin subnet 198.121.62.0/24. Figure 6-23 provides an illustration. If you compare this LSP to the LSP from Example 6-55, you can see that the route reflectors are no longer within the path between BankCorp sites.

Example 6-61 *End-to-End LSP for MH-MP-EBGP with IPv4 + Labels*

```
SanJose-PE# show ip cef vrf BankCorp 198.121.62.0
198.121.62.0/24, version 39, cached adjacency to Serial4/0
0 packets, 0 bytes
  tag information set
    local tag: VPN route head
    fast tag rewrite with Se4/0, point2point, tags imposed {21 19}
  via 196.49.1.3, 0 dependencies, recursive
    next hop 194.22.15.9, Serial4/0 via 196.49.1.3/32
    valid cached adjacency
    tag rewrite with Se4/0, point2point, tags imposed {21 19}

SuperCom-Prouter# show mpls forwarding label 21
Local  Outgoing    Prefix          Bytes tag  Outgoing   Next Hop
tag    tag or VC   or Tunnel Id    switched   interface
21     26          196.49.1.3/32   610        Et5/1      194.22.15.5

SuperComParis-ASBR# show mpls forwarding label 26
Local  Outgoing    Prefix          Bytes tag  Outgoing   Next Hop
tag    tag or VC   or Tunnel Id    switched   interface
26     19          196.49.1.3/32   560        PO10/0/0   point2point

EuroComParis-ASBR# show mpls forwarding label 19
Local  Outgoing    Prefix          Bytes tag  Outgoing   Next Hop
tag    tag or VC   or Tunnel Id    switched   interface
19     23          196.49.1.3/32   1200       AT4/1/0    10.2.1.22

EuroCom-Prouter# show mpls forwarding label 23
Local  Outgoing    Prefix          Bytes tag  Outgoing   Next Hop
tag    tag or VC   or Tunnel Id    switched   interface
23     Pop tag     196.49.1.3/32   560        AT1/1.1    point2point

Munich_PE# show mpls forwarding label 19
Local  Outgoing    Prefix            Bytes tag  Outgoing   Next Hop
tag    tag or VC   or Tunnel Id      switched   interface
19     Untagged    198.121.62.0/24[V]  \
                                     1710       Et4/0      194.69.27.17
```

Figure 6-23   *End-to-End LSP for MH MP-eBGP with IPv4 + Labels*

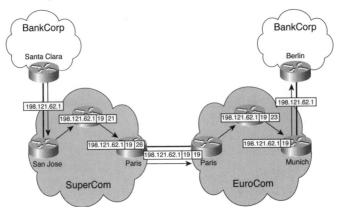

Summary

In this chapter, you saw that the base MPLS VPN architecture might not provide all of the functionality you need for certain deployment scenarios. So that you can meet the connectivity requirements for these scenarios, Cisco Systems Inc. has introduced the Carrier's Carrier and InterAS solutions.

To ease the burden of large routing tables at the PE routers, you can use the Carrier's Carrier architecture so that external routes are exchanged directly between customer sites. Any internal routes such as BGP next-hops, server addresses, and so on are exchanged with the MPLS VPN backbone.

You can establish connectivity within a VPN that can span multiple service provider footprints by using the InterAS architecture. Several options exist within this solution that provide flexible service deployment, such as Multihop and External Multiprotocol BGP support.

CHAPTER 7

Multicast VPN

Multicast is a popular feature used mainly by IP-networks of Enterprise customers. Multicast allows the efficient distribution of information between a single multicast source and multiple receivers. An example of a multicast source in a corporate network would be a financial information server provided by a third-party company such as Bloomberg's or Reuters. The receivers would be individual PCs scattered around the network all receiving the same financial information from the server. The multicast feature allows a single stream of information to be transmitted from a source device, regardless of how many receivers are active for the information from that source device. The routers automatically replicate a single copy of the stream to each interface where multicast receivers can be reached. Therefore, multicast significantly reduces the amount of traffic required to distribute information to many interested parties.

This chapter describes in detail how an MPLS VPN service provider can provide multicast services between multiple sites of a customer VPN that has an existing multicast network or is intending to deploy the multicast feature within their network. This feature is known as *multicast VPN* (mVPN) and is available from Cisco IOS 12.2(13)T onward. This chapter includes an introduction to general IP Multicast concepts, an overall description of the mVPN feature and architecture, a detailed description of each IP Multicast component modified to support the mVPN feature, and a case study that shows how you can implement mVPN in an MPLS VPN backbone.

Introduction to IP Multicast

IP multicast is an efficient mechanism for transmitting data from a single source to many receivers in a network. The destination address of a multicast packet is always a multicast group address. This address comes from the IANA block 224.0.0.0–239.255.255.255. (Before the concept of classless interdomain routing, or CIDR, existed, this range was referred to as the D-class.) A source transmits a multicast packet by using a multicast group address, while many receivers "listen" for traffic from that same group address.

Examples of applications that would use multicast are audio/video services such as IPTV, Windows Media Player, conferencing services such as NetMeeting or stock tickers, and financial information such as those that TIBCO and Reuters provide.

NOTE If you want to gain a more complete or detailed understanding of IP multicast, then read the Cisco Press book titled *Developing IP Multicast Networks* (ISBN 1-57870-077-9) or any other book that provides an overview of multicast technologies. You can obtain further information on advanced multicast topics from http://www.cisco.com/go/ipmulticast.

Multicast packets are forwarded through the network by using a *multicast distribution tree*. The network is responsible for replicating the same packet at each *bifurcation point* (the point at which the branches fork) in the tree. This means that only one copy of the packet travels over any particular link in the network, making multicast trees extremely efficient for distributing the same information to many receivers.

There are two types of distribution trees: source trees and shared trees.

Source Trees

A *source tree* is the simplest form of distribution tree. The source host of the multicast traffic is located at the root of the tree, and the receivers are located at the ends of the branches. Multicast traffic travels from the source host down the tree toward the receivers. The forwarding decision on which interface a multicast packet should be transmitted out is based on the multicast forwarding table. This table consists of a series of multicast state entries that are cached in the router. State entries for a source tree use the notation (S, G) pronounced *S comma G*. The letter *S* represents the IP address of the source, and *G* represents the group address.

NOTE The notion of direction is used for packets that are traveling along a distribution tree. When a packet travels from a source (or root) toward a receiver, it is deemed to be traveling *down the tree*. If a packet is traveling from the receiver toward the source (such as a control packet), it is deemed to be traveling *up the tree*.

A source tree is depicted in Figure 7-1. The host 196.7.25.12 at the root of the tree is transmitting multicast packets to the destination group 239.194.0.5, of which there are two interested receivers. The forwarding cache entry for this multicast stream is (196.7.25.12, 239.194.0.5).

A source tree implies that the route between the multicast source and receivers is the shortest available path; therefore, source trees are also referred to as *shortest path trees* (SPTs). A separate source tree exists for every source that is transmitting multicast packets, even if those sources are transmitting data to the same group. This means that there will be an (S, G) forwarding state entry for every active source in the network. Referring to our earlier example, if another source, such as 196.7.25.18, became active that was also transmitting to group 239.194.0.5, then an additional state entry (and a different SPT) would be created as (196.7.25.18, 239.194.0.5). Therefore, source trees or SPTs provide optimal routing at the cost of additional multicast state information in the network.

Figure 7-1   *Source Distribution Tree*

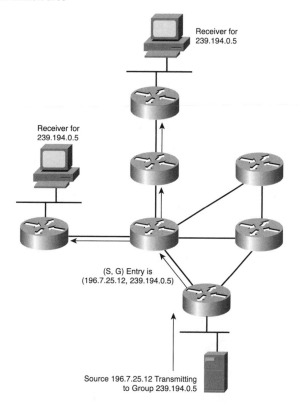

The important thing to remember about source trees is that the receiving end can only join the source tree if it has knowledge of the IP address of the source that is transmitting the group in which it is interested. In other words, to join a source tree, an explicit (S, G) join must be issued from the receiving end. (This explicit [S, G] join is issued by the last hop router, not the receiving host. The receiving host makes the last hop router aware that it wants to receive data from a particular group, and the last hop router figures out the rest.)

Shared Trees

Shared trees differ from source trees in that the root of the tree is a common point somewhere in the network. This common point is referred to as the *rendezvous point (RP)*. The RP is the point at which receivers join to learn of active sources. Multicast sources must transmit their traffic to the RP. When receivers join a multicast group on a shared tree, the root of the tree is always the RP, and multicast traffic is transmitted from the RP down toward the receivers. Therefore, the RP acts as a go-between for the sources and receivers. An RP can be the root for all multicast groups in the network, or different ranges of multicast groups can be associated with different RPs.

Multicast forwarding entries for a shared tree use the notation (*, G), which is pronounced *star comma G*. This is because all sources for a particular group share the same tree. (The multicast groups go to the same RP.) Therefore, the * or wildcard represents all sources. A shared tree is depicted in Figure 7-2. In this example, multicast traffic from the source host 196.7.25.18 and 196.7.25.12 travel to the RP and then down the tree toward the two receivers. There are two routing entries, one for each of the multicast groups that share the tree: (*, 239.194.0.5) and (*, 239.194.0.7). In a shared tree, if more sources become active for either of these two groups, there will still be only two routing entries due to the wildcard representing all sources for that group.

Figure 7-2   *Shared Distribution Tree*

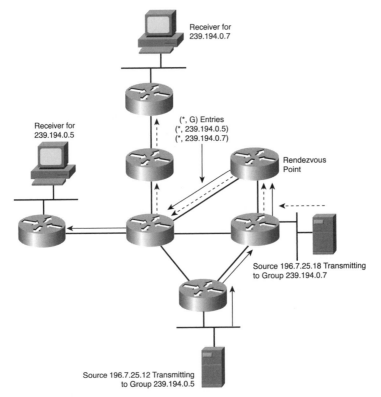

Shared trees are not as optimal in their routing as source trees because all traffic from sources must travel to the RP and then follow the same (*, G) path to receivers. However, the amount of multicast routing state information required is less than that of a source tree. Therefore, there is a trade-off between optimal routing versus the amount of state information that must be kept.

Shared trees allow the receiving end to obtain data from a multicast group without having to know the IP address of the source. The only IP address that needs to be known is that of the RP. This can be configured statically on each router or learned dynamically by mechanisms such as Auto-RP or Bootstrap Router (BSR).

Shared trees can be categorized into two types: unidirectional and bidirectional. Unidirectional trees are essentially what has already been discussed; sources transmit to the RP, which then forwards the multicast traffic down the tree toward the receivers.

In a bidirectional shared tree, multicast traffic can travel up and down the tree to reach receivers. Bidirectional shared trees are useful in an any-to-any environment, where many sources and receivers are evenly distributed throughout the network. Figure 7-3 shows a bidirectional tree. Source 196.7.25.18 is transmitting to two receivers A and B for group 239.194.0.7. The multicast traffic from the source host is forwarded in both directions as follows:

- Up the tree toward the root (RP). When the traffic arrives at the RP, it is then transmitted down the tree toward receiver A.

- Down the tree toward receiver B. (It does not need to pass the RP.)

Bidirectional trees offer improved routing optimality over unidirectional shared trees by being able to forward data in both directions while retaining a minimum amount of state information. (Remember, state information refers to the amount of (S, G) or (*, G) entries that a router must hold.)

Figure 7-3   *Bidirectional Shared Tree*

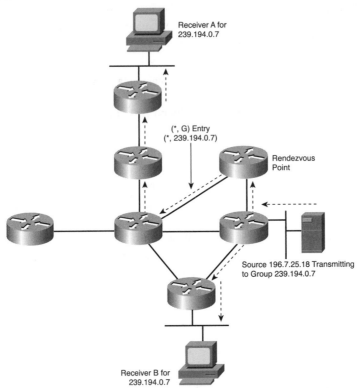

Multicast Forwarding

Packet forwarding in a router can be divided into two types: unicast forwarding and
multicast forwarding. The difference between unicast forwarding and multicast forwarding
can be summarized as follows:

- Unicast forwarding is concerned with where the packet is going.

- Multicast forwarding is concerned with where the packet came from.

In unicast routing, the forwarding decision is based on the destination address of the packet.
At each router along the path, you can derive the next-hop for the destination by finding the
longest match entry for that destination in the unicast routing table. The unicast packet is
then forwarded out the interface that is associated with the next-hop.

Forwarding of multicast packets cannot be done in the same manner because the destination
is a multicast group address that you will most likely need to forward out multiple interfaces. Multicast group addresses do not appear in the unicast routing table; therefore,

forwarding of multicast packets requires a different process. This process is called *Reverse Path Forwarding* (RPF), and it is the basis for forwarding multicast packets in most multicast routing protocols. In particular, RPF is used with Protocol Independent Multicast (PIM), which is the protocol used and described throughout this chapter.

RPF

Every multicast packet received on an interface at a router is subject to an RPF check. The RPF check determines whether the packet is forwarded or dropped and prevents looping of packets in the network. RPF operates like this:

- When a multicast packet arrives at the router, the *source* address of that packet is checked to make sure that the incoming interface indeed leads back to the source. (In other words, it is on the reverse path.)

- If the check passes, then the multicast packet is forwarded out the relevant interfaces (but not the RPF interface).

- If the RPF check fails, the packet is discarded.

The interface used for the RPF check is referred to as the *RPF interface*. The way that this interface is determined depends on the multicast routing protocol that is in use. This chapter is concerned only with PIM, which is the most widely used protocol in Enterprise networks. PIM is discussed in the next section. PIM uses the information in the unicast routing table to determine the RPF interface. Figure 7-4 shows the process of an RPF check for a packet that arrives on the wrong interface. A multicast packet from the source 196.7.25.18 arrives on interface S0. A check of the multicast routing table shows that network 196.7.25.0 is reachable on interface S1, not S0; therefore, the RPF check fails and the packet is dropped.

Figure 7-4   *RPF Check Fails*

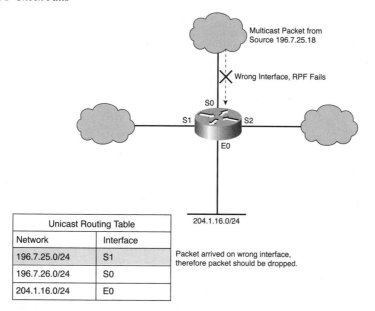

Unicast Routing Table	
Network	Interface
196.7.25.0/24	S1
196.7.26.0/24	S0
204.1.16.0/24	E0

Figure 7-5 shows the RPF check for a multicast packet that arrives on the correct interface. The multicast packet with source arrives on interface S1, which matches the interface for this network in the unicast routing table. Therefore, the RPF check passes and the multicast packet is replicated to the interfaces in the outgoing interface list (called the *olist*) for the multicast group.

Figure 7-5   *RPF Check Succeeds*

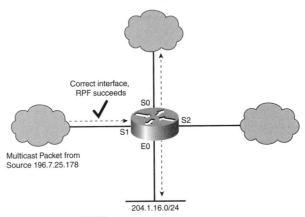

Unicast Routing Table	
Network	Interface
196.7.25.0/24	S1
196.7.26.0/24	S0
204.1.16.0/24	E0

Packet arrived on correct interface, therefore packet should be replicated.

If the RPF check has to refer to the unicast routing table for each arriving multicast packet, this will have a detrimental affect on router performance. Instead, the RPF interface is cached as part of the (S, G) or (*, G) multicast forwarding entry. When the multicast forwarding entry is created, the RPF interface is set to the interface that leads to the source network in the unicast routing table. If the unicast routing table changes, then the RPF interface is updated automatically to reflect the change.

Example 7-1 shows a multicast forwarding entry for (194.22.15.2, 239.192.20.16). You can also refer to this entry as a *multicast routing table entry*. The presence of the source in the (S, G) notation indicates that this entry is associated with a source tree or shortest path tree. The incoming interface is the RPF interface, which has been set to POS3/0. This setting matches the next-hop interface shown in the OSPF routing entry for the source 194.22.15.2. There are two interfaces in the outgoing olist: Serial4/0 and Serial4/2. The outgoing interface list provides the interfaces that the multicast packet should be replicated out. Therefore, packets that pass the RPF check from source 194.22.15.2 (they must come in on

POS3/0) that are destined to group 239.192.20.16 are replicated out interface Serial4/0 and Serial4/2.

Example 7-1   *Source Tree Multicast Forwarding Entry*

```
(194.22.15.2, 239.192.20.16), 00:03:30/00:03:27, flags: sT
  Incoming interface: POS3/0, RPF nbr 194.22.15.17
  Outgoing interface list:
    Serial4/0, Forward/Sparse-Dense, 00:03:30/00:02:55
    Serial4/2, Forward/Sparse-Dense, 00:02:45/00:02:05

Routing entry for 194.22.15.2/32
  Known via "ospf 1", distance 110, metric 2, type intra area
  Last update from 194.22.15.17 on POS3/0, 1w5d ago
  Routing Descriptor Blocks:
  * 194.22.15.17, from 194.22.15.2, 1w5d ago, via POS3/0
      Route metric is 2, traffic share count is 1
```

For completeness, a shared tree routing entry is shown in Example 7-2. This entry represents all sources transmitting to group 239.255.0.20. The RPF interface is shown to be FastEthernet0/1, which is the next-hop interface to the RP 196.7.25.1. Remember that the root of a shared tree are always the RP; therefore, the RPF interface for a shared tree is the reverse path back to the RP.

Example 7-2   *Shared Tree Multicast Forwarding Entry*

```
(*, 239.255.0.20), 2w5d/00:00:00, RP 196.7.25.1, flags: SJCL
  Incoming interface: FastEthernet0/1, RPF nbr 192.168.2.34
  Outgoing interface list:
    FastEthernet0/0, Forward/Sparse, 00:03:29/00:02:54
```

The outgoing interface lists in the preceding examples are determined by the particular multicast protocol in use.

PIM

Over the years, various multicast protocols have been developed, such as Distance Vector Multicast Routing Protocol (DVMRP), Multicast Open Shortest Path First (MOSPF), and Core Base Trees (CBT). The characteristic that these protocols have in common is that they create a multicast routing table based on their own discovery mechanisms. The RPF check does not use the information already available in the unicast routing table.

The protocol that is the most widely deployed and relevant to this chapter is PIM. As discussed previously, PIM uses the unicast routing table to discover whether the multicast packet has arrived on the correct interface. The RPF check is independent because it does not rely on a particular protocol; it bases its decisions on the contents of the unicast routing table.

Several PIM modes are available: dense mode (PIM DM), sparse mode (PIM SM), Bidirectional PIM (PIM Bi-Dir), and a recent addition known as Source Specific Multicast (SSM).

PIM DM

The deployment of PIM DM is diminishing because it has been proven to be inefficient in comparison to PIM SM. PIM DM is based on the assumption that for every subnet in the network, at least one receiver exists for every (S, G) multicast stream. Therefore, all multicast packets are pushed or flooded to every part of the network. Routers that do not want to receive the multicast traffic because they do not have a receiver for that (S, G) send a prune message back up the tree. Branches that do not have receivers are pruned off, the result being a source distribution tree with branches that have receivers. Periodically, the prune message times out, and multicast traffic begins to flood through the network again until another prune is received.

PIM SM

PIM SM is more efficient than PIM DM in that it does not use flooding to distribute traffic. PIM SM employs the pull model, in which traffic is distributed only where is it requested. Multicast traffic is distributed to a branch only if an explicit join message has been received for that multicast group. Initially, receivers in a PIM SM network join the shared tree (rooted at the RP). If the traffic on the shared tree reaches a certain bandwidth threshold, the last hop router (that is, the one to which the receiver is connected) can choose to join a shortest-path tree to the source. This puts the receiver on a more optimal path to the source.

PIM Bi-Dir

PIM Bi-Dir creates a two-way forwarding tree, as shown in Figure 7-3. All multicast routing entries for bidirectional groups are on a (*, G) shared tree. Because traffic can travel in both directions, the amount of state information is kept to a minimum. Routing optimality is improved because traffic does not have to travel unnecessarily toward the RP. Source trees are never built for bidirectional multicast groups. Bidirectional trees in the service provider network are covered in the section "Case Study of mVPN Operation in SuperCom" later in this chapter.

SSM

SSM implies that the IP address of the source for a particular group is known before a join is issued. SSM in Cisco IOS is implemented in addition to PIM SM and co-exists with IP Multicast networks based on PIM SM. SSM always builds a source tree between the receivers and the source. The source is learned through an out-of-band mechanism. Because the source is known, an explicit (S, G) join can be issued for the source tree that obviates the need for shared trees and RPs. Because no RPs are required, optimal routing is assured; traffic travels the most direct path between source and receiver. SSM is a recent innovation in multicast networks and is recommended for new deployments, particularly in the service provider core for an mVPN environment. A practical deployment of SSM is discussed in the section, "Case Study of mVPN Operation in SuperCom" later in this chapter.

Multicast is a powerful feature that allows the efficient one-to-many distribution of information. Multicast uses the concept of distribution trees, where the source is the root of the tree and the receivers are at the leaves of the tree. The routers replicate packets at each branch of the tree, known as the bifurcation point. The tree is represented as a series of multicast state entries in each router, and packets are forwarded down this tree (toward the leaves) by using RPF. There are various modes of multicast operation in networks with the most popular one being PIM SM.

Enterprise Multicast in a Service Provider Environment

The fundamental problem that service providers face today when offering native multicast services to end customers is the amount of multicast distribution information (that is [S, G] or [*, G] states) that needs to be maintained to provide the most optimal multicast traffic distribution. When a multicast source becomes active within a particular customer site, the multicast traffic must travel through the service provider network to reach all PE routers that have receivers connected to CE routers for that multicast group. To prevent unnecessary traffic delivery, the service provider must avoid sending traffic to PE routers that have no interested receivers. To accomplish this goal and achieve optimal routing, each P router in the network must maintain state information for all active customer distribution trees.

However, a problem arises in that the service provider has no visibility into how its end customers manage multicast within their enterprise. In addition, the service provider does not have control over the distribution of sources and receivers or the number of groups that the end customer chooses to use. In this situation, the P routers are required to support an unbounded amount of state information based on the enterprise customer's application of multicast.

Figure 7-6 illustrates this scenario in the SuperCom network. (This chapter uses SuperCom as the example network.) As shown in the figure, SuperCom provides native multicast services to VPN customers FastFoods and EuroBank. In this example, native multicast means that the SuperCom network provides both customers with multicast services via the global multicast routing table by using standard multicast procedures. To obtain multicast services, each EuroBank or FastFoods site must ultimately connect to a SuperCom global interface (that is, one with no VRF defined). Multicast traffic travels across the SuperCom network using standard IP multicast; no tunnels or encapsulations are used. The FastFoods organization has three active distribution trees rooted at two sources (A and B). Similarly, EuroBank has three active distribution trees rooted at three sources (C, D, and E). Each of these trees has at least one receiver that is connected to a CE somewhere in the global multicast network.

To provide optimal multicast traffic distribution, the Washington P router must hold the state information for all six trees. This applies equally to any other P and PE routers that are in the path of the distribution trees. Because all multicast routing operates in the global SuperCom table, it is possible that multicast groups that different customers use will conflict (as would be the case with multiple customers using the same RFC 1918 addressing in a unicast network). To avoid this situation, SuperCom must allocate each VPN a unique range of multicast groups.

Figure 7-6 *Supporting Native Enterprise Multicast*

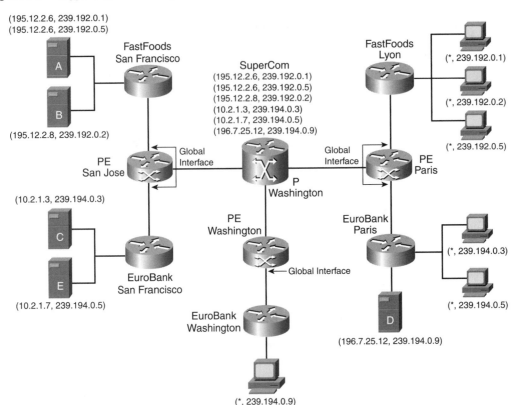

The total amount of state information that the SuperCom network must hold is determined by the way the customer deploys multicast in his network. For each unique customer source, a separate state entry exists in the global table for each multicast group that source is serving. Deploying features such as bidirectional trees reduces the amount of multicast state information required, although traffic distribution is not as optimal. Given that the amount of state information is unbounded (cannot be limited) and the service provider must allocate and manage multicast groups, the deployment of native multicast services in this manner is not recommended from a scaling and provisioning standpoint.

A common way to provide multicast over a service provider IP or MPLS VPN network is to overlay generic routing encapsulation (GRE) tunnels between CE routers. This eliminates the need for any state information to be kept in the P routers because all multicast packets between VPN sites are encapsulated by using GRE within the service provider network. This solution also allows different enterprise customers to use overlapping multicast groups. However, the disadvantage of this solution is that unless the customer implements a full mesh of GRE tunnels between CE routers, optimal multicast routing is not achieved. In fact, more bandwidth can be wasted by multicast traffic backtracking over different GRE tunnels across the P network. Further to this, Multicast over GRE is inherently unscalable due to the potential number of tunnels required and the amount of operational and management overhead.

A more scalable model for providing multicast within a VPN can be derived from the way optimal unicast routing is achieved in an MPLS VPN.

In an MPLS VPN

- A P router maintains routing information and labels for the global routing table only. It does not hold routing or state information for customer VPNs.

- A CE router maintains a routing adjacency with its PE router neighbor only. CE routers do not peer with other CE routers but still have the ability to access other CE routers in their VPN through the most optimal route that the P network provides.

As you will see, the mVPN solution that is implemented in Cisco IOS provides a scalable and efficient method of transporting multicast traffic between sites of a VPN customer and has similar characteristics mentioned in the previous bullet points.

In a service provider network that is enabled with mVPN

- A P router maintains multicast state entries for the global routing table only. It does not hold multicast state entries for customer VPNs.

- A CE router maintains a multicast PIM adjacency with its PE router neighbor only. CE routers do not have multicast peerings with other CE routers, but they can exchange multicast information with other CE routers in the same VPN.

The following sections describe the mVPN architecture as implemented by Cisco IOS.

mVPN Architecture

The mVPN solution discussed in this chapter is based on section 2 of *Multicast in MPLS/BGP VPNs* Internet draft (draft-rosen-vpn-mcast).

Section 2 of this Internet draft describes the concept of *multicast domains* in which CE routers maintain a PIM adjacency with their local PE router only, and not with other CE routers. As mentioned previously, this adjacency characteristic is identical to that used in MPLS VPNs. Enterprise customers can maintain their existing multicast configurations, such as PIM SM/PIM DM and any RP discovery mechanisms, and they can transition to an mVPN service by using multicast domains without configuration changes. P routers do not hold state information for individual customer source trees; instead, they can hold as little as a single state entry for each VPN (assuming that PIM Bi-Dir is deployed) regardless of the number of multicast groups within that VPN.

If a service provider is using PIM SM in the core (instead of PIM Bi-Dir), then the greatest amount of state information that would be required in a P router would be roughly equivalent to the number of PE routers in the backbone multiplied by the number of VPNs defined on those PE routers. This should be significantly less than the number of potential customer multicast groups. Although you can reduce the amount of P-network state information, the real point to note here is that with multicast domains, regardless of which multicast mode the service provider is using (PIM SM, Bi-Dir, SSM), the amount of state information in the core is deterministic. The core information does not depend on the customer's multicast deployment.

Customer networks are also free to use whatever multicast groups they need without the possibility of overlap with other VPNs. These groups are invisible to the P router network, in the same manner that VPN unicast routes are invisible to P routers in an MPLS VPN network.

Multicast Domain Overview

A multicast domain is a set of multicast-enabled virtual routing and forwarding instances (VRFs) that can send multicast traffic to each other. These multicast VRFs are referred to as mVRFs. Multicast domains map all of a customer's multicast groups that exist in a particular VPN to a single unique global multicast group in the P-network. This is achieved by encapsulating the original customer multicast packets within a provider packet by using GRE. The destination address of the GRE packet is the unique multicast group that the service provider has allocated for that multicast domain. The source address of the GRE packet is the BGP peering address of the originating PE router. A different global multicast group address is required for every multicast domain. Therefore, the set of all customer multicast states $(*, G^1)\ldots(*, G^N)$ can be mapped to a single (S, G) or (*, G) in the service provider network.

NOTE   The use of GRE in a multicast domain is not the same as the overlay solution in which point-to-point GRE tunnels are used between CE routers. The GRE tunnels used here are between PE routers in a multicast configuration. The tunnels can be considered point-to-multipoint connections if PIM SM is deployed or even multipoint-to-multipoint if using PIM Bi-Dir. Therefore, the use of GRE for multicast domains is inherently more efficient than GRE overlay.

Each PE router that is supporting an mVPN customer is part of the multicast domain for that customer. Multiple end customers can attach to a particular PE router, which means that the PE router can be a member of many multicast domains—one for each mVPN customer who is connected to it.

One of the major attractions of the multicast domain solution is that the P routers do not need a software upgrade to enable new multicast features to support mVPNs. Only native multicast is required in the core network to support multicast domains. The advantage of this is that native multicast is a mature technology in Cisco IOS; therefore, the operational risk is minimized in the service provider network when deploying multicast domains.

The P-network builds a default multicast distribution tree (Default-MDT) between PE routers for each multicast domain by using a unique multicast group address that the service provider allocates. These unique multicast groups are referred to as *MDT-Groups*. Each mVRF belongs to a default MDT. Therefore, the amount of state information that a P router must hold is not a function of the number of customer multicast groups in the network; instead, it is the number of VPNs. This considerably reduces the amount of state information required in a P router. If the MDT is configured as a bidirectional tree, then it is possible to have a single (*, G) multicast state entry for each VPN.

Figure 7-7 shows the concept of multicast domains in the SuperCom network. The FastFoods and EuroBank VPNs belong to separate multicast domains. The SuperCom core creates a Default-MDT for each of these multicast domains by using the MDT-group addresses 239.192.10.1 for FastFoods and 239.192.10.2 for EuroBank. The PE routers at San Jose and Paris join both Default-MDTs as they are connected to the FastFoods and EuroBank sites. The Washington PE router only needs to connect to the Default-MDT for the EuroBank VPN.

Figure 7-7 *Multicast Domains*

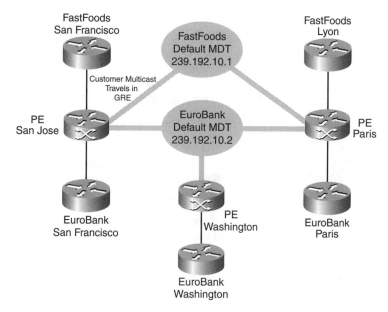

Any EuroBank or FastFoods packets that travel along these Default-MDTs are encapsulated by using GRE. The source of the outer packet is the Multiprotocol BGP peering address of the sending PE router, and the destination is the appropriate MDT-group address. GRE essentially hides the customer multicast packet from the P-network and allows us to map many multicast groups in a VPN to a single provider multicast group. The SuperCom P routers only see the source and destination of the outer IP header that SuperCom allocates. This source and destination appear as an (S, G) state entry in the SuperCom global multicast table.

Assuming that the SuperCom network has been configured with PIM Bi-Dir, only two (*, G) states are required in each P router: (*, 239.192.10.1) and (*, 239.192.10.2). This compares favorably with the six states required in the native multicast network described earlier in Figure 7-6. Also note in our example that the amount of state information in the P-network is always bounded to two entries regardless of how many new sources and groups FastFoods or EuroBank introduce.

NOTE   A P router is only aware of the PE router source addresses and the MDT-Group addresses that form the MDTs. CE router traffic traveling along an MDT is forwarded in a GRE-encapsulated packet (P-packet) using the MDT-group address as the destination (more on this in the later section, "MDTs"). The GRE P-packet uses IP only, and no MPLS label headers are applied to MDT traffic. Only pure IP multicast exists in the core.

NOTE   mVPN will be supported from IOS versions 12.2(13)T and 12.0(23)S for Cisco 7200 and 7500 series routers. Support for Cisco 10000 series routers will be available from IOS version 12.0(23)SX, Cisco 12000 series is suppored in 12.0(26)S. The initial release will permit a VPN to participate only in a single multicast domain; access to Internet multicast or other multicast domains will not be permissible. However, it is expected that this limitation will be removed in future versions of IOS.

PIM SM or SSM are the only multicast modes supported in the P-network for mVPN.

To summarize, the goals of the multicast domain solution are as follows:

- To deliver Enterprise Multicast to customers who subscribe to an MPLS VPN service
- To minimize the amount of state information in the P-network (the service provider core) while providing optimal routing
- To allow customers the freedom to choose their own multicast groups, multicast operations mode, RP placement, and so on
- To allow multicast in the P-network to be completely separated from the operation of multicast in the customer network.

The various components used to deliver multicast domains are explained in the following sections.

Multicast VRF

On a PE router, each VRF can have an associated multicast routing and forwarding table configured, referred to as a multicast VRF (mVRF). The mVRF is the PE router's view into the enterprise VPN multicast network. The mVRF contains all the multicast routing information for that VPN. This information includes the state entries for distribution trees or RP-to-group mappings (if PIM SM is being used). When a PE router receives multicast data or control packets from a CE router interface in a VRF, multicast routing such as RPF checks and forwarding will be performed on the associated mVRF.

The PE router also can configure multicast features or protocols in the context of the mVRF. For example, if the customer network were using static RP configurations (that is, it was not using Auto-RP to distribute RP information), then the PE router would need to configure the same static RP entry information that was being used in the C-network. The multicast routing protocols in Cisco IOS such as PIM, IGMP, and MSDP have been modified to operate in the context of an mVRF and as such only modify data structures and states within that mVRF.

Example 7-3 shows the PIM and MSDP commands available in the context of a VRF.

Example 7-3   *VRF-Aware Multicast Configuration Commands*

```
SuperCom_Paris(config)#ip pim vrf EuroBank ?
  accept-register      Registers accept filter
  accept-rp            RP accept filter
  bsr-candidate        Candidate bootstrap router (candidate BSR)
  register-rate-limit  Rate limit for PIM data registers
  register-source      Source address for PIM Register
  rp-address           PIM RP-address (Rendezvous Point)
  rp-announce-filter   Auto-RP announce message filter
  rp-candidate         To be a PIMv2 RP candidate
  send-rp-announce     Auto-RP send RP announcement
  send-rp-discovery    Auto-RP send RP discovery message (as RP-mapping agent)
  spt-threshold        Source-tree switching threshold
  ssm                  Configure Source Specific Multicast
  state-refresh        PIM DM State-Refresh configuration

SuperCom_Paris(config)#ip msdp vrf EuroBank ?
  default-peer         Default MSDP peer to accept SA messages from
  description          Peer specific description
  filter-sa-request    Filter SA-Requests from peer
  mesh-group           Configure an MSDP mesh-group
  originator-id        Configure MSDP Originator ID
  peer                 Configure an MSDP peer
  redistribute         Inject multicast route entries into MSDP
  sa-filter            Filter SA messages from peer
  sa-limit             Configure SA limit for a peer
  sa-request           Configure peer to send SA-Request messages to
  shutdown             Administratively shutdown MSDP peer
  timer                MSDP timer
  ttl-threshold        Configure TTL Thresold for MSDP Peer
```

In addition to the commands in the previous example, there are several multicast **show** commands that support VRF contexts. These are shown in Example 7-4.

Example 7-4 *VRF-Aware Multicast show Commands*

```
SuperCom_Paris#show ip pim vrf EuroBank ?
  autorp       Global AutoRP information
  bsr-router   Bootstrap router (v2)
  interface    PIM interface information
  mdt          Multicast tunnel information
  neighbor     PIM neighbor information
  rp           PIM Rendezvous Point (RP) information
  rp-hash      RP to be chosen based on group selected

SuperCom_Paris#show ip msdp vrf EuroBank ?
  count      SA count per AS
  peer       MSDP Peer Status
  sa-cache   MSDP Source-Active Cache
  summary    MSDP Peer Summary

SuperCom_Paris#show ip igmp vrf EuroBank ?
  groups       IGMP group membership information
  interface    IGMP interface information
  membership   IGMP membership information for forwarding
  tracking     IGMP Explicit Tracking information
  udlr         IGMP undirectional link multicast routing information
```

Example 7-5 shows the commands to enable multicast for the EuroBank VRF. The **ip multicast-routing vrf** enables multicast routing on the associated EuroBank VRF. In addition, any multicast interfaces in the EuroBank VRF will also require PIM to be enabled, as shown with the **ip pim sparse** command. The various PIM adjacencies that can exist are discussed in the following section.

Example 7-5 *Enabling Multicast in a VRF*

```
ip multicast-routing vrf EuroBank
!
interface Serial0/0
 ip vrf forwarding EuroBank
 ip address 192.168.2.26 255.255.255.252
 ip pim sparse
```

NOTE If the **ip vrf forwarding** command is removed from the PE router configuration, not only is the **ip address** command removed from any associated VRFs, but the **ip pim sparse** command is also removed.

PIM Adjacencies

Each VRF that has multicast routing enabled has a single PIM instance created on the PE router. This VRF-specific PIM instance forms a PIM adjacency with each PIM-enabled CE router in that mVRF. The customer multicast routing entries that each PIM instance creates are specific to the corresponding mVRF.

In addition to the CE router PIM adjacency, the PE router forms two other types of PIM adjacencies. The first is a PIM adjacency with other PE routers that have mVRFs in the same multicast domain. This PE router PIM adjacency is accessible through the *multicast tunnel interface* (MTI) and is used to transport multicast information between mVRFs (through a MDT) across the backbone. MDTs and MTIs are described later in this chapter. The PE router PIM adjacencies are maintained by using the same PIM instance that is used between the PE router and CE router for the associated mVRF.

The second type of PIM adjacency is created by the global PIM instance. The PE router maintains global PIM adjacencies with each of its IGP neighbors, which will be P routers, or directly connected PE routers (that are also providing a P router function). The global PIM instance is used to create the multicast distribution trees (MDTs) that connect the mVRFs.

NOTE   CE routers do not form PIM adjacencies with each other, nor does a CE router form an adjacency with a PE router by using the global PIM instance.

Figure 7-8 shows the different types of PIM adjacencies in the SuperCom network for the FastFoods VPN. A PIM adjacency exists between the San Francisco FastFoods CE router and San Jose PE router, as well as between the Lyon FastFoods CE router and the Paris PE router. Because the FastFoods mVRFs are part of the same multicast domain, a PIM adjacency is active between the San Jose and Paris PE routers. Both San Jose and Paris PE routers have separate PIM adjacency in the global table to the Washington P router.

Figure 7-8   *PIM Adjacencies*

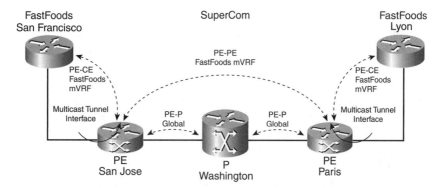

MDTs

MDTs are multicast tunnels through the P-network. MDTs transport customer multicast traffic encapsulated in GREs that are part of the same multicast domain. The two types of MDTs are as follows:

- **The Default-MDT**—An mVRF uses this MDT to send low-bandwidth multicast traffic or traffic that is destined to a widely distributed set of receivers. The Default-MDT is always used to send multicast control traffic between PE routers in a multicast domain.

- **The Data-MDT**—This MDT type is used to tunnel high-bandwidth source traffic through the P-network to interested PE routers. Data-MDTs avoid unnecessary flooding of customer multicast traffic to all PE routers in a multicast domain.

Default-MDT

When a VRF is multicast enabled (as described in Example 7-5), it must also be associated with a Default-MDT. The PE router always builds a Default-MDT to peer PE routers that have mVRFs with the same configured MDT-group address. Every mVRF is connected to a Default-MDT. An MDT is created and maintained in the P-network by using standard PIM mechanisms. For example, if PIM SM were being used in the P-network, PE routers in a particular multicast domain would discover each other by joining the shared tree for the MDT-group that is rooted at the service provider's RP.

The configuration of the Default-MDT for the FastFoods VRF is shown in Example 7-6.

Example 7-6 *Configuration of the Default-MDT*

```
ip vrf FastFoods
 rd 10:26
 route-target export 10:26
 route-target import 10:26
 mdt default 239.192.10.1
```

The example shows that only a single additional command is required for the existing VRF configuration. Upon application of the **mdt default** command, a multicast tunnel interface is created within the FastFoods mVRF, which provides access to the MDT-Group 239.192.10.1 within the SuperCom network. If other PE routers in the network are configured with the same group, then a shared or source tree is built between those PE routers.

NOTE   Enabling multicast on a VRF does not guarantee that there is any multicast activity on a CE router interface, only that there is a potential for sources and receivers to exist. After multicast is enabled on a VRF and a Default-MDT is configured, the PE router joins the Default-MDT for that domain regardless of whether sources or receivers are active. This is necessary so that the PE router can build PIM adjacencies to other PE routers in the same domain and that at the very least, mVPN control information can be exchanged.

NOTE   At present, an mVRF can belong only to a single Default-MDT; therefore, extranets cannot be formed between mVPNs.

When a PE router joins an MDT, it becomes the root of that tree, and the remote peer PE routers become leaves of the MDT. Conversely, the local PE router becomes a leaf of the MDT that is rooted at remote PE routers. Being a root and a leaf of the same tree allows the PE router to participate in a multicast domain as both a sender and receiver. Figure 7-9 illustrates the MDT root and leaves in the SuperCom network.

Figure 7-9   *MDT Roots and Leaves*

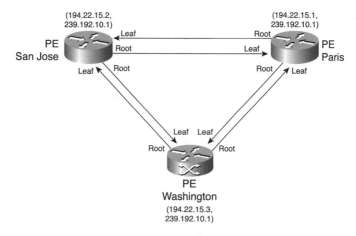

NOTE   In our example, there are three (S, G) state entries, one for each PE router root of group 239.192.10.1. You can minimize the amount of state information for the MDT in the P-network to a single (*,239.192.10.1). This can be done by either setting the PIM spt-threshold to infinity for the MDT-Group or by deploying PIM Bi-Dir. However, doing so would change the MDT from a source tree to a shared tree, which in turn could affect routing optimality.

As mentioned previously, when a PE router forwards a customer multicast packet onto an MDT, it is encapsulated with GRE. This is so that the multicast group of a particular VPN can be mapped to a single MDT-group in the P-network. The source address of the outer IP header is the PE Multiprotocol BGP local peering address, and the destination address is the MDT-Group address assigned to the multicast domain. Therefore, the P-network is only concerned with the IP addresses in the GRE header (allocated by the service provider), not the customer-specific addressing.

The packet is then forwarded in the P-network by using the MDT-Group multicast address just like any other multicast packet with normal RPF checks being done on the source address (which, in this case, is the originating PE). When the packet arrives at a PE router from an MDT, the encapsulation is removed and the original customer multicast packet is forwarded to the corresponding mVRF. The target mVRF is derived from the MDT-Group address in the destination of the encapsulation header. Therefore, using this process, customer multicast packets are tunneled through the P-network to the appropriate MDT leaves. Each MDT is a mesh of *multicast tunnels* forming the multicast domain.

In Cisco IOS, access to the MDT is represented as the MTI and is discussed in a following section. Cisco IOS creates this tunnel interface automatically upon configuration of the MDT.

NOTE   GRE, as defined in RFC 2784, is the default encapsulation method for the multicast tunnel. A future possibility is to encapsulate the customer packet with MPLS (multicast forwarding using labels). This forwarding method is described in the draft RFC farinacci-mpls-multicast, "Using PIM to Distribute Labels for Multicast Routes," which you can obtain from http://www.ietf.org/. However, at the time of writing this chapter, only pure IP encapsulation and forwarding is supported for multicast domains.

Figure 7-10 shows the process of customer packet encapsulation across an MDT.

Figure 7-10   *MDT Packet Encapsulation*

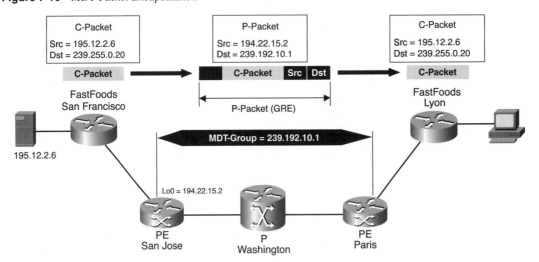

For clarity in this and further examples, any information pertaining to the customer network will be preceded by a "C-" and information pertaining to the provider network will be preceded by a "P-". For example, a packet originating from a customer network will be referred to as a C-packet, and a PIM join message in the service provider network will be referred to as a P-join.

In the example, a source at San Francisco is sending traffic to a receiver at FastFoods Lyon by using the group (*, 239.255.0.20). The Default-MDT for the FastFoods multicast domain has been defined to be 239.192.10.1, and this value is configured on each of the FastFoods VRFs. The San Jose PE router encapsulates multicast traffic destined to the group 239.255.0.20 from the source 195.12.2.6 at the FastFoods San Francisco site into a P-Packet by using GRE encapsulation. The Type-of-Service byte of the C-packet is also copied to the P-packet. The source address of the P-packet is the BGP peering address of the San Jose PE router (194.22.15.2), and the destination address is the MDT-Group (239.192.10.1). When the P-packet arrives at the Paris PE router, the encapsulation is stripped and the original C-packet is forwarded to the receiver.

NOTE   It is recommended that the MDT-group addresses for the P-network be taken from the range defined in RFC 2365, "Administratively Scoped IP Multicast." This ensures that the provision of multicast domains does not interfere with the simultaneous support of Internet multicast in the P-network.

Data-MDT

Any traffic offered to the Default-MDT (via the multicast tunnel interface) is distributed to all PE routers that are part of that multicast domain, regardless of whether active receivers are in an mVRF at that PE router. For high-bandwidth applications that have sparsely distributed receivers, this might pose the problem of unnecessary flooding to dormant PE routers. To overcome this, a special MDT group called a Data-MDT can be created to minimize the flooding by sending data only to PE routers that have active VPN receivers. The Data-MDT is created dynamically if a particular multicast stream exceeds a bandwidth threshold. Each VRF can have a pool of Data-MDT groups allocated to it.

NOTE   Note that the Data-MDT is only created for data traffic. All multicast control traffic travels on the Default-MDT to ensure that all PE routers receive control information.

When a traffic threshold is exceeded on the Default-MDT, the PE router that is connected to the VPN source of the multicast traffic can switch the (S, G) from the Default-MDT to a group associated with the Data-MDT.

NOTE   The rate at which the threshold is checked is a fixed value, which varies between router platforms. The bandwidth threshold is checked per (S, G) multicast stream rather than an aggregate of all traffic on the Default-MDT.

The group selected for the Data-MDT is taken from a pool that has been configured on the VRF. For each source that exceeds the configured bandwidth threshold, a new Data-MDT is created from the available pool for that VRF. If there are more high-bandwidth sources than there are groups available in the pool, then the group that has been referenced the least is selected and reused. This implies that if the pool contains a small number of groups, then a Data-MDT might have more than one high-bandwidth source using it. A small Data-MDT pool ensures that the amount of state information in the P-network is minimized. A large Data-MDT pool allows more optimal routing (less likely for sources to share the same Data-MDT) at the expense of increased state information in the P-network.

NOTE   The Data-MDT is triggered only by an (S, G) entry in the mVRF, not a (*, G) entry. If a customer VPN is using PIM Bi-Dir or the spt-threshold is set to infinity, then the Default-MDT is used for all traffic regardless of bandwidth.

Example 7-7 shows how to configure a Data-MDT pool for the EuroBank VRF.

Example 7-7   *Configuration of the Data-MDT*

```
ip vrf EuroBank
 rd 10:27
 route-target export 10:27
 route-target import 10:27
 mdt default 239.192.10.2
 mdt data 239.192.20.32 0.0.0.15 threshold 1 [list <access-list>]
```

The **mdt data** specifies a range of addresses to be used in the Data-MDT pool. Specifying the mask 0.0.0.15 allows you to use the range 239.192.20.32 through 239.192.20.47 as the address pool.

Because these are multicast group addresses (D-class addresses), there is no concept of a subnet; therefore, you can use all addresses in the mask range. The threshold is specified in kilobits. In this example, a threshold of 1 kilobit per second has been set, which means that if a multicast stream exceeds 1 Kbps, then a Data-MDT is created. The **mdt data** command can also limit the creation of Data-MDT to particular (S,G) VPN entries by specifying these addresses in an <access-list>.

When a PE router creates a Data-MDT, the multicast source traffic is encapsulated in the same manner as the Default-MDT, but the destination group is taken from the Data-MDT pool. Any PE router that has interested receivers needs to issue a P-join for the Data-MDT; otherwise, the receivers cannot see the C-packets because it is no longer active on the Default-MDT. For this to occur, the source PE router must inform all other PE routers in the multicast domain of the existence of the newly created Data-MDT. This is achieved by transmitting a special PIM-like control message on the Default-MDT containing the customer's (S, G) to Data-MDT group mapping. This message is called a *Data-MDT join*.

The Data-MDT join is an invitation to peer PE routers to join the new Data-MDT if they have interested receivers in the corresponding mVRF. The message is carried in a UDP packet destined to the ALL-PIM-ROUTERS group (224.0.0.13) with UDP port number 3232. The (S, G, Data-MDT) mapping is advertised by using the type, length, value (TLV) format, as shown in Figure 7-11.

Figure 7-11   *Data-MDT Join TLV Format*

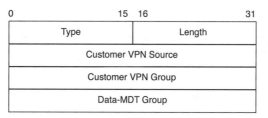

Any PE routers that receive the (S, G, Data-MDT) mapping join the Data-MDT if they have receivers in the mVRF for G. The source PE router that initiated the Data-MDT waits several seconds before sending the multicast stream onto the Data-MDT. The delay is necessary to allow receiving PE routers time to build a path back to the Data-MDT root and avoid packet loss when switching from the Default-MDT.

The Data-MDT is a transient entity that exists as long as the bandwidth threshold is being exceeded. If the traffic bandwidth falls below the threshold, the source is switched back to the Default-MDT. To avoid transitions between the MDTs, traffic only reverts to the Default-MDT if the Data-MDT is at least one minute old.

NOTE   PE routers that do not have mVRF receivers for the Data-MDT will cache the (S, G, Data-MDT) mappings in an internal table so that the join latency can be minimized if a receiver appears. The Data-MDT join message is sent every minute by the source PE-router and any cached (S, G, MDT) mappings are aged out after three minutes if they are not refreshed.

Figure 7-12 shows the operation of a Data-MDT in the SuperCom network.

Figure 7-12 *Data-MDT Operation*

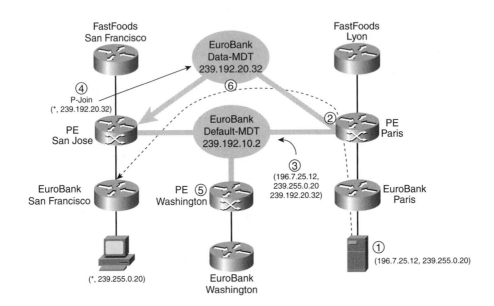

EuroBank has a high bandwidth source (196.7.25.12) located at its Paris headquarters that is servicing the EuroBank multicast group 239.255.0.20. This group has an interested receiver in EuroBank San Francisco. The following steps describe the operation of the Data-MDT:

Step 1   The source at EuroBank Paris begins to transmit. Shortly thereafter, it exceeds the bandwidth threshold.

Step 2   The Paris PE router notices that the source is exceeding the bandwidth threshold and creates a new Data-MDT from the pool configured for the EuroBank VRF, in this case 239.192.20.32.

Step 3   The Paris PE router advertises the existence of the Data-MDT via a UDP packet that contains the TLV (196.7.25.12, 239.255.0.20, 239.192.20.32). This TLV describes the Data-MDT that the customer's (S, G) is being switched over to.

Step 4   The San Jose PE router receives the (S, G, Data-MDT) mapping on the Default-MDT and issues a P-join for (*, 239.192.20.32) to the SuperCom network. This allows the San Jose PE router to join the tree for the Data-MDT in the SuperCom network.

Step 5   The PE router in Washington also receives the (S, G, Data-MDT) mapping but does not issue a P-join because no interested receivers are connected to it. Instead, the PE router caches the entry for future reference.

Step 6   After waiting for three seconds, the Paris PE router begins to transmit the multicast data for (196.7.25.12, 239.255.0.20) over the Data-MDT 239.192.20.32. The three-second delay is required to ensure that the network has had enough time to create the Data-MDT.

MTI

The MTI is the representation of access to the multicast domain in Cisco IOS. MTI appears in the mVRF as an interface called *Tunnelx*, where *x* is the tunnel number. For every multicast domain in which an mVRF participates, there is a corresponding MTI. (Note that the current IOS implementation supports only one domain per mVRF.) An MTI is essentially a gateway that connects the customer environment (mVRF) to the service provider's global environment (MDT). Any C-packets sent to the MTI are encapsulated into a P-packet (using GRE) and forwarded along the MDT. When the PE router sends to the MTI, it is the root of that MDT; when the PE router receives traffic from an MTI, it is the leaf of that MDT.

NOTE   Only a single MTI is necessary to access a multicast domain. The same MTI is used to forward traffic regardless of whether it is to the Default-MDT or to multiple Data-MDTs associated with that multicast domain.

PIM adjacencies are formed to all other PE routers in the multicast domain via the MTI. Therefore, for a specific mVRF, PE router PIM neighbors are all seen as reachable via the same MTI. The MTI is treated by an mVRF PIM instance as if it were a LAN interface. All PIM LAN procedures are valid over the MTI.

The PE router sends PIM control messages across the MTI so that multicast forwarding trees can be created between customer sites that are separated by the P-network. The forwarding trees referred to here are visible only in the C-network, not the P-network. To allow multicast forwarding between a customer's sites, the MTI is part of the outgoing interface list (olist) for the (S, G) or (*, G) states that originate from the mVRF.

The MTI is created dynamically upon configuration of the Default-MDT and cannot be explicitly configured. PIM Sparse-Dense (PIM SD) mode is automatically enabled so that various customer group modes can be supported. For example, if the customer were using PIM DM exclusively, then the MTI would be added to the olist in the mVRF with the entry marked Forward/Dense to allow distribution of traffic to other customer sites. If the PE router neighbors all sent a prune message back, and no prune override was received, then the MTI in the olist entry would be set to Prune/Dense exactly as if it were a LAN interface. If the customer network were running PIM SM, then the MTI would be added to the olist only on the reception of an explicit join from a remote PE router in the multicast domain.

NOTE   Although the MTI cannot be configured explicitly, it derives its IP properties from the same interface being used for Multiprotocol BGP peering. This is usually, but not necessarily, the loopback0 interface, and this interface *must* be multicast enabled.

The MTI is not accessible or visible to the IGP (such as OSPF or ISIS) operating in the customer network. In other words, no unicast routing is forwarded over the MTI because the interface does not appear in the unicast routing table of the associated VRF. Because the RPF check is performed on the unicast routing table for PIM, traffic received through an MTI has direct implications on current RPF procedures.

RPF Check

RPF is a fundamental requirement of multicast routing. The RPF check ensures that multicast traffic has arrived from the correct interface that leads back to the source. If this check passes, the multicast packets can be distributed out the appropriate interfaces away from the source. RPF consists of two pieces of information: the *RPF interface* and the *RPF neighbor*. The RPF interface is used to perform the RPF check by making sure that the multicast packet arrives on the interface it is supposed to, as determined by the unicast routing table. The RPF neighbor is the IP address of the PIM adjacency. It is used to forward messages such as PIM joins or prunes for the (*, G) or (S, G) entries (back toward the root of the tree where the source or RP resides). The RPF interface and neighbor are created during control plane setup of a (*, G) or (S, G) entry. During data forwarding, the RPF check is executed using the RPF interface cached in the state entry.

In an mVPN environment, the RPF check can be categorized into three types of multicast packets:

- C-packets received from a PE router customer interface in the mVRF
- P-packets received from a PE router or P router interface in the global routing table
- C-packets received from a multicast tunnel interface in the mVRF

The RPF check for the first two categories is performed as per legacy RPF procedures. The interface information is gleaned from the unicast routing table and cached in a state entry. For C-packets, the C-source lookup in the VRF unicast routing table returns a PE router interface associated with that VRF. For P-packets, the P-source lookup in the global routing table returns an interface connected to another P router or PE router. The results of these lookups are used as the RPF interface.

The third category, C-packets that are received from an MTI, is treated a little differently and requires some modification to the way the (S, G) or (*, G) state is created. C-packets in this category originated from remote PE routers in the network and have traveled across the P-network via the MDT. Therefore, from the mVRF's perspective, these C-packets must have been received on the MTI. However, because the MTI does not participate in unicast routing, a lookup of the C-source in the VRF does not return the tunnel interface. Instead, the route to the C-source will have been distributed by Multiprotocol BGP as a VPNv4 prefix from the remote PE router. This implies that the receiving interface is actually in the P-network. In this case, the RPF procedure has been modified so that if Multiprotocol BGP has learned a prefix that contains the C-source address, the RPF interface is set to the MTI that is associated with that mVRF.

NOTE   The modified RPF interface procedure is applicable only to mVRFs that are part of a single multicast domain. Although the multicast domain architecture can support multiple domains in an mVRF, the current Cisco implementation limits an mVRF to one domain.

The procedure for determining the RPF neighbor has also been modified. If the RPF interface is set to the MTI, then the RPF neighbor must be a remote PE router. (Remember that a PE router forms PIM adjacencies to other PE routers via the MTI.) The RPF neighbor is selected according to two criteria. First, the RPF neighbor must be the BGP next-hop to the C-source, as appears in the routing table for that VRF. Second, the same BGP next-hop address must appear as a PIM neighbor in the adjacency table for the mVRF. This is the reason that PIM must use the local BGP peering address when it sends hello packets across the MDT. Referencing the BGP table is done once during setup in the control plane (to create the RPF entries). When multicast data is forwarded, verification only needs to takes place on the cached RPF information.

Multiprotocol BGP MDT Updates and SSM

When a PE router creates a Default-MDT group, it updates all its peers by using Multiprotocol BGP. The Multiprotocol BGP update provides two pieces of information: the MDT-Group created and the root address of the tree (which is the BGP peering address of the PE router that originated the message). At present, this information is used only to support P-networks that use SSM. If an MDT-Group range is enabled for SSM, then the source tree is joined immediately. This differs from PIM SM, where the shared tree that is rooted at the RP is initially joined.

If an MDT-Group range has been configured to operate in SSM mode on a PE router, then that PE router needs to know the source address of the MDT root to establish an (S, G) state. This is provided in the Multiprotocol BGP update. For PE routers that do not use SSM, the information received is cached in the BGP VPNv4 table.

NOTE One of the primary advantages is that SSM does not depend on RPs, which eliminates the RP as a single point of failure. A practical example of SSM operation with MDTs is discussed later in the chapter.

The MDT-Group is carried in the BGP update message as an extended community attribute by using the type code of 0x0009. The attribute supports the AS format only and is shown in Figure 7-13.

Figure 7-13 *MDT Extended Community Attribute*

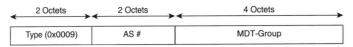

The root address of the MDT is carried in the BGP MP_REACH_NLRI attribute (AFI=1 and SAFI=128) by using the same format as a VPN-IPv4 address. We refer to it as an mVPN-IPv4 address. However, no label information is carried in the NLRI portion of the attribute. The MDT root address is carried in 2B:4B (AS # : Assigned Number) route distinguisher format but with a type code of 0x0002. The route distinguisher for the root address is shown in Figure 7-14.

NOTE The RD type code 0x0002 conflicts with the official route distinguisher format definition as described in RFC 2547bis "BGP/MPLS VPNs," available from http://www.ietf.org. This value will eventually be changed to avoid conflict with the standard.

Figure 7-14 *Route Distinguisher for MDT Root Address*

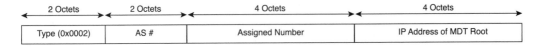

NOTE Information about Data-MDTs is not carried in Multiprotocol BGP messages. The Data-MDT join message is used for this purpose.

Figure 7-15 shows how the Default-MDT would be created by using Multiprotocol BGP updates if SuperCom were configured to operate in SSM mode only. For the purposes of this example, assume that the SSM range has been defined to be 239.192.10.0/24.

Figure 7-15 *Multiprotocol BGP Updates and SSM*

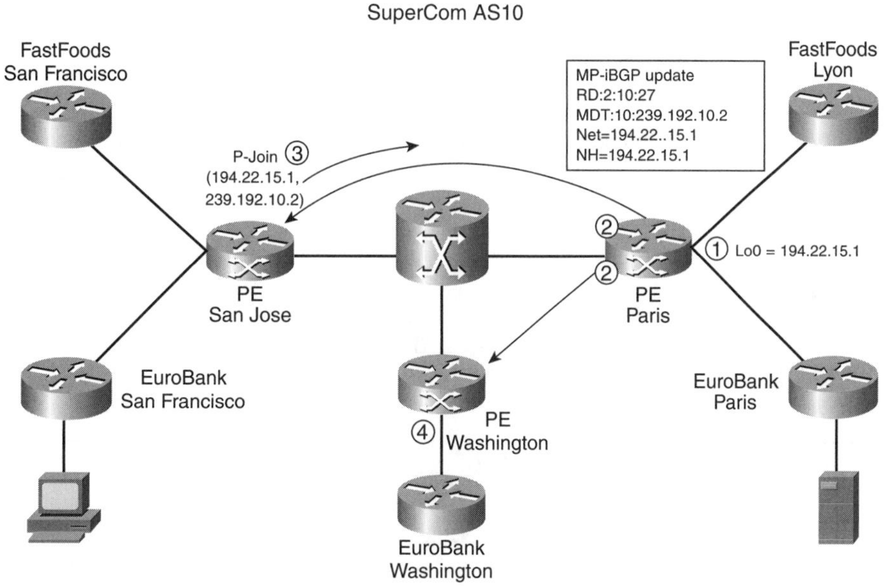

Figure 7-15 describes the creation of the Default-MDT as follows:

Step 1   The EuroBank VRF on the Paris PE router is enabled for multicast and is configured with the Default-MDT group of 239.192.10.2.

Step 2   The Paris PE router generates a Multiprotocol BGP update message to both the Washington and San Jose PE router peers. (Note: This update message is generated even if SSM is not used.) The update contains the following information:

— An MDT extended community attribute for the MDT group in the form 10:239.192.10.2, where 10 is the autonomous system number of SuperCom.

— The information in the MP_REACH_NLRI attribute contains a VPNv4 style address with a route distinguisher of **2:10:27,** where **2** is the route distinguisher type signifying that this route distinguisher is part of an MDT root address. **10:27** is the route distinguisher definition (AS:Assigned Number) from the EuroBank VRF. The IP address in the NLRI and the next-hop both use the Paris PE router BGP peering address of 194.22.15.1.

Step 3   When the San Jose PE router receives the BGP update, it immediately issues a P-join to (194.22.15.1, 239.192.10.2) by using SSM procedures. The join is issued because the San Jose PE router previously defined an mVRF to the same multicast domain (same group address of 239.192.10.2).

Step 4   The Washington PE router also receives the BGP update, but because it does not have an mVRF in that domain, it stores the update for future reference.

mVPN State Flags

Several new state flags have been created to identify multicast routing entries associated with multicast domains. These flags are shown in Table 7-1.

Table 7-1   *mVPN State Flags*

Flag	Description	Detail
Z	Multicast Tunnel	This flag appears in multicast entries in the global multicast routing table. It signifies that the multicast packets are received or transmitted on a multicast tunnel (MDT) entry. This flag appears only if mVRFs are present on the PE router that is associated with this entry. The Z flag directs that the P-packet should be de-encapsulated to reveal the C-packet.
Y	Joined MDT-Data Group	This flag appears in multicast entries for the mVRF. It signifies that data for this (*, G) or (S, G) is being received over a Data-MDT group. An entry with the Y flag signifies that this PE router received a Data-MDT join message from a source PE router and has issued a join toward it.
y	Sending to MDT-Data Group	This flag appears in multicast entries for the mVRF. It signifies that data for this (*, G) or (S, G) is being transmitted over a Data-MDT group. The y flag signifies that this PE router instigated a new Data-MDT for this customer (S, G).

Because only a single MTI exists in the mVRF per multicast domain, both the Data-MDT and the Default-MDT use the same tunnel interface for customer traffic. The **Y/y** flags are necessary to distinguish Default-MDT traffic from Data-MDT traffic and ensure that customer multicast routing entries use the correct MDT-Data group by referring to an internal table that holds the (S, G, Data-MDT) mappings.

Example 7-8 shows the value of the state flags from the Paris PE router. Do not be concerned with the context of the output shown here. A full discussion on the operation of mVPN in the SuperCom network is included in a later section.

Example 7-8   *mVPN State Flag*

```
SuperCom_Paris#show ip mroute 239.192.20.32
[snip]

(*, 239.192.20.32), 1d18h/00:03:23, RP 194.22.15.3, flags: BCZ
Bidir-Upstream: Null, RPF nbr 0.0.0.0
Outgoing interface list:
Serial4/0, Forward/Sparse, 1d18h/00:02:30
MVRF EuroBank, Forward/Sparse, 1d18h/00:00:00

SuperCom_Paris#show ip mroute vrf EuroBank 239.255.0.20
[snip]

(196.7.25.12, 239.255.0.20), 1d18h/00:03:22, flags: TY
  Incoming interface: Tunnel0, RPF nbr 194.22.15.1
  Outgoing interface list:
    Ethernet5/0, Forward/Sparse-Dense, 1d18h/00:02:50
```

The example shows output from two commands. The first command shows the entry for a
Data-MDT 239.192.20.32 in the global multicast routing table. The **Z** flag is set to show it
is associated with a multicast tunnel. The second command shows an entry in the EuroBank
mVRF for the state (196.7.25.12, 239.255.0.20). This entry happens to be receiving traffic from
the (239.192.20.32) Data-MDT in the global table as signaled by the **Y** flag, although the corre-
lation is not shown in the output. Detailed examples on the operation of the Data-MDT are
provided in the later section titled "Case Study of mVPN Operation in SuperCom."

mVPN Forwarding

Forwarding can be divided into two categories: C-packets that are received from a PE router
customer interface in mVRF (excluding the MTI), and P-packets received from a PE router
global multicast interface. To simplify things, assume that control checks such as time-to-
live (TTL) and RPF are always successful.

C-Packets Received from a PE Router Customer Multicast Interface

The following describes the steps that the router takes when a multicast packet arrives at
the PE router from a VRF interface:

Step 1   A C-Packet arrives on an VRF-configured PE router interface.

Step 2   The VRF that is configured for that interface implicitly identifies the mVRF.

Step 3   An RPF check is done on the C-packet, and if successful the C-packet is
replicated based on the contents of the olist for the (S, G) or (*, G) entry
in the mVRF. The olist might contain multicast-enabled interfaces in the
same mVRF, in which case packet forwarding follows standard multicast
procedures. The olist might also contain a tunnel interface that connects
the multicast domain.

Step 4 If the olist contains a tunnel interface, then the packet is encapsulated by using GRE, with the source being the BGP peering address of the local PE router and the destination being the MDT Group address. The decision on whether the Default-Group or the Data-MDT group is selected depends on whether the **y** flag is set on the (S, G) entry in the mVRF. The Type-of-Service byte of the C-packet is copied to the P-packet.

Step 5 The C-Packet is now a P-Packet in the global multicast routing table.

Step 6 The P-packet is forwarded all the way through the P-network by using standard multicast procedures. P routers are unaware of any mVPN activity and treat the packet as native multicast.

P-Packets Received from a PE Router Global Multicast Interface

The following describes the steps that the router takes when a multicast packet arrives at the P router from another P router or PE router in the global routing table:

Step 1 A P-packet arrives from a PE router interface in the global network.

Step 2 The P-packet's corresponding (S, G) or (*, G) entry is looked up in the global mroute table, and a global RPF check is done.

Step 3 If the RPF check is successful, the P-packet is replicated out any P-network interfaces that appear in the olist for its (S, G) or (*, G) entry. At this point, the P-packet is still being treated as native multicast.

Step 4 If the (S, G) or (*, G) entry has the **Z** flag set, then this is a Default- or Data-MDT with an associated mVRF; therefore, the P-packet must be de-encapsulated to reveal the C-packet.

Step 5 The destination mVRF of the C-packet is derived from the MDT-group address in the P-packet. The incoming MTI is also resolved from the MDT-group address.

Step 6 The C-packet is presented to the target mVRF, with the appropriate MTI set as the incoming interface. The RPF check verifies this tunnel interface.

Step 7 The C-packet is once again a native multicast packet, but it resides in the customer's network. The C-packet is replicated to all multicast-enabled interfaces in the mVRF that appears in the olist for the (S, G) or (*, G) entry.

Case Study of mVPN Operation in SuperCom

Now that the various components and procedures of mVPN have been covered, it is useful to consolidate this information into a case study of mVPN operation in the SuperCom network. Figure 7-16 shows the SuperCom network topology to be used for the case study.

Figure 7-16 *SuperCom mVPN Network*

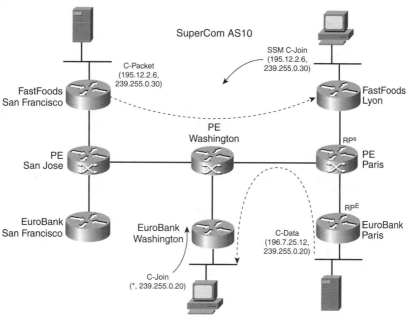

SuperCom is supporting two mVPN customers: EuroBank and FastFoods. Each of these customers is participating in a separate multicast domain via the PE routers at San Jose, Washington, and Paris.

EuroBank has three sites located at San Francisco, Washington, and Paris. One active source is connected to the Paris CE router that provides a multicast stream to an interested receiver at the Washington CE router. Even though the San Francisco CE router does not have receivers, the mVRF in the San Jose PE router still connects to the EuroBank multicast domain (in the event that a receiver does become active at the CE router). The EuroBank network has been configured with PIM SM mode, and the RP is located at the Paris CE router, denoted in Figure 7-16 by **RP^E**. RP information is statically distributed. The SuperCom network has been configured so that the Default-MDT EuroBank uses between all PE routers is 239.192.10.2 (shown previously in Figure 7-7), and the EuroBank Data-MDTs are created by using addresses from the range 239.192.20.32–239.192.20.47. FastFoods has two sites located at San Francisco and Lyon. One active source is connected to the San Francisco CE router and provides a multicast stream to an interested receiver at the Lyon CE router. The FastFoods network has been configured to operate in SSM mode; therefore, the Lyon CE router has issued a source-specific C-join to the server at FastFoods San Francisco. The SuperCom network has been configured so that the Default-MDT FastFoods uses between all PE routers is 239.192.10.1 (shown previously in Figure 7-7). The Data-MDTs are created by using addresses from the range 239.192.20.16–239.192.20.31.

NOTE	Both FastFoods and EuroBank are using the multicast range 239.255.0.0/16 for multicast services within their VPNs. This follows the convention laid out in RFC 2365 for the use of site local addressing. Because FastFoods and EuroBank are in different multicast domains, there is no conflict of the 239.255.0.0/16 range.

SuperCom is using AS 10 and has deployed PIM Bi-Dir. This means that although the routing in the core is not the most optimal, the amount of state information is kept to a minimum. The Paris PE router acts as the RP (denoted in the figure by $RP^{S)}$ and serves as the root of all MDT shared trees in the SuperCom global space. The SuperCom RP to group mapping information is distributed via Auto-RP. Later in the chapter, you will learn about the operation of PIM SSM in the SuperCom network as an alternative to PIM SM.

The San Jose, Washington, and Paris PE routers join the EuroBank multicast domain (239.192.10.2) because they have a EuroBank mVRF configured (regardless of whether receivers are active). Only the San Jose and Paris PE routers join the FastFoods multicast domain (239.192.10.1). The Washington PE router does not join the FastFoods domain because it does not have a FastFoods VRF configured. Figure 7-7 shows the logical view of the Default-MDTs in the SuperCom network.

Table 7-2 provides a summary of the topology information in the SuperCom network to assist in understanding the examples in the following sections.

Table 7-2   *SuperCom Topology Information*

Company	Site/Category	Item	Value
SuperCom Backbone	Paris (PE Router)	Lo0:	194.22.15.1/32
	San Jose (PE Router)	Lo0:	194.22.15.2/32
	Washington (PE Router)	Lo0:	194.22.15.3/32
	Circuit Addresses	PE<->CE	192.168.2.0/24
	PIM	Mode	Bidirectional
	PIM	Rendezvous Point (Auto-RP)	195.22.15.1 (SuperCom Paris)
FastFoods	San Jose (CE Router)	Subnet	195.12.2.0/24
	San Jose (CE Router)	Source Group	(195.12.2.6, 239.255.0.30)
	Lyon	Subnet	10.2.1.0/24
	PIM	Mode	SSM
	MDT	Default	239.192.10.1
	MDT	Data	239.192.20.16/28

Table 7-2   *SuperCom Topology Information (Continued)*

Company	Site/Category	Item	Value
EuroBank	Paris (CE Router)	Subnet	196.7.25.0/24
	Paris (CE Router)	Source Group	(196.7.25.12, 239.255.0.20)
	Washington (CE Router)	Subnet	196.7.26.0/24
	San Jose (CE Router)	Subnet	10.2.1.0/24
	PIM	Mode	Sparse
	PIM	Rendezvous Point (Static)	196.7.25.1 (EuroBank Paris)
	MDT	Default	239.192.10.2
	MDT	Data	239.192.20.32/28

PIM SM in the SuperCom Network

As highlighted throughout this chapter, the only requirement on the core network is that native multicast be enabled. Because we are using Auto-RP, each applicable P-network interface in SuperCom is configured with the command **ip pim sparse-dense-mode**. To keep the multicast routing state to a minimum, PIM Bi-Dir mode is also enabled on each SuperCom router with the global command **ip pim bidir-enable**. (In addition, Bi-Dir must be enabled for individual groups.)

Auto-RP is used to distribute the Default-MDT (239.192.10.0/24) and Data-MDT (239.192.20.0/24) ranges of group addresses to all other P routers and PE routers. This is accomplished by configuring the Paris PE router (the RP for SuperCom), as shown in Example 7-9.

Example 7-9   *Auto-RP Configuration for SuperCom*

```
ip access-list standard MDT-Range
 permit 239.192.10.0 0.0.0.255
 permit 239.192.20.0 0.0.0.255
!
ip pim send-rp-announce Loopback0 scope 64 group-list MDT-Range bidir
ip pim send-rp-discovery Loopback0 scope 64
```

You can verify distribution of RP information by examining the group-to-rendezvous point mapping cache on another PE router, as shown in Example 7-10.

Example 7-10   *Confirming Auto-RP Information*

```
SuperCom_Washington#show ip pim rp map
PIM Group-to-RP Mappings

Group(s) 239.192.10.0/24
  RP 194.22.15.1 (SuperCom_Paris), v2v1, bidir
    Info source: 194.22.15.1 (SuperCom_Paris), elected via Auto-RP
        Uptime: 3d15h, expires: 00:02:52
Group(s) 239.192.20.0/24
  RP 194.22.15.1 (SuperCom_Paris), v2v1, bidir
    Info source: 194.22.15.1 (SuperCom_Paris), elected via Auto-RP
        Uptime: 3d15h, expires: 00:02:55
```

The output confirms that the Default-MDT and the Data-MDT will operate in Bi-Dir mode and that the root of the shared trees created from these groups will be the Paris PE router. This means that all traffic for Default- and Data-MDTs will flow via the Paris PE router. If Bi-Dir mode were not enabled, then a shortest path tree would eventually be created for each Default- or Data-MDT by using an (S, G) pair instead of (*, G). That would create more state information in the network, but it might provide a more optimal route.

NOTE   Bi-Dir mode has only been enabled for the MDT group ranges in the SuperCom network. This does not preclude the use of other available modes such as PIM SM or SSM for other multicast groups.

PIM must also be enabled on the interface that Multiprotocol BGP uses for its peering address. This is important because the address on that interface is used as the root of the MDT and is carried in PIM hello messages via the MTI. All the SuperCom routers use loopback0 as their BGP interface and have multicast enabled, as shown in Example 7-11 for the Paris PE router.

Example 7-11   *Enabling Multicast on the BGP Peering Interface*

```
router bgp 10
 no synchronization
 no bgp default ipv4-unicast
 bgp log-neighbor-changes
 neighbor 194.22.15.2 remote-as 10
 neighbor 194.22.15.2 update-source Loopback0
 neighbor 194.22.15.3 remote-as 10
 neighbor 194.22.15.3 update-source Loopback0
 no auto-summary
 !
 [snip]

interface Loopback0
 ip address 194.22.15.1 255.255.255.255
 ip pim sparse-dense-mode
 !
```

Enabling Multicast in VRFs

After basic multicast has been enabled in the core of the SuperCom network, you can enable multicast on each of the FastFoods and EuroBank VRFs. The configurations vary slightly depending on whether a Data-MDT is required (that is, multicast sources originate from this VRF) and which multicast mode the customer is using.

Example 7-12 shows the configuration for the FastFoods VRF. Every FastFoods VRF uses the same Default-MDT of 239.192.10.1. The Data-MDT range of 239.192.20.16/28 is used for any multicast stream on the Default-MDT that exceeds 1 Kbps. Note that the **mdt data** command only needs to be applied to the PE router at San Jose because this PE router has a FastFoods source connected. However, if FastFoods VPN sources existed at other PE routers, then the same **mdt data** commands could be applied. Multicast routing is enabled on the VRF by using the **ip multicast-routing vrf** command. Each interface that is associated with the FastFoods VRF requires PIM to be enabled. Because FastFoods has chosen to use SSM, you must make the VRF aware of this fact so that it can create the correct multicast routing entries in the FastFoods mVRF. You can accomplish this with the **ip pim vrf FastFoods ssm range** command.

Example 7-12 *FastFoods mVRF Configuration*

```
ip vrf FastFoods
rd 10:26
route-target export 10:26
route-target import 10:26
mdt default 239.192.10.1
mdt data 239.192.20.16 0.0.0.15 threshold 1   ← San Jose PE only
!
ip multicast-routing vrf FastFoods
!
interface Serial4/0
ip vrf forwarding FastFoods
ip address 192.168.2.18 255.255.255.252
ip pim sparse-mode
!
ip pim vrf FastFoods ssm range FastFoods_Site_Local_Scope
!
ip access-list standard FastFoods_Site_Local_Scope
 permit 239.255.0.0 0.0.255.255
```

The EuroBank configuration shown in Example 7-13 is similar to FastFoods. (The MDT ranges differ, of course!) EuroBank is using a static RP configuration; therefore, you must configure each EuroBank VRF with a static group to RP mapping by using the command **ip pim vrf EuroBank rp-address.** The Data-MDT configuration is only required at the Paris PE router because the only source EuroBank has is in its Paris site.

Example 7-13 *EuroBank mVRF Configuration*

```
ip vrf EuroBank
 rd 10:27
 route-target export 10:27
 route-target import 10:27
 mdt default 239.192.10.2
```

continues

Example 7-13 *EuroBank mVRF Configuration (Continued)*

```
 mdt data 239.192.20.32 0.0.0.15 threshold 1 ← Paris PE only
 !
 ip multicast-routing vrf EuroBank
 !
 interface Serial0/0
  ip vrf forwarding EuroBank
  ip address 192.168.2.26 255.255.255.252
  ip pim sparse-mode
 !
 ip pim vrf EuroBank rp-address 196.7.25.1 EuroBank_Site_Local_Scope
 !
 ip access-list standard EuroBank_Site_Local_Scope
  permit 239.255.0.0 0.0.255.255
```

Multicast Tunnel Interfaces

When the Default-MDT is configured, the SuperCom PE router immediately creates a tunnel interface by using the IP characteristics from the loopback0 interface. A Multiprotocol BGP update message is then sent to all the other PE routers that are BGP peers to signal the existence of the new Default-MDT. The PE router issues a P-join to the SuperCom RP for the Default-MDT group.

Example 7-14 shows some interesting information when a Default-MDT is configured, in this case on the EuroBank VRF at the SuperCom Paris PE router. Tunnel0 is used as the MTI for the EuroBank mVRF. The interface characteristics show that traffic entering Tunnel0 is encapsulated by using GRE with a destination address of 239.192.10.2 (Default-MDT) and a source address of 194.22.15.1 (learned from loopback0).

Inside the EuroBank VRF, you can see two PIM-enabled interfaces. Serial0/0 is the connection to the EuroBank CE router in Paris, and Tunnel0 is the MTI that provides access to and from the Default-MDT. The MTI is treated as a multiaccess interface; therefore, a designated router (DR) with the IP address 194.22.15.3 has been selected by using normal PIM designated router election rules. The PIM adjacencies that are formed over the MTI are discussed in a following section. Note that the tunnel operates in SD mode and the neighbor count is 2, which corresponds to the other PE routers.

Example 7-14 *EuroBank Multicast Tunnel Interface*

```
02:05:15: %LINEPROTO-5-UPDOWN: Line protocol on Interface Tunnel0, changed
 state to up

SuperCom_Paris#show interface tunnel0
Tunnel0 is up, line protocol is up
  Hardware is Tunnel
  Interface is unnumbered. Using address of Loopback0 (194.22.15.1)
  MTU 1514 bytes, BW 9 Kbit, DLY 500000 usec,
     reliability 255/255, txload 1/255, rxload 1/255
  Encapsulation TUNNEL, loopback not set
  Keepalive not set
```

Example 7-14 *EuroBank Multicast Tunnel Interface (Continued)*

```
  Tunnel source 194.22.15.1 (Loopback0), destination 239.192.10.2, fastswitch
  TTL 255
  Tunnel protocol/transport GRE/IP Multicast, key disabled, sequencing disabled
   Checksumming of packets disabled, fast tunneling enabled
 [snip]


 SuperCom_Paris#show ip pim vrf EuroBank interface

 Address          Interface          Ver/   Nbr    Query  DR      DR
                                      Mode   Count  Intvl  Prior
 192.168.2.26     Serial0/0          v2/S   1      30     1       0.0.0.0
 194.22.15.1      Tunnel0            v2/SD  2      30     1       194.22.15.3
```

Example 7-15 shows debug output from the San Jose PE router of the BGP update message that was received from the Paris PE router when the EuroBank Default-MDT was created. The MDT extended community attribute shows that the MDT group is 239.192.10.2 and that the root of this group is 194.22.15.1, as shown in the mVPN-IPV4 address 2:10:27:194.22.15.1/32.

Example 7-15 *EuroBank MDT BGP update*

```
 BGP(2): 194.22.15.1 rcvd UPDATE w/ attr: nexthop 194.22.15.1, origin ?,
   localpref 100, extended community RT:10:27 MDT:10:239.192.10.2
 BGP(2): 194.22.15.1 rcvd 2:10:27:194.22.15.1/32
```

Example 7-16 shows the contents of the BGP VPNv4 table on the San Jose PE router for the MDT updates it has received from its peers. Two route distinguisher entries correspond to the FastFoods (2:10:26) and EuroBank (2:10:27) multicast domains. Each PE router that has advertised a Default-MDT for these domains is listed under the route distinguisher entry. As you can see, if you exclude the local San Jose PE router entry, there is one peer for FastFoods (Paris PE router 194.22.15.1), and there are two peers for EuroBank (Paris PE router and Washington PE router 194.22.15.3), as per the SuperCom topology.

Example 7-16 *Default-MDT Summary BGP VPNv4 Table*

```
 SuperCom_SanJose#show ip bgp vpnv4 all ¦ begin 2:10:26
 Route Distinguisher: 2:10:26
 *>i194.22.15.1/32    194.22.15.1               100     0 ?
 *> 194.22.15.2/32    0.0.0.0                           0 ?
 Route Distinguisher: 2:10:27
 *>i194.22.15.1/32    194.22.15.1               100     0 ?
 *> 194.22.15.2/32    0.0.0.0                           0 ?
 *>i194.22.15.3/32    194.22.15.3               100     0 ?
```

Example 7-17 shows the details of the EuroBank and FastFoods MDT entries received via Multiprotocol BGP from the Paris PE router.

Example 7-17 *Detail MDT BGP Entry*

```
SuperCom_SanJose#show ip bgp vpnv4 all 194.22.15.1
BGP routing table entry for 2:10:26:194.22.15.1/32, version 38
Paths: (1 available, best #1, no table, not advertised to EBGP peer)
  Not advertised to any peer
  Local
    194.22.15.1 (metric 66) from 194.22.15.1 (194.22.15.1)
      Origin incomplete, localpref 100, valid, internal, mdt, no-import, best
        Extended Community: RT:10:26 MDT:10:239.192.10.1
BGP routing table entry for 2:10:27:194.22.15.1/32, version 37
Paths: (1 available, best #1, no table, not advertised to EBGP peer)
  Not advertised to any peer
  Local
    194.22.15.1 (metric 66) from 194.22.15.1 (194.22.15.1)
      Origin incomplete, localpref 100, valid, internal, mdt, no-import, best
        Extended Community: RT:10:27 MDT:10:239.192.10.2
```

NOTE   As discussed previously, this BGP information is currently accessed only by SSM
procedures. All routers cache this information regardless of whether they are configured to
use SSM. Other uses for this information are currently being investigated.

Even though the BGP update contains route target extended community, it is not imported
into a VRF because of the presence of the MDT extended community attribute.

Now that the mVRFs and the MTIs have been created, it is a good time to examine the
MDTs that have been created in the core of the SuperCom network.

Multicast Distribution Trees

The SuperCom network creates a separate, bidirectional tree for each of the FastFoods and
EuroBank multicast domains by using standard PIM procedures. Example 7-18 shows the
global multicast routing table for the Paris PE router. The other PE routers that are within
the SuperCom network have similar (*, G) entries.

The multicast domains are represented by a bidirectional entry, denoted with the **B** flag. The
Z flag signifies that this entry is a multicast tunnel and that a mVRF is connected to it,
indicated by the **C** flag. The associated VRF appears in the olist of the entry. The olist entry
also shows Serial0/2, which is a global interface that connects to the other SuperCom
routers. Because the Paris PE router is the RP, the Bidir-upstream field is null. If this router
were not the RP, this field would contain the local interface in the direction of the RP.

Example 7-18 *Paris PE Global Multicast Routing Table*

```
SuperCom_Paris#show ip mroute
IP Multicast Routing Table
Flags: D - Dense, S - Sparse, B - Bidir Group, s - SSM Group, C - Connected,
```

Example 7-18 *Paris PE Global Multicast Routing Table (Continued)*

```
            L - Local, P - Pruned, R - RP-bit set, F - Register flag,
            T - SPT-bit set, J - Join SPT, M - MSDP created entry,
            X - Proxy Join Timer Running, A - Candidate MSDP Advertisement,
            U - URD, I - Received Source Specific Host Report, Z - Multicast Tunnel
            Y - Joined MDT-data group, y - Sending to MDT-data group
Outgoing interface flags: H - Hardware switched
Timers: Uptime/Expires
Interface state: Interface, Next-Hop or VCD, State/Mode

(*, 239.192.10.1), 06:00:44/00:03:12, RP 194.22.15.1, flags: BCZ
  Bidir-Upstream: Null, RPF nbr 0.0.0.0
  Outgoing interface list:
    MVRF FastFoods, Forward/Sparse-Dense, 06:00:44/00:00:00
    Serial0/2, Forward/Sparse-Dense, 06:00:44/00:02:57

(*, 239.192.10.2), 06:00:44/00:03:22, RP 194.22.15.1, flags: BCZ
  Bidir-Upstream: Null, RPF nbr 0.0.0.0
  Outgoing interface list:
    MVRF EuroBank, Forward/Sparse-Dense, 06:00:44/00:00:00
    Serial0/2, Forward/Sparse-Dense, 06:00:45/00:02:31
```

An MDT multicast entry does not necessarily have the **Z** flag set on all routers. For example, the Washington PE router has a connection only to the EuroBank CE router; therefore, it has no need to originate (be the root) or terminate (be the leaf) the FastFoods MDT (239.192.10.1). The Washington PE multicast table is shown in Example 7-19. The FastFoods MDT entry has only the **B** flag set, which means that Washington just passes traffic straight through.

Example 7-19 *Washington PE Global Multicast Routing Table*

```
SuperCom_Washington#show ip mroute
IP Multicast Routing Table
Flags: D - Dense, S - Sparse, B - Bidir Group, s - SSM Group, C - Connected,
       L - Local, P - Pruned, R - RP-bit set, F - Register flag,
       T - SPT-bit set, J - Join SPT, M - MSDP created entry,
       X - Proxy Join Timer Running, A - Candidate MSDP Advertisement,
       U - URD, I - Received Source Specific Host Report, Z - Multicast Tunnel
       Y - Joined MDT-data group, y - Sending to MDT-data group
Outgoing interface flags: H - Hardware switched
Timers: Uptime/Expires
Interface state: Interface, Next-Hop or VCD, State/Mode

(*, 239.192.10.1), 3d23h/00:03:27, RP 194.22.15.1, flags: B
  Bidir-Upstream: Serial4/0, RPF nbr 194.22.15.22
  Outgoing interface list:
    POS3/0, Forward/Sparse-Dense, 07:54:24/00:03:09
    Serial4/0, Bidir-Upstream/Sparse-Dense, 07:54:24/00:00:00

(*, 239.192.10.2), 3d23h/00:03:30, RP 194.22.15.1, flags: BCZ
  Bidir-Upstream: Serial4/0, RPF nbr 194.22.15.22
```

continues

Example 7-19 *Washington PE Global Multicast Routing Table (Continued)*

```
Outgoing interface list:
  POS3/0, Forward/Sparse-Dense, 07:54:24/00:03:30
  Serial4/0, Bidir-Upstream/Sparse-Dense, 07:54:26/00:00:00
  MVRF EuroBank, Forward/Sparse-Dense, 07:54:27/00:00:00
```

mVRF PIM Adjacencies

In each mVRF, PIM adjacencies are formed with the associated FastFoods or EuroBank CE routers, and also over the MTI to the other PE routers in the multicast domain. Example 7-20 shows the adjacencies that are formed at the Paris PE router for EuroBank and FastFoods. The example shows that the Paris PE router has created two tunnel interfaces: Tunnel0 for EuroBank and Tunnel1 for FastFoods.

For EuroBank, two PIM adjacencies have been formed over Tunnel0—one to the San Jose PE router (194.22.15.2) and the other to the Washington PE router (194.22.15.3)—because both of these PE routers have a EuroBank VRF that is multicast enabled. Because the tunnel behaves as a multiaccess medium, the designated router elected is the PE router with the highest IP address or the highest nominated priority. (In our example, all the priorities are set to a default of 1.)

Tunnel1 in the FastFoods VRF has formed a single PIM adjacency to the San Jose PE router, with that PE router also being elected the DR. The PIM adjacencies to CE routers in both VRFs are formed in the normal manner. Note that the neighbor addresses on the tunnels are also those used for BGP peering.

Example 7-20 *VRF PIM Adjacencies*

```
SuperCom_Paris#show ip pim vrf EuroBank neighbor
PIM Neighbor Table
Neighbor          Interface          Uptime/Expires      Ver   DR
Address                                                         Prio/Mode
192.168.2.25      Serial0/0          02:47:14/00:01:32 v2   1 / B S
194.22.15.2       Tunnel0            02:46:38/00:01:37 v2   1 / B S
194.22.15.3       Tunnel0            02:46:38/00:01:38 v2   1 / DR B S


SuperCom_Paris#show ip pim vrf FastFoods neighbor
PIM Neighbor Table
Neighbor          Interface          Uptime/Expires      Ver   DR
Address                                                         Prio/Mode
192.168.2.21      FastEthernet0/1    08:35:18/00:01:38 v2   1 / B S
194.22.15.2       Tunnel1            08:34:38/00:01:40 v2   1 / DR B S
```

mVRF Routing Entries

Now that the MDTs are set up and the PE router PIM adjacencies have been formed, you can look at the multicast routing tables that have been created in each of the mVRFs. Example 7-21 shows the routing tables for the EuroBank VRF at the Paris and Washington

PE routers. The San Jose PE router does not have active receivers or sources connected to the EuroBank San Francisco mVRF; therefore, its EuroBank multicast routing table is empty. For purposes of clarity, the output has been clipped to show relevant information only.

Example 7-21 *Multicast Routing Table for EuroBank VPN*

```
SuperCom_Paris#show ip mroute vrf EuroBank
[snip]
(*, 239.255.0.20), 09:15:02/00:03:02, RP 196.7.25.1, flags: S
  Incoming interface: Serial0/0, RPF nbr 192.168.2.25
  Outgoing interface list:
    Tunnel0, Forward/Sparse-Dense, 09:15:02/00:03:02

SuperCom_Washington#show ip mroute vrf EuroBank
[snip]
(*, 239.255.0.20), 4d01h/00:03:27, RP 196.7.25.1, flags: S
  Incoming interface: Tunnel0, RPF nbr 194.22.15.1
  Outgoing interface list:
    Ethernet5/0, Forward/Sparse, 4d01h/00:03:27
```

Looking at the Paris PE router (*, 239.255.0.20) routing entry, you can see that the incoming interface is Serial0/0, which connects to the EuroBank Paris CE router where the source resides. The olist contains Tunnel0, which means that any multicast traffic that is destined to this interface is encapsulated and transmitted via the Default-MDT.

There is a receiver for (*, 239.255.0.20) at the Washington PE router, which you can see in the Washington mVRF routing table. The incoming interface is Tunnel0, and the olist contains Ethernet5/0, which points to the FastFoods Washington CE router. The EuroBank Washington CE router has issued a C-join toward the EuroBank RP (196.7.25.1) over Tunnel0.

The multicast packets received from the EuroBank Paris source are de-encapsulated and forwarded to the EuroBank mVRF, not because the incoming interface is Tunnel0, but because of the global entry for the EuroBank MDT (*, 239.192.10.2) having the Z flag set. This can be confirmed by referring back to Example 7-19, which shows the Washington PE router's global multicast routing table.

The incoming Tunnel0 interface is used to verify the RPF check for the EuroBank source (196.7.25.12), as shown in Example 7-22. Notice that the RPF neighbor is the BGP peer address of the Paris PE router where 196.7.25.12 originated.

Example 7-22 *RPF Information for EuroBank Source*

```
SuperCom_Washington#show ip rpf vrf EuroBank 196.7.25.12
RPF information for Eurobank_Paris_Source (196.7.25.12)
  RPF interface: Tunnel0
  RPF neighbor: SuperCom_Paris (194.22.15.1)
  RPF route/mask: 196.7.25.0/24
  RPF type: unicast (bgp 100)
  RPF recursion count: 0
  Doing distance-preferred lookups across tables
```

The EuroBank routing tables shown here are in the PIM SM steady state; that is, the routing entries are connected to the shared tree. No source data is flowing (or the spt-threshold has not been met) from EuroBank Paris; therefore, no shortest path tree has been built back to the Paris source. If there were, you would see an (S, G) entry instead of just (*, G). If an (S, G) entry existed, then it would switch over to a Data-MDT (assuming the threshold was exceeded). You will learn the operation of the Data-MDT in a further section.

Now is a good time to look at the multicast routing entries for FastFoods, shown in Example 7-23. Once again, unnecessary information has been clipped. FastFoods is operating in SSM mode; therefore, the routing entries are denoted by the **s** flag stating that this entry is part of an SSM group. SSM does not use a RP, and it always uses a source tree (S, G) instead of a shared tree (*, G). As you can see, Tunnel1 appears in the olist at the San Jose PE router and is the incoming interface at the Paris PE router, signifying that the source is at San Jose. Initially, the traffic stream flows over the Default-MDT; when the MDT threshold is exceeded, the traffic stream switches over to the Data-MDT.

Example 7-23 *Multicast Routing Table for FastFoods VPN*

```
SuperCom_SanJose#show ip mroute vrf FastFoods
[snip]
(195.12.2.6, 239.255.0.30), 04:15:49/00:02:35, flags: sT
  Incoming interface: Serial4/0, RPF nbr 192.168.2.17
  Outgoing interface list:
    Tunnel1, Forward/Sparse-Dense, 04:15:49/00:02:35

SuperCom_Paris#show ip mroute vrf FastFoods
[snip]
(195.12.2.6, 239.255.0.30), 14:25:19/00:02:50, flags: s
  Incoming interface: Tunnel1, RPF nbr 194.22.15.2
  Outgoing interface list:
    FastEthernet0/1, Forward/Sparse, 14:25:19/00:02:50
```

The important thing to remember about these examples is that the SuperCom network is oblivious to the multicast mode of operation in the FastFoods or EuroBank networks. The MTI intrinsically supports PIM SD mode; therefore, the customer's choice of multicast mode, RP placement, or RP-to-group distribution method is of little relevance to the SuperCom network.

Data-MDT Operation

As mentioned previously, due to the absence of receivers or sources, the San Francisco EuroBank mVRF at the San Jose PE router does not have routing entries, as shown in Example 7-24. You can see that although the EuroBank mVRF is empty, the San Jose PE router is still joined to the EuroBank Default-MDT shared tree (*, 239.192.10.2), regardless of whether EuroBank San Francisco has receivers (or sources).

Example 7-24 *San Jose PE EuroBank mVRF and Global MDT Entry*

```
SuperCom_SanJose#show ip mroute vrf EuroBank
IP Multicast Routing Table
Flags: D - Dense, S - Sparse, B - Bidir Group, s - SSM Group, C - Connected,
       L - Local, P - Pruned, R - RP-bit set, F - Register flag,
       T - SPT-bit set, J - Join SPT, M - MSDP created entry,
       X - Proxy Join Timer Running, A - Candidate MSDP Advertisement,
       U - URD, I - Received Source Specific Host Report, Z - Multicast Tunnel
       Y - Joined MDT-data group, y - Sending to MDT-data group
Outgoing interface flags: H - Hardware switched
Timers: Uptime/Expires
Interface state: Interface, Next-Hop or VCD, State/Mode


SuperCom_SanJose#show ip mroute 239.192.10.2
[snip]

(*, 239.192.10.2), 03:50:40/00:02:41, RP 194.22.15.1, flags: BCZ
  Bidir-Upstream: POS3/0, RPF nbr 194.22.15.18
  Outgoing interface list:
    POS3/0, Bidir-Upstream/Sparse-Dense, 03:49:35/00:00:00
    MVRF EuroBank, Forward/Sparse-Dense, 03:50:40/00:00:00
```

This means that any traffic that the source in EuroBank Paris sends is not only received by
the Washington PE router (which has an interested receiver in its path), but the P-packet
also is replicated along the Default-MDT toward the San Jose PE router. At San Jose, the
P-packet is decapsulated, and as there is no forwarding entry for this C-packet in the
EuroBank mVRF, it is dropped. This process is illustrated in Figure 7-17.

Figure 7-17 *Unnecessary Replication of Packets in MDT*

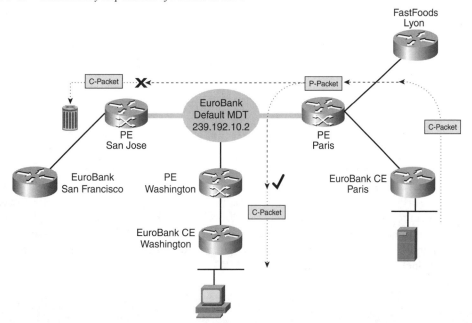

To overcome this problem, you can use a Data-MDT to send packets only to the PE routers that are interested in the traffic. In the SuperCom network, assume that the two active sources at FastFoods San Jose and EuroBank Paris have started to transmit multicast traffic. After these streams exceed the MDT threshold (set at 1 Kbps), they switch over to a separate Data-MDT. The Data-MDT group is taken from the pool of addresses configured on the respective VRF at the source PE routers (that is, San Jose PE router for FastFoods and Paris PE router for EuroBank).

The Paris PE router joins the Data-MDT (*, 239.192.20.16) for FastFoods, and the Washington PE router joins the Data-MDT (*, 239.192.20.32) for EuroBank. The Data-MDTs that are created are illustrated in Figure 7-18. Notice that the San Jose PE router does not join the EuroBank Data-MDT; therefore, it does not receive unwanted multicast traffic.

Figure 7-18   *Active Data-MDTs for EuroBank and FastFoods*

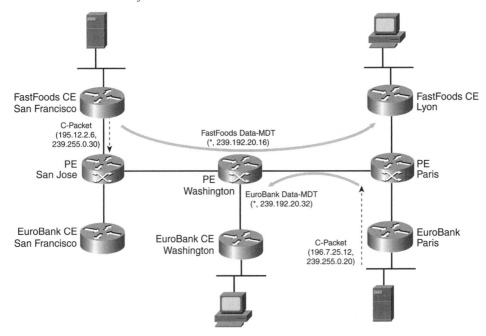

Using the EuroBank multicast stream as an example, you will see the process of creating the Data-MDT. Because EuroBank is operating in PIM SM, the initial traffic from the EuroBank Paris source is sent over the shared tree to the EuroBank Washington CE router. A source tree (196.7.25.12, 239.255.0.20) is built back to EuroBank Paris from EuroBank Washington within the mVRF context following standard PIM SM rules. This is an important step; if the source traffic were to remain on the (*, G) shared tree, then it would be ineligible to be switched to a Data-MDT.

On the other hand, the FastFoods network does not need to switch from a shared tree because it uses SSM. Therefore, all of FastFoods' traffic is always on a source tree and eligible to be switched to a Data-MDT.

Example 7-25 shows the multicast routing entries for the EuroBank mVRF at the Paris PE router. You can see that there are two entries: the shared tree entry (*, 239.255.0.20) and the newly created source tree entry (196.7.25.12, 239.255.0.20). The interesting thing about the source tree entry is that the "y" flag is set. This means that the source tree entry has switched from the Default-MDT (because the threshold was exceeded) and is now sending its traffic by using the Data-MDT via Tunnel0.

Example 7-25 *EuroBank mVRF Routing Entries at SuperCom Paris*

```
SuperCom_Paris#show ip mroute vrf EuroBank
IP Multicast Routing Table
Flags: D - Dense, S - Sparse, B - Bidir Group, s - SSM Group, C - Connected,
       L - Local, P - Pruned, R - RP-bit set, F - Register flag,
       T - SPT-bit set, J - Join SPT, M - MSDP created entry,
       X - Proxy Join Timer Running, A - Candidate MSDP Advertisement,
       U - URD, I - Received Source Specific Host Report, Z - Multicast Tunnel
       Y - Joined MDT-data group, y - Sending to MDT-data group
Outgoing interface flags: H - Hardware switched
Timers: Uptime/Expires
Interface state: Interface, Next-Hop or VCD, State/Mode

(*, 239.255.0.20), 2d02h/stopped, RP 196.7.25.1, flags: S
  Incoming interface: Serial0/0, RPF nbr 192.168.2.25
  Outgoing interface list:
    Tunnel0, Forward/Sparse-Dense, 2d02h/00:03:10

(196.7.25.12, 239.255.0.20), 00:11:06/00:03:23, flags: Ty
  Incoming interface: Serial0/0, RPF nbr 192.168.2.25
  Outgoing interface list:
    Tunnel0, Forward/Sparse-Dense, 00:11:12/00:03:10
```

When the threshold for (196.7.25.12, 239.255.0.20) was exceeded, the Paris PE router sent a Data-MDT TLV join message over the Default-MDT to the Washington and San Jose PE routers. Because the Washington PE router has an interested receiver, it immediately joined the new Data-MDT, whereas the San Jose PE router just cached the message. Example 7-26 shows the PIM debug messages that the Washington PE router output. Note that the messages shown here are from two PIM instances. PIM(1) is the instance running in the mVRF, and PIM(0) is the global instance. The Data-MDT join message indicates that EuroBank traffic for (196.7.25.12, 239.255.0.20) will be switched over to the Data-MDT group 239.192.20.32. This prompts the Washington PE router to issue a P-join for (*, 239.192.20.32) so that it can continue to receive the traffic.

Example 7-26 *EuroBank Data-MDT TLV Join Message*

```
PIM(1): MDT join TLV received for (196.7.25.12,239.255.0.20) MDT-data:
  239.192.20.32
PIM(1): MDT-data group (*,239.192.20.32) added on interface: Loopback0
PIM(0): Check RP 194.22.15.1 into the (*, 239.192.20.32) entry
PIM(0): Building triggered (*,G) Join / (S,G,RP-bit) Prune message for
  239.192.20.32
```

If you look at the routing entries for the EuroBank mVRF in the Washington PE router, as shown in Example 7-27, you see that the source tree entry has the "Y" flag set, indicating that receive traffic for (196.7.25.12,239.255.0.20) has been switched to Data-MDT.

Example 7-27 *EuroBank mVRF Routing Entries at the Washington PE*

```
SuperCom_Washington#show ip mroute vrf EuroBank
IP Multicast Routing Table
Flags: D - Dense, S - Sparse, B - Bidir Group, s - SSM Group, C - Connected,
       L - Local, P - Pruned, R - RP-bit set, F - Register flag,
       T - SPT-bit set, J - Join SPT, M - MSDP created entry,
       X - Proxy Join Timer Running, A - Candidate MSDP Advertisement,
       U - URD, I - Received Source Specific Host Report, Z - Multicast Tunnel
       Y - Joined MDT-data group, y - Sending to MDT-data group
Outgoing interface flags: H - Hardware switched
Timers: Uptime/Expires
Interface state: Interface, Next-Hop or VCD, State/Mode

(*, 239.255.0.20), 5d19h/stopped, RP 196.7.25.1, flags: S
  Incoming interface: Tunnel0, RPF nbr 194.22.15.1
  Outgoing interface list:
    Ethernet5/0, Forward/Sparse, 5d19h/00:03:24

(196.7.25.12, 239.255.0.20), 00:45:48/00:03:28, flags: TY
  Incoming interface: Tunnel0, RPF nbr 194.22.15.1
  Outgoing interface list:
    Ethernet5/0, Forward/Sparse, 00:45:48/00:03:24
```

NOTE   The procedure for creating the FastFoods Data-MDT is the same as EuroBank except that a different pool of address is used. It would be superfluous to cover the scenario again for FastFoods.

Now that the Data-MDTs have been created, the last thing to examine is the entries in the SuperCom global multicast table. Example 7-28 shows the multicast routing entries at the Paris PE router. Unnecessary information, such as Auto-RP entries, has been pruned (pardon the pun) from the output to improve readability of the example. You can see that two additional shared tree routing entries correspond to the two Data-MDTs (239.192.20.16 and 239.192.20.32). Because the Paris PE router has a receiver in the

FastFoods mVRF, it has joined the FastFoods Data-MDT and is forwarding traffic from
(*, 239.192.10.16) to the FastFoods mVRF. The Z flag indicates this is a multicast tunnel,
and the C flag indicates that an mVRF is connected. The Paris PE router is a leaf of the
(*, 239.192.10.16) entry.

Example 7-28 *Paris PE Data-MDT Routing Entries*

```
SuperCom_Paris#show ip mroute
[snip]

(*, 239.192.10.1), 2d03h/00:03:28, RP 194.22.15.1, flags: BCZ
  Bidir-Upstream: Null, RPF nbr 0.0.0.0
  Outgoing interface list:
    Serial0/2, Forward/Sparse-Dense, 1d17h/00:03:16
    MVRF FastFoods, Forward/Sparse-Dense, 2d03h/00:00:00

(*, 239.192.10.2), 2d03h/00:03:18, RP 194.22.15.1, flags: BCZ
  Bidir-Upstream: Null, RPF nbr 0.0.0.0
  Outgoing interface list:
    MVRF EuroBank, Forward/Sparse-Dense, 2d03h/00:00:00
    Serial0/2, Forward/Sparse-Dense, 2d03h/00:02:38

(*, 239.192.20.16), 00:50:15/00:03:26, RP 194.22.15.1, flags: BCZ
  Bidir-Upstream: Null, RPF nbr 0.0.0.0
  Outgoing interface list:
    Serial0/2, Forward/Sparse-Dense, 00:50:12/00:03:20
    MVRF FastFoods, Forward/Sparse-Dense, 00:50:15/00:00:00

(*, 239.192.20.32), 19:08:21/00:03:27, RP 194.22.15.1, flags: BZ
  Bidir-Upstream: Null, RPF nbr 0.0.0.0
  Outgoing interface list:
    Serial0/2, Forward/Sparse-Dense, 01:12:54/00:03:19
[snip]
```

There is something interesting about the last entry (*, 239.192.10.32), which is the Data-
MDT for EuroBank. No C flag is present, which indicates that no mVRF is connected. This
is because the Paris PE router is sending traffic to this tunnel from its connected source; the
PE router is not receiving traffic from the tunnel. The Paris PE router is the root of the
(*, 239.192.10.32) entry only.

To see how the EuroBank or FastFoods (S, G) entries are mapped to a particular Data-MDT,
you use the **show ip pim mdt** command. Example 7-29 shows the (S, G, Data-MDT)
details for both active multicast streams at the Paris PE router. The **receive** command shows
that the Paris PE router has joined the Data-MDT 239.192.20.16 for the FastFoods source
tree (195.12.2.6, 239.255.0.30). The **send** command shows that the Paris PE router is
encapsulating traffic from the EuroBank source (196.7.25.12, 239.255.0.20) and is sending
it to the Data-MDT 239.192.20.32.

Example 7-29 *FastFoods and EuroBank Data-MDT Mappings*

```
SuperCom_Paris#show ip pim vrf FastFoods receive detail

Joined MDT-data groups for VRF: FastFoods
  group: 239.192.20.16 source: 0.0.0.0 ref_count: 1
  (195.12.2.6, 239.255.0.30), 2d04h/00:03:23/00:03:00, OIF count: 1, flags: sTY

SuperCom_Paris#show ip pim vrf EuroBank mdt send
MDT-data send list for VRF: EuroBank
  (source, group)                   MDT-data group        ref_count
  (196.7.25.12, 239.255.0.20)       239.192.20.32         1
```

The example also shows a ref_count value. If the Data-MDTs in a pool for a given mVRF have been exhausted due to many active high-bandwidth sources, then Data-MDTs are reused based on the entry that has the lowest ref_count.

SSM in the SuperCom Core

You can deploy the SuperCom core with SSM instead of PIM SM. Doing so obviates the need for a RP, which in turn eliminates a single point of failure. The configuration to enable SSM for MDT groups is simple (see Example 7-30). This configuration is applied to all SuperCom routers in place of RP to MDT-group mappings. The MDT-Range access-list contains the address ranges that the SuperCom network uses for both Default-MDT and Data-MDT. This access-list is associated with SSM by using the **ip pim ssm range** global command; therefore, any multicast traffic that contains these destination group addresses uses SSM control procedures. Note that both the Default-MDT and Data-MDT ranges are part of the SSM range.

Example 7-30 *Enabling SSM*

```
ip pim ssm range MDT-Range
!
ip access-list standard MDT-Range
 permit 239.192.10.0 0.0.0.255
 permit 239.192.20.0 0.0.0.255
```

When a SuperCom PE router creates a new Default-MDT through user configuration, it is signaled by a Multiprotocol BGP update to all its peers, as discussed previously. When a local PE router receives the update, a source tree join is issued back to the originator of the BGP message if the following conditions are met:

- The Default-MDT group address matches the local SSM range.

- A local mVRF is configured with the same Default-MDT group.

Example 7-31 shows the debug output for the BGP update and the corresponding PIM join from one of the SuperCom routers. This router has received a BGP update from 194.22.15.2

(which happens to be the San Jose PE router) stating that it has created a new Default-MDT 239.192.10.2 (EuroBank VPN). Because this router meets the conditions stated previously, it immediately issues a source join to (194.22.15.2, 239.192.10.2) for the Default-MDT.

Example 7-31 *Joining the Default-MDT Using SSM*

```
BGP(2): 194.22.15.2 rcvd UPDATE w/ attr: nexthop 194.22.15.2, origin ?,
  localpref 100, extended community RT:10:27 MDT:10:239.192.10.2


BGP(2): 194.22.15.2 rcvd 2:10:27:194.22.15.2/32


PIM(0): Send v2 Join on Serial0/2 to 194.22.15.2 for (194.22.15.2/32,
  239.192.10.2), S-bit
```

How does the multicast routing table differ when you are using SSM? Compare the Paris PE router routing table in Example 7-32 using SSM with the same table using PIM Bi-Dir shown previously in Example 7-18. With PIM Bi-Dir, there were only two (*, G) shared tree entries: one for each of the EuroBank and FastFoods multicast domains. As you can see in Example 7-32, with SSM, you have five entries represented by the **s** flag. Because these are all source trees, you have more optimal routing because traffic does not have to traverse the RP.

Three of the entries in Example 7-32 are source trees that are rooted at remote PE routers. The Paris PE router has joined these source trees (by using SSM) based on Default-MDT information received in the Multiprotocol BGP update; therefore, the **I** flag has been set for these entries. The Paris PE router forwards traffic received from these entries to the corresponding mVRF in the olist. Of these three **I** entries, two are for the EuroBank Default-MDT (239.192.10.2) connecting to the San Jose and Washington PE routers, and the third is for the FastFoods Default-MDT (239.192.10.1) connecting to the San Jose PE router.

The other two routing entries in Example 7-32 do not have the **I** flag set. These entries represent the source trees for the two Default-MDTs rooted at the Paris PE router. Note the S of the (S, G) is 194.22.15.1, which is the loopback0 interface address of the Paris PE router. The remote PE routers issue a corresponding SSM join back to the Paris PE router. The outgoing interfaces point to the SuperCom core network.

Example 7-32 *Paris PE Global Multicast Routing Table Using SSM*

```
SuperCom_Paris#show ip mroute
IP Multicast Routing Table
Flags: D - Dense, S - Sparse, B - Bidir Group, s - SSM Group, C - Connected,
       L - Local, P - Pruned, R - RP-bit set, F - Register flag,
       T - SPT-bit set, J - Join SPT, M - MSDP created entry,
       X - Proxy Join Timer Running, A - Candidate MSDP Advertisement,
       U - URD, I - Received Source Specific Host Report, Z - Multicast Tunnel
       Y - Joined MDT-data group, y - Sending to MDT-data group
Outgoing interface flags: H - Hardware switched
Timers: Uptime/Expires
Interface state: Interface, Next-Hop or VCD, State/Mode
```

continues

Example 7-32 *Paris PE Global Multicast Routing Table Using SSM (Continued)*

```
(194.22.15.1, 239.192.10.1), 00:04:22/00:03:27, flags: sTZ
  Incoming interface: Loopback0, RPF nbr 0.0.0.0
  Outgoing interface list:
    Serial0/2, Forward/Sparse-Dense, 00:02:45/00:03:25

(194.22.15.2, 239.192.10.1), 00:03:02/00:02:57, flags: sTIZ
  Incoming interface: Serial0/2, RPF nbr 194.22.15.2
  Outgoing interface list:
    MVRF FastFoods, Forward/Sparse-Dense, 00:03:02/00:00:00

(194.22.15.1, 239.192.10.2), 00:04:23/00:03:25, flags: sTZ
  Incoming interface: Loopback0, RPF nbr 0.0.0.0
  Outgoing interface list:
    Serial0/2, Forward/Sparse-Dense, 00:02:47/00:03:24

(194.22.15.2, 239.192.10.2), 00:03:04/00:02:45, flags: sTIZ
  Incoming interface: Serial0/2, RPF nbr 194.22.15.2
  Outgoing interface list:
    MVRF EuroBank, Forward/Sparse-Dense, 00:03:04/00:00:00

(194.22.15.3, 239.192.10.2), 00:03:10/00:02:45, flags: sTIZ
  Incoming interface: Serial0/2, RPF nbr 194.22.15.2
  Outgoing interface list:
    MVRF EuroBank, Forward/Sparse-Dense, 00:03:10/00:00:00
```

SSM also uses the Data-MDT join message to trigger a join and switch over to the Data-MDT. The way it does this differs slightly from PIM SM. The Data-MDT join message only contains the (S, G, Data-MDT) mapping. PIM SM only requires the value of Data-MDT, so a (*, Data-MDT) P-join can be issued toward the rendezvous point by the receiving PE router. However, SSM requires the source address of the originating PE router, so that a (S-PE, Data-MDT) P-join can be issued. The value of S-PE is derived from the RPF neighbor of S in the (S, G, Data-MDT) mapping. This is verified in the debug and RPF output in Example 7-33.

Example 7-33 *Joining the Data-MDT Using SSM*

```
PIM(1): MDT join TLV received for (196.7.25.12,239.255.0.20) MDT-data:
 239.192.20.32
PIM(1): MDT-data group (194.22.15.1,239.192.20.32) added on interface: Loopback0
PIM(0): Send v2 Join on Serial4/0 to 194.22.15.22 for (194.22.15.1/3
2, 239.192.20.32), S-bit
PIM(0): Building Join/Prune message for 239.192.20.32

SuperCom_Washington#show ip rpf vrf EuroBank 196.7.25.12
RPF information for Eurobank_Paris_Source (196.7.25.12)
  RPF interface: Tunnel0
  RPF neighbor: SuperCom_Paris (194.22.15.1)
  RPF route/mask: 196.7.25.0/24
  RPF type: unicast (bgp 100)
  RPF recursion count: 0
  Doing distance-preferred lookups across tables
```

Summary

Cisco Systems Multicast-VPN feature is based on the multicast domain solution described in section 2 of draft-rosen-vpn-mcast, "Multicast in MPLS/BGP VPN," which you can find at http://www.ietf.org. Multicast domains allow a service provider to offer mVPN services to their customers by using native multicasting techniques in the core. Native multicast is a mature technology on Cisco IOS; therefore, stability of the P-network is protected because no new features or software upgrades need to be performed on the P routers.

Scalability of the solution is ensured because the P-network has no visibility into the customer's multicast network. All mVPN traffic is carried inside a single multicast tunnel for that VPN. The number of multicast tunnels in the provider network is predictable and is significantly lower than the number of potential multicast groups in all VPNs.

From the end customer's point of view, no changes need to be made in the network to connect to a mVPN service. The service provider can support all customer modes, including PIM SM, PIM DM, PIM SSM, and any type of customer rendezvous point topology.

Routing optimality is improved in the P-network via the use of special tunnels for high-bandwidth sources that ensure that enterprise multicast traffic is delivered only to PE routers that have an interested receiver.

CHAPTER 8

IP Version 6 Transport Across an MPLS Backbone

Most of today's service provider and enterprise networks are based on the version of Internet Protocol (IP, also known as IPv4) that was designed in the 1970s and early 1980s. Several years ago, a new version of IP (IP version 6, or IPv6) was standardized. IPv6 provides a larger address space and tighter integration of network services (such as IP Quality of Service) with the network-layer protocol.

IPv6 is gaining increasing acceptance, predominantly in the mobile markets. Most of the service provider or enterprise networks will need to support it in the years to come. Recently, Cisco Systems introduced a new IOS feature that allows transport of IPv6 datagrams across the Multiprotocol Label Switching (MPLS)-enabled IPv4 backbone, giving the network designers and network managers a seamless migration path toward the next-generation IP networks.

This chapter discusses the business drivers that require IPv6 deployment in today's networks, an overview of IPv6 transport across an MPLS backbone, a brief introduction to IPv6 addressing and routing, as well as in-depth design and configuration guidelines for deploying IPv6-over-MPLS transport in your network.

IPv6 Business Drivers

More than a decade ago, the Internet architects who were working within the Internet Engineering Task Force (IETF) realized that with the predicted growth in Internet usage, the current Internet would quickly run out of IP addresses. A worldwide effort was launched to design a next-generation IP (codenamed IP: next generation, or IPng). Several different proposals were submitted to the working group, including reusing the existing Open System Interconnection (OSI) protocols and running, for example, TCP on top of Connectionless Network Protocol (CLNP). However, due to a number of reasons, the working group selected another proposal that extended the IP addresses from 32 bits to 128 bits, while retaining the majority of other properties of the current IP.

While IPng was being designed, another technology, network address translation (NAT), extended the life of the existing Internet for at least a decade, if not longer. With a significant portion of IP address space dedicated to private IP addresses and with everyone deploying NAT at the edge between a private network and the public Internet, the growth in IP address utilization slowed considerably. Many people believed that IPng (officially named IP version 6, or IPv6) would follow the slim acceptance of OSI protocols and never reach wide deployment. A year or two ago, there were almost no commercially available implementations of IPv6, either in the hosts or in the networking equipment.

NOTE   NAT is described in more detail in Chapter 4, "Virtual Router Connectivity."

As is usually the case in the networking world, many completely unrelated developments have shifted the whole Internet usage paradigm and made network designers interested in IPv6 yet again. These developments include the following:

- **Changes in application concepts**—A few years ago, most applications were designed by using the client-to-server data exchange paradigm (such as a user browsing on a web server). These applications are well suited to NAT because only the servers need public IP addresses, whereas the clients can use private addresses. New applications—most notably IP telephony, Internet-wide file-sharing schemes similar to Napster, and Internet games—require client-to-client data exchange. Although you can make some of these applications work across NAT boundaries, the NAT implementations have to be continually updated to support each individual peer-to-peer application.

- **Changes in Internet access methods**—Until recently, most IP hosts were located in private enterprise networks (where the whole network would use only a few public IP addresses) or used dial-up connections to the Internet (where the public IP addresses could be recycled among several users). With the widespread deployment of broadband Internet, most home users have permanent connections to the Internet and in many cases require a constantly allocated public IP address for each home user.

- **Changes in IP platforms**—A few years ago, the widest-deployed IP platform was probably the personal computer (PC). With the predicted deployment of an IP protocol stack on mobile phones and the widespread deployment of handheld and wireless devices, there should be a significant increase in future IP addressing needs. Not surprisingly, the first users who have been asking for deployment-quality IPv6 software are the wireless and mobile phone operators.

Availability of deployment-quality IPv6 software in IP hosts and routers does not solve the primary problem of service providers who would like to deploy the IPv6 protocol. Service providers who are deploying new protocols or solutions in their network must retain the stability and functionality of their existing backbones. Therefore, the introduction of new functionally usually starts with a controlled deployment of a pilot network, which is only later followed by a tightly managed large-scale deployment. This requirement effectively rules out immediate large-scale network-wide IPv6 deployment.

Deployment of IPv6 in Existing Networks

A service provider can use various methods if it wants to deploy a pilot IPv6 network, based on the transport topology used in the network core. These methods include the following:

- If the network core is IP-based, IP tunnels can be built between edge routers that support the IPv6 protocol, as shown in Figure 8-1. These tunnels then act as point-to-point links supporting the IPv6 protocol. The IPv6 packets that are exchanged between the edge routers can be transported transparently across the backbone encapsulated in IP packets.

Figure 8-1   *IPv6 Transport Across IPv4 Tunnels*

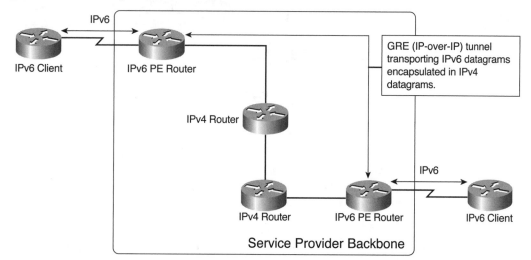

- If the network core is using Layer 2 WAN technology (Frame Relay or Asynchronous Transfer Mode [ATM]), additional virtual circuits (VCs) can be deployed directly between the edge routers to transport the IPv6 packets separately from the regular IP traffic, as shown in Figure 8-2. A similar approach also can be used in an MPLS-based core implementing circuit transport over MPLS.

Neither solution scales well in large networks; therefore, each is difficult to extend beyond a few-node pilot network. There are two reasons for this:

- The IP tunnels or virtual circuits must be configured manually unless advanced auto-discovery/auto-provisioning mechanisms are used, which introduces several restrictions and complexities.

- A full mesh of IP tunnels or virtual circuits is required between all edge routers to enable optimum end-to-end transport across the provider backbone.

Figure 8-2   *IPv6 Traffic Is Transported Through Dedicated Virtual Circuits*

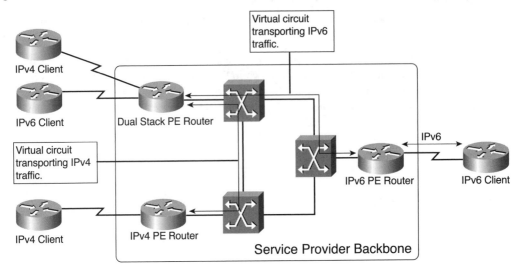

As in many other scenarios, the MPLS technology offers another alternative: the transport of IPv6 datagrams across an MPLS-enabled IPv4 backbone. This solution, known as IPv6 provider edge router (or 6PE), provides a scalable solution to the IPv6 early-deployment problem. It has the following characteristics:

- The IPv6 protocol is deployed only on selected PE routers.

- The PE routers use Multiprotocol BGP (MP-BGP) sessions to exchange IPv6 routes across the backbone.

- MPLS labels are assigned to IPv6 routes by the PE routers and exchanged directly between the PE routers (much like VPN routes).

- The IPv6 datagrams are transported across the MPLS backbone by using a two-level MPLS label stack. The first label in the label stack is the LDP-assigned label of the egress PE router. (You could also use another PE-PE Label Distribution Protocol [LDP], such as RSVP-TE.) The second label in the label stack is the PE-assigned IPv6 label.

The overall architecture of the 6PE solution is shown in Figure 8-3.

Even if you are a casual reader, you probably immediately recognized the close similarities (summarized in Table 8-1) between the 6PE solution and the MPLS VPN solution. There is only one significant difference between the two solutions: The MPLS VPN solution supports multiple instances of IPv4 on the same PE router (each one running in its isolated VRF), whereas the 6PE solution supports only a single instance of IPv6 on each PE router (using a global IPv6 routing and forwarding table).

Figure 8-3   *6PE Architecture*

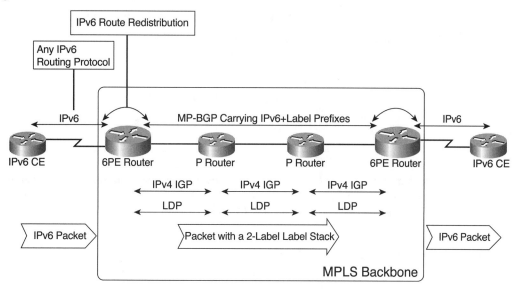

Table 8-1   *Similarities and Differences Between MPLS VPN and 6PE*

Function	MPLS VPN Implementation	6PE Implementation
PE router routing and forwarding	Each VRF is an isolated instance of IPv4 from a routing and forwarding perspective.	Each PE router has a global IPv6 routing and forwarding table.
Exchange of routes between PE routers	Route distinguishers are prepended to IPv4 routes, resulting in VPNv4 routes. A label is assigned to each VPNv4 route. VPNv4 routes and associated labels are exchanged between PE routers in MP-BGP updates.	Native IPv6 prefixes are exchanged between the PE routers. In some IOS implementations, a fixed set of 16 labels is assigned to the 6PE functionality. In other implementations, each IPv6 route is assigned a dedicated label.
Building the forwarding table	MPLS label imposition is configured in the forwarding table for routes received from a remote PE router. The top label in the label stack is the LDP-label associated with the MP-BGP next-hop, and the next label is the label received in the MP-BGP update. Both labels are placed in the forwarding table.	Identical.

continues

Table 8-1 *Similarities and Differences Between MPLS VPN and 6PE (Continued)*

Function	MPLS VPN Implementation	6PE Implementation
Packet forwarding	Label stack is prepended to ingress packets received from the CE routers. Packet transport across the provider backbone is based on the top label in the label stack, and the remote PE router acts on the bottom label in the label stack.	Identical.

This chapter will now move on to a quick introduction to IPv6, followed by an in-depth discussion of 6PE concepts and design scenarios. The 6PE concepts and design scenarios will be illustrated with the familiar SuperCom case study.

Quick Introduction to IPv6

This section discusses the basics of IPv6 to allow those of you who are not familiar with IPv6 to follow the discussions in this chapter. If you are interested in an in-depth description of IPv6, you can find more information at http://www.cisco.com/go/ipv6.

IPv6 Addressing

IPv6 uses 128-bit addresses, displayed as a sequence of 16-bit fields, separated by colons. For example, 1234:5678:0000:0000:0000:005c:7113:dfae is a valid IPv6 address. To reduce the typing efforts, you can omit leading zeroes in each 16-bit field. Therefore, you could write the previous address in shorter form as 1234:5678:0:0:0:5c:7113:dfae. Furthermore, because long sequences of zeroes are expected to be quite common in IPv6 addresses, you can replace a series of contiguous zero-value 16-bit fields with a double colon. Therefore, you can shorten the previous IPv6 address to 1234:5678::5c:7113:dfae.

NOTE   To ensure unambiguous interpretation of IPv6 addresses, you can use the double colon only once within an IPv6 address. If you were to use the double colon two or more times, the sequence between double colons (such as the string 3456 in sequence 1234::3456::9abc) could be placed in multiple positions within the 128 bits, creating ambiguous IPv6 addresses.

IPv6 addresses are divided into a variable-length prefix and a host portion (similar to IPv4 addresses). The address prefix is composed of a number of (administratively defined) fields that will not be discussed here. The host portion of an IPv6 address is usually a 64-bit long *Interface ID*, computed from the MAC address of the router or host interface, as shown in Figure 8-4.

NOTE	IPv6 prefixes are written with the standard prefix notation. For example, you would write a 20-bit long IPv6 prefix that starts with 1234:a000 as 1234:a000::/20. (Even though only the 20 most significant bits are non-zero, you still need to write the leading 32 bits.)

Figure 8-4   *IPv6 Address Structure*

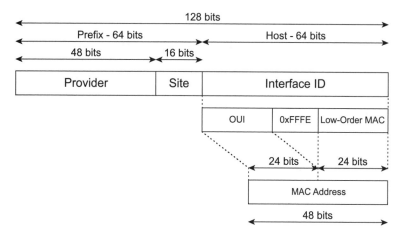

You can set various parts of the IPv6 address to special values in the destination IPv6 address to indicate to an IPv6 host or router a variety of IPv6 datagram delivery methods as follows:

- Anycast addresses (identical to subnet broadcast in IPv4), where the host portion of the IPv6 address is zero.

- Unicast addresses, which are identical to IPv4 unicast addresses, where the host portion of the IPv6 address is non-zero.

- Multicast addresses starting with FF00::/8 (most significant 8 bits are all ones). The traditional IPv4 all-ones local multicast address is replaced with IPv6 address FF02::1 (all-nodes link-scope multicast address).

The unicast IPv6 address space is administratively divided into public and private portions of the IPv6 address space based on the first bits of the IPv6 address as follows:

- Address space 0::/96 provides compatibility with existing IPv4 addresses. The IPv4 address is simply copied into the low-order 32 bits of the IPv6 address with the rest of the IPv6 address being zero. The IPv4-compatible IPv6 addresses are assigned to nodes with dual protocol stacks and are used to establish automatic IPv6 tunnels across an IPv4 backbone.

NOTE   IPv4-compatible IPv6 addresses can use IPv4-compatible syntax, where the value of the last 32 bits is expressed as dotted decimal, such as ::192.168.1.1.

- Address space 2000::/3 is currently assigned to global IPv6 addresses, which can be aggregated.
- Address space FEC0::/10 is the private address space (called site-local address space), similar to network 10.0.0.0/8 in IPv4.
- Address space FE80::/10 is link-local address space, in which the link IPv6 addresses are automatically constructed from the FE80::/10 prefix and 64-bit interface identifier. This address space serves a similar function as unnumbered IPv4 links. IPv6 routers should not forward packets that have link-local source or destination addresses.

IPv6 also defines two special addresses:

- ::1 is the loopback address. Packets that have ::1 as the source or the destination address will never leave an IPv6 host or router.
- :: (all-zeroes) is the unspecified address, which is used in automatic address assignment during the host initialization process (similar to using an all-zero IP address in DHCP requests).

The public IPv6 address space is strictly aggregatable; a customer who is changing his Internet service provider (ISP) must renumber the whole network. However, the network renumbering in IPv6 networks is significantly simpler than the network renumbering in IPv4 networks. Each IPv6 host is required to support more than one IPv6 address on each interface, giving the network designers the ability to configure overlapping "old" and "new" IPv6 subnets in the network simultaneously.

IPv6 Neighbor Discovery

As computer networking evolved, first with the introduction of lower-cost workstations and later with the deployment of IP on personal computers, several protocols were designed to ease the administrative tasks involved with large-scale deployment of IP devices. Initially, IPv4 did not support automatic address assignment or host configuration; all IP-related parameters had to be configured manually on every IP host. Many add-on protocols were later developed within the IPv4 suite of protocols to address these issues. These add-on protocols included Bootstrap Protocol (BOOTP) and Dynamic Host Configuration Protocol (DHCP), which handle address assignment, and ICMP Router Discovery Protocol (IRDP) or DHCP, which can be used for router discovery (DHCP through a default gateway option).

In IPv6, most of these tasks are handled by a single protocol, redesigned ICMP, which can, among other things, perform the following tasks:

- Neighbor discovery.
- Layer 3 to Layer 2 mapping (ARP in IPv4).

- Verification of neighbor reachability.

- Checking the uniqueness of the interface identifier in the autoconfiguration process.

- Automatic address assignment. With stateless autoconfiguration, a node can get an IPv6 address with no involvement from a central server. (No DHCP server is necessary with IPv6.)

- Router discovery.

- Verification of forwarding path availability. (A host can query the next-hop router to inquire whether the path to the destination is still available.)

- Redirection of packets sent to the wrong router (identical to IPv4 ICMP redirect messages).

As you can see from the preceding list, several tasks handled by different protocols within the IPv4 protocol suite are handled by a single protocol within the IPv6 address suite. Moreover, IPv6 supports many mechanisms that were unavailable on most IPv4 hosts (such as neighbor discovery and verification of forwarding path availability).

IPv6 Routing

Technically, IPv6 routing is similar to IPv4 routing. The major difference is the administrative requirement for strict aggregation of public IPv6 prefixes. Like IPv4 routing, IPv6 routing is prefix based, with the packets being forwarded toward the most specific matching prefix.

Most of the IPv4 routing protocols have been modified to support IPv6, including Routing Information Protocol (RIP), Intermediate System-to-Intermediate System (IS-IS), Open Shortest Path First (OSPF), and Border Gateway Protocol (BGP). Some minor modifications were made to RIP, IS-IS, and BGP as follows:

- RIP updates carry IPv6 prefixes instead of IPv4 prefixes.

- New type-length-value (TLV) pairs have been defined in IS-IS to support IPv6 routing.

- A new address family within standard Multiprotocol BGP is used to exchange external IPv6 routes.

OSPF-for-IPv6 is a completely new protocol that has only conceptual similarity with its IPv4 counterpart. Not surprisingly, OSPF for IPv6 is the last IPv6 routing protocol to be implemented in Cisco IOS.

Configuring IPv6 in Cisco IOS

IPv6 configuration in Cisco IOS is similar to configuring any other routing protocol. It involves the following steps:

1 The IPv6 routing must be enabled with a global configuration command **ipv6 unicast-routing**.

2 IPv6 addresses must be configured on the router interfaces with the **ipv6 address** *prefix/length* command.

3 Alternatively, unnumbered interfaces can be configured with **ipv6 unnumbered** *interface*, or you can decide to enable an interface for IPv6 processing using only link-local addresses on that subnet with the **ipv6 enable** command.

4 Names can be assigned to IPv6 addresses with the **ipv6 host** *name address* command, or you can use a DNS server, specified with the **ip name-server** command for name/address resolution.

NOTE   The **ip name-server** command accepts IPv4 and IPv6 addresses to support DNS servers reachable over IPv4 or IPv6.

IPv6 Interior Routing Protocol Configuration

The interior routing protocol configuration closely follows the IS-IS configuration process in IPv4. An IPv6 interior routing protocol (RIP or IS-IS) is configured in a two-step process:

1 An interior routing protocol (RIP or IS-IS) is configured and started.

2 The routing protocol is applied to an interface with an interface-level configuration command.

Table 8-2 summarizes the commands used to configure IPv6 RIP and IPv6 IS-IS.

Table 8-2   *Configuring Interior Routing Protocols with IPv6*

Command Syntax	Description
ipv6 router rip *name*	This global configuration command starts the IPv6 RIP process.
ipv6 rip *name* **enable**	This interface-level configuration command starts the selected IPv6 RIP process on the specified interface.
ipv6 rip *name* **default-information originate**	This interface-level command inserts a default route in the selected IPv6 RIP process and starts announcing the default route over the selected interface.
router isis *name*	This global configuration command starts an IS-IS routing process.
net *NET*	This router-level configuration command configures an IS-IS Network Entity Title (NET) for the routing process.

Table 8-2   *Configuring Interior Routing Protocols with IPv6 (Continued)*

Command Syntax	Description
ipv6 router isis *name*	This interface-level configuration command enables IS-IS routing on the selected interface.
address-family ipv6	This router-level configuration command selects the IPv6 address family configuration within the IS-IS routing process. The standard **distance**, **maximum-paths**, **default-information**, or **summary-prefix** commands can then be used to configure IPv6 IS-IS parameters.

Most of the other routing protocol concepts known from IPv4 are already available in Cisco IOS implementation of IPv6, including these:

- Standard access lists that are configured with the **ipv6 access-list** command.

- Route maps that can be used to control route redistribution. The route maps have been extended with additional **match** commands to support the IPv6 prefix and next-hop matching, including **match ipv6 address**, **match ipv6 next-hop**, and **match ipv6 route-source** commands.

- Route redistribution configured with the **redistribute** command. As with IPv4, route redistribution can be configured between routing protocols or between levels within the IS-IS routing protocol.

- Route filters configured with the **distribute-list** command.

IPv6 BGP Configuration

Understanding the concept of IPv6 BGP configuration is extremely simple for network engineers who have already mastered the concept of BGP address-families by deploying MPLS VPN solutions.

The IPv6 BGP configuration of a Cisco router involves the following steps:

1 Starting the BGP routing process with the **router bgp** *as-number* command.

2 Specifying BGP neighbors in the BGP router configuration with the **neighbor** command.

NOTE   The BGP **neighbor** command accepts IPv4 and IPv6 addresses as BGP neighbors.

---

3 Enabling the exchange of IPv6 prefixes with the **neighbor activate** command issued under the **address-family ipv6**.

Most of the standard BGP mechanisms are available within IPv6 BGP, such as the following:

- Advertising IPv6 prefixes with the **network** statement or the **redistribute** command
- Specifying the BGP source address with the **neighbor** *ipv6-address* **update-source** *ipv6-enabled-interface* configuration command.

NOTE   The **neighbor** *ipv6-address* **update-source** command is only meaningful if you configure a BGP session between IPv6 endpoints.

- Configuring BGP peer groups within the IPv6 address family
- Using inbound and outbound route maps and other BGP filters

---

NOTE   BGP route aggregation with the **aggregate-address** command is currently not supported in IPv6 BGP.

In-Depth 6PE Operation and Configuration

As already discussed in the introduction to this chapter, the IPv6-over-MPLS transport (6PE) uses concepts that are similar to the MPLS VPN architecture, as follows:

- IPv6 routes are exchanged between the PE routers and the CE routers. Contrary to MPLS VPN architecture, these routes are entered into the global IPv6 routing table on the PE routers, whereas in the MPLS VPN architecture, the VPNv4 routes are entered in the virtual routing and forwarding instance (VRF) tables. (As of the publication of this book, Cisco IOS does not support IPv6 VPNs.)
- Labels are assigned to local IPv6 routes as they are redistributed into IPv6 BGP.
- IPv6 routes and associated labels are exchanged between PE routers in MP-BGP sessions running between IPv4 endpoints.
- The IPv6 Cisco Express Forwarding (CEF) forwarding table is built on the ingress PE routers by using the LDP-assigned or Resource Reservation Protocol (RSVP)-traffic engineering (TE)-assigned label for the IPv4 next-hop and MP-BGP-propagated label for the destination IPv6 prefix.
- IPv6 packets received by the ingress PE routers are CEF-switched, labeled with an MPLS label stack, and forwarded along an LSP toward the egress PE router.
- When the egress PE router receives incoming labeled packets, it performs a label lookup. The MPLS label might point to an aggregate IPv6 route, in which case the egress PE router must perform an additional IPv6 lookup before it forwards the packet toward the destination CE router.

This section offers an in-depth description of every component of the 6PE solution listed previously, together with the associated Cisco IOS configuration and monitoring commands. The SuperCom backbone, shown in Figure 8-5, is used as a sample network deploying pilot IPv6 services.

Figure 8-5   *SuperCom IPv6 Pilot Network*

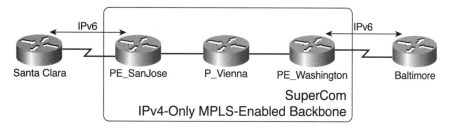

The SuperCom service provider decided to deploy a pilot IPv6 network between the San Jose and Washington PE routers. The pilot IPv6 backbone that operates across the SuperCom MPLS backbone supports test sites in Baltimore and Santa Clara. The IPv6 address ranges of the Baltimore and Santa Clara test sites as well as the IPv6 addresses used in the SuperCom backbone are outlined in Table 8-3. Link-local addresses (not shown in the table) are used on the PE-CE links.

Table 8-3   *IPv6 and Relevant IPv4 Address Assignment for SuperCom Backbone and Pilot Sites*

Company	Site	Subnet
CE routers	Santa Clara	1205:6700:0:1::/64
	Baltimore	1205:6700:0:2::/64
SuperCom	San Jose (Loopback 0)	1307:8000::2/128 194.22.15.2/32
	Washington (Loopback 0)	1307:8000::3/128 194.22.15.3/32

IPv6 Route Exchange Between PE Routers and CE Routers

The first step in 6PE solution deployment is the establishment of a routing protocol between the PE routers and the CE routers, which follows the standard IPv6 design and configuration rules and will not be covered in detail in this chapter. The SuperCom designers decided to use IPv6 RIP as the PE-CE routing protocol. One-way redistribution (RIPv6 to MP-BGP) will be used to simplify the IPv6 routing setup, and the PE routers will advertise the IPv6 default route to the CE routers in IPv6 RIP updates, as shown in Figure 8-6. The resulting configurations on the PE routers and the CE routers are included in the following examples.

Figure 8-6   *IPv6 Access Routing in SuperCom Pilot Network*

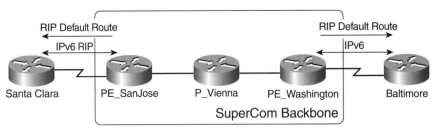

As the first configuration step, an IPv6 address is configured on the LAN interface of the Santa Clara CE router. The WAN interface of the CE router uses a link-local address, and RIP is configured on LAN and WAN interfaces of the Santa Clara router, as shown in Example 8-1.

Example 8-1   *Santa Clara CE Router Initial Configuration*

```
SantaClara#
interface Ethernet0/0
 no ip address
 ipv6 address 1205:6700:0:1::1/64
 ipv6 rip RTR enable
!
interface Serial0/0
 description *** Link to PE_SanJose ***
 no ip address
 ipv6 enable
 ipv6 rip RTR enable
!
ipv6 router rip RTR
```

The IPv4 and IPv6 addresses are configured on the loopback interface of the San Jose PE router, and **ipv6 enable** enables forwarding of IPv6 datagrams on the PE-CE link by using a link-local IPv6 address on this interface.

NOTE   You do not have to specify the link-local IPv6 address when using the **ipv6 enable** command. The link-local IPv6 address used on the interface is automatically computed from the MAC address of the interface.

The loopback interface belongs to an IPv6 routing process (IPv6 RIP) and an IPv4 routing process (integrated IS-IS). IPv6 RIP is also configured on the PE-CE WAN interface, as shown in Example 8-2. The IPv6 default route is announced from the San Jose PE router to the Santa Clara CE router via IPv6 RIP.

Example 8-2 *San Jose PE Router Initial Configuration*

```
PE_SanJose#
interface Loopback0
 ip address 194.22.15.2 255.255.255.255
 ip router isis
 ipv6 address 1307:8000::1/128
 ipv6 rip RIPv6 enable
!
interface Serial1/0
 description *** Link to Santa Clara site ***
 no ip address
 ipv6 enable
 ipv6 rip RIPv6 enable
 ipv6 rip RIPv6 default-information originate
!
ipv6 router rip RIPv6
```

The initial configuration of the Washington PE router (shown in Example 8-3) is similar to the initial configuration of the San Jose PE router with an IPv4 address and IPv6 address configured on the loopback interface, which belongs to the IPv4 and IPv6 routing processes. The PE-CE WAN link uses link-local IPv6 address and participates in IPv6 RIP routing.

Example 8-3 *Washington PE Router Initial Configuration*

```
PE_Washington#
interface Loopback0
 ip address 194.22.15.3 255.255.255.255
 ip router isis
 ipv6 address 1307:8000::3/128
 ipv6 rip RIPv6 enable
!
interface Serial5/0
 description *** Link to Baltimore site ***
 no ip address
 ipv6 enable
 ipv6 rip RIPv6 enable
 ipv6 rip RIPv6 default-information originate
!
ipv6 router rip RTR
```

The initial configuration of the Baltimore CE router (shown in Example 8-4) is similar to the initial configuration of the Santa Clara CE router. The IPv6 subnet is configured on the LAN interface, and a link-local IPv6 address is used on the WAN interface. Both interfaces participate in the IPv6 RIP routing process.

Example 8-4   *Baltimore CE Router Initial Configuration*

```
Baltimore#
interface Ethernet0/0
 no ip address
 ipv6 address 1205:6700:0:2::1/64
 ipv6 rip RTR enable
!
interface Serial0/0
 description *** Link to PE_Washington ***
 no ip address
 ipv6 enable
 ipv6 rip RTR enable
!
ipv6 router rip RTR
```

With the IPv6 routing configured on the PE routers and the CE routers, the IPv6 routing tables on the PE routers will contain the local routes and the routes received from the attached CE routers. (The IPv6 routing table from PE_SanJose is included in Example 8-5.)

Example 8-5   *IPv6 Routing Table on PE_SanJose*

```
PE_SanJose#show ipv6 route
IPv6 Routing Table - 5 entries
Codes: C - Connected, L - Local, S - Static, R - RIP, B - BGP
       I1 - ISIS L1, I2 - ISIS L2, IA - ISIS interarea
R    1205:6700:0:1::/64 [120/2]
     via FE80::206:28FF:FEE9:9E80, Serial1/0
LC   1307:8000::1/128 [0/0]
     via ::, Loopback0
L    FE80::/10 [0/0]
     via ::, Null0
L    FF00::/8 [0/0]
     via ::, Null0
```

The IPv6 routing tables on the CE routers contain the local routes, the routes advertised by the attached PE router, and the default IPv6 route. (The IPv6 routing table from the SantaClara CE router is shown in Example 8-6.)

Example 8-6   *IPv6 Routing Table on Santa Clara CE Router*

```
SantaClara#show ipv6 route
IPv6 Routing Table - 6 entries
Codes: C - Connected, L - Local, S - Static, R - RIP, B - BGP
       I1 - ISIS L1, I2 - ISIS L2, IA - ISIS interarea
Timers: Uptime/Expires

L    1205:6700:0:1::1/128 [0/0]
     via ::, Ethernet0/0, 2d19h/never
C    1205:6700:0:1::/64 [0/0]
     via ::, Ethernet0/0, 2d19h/never
R    1307:8000::1/128 [120/2]
     via FE80::208:20FF:FE3D:541C, Serial0/0, 19:10:54/00:02:31
```

Example 8-6   *IPv6 Routing Table on Santa Clara CE Router (Continued)*

```
L   FE80::/10 [0/0]
      via ::, Null0, 2d19h/never
L   FF00::/8 [0/0]
      via ::, Null0, 2d19h/never
R   ::/0 [120/2]
      via FE80::208:20FF:FE3D:541C, Serial0/0, 19:21:09/00:02:31
```

MP-BGP Session Establishment and Route Redistribution

The second step in the 6PE solution deployment is the establishment of inter-PE Multiprotocol BGP sessions and the redistribution of PE-CE routes into the IPv6 Multiprotocol BGP, as shown in Figure 8-7.

Figure 8-7   *MP-BGP IPv6 Routing in the SuperCom Network*

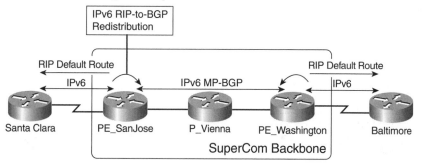

Although MP-BGP will carry the IPv6 prefixes, the sessions between the PE routers must be established between IPv4 endpoints. This ensures that the MP-BGP next-hop is an IPv4 address associated with an LDP-assigned label-switched path (LSP) across the MPLS backbone. This section focuses on a simple example in which the MP-BGP sessions are established directly between the PE routers. A more complex example including BGP route reflectors in the MPLS backbone will be presented at the end of this chapter.

The configuration tasks in this step are the same as when deploying an MPLS VPN solution:

1   Internal BGP sessions running over IPv4 are configured between PE routers by using the loopback interfaces as the source IP addresses of the BGP sessions.

NOTE   With the introduction of IPv6, Cisco IOS supports running BGP sessions between IPv6 endpoints. However, the 6PE solution requires BGP sessions between IPv4 endpoints.

2   The exchange of IPv6 routes is activated over these sessions by using the **neighbor activate** command within the **address-family ipv6** of the BGP routing process.

3 IGP routes are redistributed into MP-BGP by using the **redistribute** command within
address-family ipv6. In the SuperCom network, the IPv6 RIP routes as well as the
connected IPv6 subnets are redistributed into MP-BGP, resulting in the BGP
configurations shown in Examples 8-7 and 8-8.

Example 8-7 *IPv6 BGP Configuration on PE_SanJose*

```
PE_SanJose#
router bgp 10
 neighbor 194.22.15.3 remote-as 10
 neighbor 194.22.15.3 update-source Loopback0
 !
 address-family ipv6
 neighbor 194.22.15.3 activate
 redistribute rip RIPv6
 redistribute connected
```

Example 8-8 *IPv6 BGP Configuration on PE_Washington*

```
PE_Washington#
router bgp 10
 neighbor 194.22.15.2 remote-as 10
 neighbor 194.22.15.2 update-source Loopback0
 !
 address-family ipv6
 neighbor 194.22.15.2 activate
 redistribute rip RIPv6
 redistribute connected
```

After the MP-BGP sessions are active, the IPv6 routes are exchanged between the PE
routers, as can be verified with the **show bgp ipv6** command, shown in Example 8-9 on the
Washington PE router.

Example 8-9 *IPv6 BGP Table on PE_Washington*

```
PE_Washington#show bgp ipv6
BGP table version is 3, local router ID is 194.22.15.3
Status codes: s suppressed, d damped, h history, * valid, > best, i - internal
Origin codes: i - IGP, e - EGP, ? - incomplete

   Network          Next Hop         Metric LocPrf Weight Path
* i1205:6700:0:1::/64
                    ::FFFF:194.22.15.2
                                        2    100      0 ?
*> 1205:6700:0:2::/64
                    ::                  2         32768 ?
* i1307:8000::1/128 ::FFFF:194.22.15.2
                                        0    100      0 ?
*> 1307:8000::3/128 ::                  0         32768 ?
```

The global IPv6 BGP table on the Washington PE router contains two locally originated IPv6 routes: the local loopback interface and the subnet that is received from the Baltimore site via IPv6 RIP. It also contains two BGP routes that are received from the San Jose PE router. Please note that the remote IPv6 BGP routes are not used. A more detailed investigation using the **show bgp ipv6** *prefix* command (shown in Example 8-10) reveals that the Washington PE router considers the San Jose PE router unreachable.

Example 8-10 *SantaClara Subnet in the BGP Table on PE_Washington*

```
PE_Washington#show bgp ipv6 1205:6700:0:1::/64
BGP routing table entry for 1205:6700:0:1::/64, version 0
Paths: (1 available, no best path)
  Not advertised to any peer
  Local
    ::FFFF:194.22.15.2 (inaccessible) from 194.22.15.2 (194.22.15.2)
      Origin incomplete, metric 2, localpref 100, valid, internal
```

The reason for this seemingly unexpected behavior is simple; if you want to ensure IPv6 transport between IPv6 BGP peers, the BGP next-hop (expressed as an IPv6 address) must be reachable, guaranteeing that an end-to-end IPv6 path exists between the BGP peers.

NOTE   Even if the BGP session is established between IPv4 endpoints, the BGP next-hop address assigned to an IPv6 prefix is an IPv6 address derived from an IPv4 BGP endpoint and must be reachable through the IPv6 forwarding table.

With the traditional IPv4/IPv6 tools, you cannot satisfy the requirement that the remote IPv4 BGP next-hop is reachable as an IPv6 address without deploying IPv6 across the whole backbone. The only solution to this design problem is the 6PE solution, which somewhat relaxes the IPv6 BGP next-hop checks, as you'll see in the next section.

Labeled IPv6 MP-BGP Prefixes

The 6PE solution replaces the requirement for an end-to-end IPv6 path between the BGP endpoints with a requirement for an end-to-end LSP between the IPv4 endpoints of the MP-BGP session. To ensure successful transport of IPv6 datagrams across this LSP, a label stack must be used and the MPLS labels assigned to IPv6 prefixes (the second label in the label stack) must be exchanged between the PE routers together with the IPv6 prefixes. This functionality is enabled with a single command, **neighbor send-label**, configured within the **address-family ipv6** of the BGP routing process.

NOTE   From the configuration perspective, the need to enable MPLS label exchange manually is one of the major differences between MPLS VPN and 6PE configuration. Labels are always exchanged for the VPNv4 address family, whereas the label exchange for the IPv6 address family must be configured manually.

The Cisco IOS implementation of the 6PE solution combines the transport of IPv6 prefixes with MP-BGP, as specified in RFC 2545 with the transport of labeled prefixes with MP-BGP as specified in RFC 3107. According to RFC 3107, the IPv6 prefix and the MPLS label together form the Network Layer Reachability Information (NLRI) of MP-BGP.

The capability to exchange labeled IPv6 prefixes between BGP neighbors is negotiated with BGP capability advertisement, as specified in RFC 2842. Labeled IPv6 prefixes are exchanged between BGP neighbors only if both neighbors advertise the IPv6 capability together with the new IPv6 + Labels capability.

NOTE   If only one of the BGP neighbors advertises the IPv6 capability, unlabeled IPv6 routes are exchanged on that BGP session. This scenario requires an end-to-end IPv6 path between these neighbors.

With the exchange of labeled IPv6 prefixes configured in the SuperCom backbone (see Example 8-11), the San Jose and Washington PE routers agree on exchanging labeled IPv6 prefixes, which you can verify with the **show ip bgp neighbor** command (output shown in Example 8-12).

Example 8-11 *Configuring MP-BGP Exchange of Labeled IPv5 Prefixes*

```
PE_SanJose#
router bgp 10
 address-family ipv6
  neighbor 194.22.15.3 send-label

PE_Washington#
router bgp 10
 address-family ipv6
  neighbor 194.22.15.2 send-label
```

Example 8-12 *IPv6 + Labels Capability Negotiated Between PE_Washington and PE_SanJose*

```
PE_Washington#show ip bgp neighbor
BGP neighbor is 194.22.15.2, remote AS 10, internal link
  BGP version 4, remote router ID 194.22.15.2
  BGP state = Established, up for 00:01:08
  Last read 00:00:08, hold time is 180, keepalive interval is 60 seconds
  Neighbor capabilities:
    Route refresh: advertised and received(old & new)
    Address family IPv4 Unicast: advertised and received
    Address family IPv6 Unicast: advertised and received
    ipv6 MPLS Label capability: advertised and received
  Received 1233 messages, 0 notifications, 0 in queue
  Sent 1233 messages, 0 notifications, 0 in queue
  Default minimum time between advertisement runs is 5 seconds
```

As soon as the **neighbor send-label** command is configured in the BGP routing process, the PE router must allocate labels for IPv6 routes and assign those labels to all IPv6 routes that originate in the IPv6 BGP table. The labels allocated by the 6PE solution can be inspected with the **show mpls forwarding** command, which produces the output in Example 8-13 on the Washington PE router.

Example 8-13 *Local Labels Allocated by the 6PE Solution on PE_Washington*

```
PE_Washington#show mpls forwarding-table
Local  Outgoing    Prefix           Bytes tag  Outgoing   Next Hop
tag    tag or VC   or Tunnel Id     switched   interface
16     Pop tag     194.22.15.16/30  0          Se5/3      194.22.15.25
17     17          194.22.15.2/32   0          Se5/3      194.22.15.25
18     Pop tag     194.22.15.4/32   0          Se5/3      194.22.15.25
19     Aggregate   IPv6             2490
20     Aggregate   IPv6             0
21     Aggregate   IPv6             0
```

Contrary to the MPLS VPN implementation, where a separate label is assigned to each VPNv4 route, a fixed set of no more than 16 labels is assigned to all IPv6 routes supported with the 6PE functionality.

NOTE   Different Cisco IOS releases use different label allocation strategies. Some releases allocate a pool of 16 labels and share the same label between multiple IPv6 routes if needed. Other releases allocate one label for each IPv6 route, eliminating the extra IPv6 lookup at the egress 6PE router. Fortunately, the label assignment strategy is egress PE router-specific and does not affect the overall 6PE architecture.

Because the number of IPv6 routes in any PE router could easily exceed 16 routes, all of these labels act as aggregate labels (see the discussion of effects of IP route summarization on MPLS LSPs in Volume I of *MPLS and VPN Architectures*), requiring an additional IPv6 lookup in the egress PE router.

NOTE   From the perspective of the 6PE solution, a single label would be enough to support the end-to-end transport of IPv6 datagrams between PE routers. Sixteen labels are used to ensure load sharing in the MPLS core based on the second label in the label stack.

The MPLS labels assigned to individual IPv6 prefixes by both the local PE router and remote PE routers can be inspected with the **show bgp labels** command, which produces the printout in Example 8-14 on the Washington PE router.

Example 8-14 *MPLS Labels Associated with IPv6 BGP Routes on PE_Washington*

```
PE_Washington#show bgp labels
    Network            Next Hop       In label/Out label
    1205:6700:0:1::/64
                       ::FFFF:194.22.15.2
                                           nolabel/22
    1205:6700:0:2::/64
                       ::              20/nolabel
    1307:8000::1/128 ::FFFF:194.22.15.2
                                           nolabel/23
    1307:8000::3/128 ::              21/nolabel
```

As with the corresponding MPLS VPN output, the **show bgp labels** printout is nonintuitive and requires careful inspection of the incoming and outgoing labels as follows:

- The locally originated IPv6 BGP routes have an incoming label (which the other PE routers will use to reach these destinations), but no outgoing label (much like VPNv4 routes).

NOTE   The locally originated IPv6 routes will have outgoing labels only when the Cisco IOS supports the IPv6 LDP between the PE routers and the CE routers.

- The IPv6 BGP routes received from remote PE routers have an outgoing label (which is used by the local PE router to build the IPv6 CEF table), but no incoming label.

NOTE   Similarly to the locally originated IPv6 routes, the incoming label will only make sense with the support of IPv6 LDP between the PE routers and the CE routers.

With the exchange of MPLS labels attached to IPv6 routes, the BGP next-hop check in Cisco IOS is slightly modified. An IPv6 BGP route is considered reachable if the IPv6 BGP next-hop is an IPv4-compatible address *and* the PE router has received a label for the IPv4 address from its downstream neighbor, indicating there is an end-to-end LSP toward the remote BGP peer. You can verify this relaxation by inspecting the IPv6 BGP table on the Washington PE router (shown in Example 8-15). As soon as the exchange of labeled IPv6 prefixes is configured, the IPv6 MP-BGP routes that are received from the San Jose PE router are selected and installed in the IPv6 routing table.

Example 8-15 *BGP Table on PE_Washington*

```
PE_Washington#show bgp ipv6
BGP table version is 5, local router ID is 194.22.15.3
Status codes: s suppressed, d damped, h history, * valid, > best, i - internal
Origin codes: i - IGP, e - EGP, ? - incomplete

   Network           Next Hop          Metric LocPrf Weight Path
*>i1205:6700:0:1::/64
                     ::FFFF:194.22.15.2
                                           2    100       0 ?
*>  1205:6700:0:2::/64
                     ::                    2            32768 ?
*>i1307:8000::1/128 ::FFFF:194.22.15.2
                                           0    100       0 ?
*>  1307:8000::3/128 ::                    0            32768 ?
```

The IPv6 routing table on the Washington PE router (displayed in Example 8-16) also indicates that the IPv6 BGP destinations are reachable via IPv6-MPLS (indicating the deployment of 6PE solution).

Example 8-16 *IPv6 Routing Table on PE_Washington*

```
PE_Washington#show ipv6 route
IPv6 Routing Table - 6 entries
Codes: C - Connected, L - Local, S - Static, R - RIP, B - BGP
       I1 - ISIS L1, I2 - ISIS L2, IA - ISIS interarea
B   1205:6700:0:1::/64 [200/0]
     via ::FFFF:194.22.15.2, IPv6-mpls
R   1205:6700:0:2::/64 [120/2]
     via FE80::230:94FF:FE9B:D940, Serial5/0
B   1307:8000::1/128 [200/0]
     via ::FFFF:194.22.15.2, IPv6-mpls
LC  1307:8000::3/128 [0/0]
     via ::, Loopback0
L   FE80::/10 [0/0]
     via ::, Null0
L   FF00::/8 [0/0]
     via ::, Null0
```

IPv6 Datagram Forwarding Across an MPLS Backbone

The 6PE solution enables IPv6 datagram forwarding across an MPLS-enabled IPv4-only backbone in which the P routers do not support the IPv6 protocol. The IPv6 datagrams transported across the backbone therefore have to be encapsulated in an MPLS frame by the ingress PE router. Similarly to the IPv4 MPLS implementation, the MPLS label stacks associated with the IPv6 routes are stored in the CEF table called forwarding information base (FIB). Due to this dependency, the IPv6 CEF must be enabled on the PE routers with the **ipv6 cef** command so that the label imposition on incoming IPv6 datagrams is enabled.

After the IPv6 CEF switching has been enabled, you can use the **show ipv6 cef** command to inspect the IPv6 FIB and the MPLS labels that are imposed in front of the IPv6 datagrams. The IPv6 FIB from the Washington PE router is displayed in Example 8-17.

Example 8-17 *IPv6 FIB on PE_Washington*

```
PE_Washington#show ipv6 cef
1205:6700:0:1::/64
     nexthop ::FFFF:194.22.15.2
     fast tag rewrite with Se5/3, 194.22.15.25, tags imposed: {17 22}
1205:6700:0:2::/64
     nexthop FE80::230:94FF:FE9B:D940 Serial5/0
1307:8000::1/128
     nexthop ::FFFF:194.22.15.2
     fast tag rewrite with Se5/3, 194.22.15.25, tags imposed: {17 23}
1307:8000::3/128
  Receive
FE80::/10
  Receive
FF00::/8
  Receive
```

As expected, the IPv6 routes received from the San Jose PE router have a label stack associated with them. The first label in the label stack, {17}, is the LDP label assigned to the BGP next-hop (PE_SanJose) by the downstream neighbor (P_Vienna). The second label in the stack, {22} or {23}, is the one assigned to the IPv6 route by the remote PE router. You can use the **show ip cef** or the **show mpls ip bindings** command to check the correctness of the first label in the label stack and the **show bgp labels** command to check the correctness of the second label in the label stack. The output from the Washington PE router is displayed in Example 8-18.

Example 8-18 *Labels Used in IPv6 Label Stack on PE_Washington*

```
PE_Washington#show ip cef 194.22.15.2
194.22.15.2/32, version 16, cached adjacency 194.22.15.25
0 packets, 0 bytes
  tag information set
    local tag: 17
    fast tag rewrite with Se5/3, 194.22.15.25, tags imposed: {17}
  via 194.22.15.25, Serial5/3, 0 dependencies
    next hop 194.22.15.25, Serial5/3
```

Example 8-18 *Labels Used in IPv6 Label Stack on PE_Washington (Continued)*

```
      valid cached adjacency
      tag rewrite with Se5/3, 194.22.15.25, tags imposed: {17}
PE_Washington#show bgp labels
   Network           Next Hop      In label/Out label
   1205:6700:0:1::/64
                      ::FFFF:194.22.15.2
                                    nolabel/22
   1205:6700:0:2::/64
                      ::            20/nolabel
   1307:8000::1/128 ::FFFF:194.22.15.2
                                    nolabel/23
   1307:8000::3/128 ::             21/nolabel
```

With the IPv6 CEF being configured on the Washington and San Jose PE routers, the end-to-end IPv6 path between the Santa Clara and Baltimore sites is operational, and the end users can execute the **trace ipv6** command on the CE routers to verify it, as shown in Example 8-19.

Example 8-19 *IPv6 Trace from Santa Clara to Baltimore*

```
SantaClara#trace ipv6

Target IPv6 address: baltimore
Source IPv6 address: santaclara
Numeric display? [no]:
Timeout in seconds [3]:
Probe count [3]:
Minimum Time to Live [1]:
Maximum Time to Live [30]:
Priority [0]:
Port Number [33434]:
Type escape sequence to abort.
Tracing the route to Baltimore (1205:6700:0:2::1)

  1 1307:8000::1 4 msec 0 msec 4 msec
  2  *  *  *
  3 1307:8000::3 0 msec 0 msec 4 msec
  4 Baltimore (1205:6700:0:2::1) 4 msec 4 msec 0 msec
```

NOTE   You must use the extended IPv6 **trace** command in the SuperCom pilot because the PE-CE links use link-local addresses, which are not usable as the source IPv6 addresses of regular IPv6 datagrams.

The **trace** output includes the ingress PE router (PE_SanJose – 1307:8000::1), the egress PE router (PE_Washington – 1307:8000::3), and the target CE router.

The **trace** output also includes a number of unreachable intermediate hops—the P routers that are unable to send the IPv6 ICMP replies back to the CE routers.

NOTE	The ICMP replies being generated by the intermediate P routers have always presented a problem because the P routers have no information about the destination of the transported datagram or the network-layer protocol being transported.
	An interim solution, documented in Chapter 5, "Advanced MPLS Topics" of Volume I of *MPLS and VPN Architectures*, was developed to support IPv4 MPLS backbones. Using this solution, the P routers send an IPv4 ICMP reply to the packet originator using the labels that are attached to the incoming datagram, hoping that the egress PE router will forward the packet back to the origination. The solution works for IPv4 datagrams only and fails completely when faced with IPv6 datagrams that are transported across the MPLS backbone.

The service providers who deploy pilot IPv6 backbones can accept this somewhat undesired behavior or they can optimize the end user experience by disabling the IPv6-to-MPLS TTL propagation with the **no mpls ip propagate-ttl forwarded** command. This command makes the MPLS backbone completely invisible to the CE routers, resulting in a clean IPv6 **trace** between the CE routers, as shown in Example 8-20. For a detailed description of this command, please refer to Chapter 5 of Volume I of the *MPLS and VPN Architectures* book.

Example 8-20   *IPv6 Trace from Santa Clara to Baltimore with Disabled TTL Propagation in SuperCom Backbone*

```
SantaClara#trace ipv6

Target IPv6 address: baltimore
Source IPv6 address: santaclara
Numeric display? [no]:
Timeout in seconds [3]: 1
Probe count [3]:
Minimum Time to Live [1]:
Maximum Time to Live [30]: 5
Priority [0]:
Port Number [33434]:
Type escape sequence to abort.
Tracing the route to Baltimore (1205:6700:0:2::1)

  1 1307:8000::1 0 msec 4 msec 0 msec
  2 1307:8000::3 4 msec 4 msec 4 msec
  3 Baltimore (1205:6700:0:2::1) 4 msec 4 msec 0 msec
```

NOTE	When TTL propagation is disabled in an MPLS VPN backbone, a user who executes a **trace** on a CE router will usually not see the egress PE router because that router performs only a label lookup and is not affected with the IP TTL. In the 6PE case, the labels that the egress PE routers assign to IPv6 prefixes are aggregate labels, and the egress PE router performs an IPv6 lookup and corresponding decrement of IPv6 TTL, making it visible to the IPv6 **trace** command.

The results of the IPv6 trace across the SuperCom backbone raise an interesting issue: The egress PE router receives the incoming IPv6 **trace** datagram over an MPLS LSP, not over a physical interface. The source IPv6 address of the returning ICMP packet is usually the IPv6 address of the incoming interface, whereas the incoming MPLS LSP has no associated IPv6 address. Which IPv6 address would then be used to send ICMP packets as responses to the IPv6 packets with TTL=1?

The Cisco IOS 6PE implementation addresses this concern. One of the global IPv6 addresses configured on the router is chosen as the address used as the source IPv6 address in ICMP replies. As usual, loopback interfaces are preferred in the address selection process. You can also manually specify the IPv6 address you want to use in the ICMP responses to packets received over MPLS LSP with the **mpls ipv6 source-interface** command.

Complex 6PE Deployment Scenarios

This section shows how you can use the 6PE functionality in more complex network design scenarios. These scenarios will include BGP route reflectors and BGP confederations as well as interautonomous system 6PE functionality.

BGP Route Reflectors

BGP route reflectors are the most common method of scaling BGP-based networks and are commonly used in larger service provider networks. The concept of BGP route reflectors is explained in great detail in *Internet Routing Architectures*, published by Cisco Press. The use of BGP route reflectors in an MPLS VPN environment is addressed in Volume I of *MPLS and VPN Architectures*. Advanced BGP route reflector scenarios are described earlier in Chapter 6, "Large-Scale Routing and Multiple Service Provider Connectivity" of this book, which addresses various designs where route reflectors are linked between adjacent service provider networks. In this section, you'll see how the introduction (or presence) of route reflectors in a service provider network affects the 6PE functionality.

The primary function of BGP route reflectors is to propagate routes received from internal BGP neighbors to other internal BGP neighbors while ensuring (with additional BGP attributes) that these routes do not start looping inside the autonomous system. While reflecting the routes, the BGP route reflectors are not allowed to change the reflected route (NLRI), its next-hop, or any other BGP attributes attached to the route.

The fact that the route reflectors do not change the NLRI (which combines an IPv6 prefix and an MPLS label when the 6PE functionality is used) or the next-hop (the IPv4 address of the PE router translated into an IPv6 address) makes them transparent to the 6PE functionality. There are, however, a few design rules that you must consider in 6PE networks with route reflectors:

- The BGP route reflectors must support the 6PE functionality to be able to accept and propagate IPv6 + Labels prefixes.

- IPv6 routing must be enabled on BGP route reflectors; otherwise, you will not be able to configure the IPv6 BGP address family on the route reflectors.

- The IPv6 + Labels MP-BGP session must be activated between route reflectors and their neighbors.

- Route reflecting must be configured within the IPv6 address family (similarly to the requirement that route reflecting be configured separately for the VPNv4 address family).

Not all service providers will want to deploy the 6PE functionality (which might require deployment of newer IOS release) in their route reflectors. Other service providers would like to avoid the additional burden placed on the route reflectors with the introduction of another address family. (Although this burden will be small initially, it will grow with the expansion of the IPv6 Internet.) In both cases, deploying dedicated 6PE route reflectors can solve the problem. Alternatively, you can use a combination of VPNv4 and 6PE routes on one set of route reflectors and IPv4 on another set.

Imagine that the SuperCom service provider has already deployed a BGP route reflector in its MPLS VPN backbone. This route reflector has the loopback IP address 194.22.15.100 and is adjacent to the Vienna P router. The BGP sessions among PE routers in Paris, San Jose, and Washington would then be replaced by a hub-and-spoke topology of BGP sessions, shown in Figure 8-8. The relevant parts of the router configuration of the RR_Vienna and modified configuration of the SanJose PE router are shown in Examples 8-21 and 8-22.

Figure 8-8   *BGP Route Reflector in SuperCom Network*

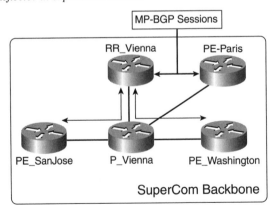

Example 8-21 *Configuration of RR_Vienna*

```
router bgp 10
 no synchronization
 neighbor 194.22.15.1 remote-as 10
 neighbor 194.22.15.1 update-source Loopback0
 neighbor 194.22.15.1 route-reflector-client
 neighbor 194.22.15.2 remote-as 10
 neighbor 194.22.15.2 update-source Loopback0
 neighbor 194.22.15.2 route-reflector-client
 neighbor 194.22.15.3 remote-as 10
 neighbor 194.22.15.3 update-source Loopback0
 neighbor 194.22.15.3 route-reflector-client
 no auto-summary
 !
 address-family vpnv4
 neighbor 194.22.15.1 activate
 neighbor 194.22.15.1 route-reflector-client
 neighbor 194.22.15.1 send-community extended
 neighbor 194.22.15.2 activate
 neighbor 194.22.15.2 route-reflector-client
 neighbor 194.22.15.2 send-community extended
 neighbor 194.22.15.3 activate
 neighbor 194.22.15.3 route-reflector-client
 neighbor 194.22.15.3 send-community extended
```

Example 8-22 *Modified Configuration of PE_SanJose*

```
router bgp 10
 neighbor 194.22.15.100 remote-as 10
 neighbor 194.22.15.100 update-source Loopback0
 no auto-summary
 !
 address-family vpnv4
 neighbor 194.22.15.100 activate
 neighbor 194.22.15.100 send-community extended
```

If the same route reflector is used to reflect the IPv6 + Labels address family between the San Jose and Washington PE routers, the IPv6 routing will have to be configured on the RR_Vienna, and the IPv6 + Labels address family will have to be activated for the San Jose and Washington PE router BGP neighbors, as shown in Example 8-23.

Example 8-23 *PE Configuration on RR_Vienna*

```
ipv6 unicast-routing
!
router bgp 10
 address-family ipv6
 neighbor 194.22.15.2 activate
 neighbor 194.22.15.2 route-reflector-client
 neighbor 194.22.15.2 send-label
 neighbor 194.22.15.3 activate
 neighbor 194.22.15.3 route-reflector-client
 neighbor 194.22.15.3 send-label
```

Alternatively, the SuperCom engineers might want to deploy a 6PE-specific BGP route reflector (with the loopback IP address 194.22.15.101) that would be used exclusively to support the IPv6 pilot, as shown in Figure 8-9. This route reflector, which is not part of a production network, can then run a less-tested IOS release because its failure will not affect the production MPLS VPN backbone.

Figure 8-9   *Dedicated 6PE BGP Route Reflector*

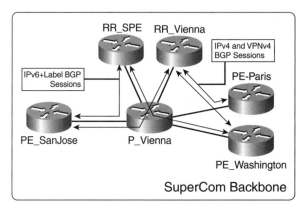

The BGP router configuration of the San Jose and Washington PE routers will need to include this new BGP neighbor. Only the IPv6 + Labels address family will be activated on the new BGP sessions, as shown in Example 8-24. The BGP configuration of the RR_6PE is almost identical to the RR_Vienna configuration in Example 8-21.

Example 8-24   *Support for Dedicated 6PE Route Reflector Configured on PE_SanJose*

```
PE_SanJose(config)#
router bgp 10
 neighbor 194.22.15.101 remote-as 10
 neighbor 194.22.15.101 update-source Loopback0
 no neighbor 194.22.15.101 activate
 !
 address-family ipv6
 neighbor 194.22.15.101 activate
 neighbor 194.22.15.100 send-label
```

6PE Deployment in Networks Using BGP Confederations

Another solution addressing the scalability issues of the IBGP sessions is the BGP confederations, which are used significantly less often than the BGP route reflectors. When using BGP confederations, the autonomous system is internally divided into a number of smaller autonomous systems, called member autonomous systems. The EBGP sessions between the member autonomous systems behave like EBGP sessions with respect to BGP route propagation rules. The only difference between intraconfederation EBGP sessions and the real EBGP sessions is that most of the BGP attributes (with the exception of AS-path) remain unchanged when a prefix is propagated across an intraconfederation EBGP session.

BGP confederations can be used in two common design scenarios:

- The whole autonomous system (all member autonomous systems) uses one IGP and the BGP next-hop is unchanged on an intraconfederation EBGP session. This design is compatible with the 6PE functionality because the NLRI (IPv6 prefix + label) and the BGP next-hop are unchanged as the IPv6 + Labels prefix is propagated across the autonomous system.

- Each member autonomous system uses a separate IGP, and the BGP next-hop is changed on an intraconfederation EBGP session with the **neighbor next-hop-self** command. This design is *not* compatible with the 6PE functionality because the current 6PE implementation in Cisco IOS does not provide the ability to re-originate the MPLS label if the BGP next-hop is changed.

There is another restriction associated with deploying 6PE functionality in BGP networks using BGP confederations: There must be a path between each pair of 6PE-enabled routers on which all member-AS boundary routers support the IPv6 functionality. IPv6 routing must be configured on all these routers together with the exchange on IPv6 + Labels prefixes across intraconfederation EBGP sessions.

Inter-AS 6PE Deployment

The deployment of 6PE functionality across multiple service providers is best handled with a design in which each service provider uses the 6PE functionality internally and exchanges the IPv6 traffic with adjacent service providers using native IPv6 packet forwarding. Consider, for example, a scenario in which the IPv6 customer of SuperCom would like to connect a third IPv6 site connected to another service provider, as shown in Figure 8-10. (The internal details of the EastCom backbone are not known to the SuperCom engineers.)

In this scenario, the best solution is for each service provider to consider the other service provider as a CE router that uses IPv6 BGP to exchange IPv6 prefixes. Native IPv6 BGP running between IPv6 endpoints can be used between these service providers to exchange IPv6 prefixes.

Figure 8-10 *Extended IPv6 Pilot*

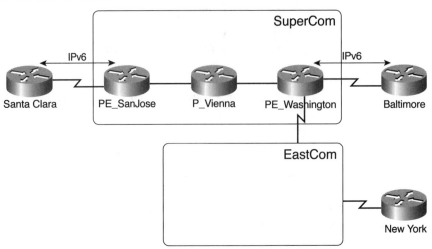

The relevant parts of the Washington PE router configuration are shown in Example 8-25.

Example 8-25 *Native IPv6 BGP Session Configured Between PE_Washington and EastCom PE Router*

```
interface Serial5/0
 description *** Link to EastCom ***
 no ip address
 ipv6 address 1307:8000:1::1/120
 ipv6 enable
!
router bgp 10
 bgp log-neighbor-changes
 neighbor 1307:8000:1::2 remote-as 65001
!
address-family ipv6
 neighbor 1307:8000:1::2 activate
```

After the IPv6 BGP session between SuperCom and EastCom is established, the
Washington PE router receives IPv6 BGP prefix information from the EastCom router, as
shown in Example 8-26.

Example 8-26 *IPv6 Prefix for NewYork Site Received by PE_Washington*

```
PE_Washington#sh bgp ipv6 1205:6700:0:3::/64
BGP routing table entry for 1205:6700:0:3::/64, version 8
Paths: (1 available, best #1, table Global-IPv6-Table)
  Advertised to non peer-group peers:
  194.22.15.2
  5001
    1307:8000:1::2 from 1307:8000:1::2 (10.0.0.1)
      Origin IGP, localpref 100, valid, external, best
```

When the IPv6 prefix is propagated to the SanJose PE router over an IPv6 + Labels MP-BGP session, the BGP next-hop is automatically changed to the IPv4 address of the Washington PE router (translated, of course, into an IPv6 address), requiring no additional configuration on the Washington or SanJose PE routers. The IPv6 BGP prefix that the SanJose PE router receives is shown in Example 8-27.

Example 8-27 *NewYork IPv6 Prefix on PE_SanJose*

```
PE_SanJose#sh bgp ipv6 1205:6700:0:3::/64
BGP routing table entry for 1205:6700:0:3::/64, version 12
Paths: (1 available, best #1, table Global-IPv6-Table)
  Not advertised to any peer
  5001
    ::FFFF:194.22.15.3 (metric 30) from 194.22.15.3 (194.22.15.3)
      Origin IGP, localpref 100, valid, internal, best
```

Summary

The 6PE solution (IPv6 transport across IPv4-only MPLS backbone) allows a seamless nonintrusive deployment of IPv6 pilot networks across existing IPv4 cores without the complexities associated with other early-deployment solutions (such as IPv6 tunnels across IPv4 backbones). The solution is similar in its concept to the MPLS VPN solution; IPv6 MP-BGP is extended with the capability to exchange MPLS labels associated with IPv6 prefixes between the PE routers. The labels associated with IPv6 prefixes are then used together with LDP-allocated labels to IPv4 BGP next-hops to build MPLS label stacks in IPv6 FIB tables. The MPLS label stacks, when imposed in front of IPv6 datagrams, enable transparent transport of IPv6 datagrams from an ingress PE router over an IPv4-only MPLS backbone to an egress PE router, which performs another IPv6 lookup and forwards the IPv6 datagram toward its final destination.

PART IV

Troubleshooting

CHAPTER 9

Troubleshooting of MPLS-Based Solutions

All of the previous chapters in this book have discussed a variety of advanced or new Multi-protocol Label Switching (MPLS)-based applications, ranging from remote access, support of new routing protocols, and multi-virtual private network (VPN) operation of CE routers to the inclusion of new IP services within the MPLS VPN architecture, including security and IP multicast. This chapter focuses on troubleshooting service provider networks designed around MPLS-based solutions.

Because the MPLS-based solutions encompass a large solution space, it's almost impossible to cover all troubleshooting scenarios in one chapter. As is usually the case when tackling complex topics in limited space, this chapter provides a generic blueprint that you can tailor to individual preferences, troubleshooting styles (starting with the most obvious tests versus methodically testing everything from scratch), and individual MPLS-based solutions. This chapter also presents troubleshooting scenarios for two of the most common MPLS-based solutions: Internet services running across an MPLS backbone, and VPN services offered on top of MPLS VPN technology.

Introduction to Troubleshooting of MPLS-Based Solutions

Most MPLS-based solutions (with the notable exception of MPLS quality of service [QoS], which is not covered in this book) follow the same conceptual architecture: customer control plane operation, provider control plane operation, and data plane operation.

Customer Control Plane Operation

The following functions are performed by the customer control plane:

- Customer routing information is exchanged between PE routers and CE routers.

- Customer routing information is propagated between PE routers, most commonly with the help of Multiprotocol Border Gateway Protocol (MP-BGP). MPLS labels are exchanged together with the customer routing information to facilitate the data forwarding with an MPLS label stack.

- Customer routing information received across the MPLS backbone is propagated to CE routers.

Provider Control Plane Operation

Most MPLS-based solutions rely on an end-to-end label-switched path (LSP) between PE routers for customer data forwarding. These paths need to be built throughout the service provider network before customer data can be forwarded successfully. Label Distribution Protocol (LDP) is usually used to build these paths. In some (rarer) cases, MPLS traffic engineering (MPLS-TE) is used directly between the PE routers to build the traffic-engineered LSPs directly between PE routers. There are also networks that would use generic route encapsulation (GRE) tunnels directly between the PE routers, in which case the LSP is only a single hop long.

Data Plane Operation

Most of the MPLS setup and deployment problems occur in the control plane; after the routing information has been exchanged between PE routers and CE routers and the LSP has been built between PE routers, the MPLS-based data forwarding across the Provider network (P-network) usually works. There are, however, a few situations in which the data plane functionality causes network-wide problems. The three most common problems are these:

- There is no end-to-end LSP between the PE routers. Although this is a provider control plane problem, it usually manifests itself on the data plane.

- The MPLS label stack is not imposed on customer datagrams because Cisco Express Forwarding (CEF) is not operational on the ingress interface.

- A Layer 2 device (most commonly a LAN switch) between MPLS nodes cannot handle the increase in Layer 2 payload size that is caused by MPLS label stack imposition. Refer to the section "Oversized Packet Issues" later in this chapter for more details.

The troubleshooting of any MPLS-based solution usually involves more than one component of the solution. Because the MPLS forwarding in the service provider backbone is crucial to the deployment of MPLS-based solutions, it makes sense to check the correct MPLS forwarding in the backbone before focusing on customer routing information exchange or forwarding of customer datagrams.

A typical MPLS troubleshooting session includes the following steps:

1. Check the MPLS forwarding across the service provider backbone. Fix the P-network label distribution process or the P-network forwarding issues if necessary.

2. Check the routing information exchange between CE routers and PE routers, between the PE routers across the MPLS backbone, and between PE routers and CE routers.

3. Check the customer datagram forwarding.

All three steps are described in more detail later in this chapter. This chapter focuses primarily on MPLS VPN as the MPLS application running across the P-network. You can easily apply the procedures discussed here to any other MPLS applications discussed in previous chapters of this book.

Troubleshooting the MPLS Backbone

MPLS is simple to configure and troubleshoot. Not many things can go wrong, and recent IOS versions (such as IOS release 12.2) check most of the prerequisites for successful MPLS operation before MPLS-related configuration commands can be entered.

NOTE   MPLS is so transparent in simple IP networks that do not use advanced MPLS features (such as BGP running only on the edge routers) or MPLS applications (MPLS VPNs or MPLS-TE) that it is sometimes hard to detect that MPLS is not operational. The first problems usually arise when you are trying to deploy advanced MPLS features.

If you encounter MPLS-related problems in your network, you should check the following things first. (The next section contains detailed instructions on how to perform these checks.)

- Is CEF enabled? MPLS requires CEF because it is the only switching mechanism that can provide the necessary forwarding structures required by the MPLS label imposition component.
- Is MPLS enabled on all routers?
- Is MPLS disabled on any of the interfaces?

Before going in depth into MPLS troubleshooting, it is always valuable to first perform a simple test described in the following section to verify whether the end-to-end LSP between the PE routers is operational. This test usually also yields the IP address of the router causing the LSP to break.

NOTE   Under some rare circumstances, the end-to-end LSP check might work, but the LSP between the PE routers would still be broken. If the customer datagram forwarding still does not work after you have checked all the other potential problems, you might have encountered such a broken LSP. At that point, you would need to perform in-depth MPLS troubleshooting.

Verifying End-to-End LSP

One of the most common reasons for end-to-end MPLS connectivity problems is a broken LSP. In many applications (such as MPLS VPN or MP-BGP running only on edge routers), an LSP should span the whole MPLS network, from ingress label switch router (LSR) to egress LSR. In these cases, the LSRs in the middle of the network usually cannot propagate unlabeled packets sent from ingress to egress LSR; therefore, a break in the LSP results in a loss of connectivity.

There are three common reasons for a break in an end-to-end LSP:

- An LSR in the path performs address summarization.
- An IP router in the path does not support MPLS.
- The P-network is using Open Shortest Path First (OSPF) as its interior routing protocol, and the subnet mask on the PE router's loopback interface is not equal to /32.

NOTE   By default, OSPF announces all loopback interfaces with the /32 subnet mask regardless of the actual subnet mask configured on the interface. The mismatch between the subnet mask announced with OSPF and the subnet mask announced with LDP breaks the last hop in the LSP.

You can easily check whether there is an operational end-to-end LSP between a pair of PE routers with the help of TTL propagation on the ingress PE router. The printouts included in the procedure that follows use a sample network shown in Figure 9-1.

Figure 9-1   *IP Addressing in the Sample Network*

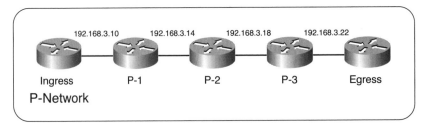

Use the following procedure to check the end-to-end LSP between a pair of LSRs:

Step 1   Enable time-to-live (TTL) propagation for local packets on the ingress LSR with the **mpls ip propagate-ttl local** command. Perform the trace from the ingress LSR toward the egress LSR. You should see all LSRs in the forwarding path with MPLS labels displayed at every hop except the last one, as shown in Example 9-1.

Example 9-1   *Traceroute from Ingress LSR to Egress LSR with TTL Propagation Enabled*

```
Ingress#trace Egress

Type escape sequence to abort.
Tracing the route to Egress (192.168.3.1)

  1 192.168.3.10 [MPLS: Label 20 Exp 0] 913 msec 1202 msec 1034 msec
  2 192.168.3.14 [MPLS: Label 22 Exp 0] 1013 msec 902 msec 901 msec
  3 192.168.3.18 [MPLS: Label 23 Exp 0] 1102 msec 1102 msec 377 msec
  4 192.168.3.22 1190 msec 1005 msec 789 msec
```

Step 2 Disable the TTL propagation for local packets on the ingress LSR with
the **no mpls ip propagate-ttl local** command and perform the same
trace command. You should see only the last LSR in the forwarding path,
as shown in Example 9-2.

Example 9-2 *Traceroute from Ingress LSR to Egress LSR with TTL Propagation Disabled*

```
Ingress#trace Egress

Type escape sequence to abort.
Tracing the route to Egress (192.168.3.1)

  1 192.168.3.22 1190 msec 1005 msec 789 msec
```

If, however, a device in the forwarding path breaks the LSP (for example, due to route
summarization), then the **trace** command (with TTL disabled) shows more than one hop
but probably less than the whole forwarding path (as displayed by the **trace** command with
TTL propagation enabled). An example indicating a broken LSP due to route summarization on P-2 is displayed in Example 9-3. The first IP address in the example is usually the
IP address of the router where the LSP breaks, which is the ideal starting point for your
troubleshooting.

Example 9-3 *Traceroute from Ingress LSR to Egress LSR Along a Broken LSP (TTL Propagation Is Disabled)*

```
Ingress#trace Egress

Type escape sequence to abort.
Tracing the route to Egress (192.168.3.1)

  1 192.168.3.14 208 msec 309 msec 677 msec
  2 192.168.3.18 789 msec 970 msec 729 msec
  3 192.168.3.22 901 msec 1098 msec 629 msec
```

Other Quick Checks

After you have verified that the LSP between PE routers is broken, you should perform a
few more quick MPLS-related checks before you go into in-depth MPLS troubleshooting:

• Is CEF enabled globally on every router in the path?

You verify proper operation of CEF with the **show ip cef summary** monitoring
command, which should produce a printout similar to the one shown in Example 9-4.

Example 9-4 *Correct show ip cef summary Printout*

```
Router#show ip cef summary
IP CEF with switching (Table Version 87), flags=0x0
  51 routes, 0 reresolve, 0 unresolved (0 old, 0 new)
  54 leaves, 30 nodes, 37896 bytes, 90 inserts, 36 invalidations
  0 load sharing elements, 0 bytes, 0 references
  universal per-destination load sharing algorithm, id E2D347E4
  2 CEF resets, 1 revisions of existing leaves
  refcounts:  1038 leaf, 995 node

Adjacency Table has 5 adjacencies
```

If, however, CEF is not enabled on the router, then the same command results in a similar printout with a small error notification at the end (highlighted in Example 9-5).

Example 9-5 *show ip cef summary Printout with CEF Disabled*

```
Router#show ip cef summary
IP CEF without switching (Table Version 61), flags=0x0
  0 routes, 0 reresolve, 0 unresolved (0 old, 0 new)
  0 leaves, 0 nodes, 0 bytes, 78 inserts, 78 invalidations
  0 load sharing elements, 0 bytes, 0 references
  universal per-destination load sharing algorithm, id 01C20606
  3 CEF resets, 0 revisions of existing leaves
  refcounts:  0 leaf, 0 node

%CEF not running
```

- Is MPLS enabled?

  You verify LSR-wide MPLS operation with the **show mpls forwarding-table** command, which should produce a printout similar to that shown in Example 9-6.

Example 9-6 *Correct show mpls forwarding-table*

```
Router#show mpls forwarding-table
Local  Outgoing    Prefix           Bytes tag  Outgoing   Next Hop
tag    tag or VC   or Tunnel Id     switched   interface
16     Untagged    192.168.21.0 255.255.255.0  \
                                    0          Se0/0.1    point2point
17     Untagged    192.168.20.0 255.255.255.0  \
                                    0          Se0/0.2    point2point
18     18          192.168.22.0 255.255.255.0  \
                                    0          Se0/0.1    point2point
19     21          192.168.3.2 255.255.255.255   \
                                    0          Se0/0.1    point2point
20     22          192.168.3.1 255.255.255.255   \
                                    0          Se0/0.1    point2point
```

If, however, you have not configured MPLS on the LSR, then the same command displays an error message similar to the one shown in Example 9-7.

Example 9-7   *show mpls forwarding-table Printout with MPLS Disabled*

```
Router#show mpls forwarding-table
Tag switching is not operational.
CEF or tag switching has not been enabled.
No TFIB currently allocated.
```

There is also a third possibility: MPLS has been enabled but, for some reason, CEF has been disabled afterward. (Cisco IOS does not allow you to configure MPLS with CEF disabled from IOS release 12.2 onward.) In this case, the **show mpls forwarding-table** command indicates that MPLS is not operational due to lack of CEF support, as shown in Example 9-8.

Example 9-8   *show mpls forwarding-table Printout with CEF Disabled*

```
Router#show mpls forwarding-table
Tag switching is not operational.
CEF or tag switching has not been enabled.
Local   Outgoing   Prefix        Bytes tag  Outgoing   Next Hop
tag     tag or VC  or Tunnel Id  switched   interface
```

- Is MPLS enabled on all interfaces?

   When you have verified the overall MPLS status on a LSR, you should check the MPLS status of individual interfaces with the **show mpls interface** command, which produces printout similar to the one in Example 9-9.

Example 9-9   *show mpls interface Printout*

```
Router#show mpls interfaces
Interface      IP    Tunnel   Operational
Serial0/0.1    Yes   No       Yes
Serial0/0.2    Yes   No       Yes
Serial0/0.5    Yes   No       Yes
```

The **show mpls interface** printout indicates whether MPLS has been configured on an interface (the **IP** column) and whether it is operational (the **Operational** column). New IOS releases with LDP support display the LDP configured (TDP or LDP) on the interface in the **IP** column.

NOTE   The **show mpls interface** command displays only the interfaces on which MPLS has been configured.

For proper and secure MPLS operation in your network, enable MPLS on all links between your core routers and disable it on all links that connect your core routers to insecure devices (external networks or customer routers)—unless, of course, you have deployed the Carrier's Carrier solution.

NOTE   MPLS is always operational on frame-mode MPLS interfaces that do not support per-protocol negotiation between adjacent routers (such as LAN interfaces, Frame Relay links, or HDLC links). A router indicates that MPLS is not operational over a PPP link if the MPLS-specific LCP is not negotiated successfully. Similarly, a router marks an ATM interface in LC-ATM mode where the LDP has not been started as nonoperational.

MPLS Control Plane Troubleshooting

If the quick checks have not discovered obvious problems, it is time to go into in-depth troubleshooting. Start with the control plane troubleshooting first because the data plane does not work properly until the labels are exchanged between adjacent LSRs through the control plane protocols (Tag Distribution Protocol [TDP] or LDP). The control plane operation is displayed in Figure 9-2.

Figure 9-2   *Control Plane Operations in an LSR*

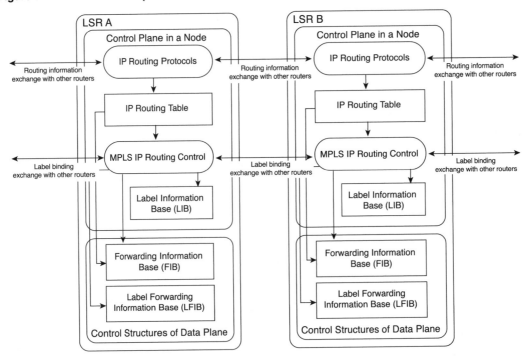

Control plane troubleshooting is focused primarily on the presence of TDP/LDP sessions between adjacent routers and the exchange of labels. In-depth troubleshooting of TDP/LDP operation and label exchange is usually a result of software error and is best left to Cisco Systems engineers.

Verify Local TDP/LDP Parameters

Start the control plane troubleshooting by verifying the TDP/LDP settings of the local router with the **show tag-switching tdp parameters** (for TDP) or **show mpls ldp parameters** (for LDP). These commands result in a printout similar to the one shown in Example 9-10. Parameters in your printout should not deviate too much from the ones in Example 9-10 unless you have manually changed TDP settings.

Example 9-10 *show tag-switching tdp parameters Printout*

```
Router#show tag-switching tdp parameters
 Protocol version: 1
 Downstream tag pool: min tag: 16; max_tag: 100000
 Session hold time: 180 sec; keep alive interval: 60 sec
 Discovery hello: holdtime: 15 sec; interval: 5 sec
 Discovery directed hello: holdtime: 180 sec; interval: 5 sec
```

NOTE   Most commonly, a mismatch in TDP hello and hold timers between adjacent LSRs causes TDP failures (detailed in the next section). In large networks or in stress-test environments, where a single LSR must allocate more than 100,000 labels (such as an asynchronous system boundary router connecting two MPLS VPN networks), you must change the maximum label with the **mpls label range** configuration command.

Verify Correct Operation of TDP/LDP Hello Protocol

Next, check the correct operation of the TDP/LDP hello protocol with the **show tag-switching tdp discovery** or **show mpls ldp discovery** commands. These commands display all MPLS-enabled interfaces and the neighbors present on them in a printout similar to the one in Example 9-11.

Example 9-11 *show tag-switching tdp discovery Printout*

```
Router#show tag-switching tdp discovery
Local TDP Identifier:
    192.168.3.5:0
TDP Discovery Sources:
    Interfaces:
        Serial0/0.1: xmit
        Serial0/0.2: xmit/recv
            TDP Id: 192.168.3.3:0
```

The printout should display at least one TDP/LDP neighbor being present through each MPLS-enabled interface. MPLS-enabled interfaces that have no neighbors present on them (like the Serial0/0.1 interface in the previous printout) indicate faulty MPLS operation. The command printout displays only the keyword **xmit** next to interfaces that have no MPLS neighbors.

The TDP/LDP hello protocol might not discover adjacent LSRs for several reasons, but the following ones occur most commonly:

- MPLS is not configured on the adjacent LSR or on the connecting interface in the adjacent LSR. Perform the quick checks from the previous section on the adjacent LSR.

- There is a protocol mismatch between adjacent LSRs. For example, one of the LSRs might support only TDP, whereas the other supports only LDP. It is also possible that one end of the link has been configured for TDP operation, whereas the other end has been configured for LDP operation. If your LSR is running IOS release 12.0ST, 12.2T, or 12.3 or greater, you can make it bilingual with the **mpls label protocol both** interface configuration command.

- An access list is blocking incoming UDP packets from adjacent LSRs. Check for the presence of access lists with the **show ip interface** command and verify their content with the **show access-list** command.

NOTE   After you have verified that your LSR can see adjacent LSRs, you must perform the same tests on all adjacent LSRs. TDP or LDP sessions start only after both LSRs can see each other.

Sometimes you will encounter an even stranger symptom: Your LSR detects the adjacent LSR but claims there is no route to the adjacent LSR, as shown in Example 9-12.

Example 9-12   *show tag-switching tdp discovery Printout with No Route to the Adjacent LSR*

```
Router#show tag-switching tdp discovery
Local TDP Identifier:
    192.168.3.3:0
TDP Discovery Sources:
    Interfaces:
        Serial0/0.1: xmit/recv
            TDP Id: 192.168.3.5:0
        Serial0/0.2: xmit
        Serial0/0.5: xmit/recv
            TDP Id: 192.168.3.2:0; no route
```

The explanation for this behavior is simple. As you might remember from Chapter 2, "Frame-Mode MPLS Operation," in Volume 1 of *MPLS and VPN Architectures*, the TDP or LDP sessions are run between *TDP identifiers* of the adjacent LSRs (usually the IP addresses of the loopback interfaces). These IP addresses must be reachable from the adjacent LSRs; otherwise, the TCP session cannot be established. In our printout, the IP address 192.168.3.2 (the TDP identifier of LSR reachable through the interface Serial0/0.5) is not reachable by the local router. To fix this error, inspect your routing protocol configurations and ensure that the IP addresses used for TDP identifiers are announced to adjacent LSRs. For more details, please refer to Chapter 2 of *MPLS and VPN Architectures, Volume 1*.

Check TDP/LDP Sessions

With the adjacent LSRs successfully exchanging the TDP/LDP hello packets, the TDP/
LDP session should start immediately. To verify the state of the TDP sessions, use the **show
tag-switching tdp neighbor** command. Similarly, use the **show mpls ldp neighbor**
command to verify the state of LDP sessions.

NOTE   The **show mpls ldp** commands are available only in Cisco IOS releases that support LDP
(IOS releases 12.0ST, 12.2T, and all mainstream releases starting with IOS release 12.3).
In these releases, the **show mpls ldp** commands also display the state of the TDP sessions
or neighbors.

The **show tag-switching tdp neighbor** command produces printout similar to that shown
in Example 9-13. In this command, you should see TDP/LDP sessions being established
with all neighbors displayed in the **show tag-switching tdp discovery** printout.

Example 9-13 *show tag-switching tdp discovery Printout*

```
Router#show tag-switching tdp neighbor
Peer TDP Ident: 192.168.3.5:0; Local TDP Ident 192.168.3.3:0
        TCP connection: 192.168.3.5.11002 - 192.168.3.3.711
        State: Oper; PIEs sent/rcvd: 83/47; ; Downstream
        Up time: 00:37:52
        TDP discovery sources:
          Serial0/0.1
        Addresses bound to peer TDP Ident:
          192.168.3.17    192.168.3.14    192.168.3.5
Peer TDP Ident: 192.168.3.2:0; Local TDP Ident 192.168.3.3:0
        TCP connection: 192.168.3.2.711 - 192.168.3.3.11001
        State: Oper; PIEs sent/rcvd: 4/4; ; Downstream
        Up time: 00:00:24
        TDP discovery sources:
          Serial0/0.5
        Addresses bound to peer TDP Ident:
          192.168.22.3    192.168.3.18    192.168.3.21    150.1.31.5
          150.1.32.1      192.168.3.26    192.168.3.2
```

The **show tag-switching tdp neighbor** command displays the details of the TCP
connection between the adjacent LSRs, the status of the TDP/LDP session (the established
session is indicated with the *State: Oper* printout), the interfaces through which the adjacent
LSR is reachable (displayed in the *TDP discovery sources* section of the printout), and the
IP addresses configured on the adjacent LSR (shown in the *Addresses bound to peer TDP
Ident* section).

There are only a few reasons why the TDP or LDP session between adjacent LSRs would not start after the neighbor had been discovered through the TDP or LDP hello protocol:

- There is no route to the TDP/LDP identifier of the adjacent LSR.

- An incoming access list is blocking TCP packets.

See the previous section for more details on solving these problems.

Check the Label Exchange

After you have verified that the TDP or LDP sessions exist between adjacent LSRs, check whether the LSRs have assigned labels to the IP prefixes under consideration. The command to display the label information base (LIB) is the **show tag-switching tdp bindings** or **show mpls ldp bindings** command (depending on the IOS release you are using). These commands display the labels that the local LSR and all adjacent LSRs assign to a specified IP prefix (or all IP prefixes), as shown in Example 9-14.

NOTE   The **show tag-switching tdp bindings** command displays only the labels assigned to IP prefixes by local and adjacent LSRs—it does not display the labels actually used in MPLS labeled datagram forwarding.

Example 9-14 *show tag-switching tdp bindings Printout*

```
Router#show tag-switching tdp bindings 192.168.3.1 32
  tib entry: 192.168.3.1 255.255.255.255, rev 14
      local binding:  tag: 21
      remote binding: tsr: 192.168.3.2:0, tag: 23
      remote binding: tsr: 192.168.3.3:0, tag: 21
```

NOTE   LSRs that use *independent control* label assignment, including all Cisco routers, should assign a label to any IP prefix, except those learned through use of BGP. LSRs that use *ordered control* label assignment, including most Cisco ATM switches, should assign labels only when asked to do so by the upstream neighbors (downstream-on-demand label allocation). Please refer to Chapter 2 of *MPLS and VPN Architectures, Volume 1* for more details on label assignment modes.

In any case, the label that the next-hop LSR assigns should be visible in the local LIB; otherwise, you will not have end-to-end MPLS forwarding.

You should follow two paths of investigation when the LIB contents do not match your expectations:

- LSRs assign labels only to non-BGP prefixes in their IP routing table. If the next-hop LSR has not provided a label to a prefix in the IP routing table of the local LSR, it might be because the next-hop LSR has a different prefix in its IP routing table (possibly due to route summarization).

- Label distribution is further filtered with an access list specified with the **tag-switching advertise-tag** command. If the downstream LSR is using a misconfigured label advertising access list, the LSR under inspection will not receive a label although it was assigned (but not distributed) by the downstream LSR. A good method to catch this symptom is to inspect the output of the **show mpls forwarding-table** command (a sample printout is available in Example 9-6), looking for *untagged* outgoing labels for destinations that are reachable through downstream P routers.

MPLS Data Plane Troubleshooting

With the MPLS control plane working properly, the MPLS data plane should work without further troubleshooting. There are, however, two cases in which the MPLS operation on the data plane might be affected:

- CEF switching might not be functional on individual interfaces.
- Non-MPLS devices in the forwarding path might affect propagation of labeled packets.

Monitoring Interface-Level CEF

Configuring CEF on the LSR does not guarantee that the CEF switching will be performed on all interfaces. For example, you can disable CEF switching on an individual physical interface with the **no ip route-cache cef** interface configuration command. You can verify proper CEF operation on an individual interface with the **show cef interface** command. Proper CEF operation is indicated with a printout similar to the one in Example 9-15. (The critical line in the printout is highlighted.)

Example 9-15 *show cef interface Printout*

```
Router#show cef interface serial 0/0
Serial0/0 is up (if_number 4)
  Corresponding hwidb fast_if_number 11
  Corresponding hwidb firstsw->if_number 4
  Internet Protocol processing disabled
  Hardware idb is Serial0/0
  Fast switching type 5, interface type 56
  IP CEF switching enabled
  IP CEF Feature Fast switching turbo vector
  Input fast flags 0x1, Output fast flags 0x0
  ifindex 2(2)
  Slot 0 Slot unit 0 VC -1
  Transmit limit accumulator 0x0 (0x0)
  IP MTU 1500
```

CEF might be configured on an interface but not be operational if the interface uses an encapsulation method that CEF does not support (for example, in Cisco IOS release 12.2, CEF is not enabled on Ethernet subinterfaces that have 802.1q encapsulation) or if you have configured another IOS feature on the interface that is not compatible with CEF (such as generic traffic shaping).

NOTE
Interface-level CEF switching is needed only on ingress interfaces that receive IP packets on which the ingress LSR performs the label imposition process. CEF switching is not needed to forward labeled packets or to forward unlabeled IP packets.

Oversized Packet Issues

Another common data plane problem has nothing to do with the LSRs but with the Layer 2 devices inserted between them (most commonly LAN switches). The MPLS label imposition process increases the size of an IP packet by 4 bytes per label imposed. The resulting packet might be too large for the physical media it must traverse, resulting in a need for packet fragmentation. For example, a 1500-byte packet with three labels results in a 1530 byte Ethernet frame (12 bytes for the labels and 18 bytes for the Ethernet header/ trailer). However, not all applications support packet fragmentation and reassembly (for example, Path MTU discovery fails when performed over poorly configured firewalls), forcing the network designer to extend the maximum length of the packet on the physical media. This action might, on the other hand, adversely impact the operation of some LAN switches that do not support large frames (also called *giant frames*).

NOTE
Some equipment manufacturers refer to frames only slightly larger than the maximum frame size specified in the Ethernet standards as *baby giants*.

The labeled packet size issue usually affects only the forwarding of large packets, resulting in an interesting symptom: The **ping** command works between the two endpoints, but the applications cannot pass useful data. To test for the presence of this symptom, perform the extended **ping** from the ingress to the egress router with varying packet sizes. If the **ping** command displays packet loss at packet sizes, you probably have an LSR that does not support full-size IP packets with imposed labels or a Layer 2 device that does not support giant frames in the forwarding path.

NOTE
Please refer to Example 9-16 for a sample troubleshooting session.

MPLS VPN Troubleshooting

Contrary to MPLS, which is simple to configure and troubleshoot, MPLS VPN technology encompasses a number of underlying concepts and technologies, ranging from various routing protocols (such as Routing Information Protocol [RIP], Open Shortest Path First [OSPF], and Border Gateway Protocol [BGP]) to complex routing designs, including controlled two-way redistribution between routing protocols, usually controlled with **access-lists** or **route-maps**.

This section focuses exclusively on the MPLS VPN-specific troubleshooting topics. You can find an in-depth discussion of the underlying technologies in a number of Cisco Press books, including these:

- *Advanced IP Network Design* by Don Slice, Russ White, and Alvaro Retana (ISBN: 1578700973)

- *Routing TCP/IP, Volume I* and *Routing TCP/IP, Volume II* by Jeff Doyle (ISBN: 1578700418 and 1578700892)

- *Internet Routing Architectures* by Sam Halabi (ISBN: 157870233X)

- *Large-Scale IP Network Solutions* by Khalid Raza and Mark Turner (ISBN: 1578700841)

- *Building Scalable Cisco Networks* by Catherine Paquet and Diane Teare (ISBN: 1578702283)

MPLS VPN troubleshooting sometimes involves in-depth troubleshooting of the routing protocols deployed between the PE routers and CE routers. Various routing protocols supported between PE routers and CE routers are discussed in the following Cisco Press books:

- RIP in *Routing TCP/IP, Volume I* and *Routing TCP/IP, Volume II* by Jeff Doyle (ISBN: 1578700418 and 1578700892)

- BGP in *Internet Routing Architectures* by Sam Halabi (ISBN: 157870233X)

- OSPF in *OSPF Network Design Solutions* by Thomas M. Thomas (ISBN: 1578700469)

- EIGRP in *EIGRP Network Design Solutions* by Ivan Pepelnjak (ISBN: 1578701651)

- IS-IS in *IS-IS Network Design Solutions* by Abe Martey (ISBN: 1578702208)

NOTE   These references are provided solely for your convenience and do not necessarily represent an endorsement by the authors of this book.

This chapter uses a simple MPLS VPN network having just one customer with two CE routers and three PE routers (one acting as a route reflector), shown in Figure 9-3.

Figure 9-3 *Sample MPLS VPN Network*

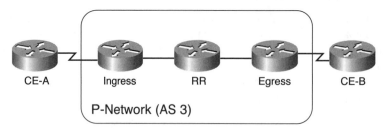

Quick MPLS VPN Checks

As always, you should start your troubleshooting efforts with a few quick checks to verify that you are using the right tools to troubleshoot the problem.

Following are the quick checks in the MPLS VPN case:

- Can you ping between CE routers?
- Is there an end-to-end LSP between ingress and egress PE routers?
- Is CEF enabled on PE-CE interfaces?

NOTE   The end-to-end LSP test was covered in the "Verifying End-to-End LSP" section earlier in this chapter.

When these quick checks fail to resolve your problem, it is time for more in-depth MPLS VPN troubleshooting.

Pinging Between the CE Routers

The first check you should always perform is the connectivity check between the CE routers. Many problems reported to be network problems turn out to be end host, application software, or even end user problems.

The simplest connectivity check is the **ping** from the ingress CE router to the egress CE router. However, even this well-proven method can fail in interesting ways in an MPLS VPN environment. Some MPLS VPN networks do not propagate PE-CE circuit subnets to other sites either by design or by omission. In these networks, the simple **ping** from a CE router to another CE router always fails. The packets that the pinging router sends use the IP interface configured on the CE-PE link as the source IP address, and the pinged router has no return path.

NOTE	The question "Should the PE-CE circuit subnets be included in the VPN routing?" has no clear answer. Intuitively, the answer would be "yes," but some designs do not include these subnets in VPN routing for good reasons. If you think the PE-CE subnets should be part of VPN routing but they are not propagated between PE routers, you have probably forgotten to configure **redistribute connected** in the VRF address family configuration within the BGP routing process.

The proper way of using **ping** in the MPLS VPN environment is the extended **ping** using the IP address configured on the LAN interface of the CE router as the source IP address. If this **ping** works, the MPLS VPN network is probably working correctly. However, to ensure that the user applications do not encounter unexpected problems, you should always perform the extended ping with various packet sizes to verify that there are no hidden problems related to IP packet fragmentation within the provider backbone. As discussed previously in this chapter, the label imposition process increases the size of an IP packet. The resulting packet might be too large for the physical media it needs to traverse, resulting in a need for packet fragmentation, which might fail for various reasons (including incorrect operation of Path MTU discovery due to misconfigured **access-lists**).

It is easy to check for this condition through the extended **ping** with varying packet sizes performed on the CE router. Start the extended **ping** on the ingress CE router and specify the following parameters (as shown in Example 9-16):

- Source address is the IP address of the LAN interface on the CE router.
- The Don't Fragment bit is set (to prevent fragmentation in the MPLS VPN network to interfere with the test).
- Packet sizes vary from MTU size minus 32 bytes (8 labels in label stack — a condition you should almost never encounter) to the MTU size (1500 bytes in most networks).

If the extended **ping** starts losing packets as you near the MTU size, you have to check the MTU sizes in your MPLS VPN network and the *giant* frame support on your LAN switches, as detailed in previous sections of this chapter.

In Example 9-16, the responses stopped coming back at packet size 1497 (1480 plus 17 successful responses), indicating that the network cannot propagate labeled packets larger than 1500 bytes (1496 bytes of IP payload plus one label in the label stack).

Example 9-16 *Extended PING with Sweeping Packet Sizes*

```
CE-A#ping
Protocol [ip]:
Target IP address: 203.1.0.1
Repeat count [5]: 1
Datagram size [100]:
Timeout in seconds [2]:
Extended commands [n]: y
```

continues

Example 9-16 *Extended PING with Sweeping Packet Sizes (Continued)*

```
Source address or interface: 203.1.4.1
Type of service [0]:
Set DF bit in IP header? [no]: y
Validate reply data? [no]:
Data pattern [0xABCD]:
Loose, Strict, Record, Timestamp, Verbose[none]:
Sweep range of sizes [n]: y
Sweep min size [36]: 1480
Sweep max size [18024]: 1500
Sweep interval [1]:
Type escape sequence to abort.
Sending 21, [1480..1500]-byte ICMP Echos to 203.1.0.1, timeout is 10 seconds:
!!!!!!!!!!!!!!!!!!!M.M.
Success rate is 80 percent (17/21), round-trip min/avg/max = 448/457/471 ms
```

Check for CEF Switching

Similar to pure MPLS operation, in most IOS releases, MPLS VPN relies on CEF switching
of packets received from the CE router by the PE router. CEF must be configured on the PE
router (which is usually not an issue because MPLS would not work otherwise) as well as
on individual PE-CE interfaces. You can verify proper CEF operation on an individual
interface with the **show cef interface** command. Proper CEF operation is indicated with a
printout similar to Example 9-17. (The critical line in the printout is highlighted.)

Example 9-17 *show cef interface Printout*

```
Router#show cef interface serial 0/0
Serial0/0 is up (if_number 4)
  Corresponding hwidb fast_if_number 11
  Corresponding hwidb firstsw->if_number 4
  Internet Protocol processing disabled
  Hardware idb is Serial0/0
  Fast switching type 5, interface type 56
  IP CEF switching enabled
  IP CEF Feature Fast switching turbo vector
  Input fast flags 0x1, Output fast flags 0x0
  ifindex 2(2)
  Slot 0 Slot unit 0 VC -1
  Transmit limit accumulator 0x0 (0x0)
  IP MTU 1500
```

Sometimes CEF is configured on an interface but is not operational because the interface
uses an encapsulation method that CEF does not support or because you have configured
another IOS feature on the interface that is incompatible with CEF. A common example in
the MPLS VPN environment includes configuring generic traffic shaping (GTS) on the PE-
CE interface because this feature is incompatible with CEF switching.

In-Depth MPLS VPN Troubleshooting

In-depth MPLS VPN troubleshooting is usually performed exclusively on the control plane. The few MPLS VPN-specific errors that can occur on the data plane are almost always a result of a software bug and are best left to the Cisco Systems engineers.

To understand the steps in MPLS VPN troubleshooting, it is worth re-examining the steps that an IP prefix undertakes as it is propagated from the egress CE router to the ingress CE router, as shown in Figure 9-4.

NOTE   You might be confused by the claim that the IP prefix is propagated from the egress CE router to the ingress CE router. However, you must remember that the IP prefixes are propagated in the opposite direction of the data flow (always from downstream toward upstream routers). The egress CE router must announce its IP prefixes to the ingress CE router to enable the packet flow in the opposite direction.

Figure 9-4   *Route Propagation Across MPLS VPN Network*

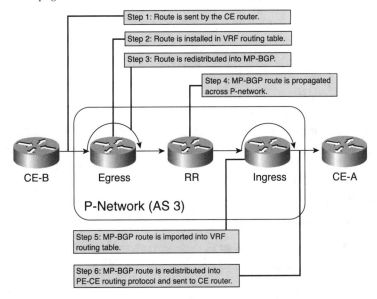

The following steps are needed to transport an IP prefix across the MPLS VPN backbone:

Step 1   The egress CE router sends the prefix to the PE router through a CE-PE routing protocol. Alternatively, the prefix is configured statically on the PE router.

Step 2   The PE router installs the prefix into one or more VRF routing tables.

Step 3 The IP prefix is redistributed from the routing table into the MP-BGP table. In this process, the IP prefix is prepended with the route distinguisher. Various BGP attributes, including extended community route target (RT), are attached to the MP-BGP route.

Step 4 The MP-BGP prefix is propagated across the MPLS VPN network.

Step 5 Best MP-BGP prefixes received by Ingress PE router are installed in VRF routing tables configured on the PE router based on the RT attached to the MP-BGP prefix and the RT configured for import in the VRF.

Step 6 Prefixes from the VRF routing table are redistributed into the PE-CE routing protocol and propagated to the ingress CE router.

Based on the process of propagating IP prefixes between customer sites, the MPLS VPN troubleshooting should follow these major steps:

Step 1 Check the CE-PE routing exchange.

Step 2 Check the route export functionality.

Step 3 Check the propagation of MPLS VPN routes.

Step 4 Check the route import functionality.

Step 5 Check the PE-CE routing exchange.

Egress CE-PE Routing Exchange

The egress CE-PE routing exchange is verified by using the **show ip route vrf** *protocol* command on the egress PE router, where *protocol* stands for the PE-CE routing protocol used in the VRF under observation. (A sample printout is included in Example 9-18.) Verify that the route to the customer LAN is present in the VRF routing table and that it points to the expected outgoing interface and next-hop.

Example 9-18 *VRF Routing Table on a PE Router*

```
PE4#show ip route vrf vpna rip
R      203.1.4.0 255.255.255.0 [120/1] via 150.1.31.18, 00:00:24, Serial0/0.100
       203.1.0.0 255.255.255.255 is subnetted, 4 subnets
R         203.1.0.4 [120/1] via 150.1.31.18, 00:00:24, Serial0/0.100
```

If you do not see the customer route in the VRF routing table, check the PE-CE routing protocol configuration on both PE and CE routers. The best command to use is the **show ip protocols [vrf** *name*] command that displays the actual settings of the routing protocols in a VRF. The sample printout in Example 9-19, taken from the egress PE router, shows the following:

1 RIP is running in the VRF vpna.

2 RIP is redistributed into BGP.

3 RIP is running on interface Serial0/0.100 (interface toward the CE router).

4 RIP version 2 is running.

5 The RIP routing protocol is receiving updates from IP address 150.1.31.18 (CE router).

Example 9-19 *show ip protocols Printout on the Egress PE Router*

```
Egress#show ip protocols vrf vpna
Routing Protocol is "rip" (1)
  Sending updates every 30 seconds, next due in 24 seconds
  Invalid after 180 seconds, hold down 180, flushed after 240
  Outgoing update filter list for all interfaces is not set
  Incoming update filter list for all interfaces is not set
  Redistributing: rip, bgp 3(2)
  Default version control: send version 2, receive version 2
    Interface          Send  Recv  Triggered RIP  Key-chain
    Serial0/0.100(3)     2     2(4)
  Maximum path: 4
  Routing for Networks:
    150.1.0.0
  Routing Information Sources:
    Gateway       Distance      Last Update
    150.1.31.18(5)      120      00:00:22
  Distance: (default is 120)
```

Some of the most common mistakes that you can find in this troubleshooting step (apart from the usual routing protocol configuration errors) include the following:

- The PE-CE routing protocol is not configured. (The operator configured the global routing protocol, not the VRF routing protocol.)

- RIP version 1 is running in the VRF. RIP version 1 is not supported in MPLS VPN environments.

- Auto-summary is configured in the routing protocol. Customers who have migrated to MPLS VPN environments usually have discontiguous subnets that require routing protocol auto-summarization to be turned off.

- OSPF routes are received from the CE router with the down bit set because another PE router redistributed them into OSPF.

- Customer BGP routes are ignored because they are propagated between customer sites that use the same BGP autonomous system number.

In this step, you might also notice undesired behavior of multihomed customer sites that use routing protocols other than BGP. These sites might receive MPLS VPN routes from one PE router and send them to another PE router, as shown in Figure 9-5. Because the CE routes always take precedence over IBGP routes exchanged between PE routers (administrative distance of internal BGP is 200), transit traffic flows over a multihomed customer site. Clearly, this is undesired behavior because the customer sites in an MPLS VPN solution should not act as transit points. An example of such a setup is displayed in Figure 9-5.

Figure 9-5   *Transit Traffic Passing Through a Customer Site*

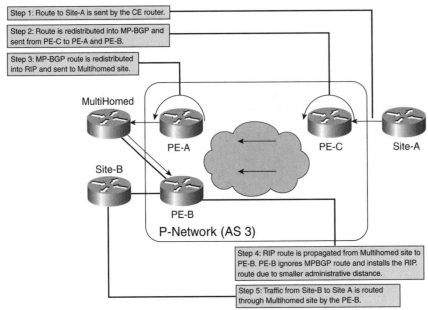

The following sequence of events occurs in the sample network:

1 Site-A sends its routes to PE-C.

2 The routes from Site-A are redistributed into MP-BGP and propagated to PE-A and PE-B. Both PE routers install the MP-BGP route into their VRF routing tables. Traffic flow from Site-B to Site-A is optimal.

3 The MP-BGP route is redistributed into RIP on PE-A and propagated to the multihomed site.

4 The multihomed site forwards the received RIP route to its other neighbor, PE-B. At this moment, PE-B has two routes available toward Site-A: Internal MP-BGP route with administrative distance 200, and RIP route with administrative distance 120. Therefore, PE-B installs the RIP route into its VRF routing table and ignores the MP-BGP route it receives from PE-C.

5 Traffic flow from Site-B to Site-A is no longer optimal because it follows the route PE-B ➠ multihomed ➠ PE-A ➠ PE-C ➠ Site-A.

NOTE   The easiest fix to the problem illustrated in Figure 9-5 is a consistent deployment of BGP on all multihomed sites. Most other solutions involve changing the administrative distance of individual routing protocols or even individual routes within a routing protocol and should be avoided.

Route Export

When you have verified that the egress PE router has received the route from the CE router (and that you have fixed potential errors), verify that the route received from the CE router is redistributed into BGP by using the **show ip route vrf** *name prefix* command, as shown in Example 9-20. The most important line in the printout is the *Advertised by bgp* line indicating that the customer's IP prefix is indeed advertised by MP-BGP.

NOTE	One of the most common MPLS VPN configuration mistakes is the omission of route redistribution into BGP, without which the connectivity between PE routers cannot be established.

Example 9-20 *Detailed show ip route Printout on PE Router*

```
Egress#show ip route vrf vpna 203.1.4.0
Routing entry for 203.1.4.0 255.255.255.0
  Known via "rip", distance 120, metric 1
  Redistributing via rip, bgp 3
  Advertised by bgp 3
  Last update from 150.1.31.18 on Serial0/0.100, 00:00:20 ago
  Routing Descriptor Blocks:
  * 150.1.31.18, from 150.1.31.18, 00:00:20 ago, via Serial0/0.100
      Route metric is 1, traffic share count is 1
```

After you verify that the customer route is redistributed into MP-BGP, verify the route distinguisher and RT attached to the customer route with the **show ip bgp vpnv4 vrf** *name prefix* command shown in Example 9-21. The route distinguisher value is shown in the *BGP routing table entry for* line, and the RT is shown in the *Extended Community* line.

Example 9-21 *BGP Prefix in Egress PE Router*

```
Egress#show ip bgp vpnv4 vrf vpna 203.1.4.0
BGP routing table entry for 3:10:203.1.4.0/24, version 9
Paths: (1 available, best #1, table vpna)
  Advertised to non peer-group peers:
  192.168.3.3
  Local
    150.1.31.18 from 0.0.0.0 (192.168.3.4)
      Origin incomplete, metric 1, localpref 100, weight 32768, valid, sourced,
best
      Extended Community: RT:3:10
```

If you get unexpected route distinguisher or RT values, check the VRF configuration with the **show ip vrf detail** command, which results in a printout similar to Example 9-22.

Example 9-22 *VRF Definition on Egress Router Shows Export Route Map*

```
Egress#show ip vrf detail
VRF vpna; default RD 3:10
  Interfaces:
    Serial0/0.100
  Connected addresses are not in global routing table
  Export VPN route-target communities
    RT:3:10
  Import VPN route-target communities
    RT:3:10
  No import route-map
  Export route-map: SetRT
```

Another common source of unexpected RT values is the export route maps, where users tend to forget the **additive** keyword in the **set extcommunity** command. For example, a route map shown in Example 9-23 erases the route target 3:10 from a matching prefix when used in the VRF *vpna* on *egress* PE router and replaces it with route target 3:22, as displayed in Example 9-24.

Example 9-23 *Export Route Map Used on Egress Router*

```
route-map SetRT permit 10
 match ip address prefix-list SetRT
 set extcommunity rt  3:22
```

Example 9-24 *Default VRF Community Is Lost Due to Export Route Map*

```
PE4#show ip bgp vpnv4 vrf vpna 203.1.0.4
BGP routing table entry for 3:10:203.1.0.4/32, version 33
Paths: (1 available, best #1, table vpna)
  Advertised to non peer-group peers:
  192.168.3.3
  Local
    150.1.31.18 from 0.0.0.0 (192.168.3.4)
      Origin incomplete, metric 1, localpref 100, weight 32768, valid, sourced,
best
      Extended Community: RT:3:22
```

Propagation of MPLS VPN Routes

The routes that the egress PE router redistributes into MP-BGP need to be propagated to the ingress PE router. Verify that the ingress PE router receives the BGP route with the **show ip bgp vpnv4 rd** *target prefix* command, a sample of which is shown in Example 9-25.

Example 9-25 *MP-BGP Route Received from Egress Router*

```
Ingress#show ip bgp vpnv4 rd 3:10 203.1.4.0
BGP routing table entry for 3:10:203.1.4.0/24, version 21
Paths: (1 available, best #1, table vpna)
  Not advertised to any peer
  Local
    192.168.3.2 (metric 10) from 192.168.3.2 (192.168.3.2)
      Origin incomplete, metric 3, localpref 100, valid, internal, best
      Extended Community: RT:3:10
```

An MP-BGP route might not be propagated from the *egress* to *ingress* PE router for several reasons:

- A VPNv4 session between the PE routers has not been activated. Verify that the VPNv4 sessions are active with the **show ip bgp neighbor** command, which results in a printout similar to the one in Example 9-26.

Example 9-26 *BGP Session Established with Another PE Router*

```
Ingress#show ip bgp neighbor 192.168.3.2
BGP neighbor is 192.168.3.2,  remote AS 3, internal link
  BGP version 4, remote router ID 192.168.3.2
  BGP state = Established, up for 00:41:40
  Last read 00:00:40, hold time is 180, keepalive interval is 60 seconds
  Neighbor capabilities:
    Route refresh: advertised and received(new)
    Address family IPv4 Unicast: advertised and received
    Address family VPNv4 Unicast: advertised and received
  Received 60 messages, 0 notifications, 0 in queue
  Sent 51 messages, 0 notifications, 0 in queue
  Route refresh request: received 0, sent 0
  Default minimum time between advertisement runs is 5 seconds
```

- VPNv4 sessions might be active, but the route reflector clients have not been configured on the VPNv4 sessions. (The route reflector clients must be configured separately for each address family.) Verify the proper route reflector client configuration on the route reflector with the **show ip bgp neighbor** command. Focus on the information displayed about the VPNv4 address family, as shown in Example 9-27.

Example 9-27 *BGP Route Reflector Client Configured on VPNv4 Session*

```
RR#show ip bgp neighbor 192.168.3.1
BGP neighbor is 192.168.3.1,  remote AS 3, internal link
  BGP version 4, remote router ID 192.168.3.1
  BGP state = Established, up for 00:44:11
  Last read 00:00:10, hold time is 180, keepalive interval is 60 seconds
  Neighbor capabilities:
    Route refresh: advertised and received(new)
    Address family IPv4 Unicast: advertised and received
    Address family VPNv4 Unicast: advertised and received
  Received 54 messages, 0 notifications, 0 in queue
  Sent 63 messages, 0 notifications, 0 in queue
  Route refresh request: received 0, sent 0
  Default minimum time between advertisement runs is 5 seconds

[... part of the printout deleted ...]

 For address family: VPNv4 Unicast
  BGP table version 41, neighbor version 41
  Index 1, Offset 0, Mask 0x2
  Route-Reflector Client
  3 accepted prefixes consume 180 bytes
  Prefix advertised 24, suppressed 0, withdrawn 0
  Number of NLRIs in the update sent: max 4, min 0
```

continues

Example 9-27 *BGP Route Reflector Client Configured on VPNv4 Session (Continued)*

```
Connections established 1; dropped 0
Last reset never
```

- The PE router might drop an MP-BGP route if it has no matching route target. (None of the route targets attached to the route are configured in a VRF.) In this case, verify the VRF settings with the **show ip vrf detail** command.

Route Import

The best MP-BGP route that a remote PE router receives is imported into the VRF routing table (assuming there is a match in route targets configured in the VRF and route targets attached to the route). Verify that the route is inserted into the VRF routing table with the **show ip route vrf** *name prefix* command, as shown in Example 9-28.

NOTE   In complex environments that have multihomed customer sites, a PE router might receive more than one MP-BGP route toward the same destination. In these cases, standard BGP route selection rules determine which route is the best route (regardless of route targets attached to the route). You can use any BGP attribute to influence the route selection process; however, you are advised not to use the MED attribute if you redistribute BGP routes into RIP or OSPF because the RIP/OSPF metric of the redistributed route is taken from the MED attribute.

Example 9-28 *MP-BGP Route Inserted in the VRF Routing Table*

```
Ingress#show ip route vrf vpna 203.1.4.0
Routing entry for 203.1.4.0 255.255.255.0
  Known via "bgp 3", distance 200, metric 3, type internal
  Redistributing via rip
  Advertised by rip metric transparent
  Last update from 192.168.3.2 00:14:42 ago
  Routing Descriptor Blocks:
  * 192.168.3.2 (Default-IP-Routing-Table), from 192.168.3.2, 00:14:42 ago
      Route metric is 3, traffic share count is 1
      AS Hops 0
```

There are three main reasons that a route the ingress PE router receives is not imported into the VRF:

- Mismatch in route targets, which can be verified easily with the **show ip vrf detail** command.
- Misconfigured **import map**. The printout shown in Example 9-29 includes a sample configuration error where the VRF refers a nonexistent route map. As you can see in the printout, the MP-BGP route is received by the *ingress* PE router but not inserted into the VRF routing table. Further investigation reveals that the **route-map** that the **import map** command refers to does not exist.

- Maximum VRF route limit has been exceeded.

Example 9-29 *MP-BGP Route Not Inserted Due to Import Map Configuration Error*

```
Ingress#show ip bgp vpnv4 rd 3:10 203.1.4.0
BGP routing table entry for 3:10:203.1.4.0/24, version 67
Paths: (1 available, best #1, table NULL)
  Not advertised to any peer
  Local
    192.168.3.2 (metric 10) from 192.168.3.2 (192.168.3.2)
      Origin incomplete, metric 3, localpref 100, valid, internal, best
      Extended Community: RT:3:10
Ingress#show ip route vrf vpna
Codes: C - connected, S - static, I - IGRP, R - RIP, M - mobile, B - BGP
       D - EIGRP, EX - EIGRP external, O - OSPF, IA - OSPF inter area
       N1 - OSPF NSSA external type 1, N2 - OSPF NSSA external type 2
       E1 - OSPF external type 1, E2 - OSPF external type 2, E - EGP
       i - IS-IS, L1 - IS-IS level-1, L2 - IS-IS level-2, ia - IS-IS inter area
       * - candidate default, U - per-user static route, o - ODR
       P - periodic downloaded static route

Gateway of last resort is not set

R    203.1.1.0 255.255.255.0 [120/1] via 150.1.31.2, 00:00:01, Serial0/0.100
     203.1.0.0 255.255.255.255 is subnetted, 1 subnets
R       203.1.0.1 [120/1] via 150.1.31.2, 00:00:01, Serial0/0.100
     150.1.0.0 255.255.255.252 is subnetted, 1 subnets
C       150.1.31.0 is directly connected, Serial0/0.100
Ingress#show ip vrf detail
VRF vpna; default RD 3:10
  Interfaces:
    Serial0/0.100
  Connected addresses are not in global routing table
  Export VPN route-target communities
    RT:3:10
  Import VPN route-target communities
    RT:3:10
  Import route-map: NoSuchMap
  No export route-map
Ingress#show route-map NoSuchMap
route-map NoSuchMap not found
```

NOTE	Route import is a periodic process controlled by the **bgp scan-time import** parameter, which has a default value of 15 seconds. Therefore, there could be a 15-second gap between the time that the MP-BGP route is received and the time that it appears in the VRF routing table. Similarly, any configuration change takes effect within the next 15 seconds.

Redistribution of MPLS VPN Routes and Ingress PE-CE Routing Exchange

The last, but often misconfigured, part of the MPLS VPN route propagation process is the sending of the routes received via MP-BGP from remote customer sites to the CE router. Common configuration errors in this part include the following:

* Routes not being redistributed from MP-BGP into the PE-CE routing protocol
* Routes being redistributed with illegal metric

NOTE   A less common design error occurs in networks that use MED to propagate the IGP metric across the MP-BGP backbone. If you mix routing protocols in such a design (or manually change MED values), you could end up in a situation in which a route is not propagated to a RIP neighbor because the RIP hop count transferred from the BGP MED attribute is too high.

You can verify whether a route is redistributed from MP-BGP into the PE-CE routing protocol with the **show ip route vrf** *name prefix* command. A printout taken from the ingress router is included in Example 9-30.

Example 9-30 *MP-BGP Route Received from Another PE Router Is Not Advertised to CE Router*

```
Ingress#show ip route vrf vpna 203.1.4.0
Routing entry for 203.1.4.0 255.255.255.0
  Known via "bgp 3", distance 200, metric 3, type internal
  Redistributing via rip
  Last update from 192.168.3.2 00:16:00 ago
  Routing Descriptor Blocks:
  * 192.168.3.2 (Default-IP-Routing-Table), from 192.168.3.2, 00:16:00 ago
      Route metric is 3, traffic share count is 1
      AS Hops 0
```

In the **show ip route vrf** *name prefix* printout, check the following:

* Presence of *Redistributing via protocol* line, indicating that the MP-BGP route is redistributed into the PE-CE routing protocol
* Presence of *Advertised by protocol metric value* line, indicating that the route is actually announced to the CE router

In Example 9-30, the route is not advertised to the CE routers because it is redistributed from MP-BGP into RIP with the default metric value of 16, which equals RIP infinity (indicating unreachable route). After the PE router configuration is fixed, the PE router starts announcing the RIP route to the CE routers (see Example 9-31).

Example 9-31   *Route Is Advertised to the CE Router After the Redistribution Metric Is Fixed*

```
Ingress#conf t
Enter configuration commands, one per line.  End with CNTL/Z.
Ingress(config)#router rip
Ingress(config-router)#address-family ipv4 vrf vpna
Ingress(config-router-af)#redistribute bgp 3 metric 2
Ingress(config-router-af)#^Z
Ingress#
Ingress#show ip route vrf vpna 203.1.4.0
Routing entry for 203.1.4.0 255.255.255.0
  Known via "bgp 3", distance 200, metric 3, type internal
  Redistributing via rip
  Advertised by rip metric 2
  Last update from 192.168.3.2 00:16:47 ago
  Routing Descriptor Blocks:
  * 192.168.3.2 (Default-IP-Routing-Table), from 192.168.3.2, 00:16:47 ago
      Route metric is 3, traffic share count is 1
      AS Hops 0
```

Summary

In this chapter, you saw guidelines for troubleshooting MPLS-based solutions. Most of these solutions require an end-to-end LSP between routers at the edge of the P-network. Therefore, checking this LSP with a **trace** command in combination with disabled TTL propagation is always a good starting point. Should you find that the LSP works as expected, focus on the troubleshooting of the solution that is deployed on top of the MPLS backbone; otherwise, fix the MPLS backbone first.

Let's also conclude this chapter with a short note on the troubleshooting process itself. This chapter presented only one of the possible approaches to MPLS troubleshooting. You will, over time and based on your experience, probably find another approach that will give you quicker results based on errors you encounter most commonly in your network. For example, you might want to start with the end-to-end LSP check first, check for problems with large packet propagation next, and only then go to further troubleshooting steps. However, the distribution of common errors varies from one network to another; therefore it is impossible to give you a recipe that will be optimal in all circumstances.

The MPLS backbone troubleshooting should start with a few quick checks performed on all LSRs in your network:

- Is CEF switching enabled on the LSR?
- Is MPLS enabled on the LSR?
- Is MPLS enabled on all interfaces?

If these quick checks do not solve your problem, you have to go into control-plane trouble-shooting and perform the following checks:

- Are adjacent LSRs discovered through the TDP/LDP hello protocol?
- Do the LSRs have routes to the TDP/LDP identifier of the adjacent LSR?
- Is the TCP session established after the adjacent LSR is discovered?
- Are the labels exchanged between adjacent LSRs?

After you have verified that the control plane works correctly and that the TDP/LDP sessions are established and labels are exchanged, verify the correct operation of the MPLS data plane with the following checks:

- Is CEF operational on the ingress interface where the label imposition is performed on the IP packets?
- Is there an end-to-end LSP between the ingress and egress LSR?
- Does the problem you are troubleshooting affect only large packets?

In the MPLS VPN environment, the common errors include these:

- The reported problem is not really an MPLS VPN problem or even network problem, but an application or user problem.
- The MPLS backbone does not support a large enough MTU size.
- End-to-end LSP is broken between the ingress and egress PE routers.

If these quick checks do not solve your problem, you must go into MPLS-VPN trouble-shooting and verify all steps in MPLS VPN route propagation:

- Exchange of routing information from CE router to PE router
- Redistribution of customer route into MP-BGP (also check for correct values of RD and RT at this step)
- Propagation of MP-BGP route across MPLS VPN backbone
- Import of MP-BGP route into VRF routing table on the receiving PE router
- Redistribution of MP-BGP route into PE-CE routing protocol and propagation of the redistributed route to the CE router.

INDEX

Numerics

6PE (IPv6 provider edge router), 392, 400
    designing with BGP confederations, 419
    designing with BGP route reflectors, 415–418
    inter-AS 6PE deployment, 419–421
    inter-MP-BGP session establishment, 405–407
    IPv6 datagram forwarding across MPLS
      backbone, 412–415
    IPv6 route exchange between CE and PE
      routers, 401–404
    labeled IPv6 MP-BGP prefixes, configuring,
      407–411
    route redistribution, 405–407
    versus MPLS VPN, 392

A

AAA (authentication, authorization and accounting)
    authentication
      CE-to-CE, 238–240
      LCP, 28
      neighbor authentication, 230–231
      between PE routers, 235–236
      on PE/CE circuits, 232, 234–235
      on P-networks, 236–237
    per-VRF AAA, 105–110
    RADIUS, 33–35
      AV pairs, 35–36
      VSAs, 35–36
access protocols
    DHCP, 36–37
    PPP, 27
      L2TP, 29–30
      LCP, 27–29
      RADIUS, 33–35
        AV pairs, 35–36
        VSAs, 35–36
      VPDNs, 31–33

access technology integration with MPLS-based
    VPNs, 17
accessing common services with PE-NAT, 205–208
access-lists, limiting access to PE/CE circuits,
    252–256
address pools, ODAPs, 99–105
addressing, IPv6, 394
    interface ID, 394
    public address space, 396
advanced MPLS VPN remote access features of
    Cisco IOS Software
      ODAPs, 99–105
      per-VRF AAA, 105–110
Advertising Router field (LSA), 124
antilabel spoofing, 230
applications (MPLS), 13
architecture
    control plane
      troubleshooting, 432
      verifying label exchange, 436–437
      verifying local TDP/LDP parameters, 433
      verifying TDP/LDP Hello protocol,
        433–434
      verifying TDP/LDP session state, 435
    customer control plane, 425
    data plane, 426
      troubleshooting, 437–438
    point-to-point, 6–16, 23–24, 28–31, 34–40, 49,
      51, 58, 63, 75–94, 100, 107, 112, 118–153,
      163–165, 170–171, 175–179, 185–188,
      197–207, 214, 226–239, 257–272, 277, 281,
      287–306, 315, 317, 321, 324, 330, 335–336,
      338–367, 379–380, 391–405, 416–432,
      440–446
    provider control plane, 426
ATM (Asynchronous Transfer Mode)
    PPPoA, configuring DSL access to MPLS
      VPN, 82–85
attributes (BGP), UPDATE authenticator, 240

F

G

H

I

N

Wouldn't it be great

if the world's leading technical publishers joined forces to deliver their best tech books in a common digital reference platform?

They have. Introducing
InformIT Online Books
powered by Safari.

■ **Specific answers to specific questions.**
InformIT Online Books' powerful search engine gives you relevance-ranked results in a matter of seconds.

■ **Immediate results.**
With InformIt Online Books, you can select the book you want and view the chapter or section you need immediately.

■ **Cut, paste and annotate.**
Paste code to save time and eliminate typographical errors. Make notes on the material you find useful and choose whether or not to share them with your work group.

■ **Customized for your enterprise.**
Customize a library for you, your department or your entire organization. You only pay for what you need.

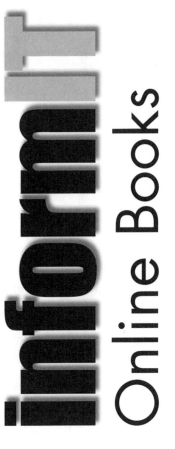

Get your first 14 days FREE!
InformIT Online Books is offering its members a 10 book subscription risk-free for 14 days. Visit **http://www.informit.com/onlinebooks/cp** for details.

informit.com/onlinebooks/cp

Train with authorized Cisco Learning Partners.

Discover all that's possible on the Internet.

One of the biggest challenges facing networking professionals is how to stay current with today's ever-changing technologies in the global Internet economy. Nobody understands this better than Cisco Learning Partners, the only companies that deliver training developed by Cisco Systems.

Just go to **www.cisco.com/go/training_ad**. You'll find more than 120 Cisco Learning Partners in over 90 countries worldwide.* Only Cisco Learning Partners have instructors that are certified by Cisco to provide recommended training on Cisco networks and to prepare you for certifications.

To get ahead in this world, you first have to be able to keep up. Insist on training that is developed and authorized by Cisco, as indicated by the Cisco Learning Partner or Cisco Learning Solutions Partner logo.

Visit **www.cisco.com/go/training_ad** today.

CISCO SYSTEMS

EMPOWERING THE
INTERNET GENERATION™

Copyright © 2001 Cisco Systems, Inc. All rights reserved. Empowering the Internet Generation is a service mark, and Cisco, Cisco Systems, and the Cisco Systems logo are registered trademarks of Cisco Systems, Inc. or its affiliates in the U.S. and certain other countries. *Valid as of December 15, 2000.

Cisco Press

Learning is serious business.

Invest wisely.

ciscopress.com

CCIE Security

Network Security Principles and Practices (CCIE Professional Development)

Saadat Malik

1-58705-025-0 • **Available Now**

Network Security Principles and Practices is a comprehensive guide to network security threats and the policies and tools developed specifically to combat those threats. Starting with a general discussion of network security concepts and design philosophy, the book shows readers how they can build secure network architectures from the ground up. Taking a practical, applied approach to building security into networks, the book focuses on showing readers how to implement and verify security features and products in a variety of environments. Security aspects of routing protocols are discussed and various options for choosing and using them analyzed. The book goes into a detailed discussion of the security threats posed by increasingly prevalent LAN to LAN virtual private networks and remote access VPN installations and how to minimize large vulnerabilities caused by these non-traditional network portals. Firewalls, including the PIX and IOS® Firewalls, and underlying protocols are presented in depth. Intrusion detection is fully examined. The book shows the reader how to control dial-in access by setting up access servers with AAA, PPP, TACACS+, and RADIUS. Finally, protections at the service provider are discussed by showing the reader how to provision security at the service provider level.

CCIE® Practical Studies: Security (CCIE Self-Study)

Andrew Mason, Dmitry Bokotey

1-58705-110-9 • **Available June 2003**

The Cisco Certified Internetworking Expert (CCIE) Certification from Cisco Systems is the most prestigious certification in the networking industry. In 2001, Cisco exam with a one-day intensive lab exam is a highly sought after affirmation of a networkers security skills. A key to success in the intensive lab exam is hands-on understanding of how the security principles and concepts are executed in a real network. *CCIE Practical Studies: Security* provides a series of lab scenarios that help a CCIE candidate or advanced-level networker gain that expertise. The labs show how, with or without a lab of actual equipment, different concepts are applied. Chapters include background and technology overviews, directions on how to set up a practice lab, case study-based scenarios that show the step-by-step implementation of these concepts, and comprehensive labs that mimic those in the one-day lab exam. *CCIE Practical Studies: Security* serves as an invaluable guide in gaining networking security experience and in CCIE testing success.

Learning is serious buisiness. **Invest wisely.**

Cisco Press

Learning is serious business.

Invest wisely.

General CCIE

CCIE Routing and Switching
Exam Certification Guide
Anthony Bruno, CCIE
1-58720-053-8 • **Available Now**

CCIE Routing and Switching Exam Certification Guide covers the general networking topics listed in the Routing and Switching (#350-001) and Communications and Services CCIE Qualification Exams. This book will help the reader increase and reinforce their knowledge in each general networking area to prepare for the qualifying exam; it serves as a complete self-assessment tool for candidates to identify weak spots in their knowledge that require additional review. As with all Exam Certification Guides from Cisco Press, each chapter has a "Do I know this already?" pre-chapter quiz and other standard elements like the accompanying CD-ROM with exams that will help the reader practice for the test. In addition to building confidence as an exam preparation resource, this book provides network engineers, designers, and architects with an all-around reference to keep them on top of the latest and most important networking technologies and techniques.

CCIE Practical Studies, Volume 1
Karl Solie, CCIE
1-58720-002-3 • **Available Now**

While the popularity of the CCIE Exam grows amongst technology professionals, the fail rate is still quite high, over 80% (approx.). *CCIE™ Practial Studies, Volume I* focuses on the lab portion of the exam, where most fail. It includes in-depth coverage for over 70 labs scenarios as well as how to design and implement basic to complicated networks.

Cisco Press Security

Troubleshooting IP Routing Protocols
(CCIE Professional Development)

Zaheer Aziz, CCIE; Johnson Liu, CCIE;
Abe Martey, CCIE; Faraz Shamin; CCIE

1-58705-019-6 • **Available Now**

As the Internet continues to grow exponentially, the need for network engineers to build, maintain and troubleshoot the growing number of component networks has also increased significantly. Since network troubleshooting is a practical skill that requires on-the-job experience, it has become critical that the learning curve to gain expertise in internetworking technologies be reduced to quickly fill the void of skilled network engineers needed to support the fast growing internet.

Troubleshooting Remote Access Networks
(CCIE Professional Development)

Plamen Nedeltchev

1-58705-076-5 • **Available Now**

Troubleshooting Remote Access Networks helps you understand underlying technologies and gain insight into the challenges, issues, and best practices for supporting remote access networks. Covering fundamental concepts, design issues, provisioning, DSL and Cable connectivity options, central office operations, authentication techniques, and troubleshooting, this book serves as a comprehensive tool to resolving remote access issues. In-depth analysis of essential remote access technologies provides greater insight into Dial, ISDN, Frame Relay, and VPNs. With a focus specifically on the more popular enterprise applications of these technologies, each major section discusses troubleshooting methodology and scenarios. The methodology walks readers through the process of identifying, isolating, and correcting common failures. This structured approach helps limit the inclination to attack network failures in a more random fashion, which is not nearly as efficient. Explanations of typical symptoms, problems, show commands, and debug information are also extensive.

ciscopress.com

Cisco Press Security

CCSP™ Cisco Secure PIX® Firewall Advanced Exam Certification Guide (CCSP Self-Study)
Christian Degu, Greg Bastien
1-58720-067-8 • **Available No**

The CSPFA exam is one of the five component exams to the CCSP certification. *CCSP Cisco Secure PIX Firewall Advanced Exam Certification Guide* provides CSPFA exam candidates with a comprehensive preparation tool for testing success. With pre- and post-chapter tests, a CD-ROM-based testing engine with more than 200 questions, and comprehensive training on all exam topics, this title brings the proven exam preparation tools from the popular Cisco Press Exam Certification Guide series to the CSPFA candidate. It also serves as a learning guide for networkers interested in learning more about working with the PIX Firewall line of products.

CCSP Cisco Secure VPN Exam Certification Guide
John Roland, Mark Newcomb
1-58720-070-8 • **Available Now**

As security demands continue to increase for enterprise and service provider networks, the number of employees working from remote locations requiring an efficient and rapid virtual private network connection grows as well. The Cisco Secure line of products and services are focused on providing the seamless operation of these remote networks with the maximum level of security available. Organizations using this suite of products and services need networking professionals with proven skills at getting the highest levels of both security and network operability. This need has created a booming demand for the Cisco Systems security certifications that verify those skills and abilities. The CSVPN exam is one of the components of the Cisco Systems security designation. CSS-1 Cisco Secure VPN Exam Certification Guide provides CSVPN exam candidates with a comprehensive preparation tool for testing success. With pre- and post-chapter tests, a CD-ROM-based testing engine with more than 200 questions, and comprehensive training on all exam topics, this title brings the proven exam preparation tools from the popular Cisco Press Exam Certification Guide series to the CSVPN candidate.

ciscopress.com

Learning is serious buisiness.   **Invest wisely.**

MPLS and VPN Architectures

Ivan Pepelnjak and Jim Guichard

1587050021 • **Available Now**

Multiprotocol Label Switching (MPLS) provides the mechanisms to perform label switching, which is an innovative technique for high-performance packet forwarding. This book provides an in-depth study of MPLS technology, including MPLS theory and configuration, network design issues, and case studies. The MPLS/VPN architecture and all of its mechanisms are explained with configuration examples and suggested deployment guidelines. MPLS and VPNs provides the first in-depth discussion particular to Cisco's MPLS architecture. The book covers MPLS theory and configuration, network design issues, and case studies as well as one major MPLS application: MPLS-based VPNs. The MPLS/VPN architecture and all of its mechanisms are explained with configuration examples, suggested design and deployment guidelines, and extensive case studies.

MPLS and VPN Architectures (CCIP Edition)

Ivan Pepelnjak and Jim Guichard

1587050811 • **Available Now**

MPLS and VPN Architectures, CCIP Edition, is a practical guide to understanding, designing, and deploying MPLS-based VPNs. This book covers MPLS theory and configuration, network design issues, and one major MPLS application: MPLS-based VPNs. The MPLS/VPN architecture and all its mechanisms are explained with configuration examples, suggested design and deployment guidelines, and extensive case studies.